Quantum
Software

Iaakov Exman • Ricardo Pérez-Castillo •
Mario Piattini • Michael Felderer

Editors

Quantum Software

Aspects of Theory and System Design

 Springer

Editors

Iaakov Exman (iD)
School of Computer Science
Holon Institute of Technology (HIT)
Holon, Israel

Mario Piattini (iD)
Institute of formation Systems and
Technologies
University of Castilla-La Mancha (UCLM)
Ciudad Real, Spain

Ricardo Pérez-Castillo (iD)
Faculty of Social Sciences and Information
Technology
University of Castilla-La Mancha (UCLM)
Talavera de la Reina, Spain

Michael Felderer (iD)
Institute of Software Technology
German Aerospace Center (DLR)
Cologne, Germany

University of Innsbruck
Innsbruck, Austria

University of Cologne
Cologne, Germany

ISBN 978-3-031-64135-0   ISBN 978-3-031-64136-7   (eBook)
https://doi.org/10.1007/978-3-031-64136-7

Open Access sponsored by University of Innsbruck, Innsbruck, Austria.

This Springer imprint is published by the registered company Springer Nature Switzerland AG
The registered company address is: Gewerbestrasse 11, 6330 Cham, Switzerland

To Michal my wife, companion for life,
and to our children.
—Iaakov Exman

To my son and daughter.
In the superposition of life's infinite
possibilities,
you both are my brightest outcomes.
—Ricardo Perez-Castillo

To Juan Carlos Trujillo, excellent
professional and friend.
—Mario Piattini

To Angelika and Konstantin for enriching my
private life. To the staff of the DLR Institute
of Software Technology for inspiring my
professional life.
—Michael Felderer

The four editors would like to thank all the
participants of the Innsbruck Symposium for
fostering a creative atmosphere that inspired
this book.
We extend special gratitude to the chapter
authors for their outstanding contributions,
which have made this book a significant
reality.
We also wish to thank the University of
Innsbruck for its support in making this book
open access.

Preface

Overview

Quantum software before hardware? This is just one of the questions triggered in the reader's mind by this book. Sometimes, there is a single answer. Oftentimes, it offers several answers. Other times, the answer provokes further thoughts. This is not supposed to be a one-time-read book. It is expected to be perceived in an easily grasped place on the shelf, to be consulted again and again.

This book's title is not a question. It stands as a clear statement, conveying basic ideas intended to resist challenges over time, like those deep theories proposed before the ultimate convincing experiments are performed. The book editors are perfectly aware of the current quantum computing stage, coined NISQ—Noise Intermediate-Scale Quantum—era by John Preskill [1], and the still competitive arena between hardware technologies. NISQ means that quantum processors have a limited number of qubits, not enough for error correction fault-tolerance in the noisy environment, but still susceptible to quantum decoherence.

In any case, regardless of whether fault-tolerant quantum computers are achieved in the more or less near future, it is certain that we are already witnessing the quantum advantage and that in order for it to become a widespread reality, adequate quantum software is needed.

This book focuses precisely on the different aspects to be taken into account in software, from the most fundamental and theoretical to the most applied aspects of quantum software engineering.

Organization

After an introductory chapter [2]—overviewing the contents of the subsequent chapters—the book is composed of three parts.

It starts with a theoretical part on quantum software, as a bold declaration that quantum software theory is deep and valuable independent of the existence of specific practical quantum hardware. It is based upon the claim, supported elsewhere, that quantum software is the more general theory subsuming classical and hybrid software system theories.

The second, more extensive, part deals with quantum software system and engineering design. The quality of this part follows from comparison of the liberal diversity, of sometimes conflicting views and approaches to design, enabling the reader to make a well-pondered rational choice of preference.

The book concludes with a third part, referring to multiple software applications and corresponding laboratory experience, in order to understand their implications in practice, and avoid repeating past mistakes.

Target Readership

This book should be of interest to industry professionals and researchers in academia, who are either producing or applying quantum software systems in their work or are considering their potential utility in the future. Furthermore, this text could be beneficial for practitioners already experienced with classical software engineering who desire to understand the fundamentals of quantum software, including the underlying technology, programming techniques, and possible applications.

In a teaching environment, it can be used as a reference book, or selected chapters can be used directly as reading material, from each of the book's three parts, theoretical, system design, or actual applications.

Overall, any standard first year STEM—Science, Technology, Engineering, and Mathematics—bachelor's degree studies will suffice. Certain chapters demand a slightly greater mathematical/physical maturity, as the reader may perceive. Concerning quantum computing knowledge, if needed, one may consult either a general well-known book on computation and information, such as *Quantum Computation and Quantum Information* by Nielsen and Chuang [3] or relevant chapters of *Quantum Software Engineering* by Serrano et al. [4].

Conclusion

There are several possible ways to get the best benefits from this book. These depend on the reader's perspective and on the particular areas of interest.

One can work hard on a single chapter, analyzing in depth each of its topics. One may even contact the chapter authors for further discussion. Another possibility, especially referring to the book's second part on system design, is to take a comparative approach of some of the relevant chapters. This is also possible concerning the book's third part on applications and laboratory experience.

Referring to open issues and future research directions, each of the book's chapters points out its most pressing issues of relevance.

One must very carefully take into account previous lessons of the history of science and technology to make a reasonable assessment of the future of quantum software, with respect to the ever-accelerating and always surprising computing areas. There have been well-known cases of misjudgment in the past decades. A very high official of a big computing company—that still exists! despite the misjudgment—expressed the idea that the total number of computers on planet Earth will be five or six, i.e., roughly proportional to the number of big powers among the nations. Another high official of a computing company with 500,000 employees said that he does not understand why people would wish to have a personal computer at home; the company did not survive this prophecy. So, it is only safe to state that the future will be much more interesting than our wildest imagination.

Holon, Israel   Iaakov Exman
Talavera de la Reina, Spain   Ricardo Pérez-Castillo
Ciudad Real, Spain   Mario Piattini
Cologne, Germany   Michael Felderer

References

[1] Preskill, J.: Quantum Computing in the NISQ era and beyond. arXiv:1801. 00862 (2018). https://doi.org/10.48550/arXiv.1801.00862

[2] Felderer, M., Perez-Castillo, R., Piattini, M., Exman, I.: A novel perception of quantum software: theoretical, engineering and application aspects (Chapter 1). In: Quantum Software – Aspects of Theory and System Design. Springer-Nature, Cham (2024)

[3] Nielsen, M.A., Chuang, I.L.: Quantum Computation and Quantum Information. Cambridge University Press, Cambridge (2010)

[4] Serrano, M.A., Perez-Castillo, R., Piattini, M. (eds.): Quantum Software Engineering. Springer-Nature, Cham (2022)

Acknowledgments

We express gratitude for the support of the University of Innsbruck enabling the open access publication of this book. Furthermore, we acknowledge the support of PID2022-137944NB-I00 (SMOOTH Project) and PDC2022-133051-I00 (QU-ASAP Project) funded by MCIN/AEI/10.13039/501100011033 and by the European Union NextGenerationEU/PRTR, QSERV-UCLM (PID2021-124054OB-C32) financed by the Spanish Ministry of Science and Innovation (MICINN), and the financial support for the execution of applied research projects, within the framework of the University of Castilla-La Mancha (UCLM) Own Research Plan, co-financed at 85% by the European Regional Development Fund (FEDER) UNION (2022-GRIN-34110).

Contents

Contributors

Rui Abreu Faculty of Engineering of University of Porto & INESC-ID, Lisboa, Portugal

Raul Barba-Rojas Escuela Superior de Informatica (ESI-CR), Ciudad Real, Spain

Achim Basermann Institute of Software Technology, German Aerospace Center (DLR), Cologne, Germany

Jose Campos Faculty of Engineering of University of Porto & LASIGE, Faculdade de Ciencias, Universidade de Lisboa, Lisbon, Portugal

Cecilia Carbonelli Infineon Technologies AG, Neubiberg, Germany

Andrea De Lucia SeSa Lab - University of Salerno, Salerno, Italy

Manuel De Stefano SeSa Lab - University of Salerno, Salerno, Italy

Dario Di Nucci SeSa Lab - University of Salerno, Salerno, Italy

Michael Epping Institute of Software Technology, German Aerospace Center (DLR), Cologne, Germany

Alexander Erhard Alpine Quantum Technologies GmbH, Innsbruck, Austria

Iaakov Exman HIT - Holon Institute of Technology, Holon, Israel

Benedikt Fauseweh Institute of Software Technology, German Aerospace Center (DLR), Cologne, Germany

Michael Felderer Institute of Software Technology, German Aerospace Center (DLR), Cologne, Germany
University of Innsbruck, Innsbruck, Austria
University of Cologne, Cologne, Germany

Thomas Feldker Alpine Quantum Technologies GmbH, Innsbruck, Austria

Daniel Fortunato Faculty of Engineering of University of Porto & Artificial Intelligence and Computer Science Laboratory, Porto, Portugal

Albert Frisch Alpine Quantum Technologies GmbH, Innsbruck, Austria

Jose Garcia-Alonso Quercus Software Engineering Group, University of Extremadura, Caceres, Spain

Florian Girtler Alpine Quantum Technologies GmbH, Innsbruck, Austria

Max Hettrich Alpine Quantum Technologies GmbH, Innsbruck, Austria

Jose Luis Hevia aQuantum, Madrid, Spain

Wilfried Huss Alpine Quantum Technologies GmbH, Innsbruck, Austria

Georg Jacob Alpine Quantum Technologies GmbH, Innsbruck, Austria

Luis Jimenez-Navajas aQuantum, Faculty of Social Sciences & IT, University of Castilla-La Mancha, Talavera de la Reina, Spain

Mathias Jung University of Wurzburg, Wurzburg, Germany

Jose A. Cruz Lemus Escuela Superior de Informatica (ESI-CR), Ciudad Real, Spain

Elisabeth Lobe Institute of Software Technology, German Aerospace Center (DLR), Cologne, Germany

Malte Lochau University of Siegen, Siegen, Germany

Sebastian Luber Infineon Technologies AG, Neubiberg, Germany

Christine Maier Alpine Quantum Technologies GmbH, Innsbruck, Austria

Aurelio Martinez aQuantum, Madrid, Spain

Wolfgang Mauerer Technical University of Applied Sciences Regensburg, Regensburg, Germany
Siemens AG, Regensburg, Germany

Gregor Mayramhof Alpine Quantum Technologies GmbH, Innsbruck, Austria

Enrique Moguel Quercus Software Engineering Group, University of Extremadura, Caceres, Spain

Thomas Monz Alpine Quantum Technologies GmbH, Innsbruck, Austria
Institut für Experimentalphysik, Universität Innsbruck, Innsbruck, Austria

Juan M. Murillo Quercus Software Engineering Group, University of Extremadura, Caceres, Spain

Ezequiel Murina aQuantum, Madrid, Spain

Daniel Nigg Alpine Quantum Technologies GmbH, Innsbruck, Austria

Fabio Palomba SeSa Lab - University of Salerno, Salerno, Italy

Fabiano Pecorelli Jheronimus Academy of Data Science, Hertogenbosch, Netherlands

Ricardo Pérez-Castillo UCLM - University of Castilla-La Mancha, Talavera de la Reina, Spain

Guido Petersen aQuantum, Madrid, Spain

Mario Piattini UCLM - University of Castilla-La Mancha, Ciudad Real, Spain

Rudolf Ramler Software Competence Center Hagenberg, Hagenberg, Austria

Moises Rodrigues Escuela Superior de Informatica (ESI-CR), Ciudad Real, Spain

Melven Röhrig-Zöllner Institute of Software Technology, German Aerospace Center (DLR), Cologne, Germany

Ina Schäfer Karlsruhe Institute of Technology, Karlsruhe, Germany

Gary Schmiedinghoff Institute of Software Technology, German Aerospace Center (DLR), Cologne, Germany

Chistoph Schroth Fraunhofer IESE, Kaiserslautern, Germany

Peter K. Schuhmacher Institute of Software Technology, German Aerospace Center (DLR), Cologne, Germany

Yoshinta Setyawati Institute of Software Technology, German Aerospace Center (DLR), Cologne, Germany

Christian Sommer Alpine Quantum Technologies GmbH, Innsbruck, Austria

Davide Taibi University of Oulu, Oulu, Finland

Juris Ulmanis Alpine Quantum Technologies GmbH, Innsbruck, Austria

Alexander Weinert Institute of Software Technology, German Aerospace Center (DLR), Cologne, Germany

Etienne Wodey Alpine Quantum Technologies GmbH, Innsbruck, Austria

Mederika Zangerl Alpine Quantum Technologies GmbH, Innsbruck, Austria

A Novel Perception of Quantum Software: Theoretical, Engineering, and Application Aspects

Michael Felderer (ID), **Ricardo Pérez-Castillo** (ID), **Mario Piattini** (ID), and **Iaakov Exman** (ID)

Abstract The chapter discusses the importance of quantum software and defines it as a multifaceted concept comprising a theoretical, engineering, and application viewpoint. Hence, it covers aspects of quantum software theory, quantum software systems, as well as quantum software laboratory. The chapter also outlines the entire book and its individual chapters structured into three parts on quantum software theory, quantum software system design, as well as quantum software laboratory and applications.

Keywords Quantum computing · Software engineering · Theory and experiments

M. Felderer
Institute of Software Technology, German Aerospace Center (DLR), Cologne, Germany

University of Innsbruck, Innsbruck, Austria

University of Cologne, Cologne, Germany
e-mail: Michael.Felderer@dlr.de

R. Pérez-Castillo (✉)
UCLM – University of Castilla-La Mancha, Talavera de la Reina, Spain
e-mail: Ricardo.PDelCastillo@uclm.es

M. Piattini
UCLM – University of Castilla-La Mancha, Ciudad Real, Spain
e-mail: Mario.Piattini@uclm.es

I. Exman
HIT – Holon Institute of Technology, Holon, Israel
e-mail: iaakov@hit.ac.il

© The Author(s) 2024   1
I. Exman et al. (eds.), *Quantum Software*,
https://doi.org/10.1007/978-3-031-64136-7_1

1   Introduction

Quantum computing itself is a computational paradigm that explicitly uses properties of subatomic particles such as superposition, entanglement, and interference to achieve asymptotical speedups over classical algorithms on certain tasks [1]. It is gaining considerable attention from industry, academia, and public authorities alike and has been making great progress in recent years. In order to meet its expectations, not only hardware for quantum computing but also software is required. Quantum software is a key enabler for quantum computing and, as classical software, encompasses multiple facets.

As classical software, also quantum software is a multifaceted concept with several aspects. It covers algorithms, system software, application software, entire ecosystems, and hybrid systems, as well as suitable software and systems engineering concepts. In addition, new theoretical foundations for the concept of quantum software are required as well as concrete applications. This book aims to cover all these aspects and is therefore divided into three parts: Part I is on quantum software theory, Part II on quantum software system design, and Part III on the quantum software applications and laboratory.

The three parts of the book provide the reader with three different perspectives on quantum software. The first part takes the theoretical viewpoint into account. It emphasizes that one needs more than just informal software development models. The time has come to apply mathematical theories enabling convincing verification of the correctness of quantum software systems. The second part focuses on the software and system engineering viewpoint. Its goal is to show that in contrast to a dogmatic fixation on a single approach, one should take the variety of existing approaches into account to design novel quantum software systems. The third part of the book focuses on the laboratory and application perspective. Quantum software applications and laboratory experience are essential to avoid past mistakes and make quantum computing and its software a success.

The multiplicity of the sometimes conflicting perspectives offered by the different chapters of this book forces consideration of distinct factors involved in a problem, facilitating the path to the problem solution. The freedom afforded by the large variety of approaches is a blessing to be explored and not an impediment to rational decisions, as we try hard to demonstrate in this book. Moreover, it is an additional way to change how a quantum software system is perceived.

The following sections summarize the contributions of the individual chapters. Section 2 summarizes the two chapters on quantum software theory. Section 3 summarizes the six chapters on quantum software system design. Section 4 summarizes the four chapters on quantum software laboratory and applications.

2 Quantum Software Theory

Quantum computing requires theoretical considerations about the nature of quantum software. Quantum software adds additional aspects to the software engineering body of knowledge [2]. It is the result of a special combination of quantum and software. Two key aspects are modularity—separating modules, the meaningful subsystems of a system—and entanglement—linking modules when needed, in order to enable quantum software to run, e.g., in a simulation. Richard P. Feynman's visionary 1982 article entitled "Simulating Physics with Computers" [3] is a pioneer in the field of quantum computing. This is due to Feynman's inimitable style and his extensive analysis of the difficulties of quantum simulation of nature.

The second chapter, entitled "Simulating Quantum Software with Density Matrices: Reading Feynman on Fast-Forward," provides a novel reinterpretation of Feynman's paper [3] as a "quantum software" precursor. Feynman's proposal to represent the simulated system by a density matrix opens the way toward a mathematical quantum software systems theory. Density matrix modularization leads to *software modules* as high-level abstractions unifying conceptual software units, stimulating new software-related questions and novel quantum solutions. This chapter defines quantum software in terms of a conceptual software perspective and the density matrix as the rigorous bridge between concepts and qubits.

The third chapter, entitled "Superoperators for Quantum Software Engineering," reviews a superoperator-based approach to quantum dynamics. The approach is supposed to be concrete enough to be useful in quantum software and systems engineering, which necessitates gaining an understanding of quantum programming languages and possible approaches to equip them with formal semantics. The chapter discusses one particularly important superoperator-based formalism, i.e., linear superoperators acting on density operators. The chapter tailors the formalism toward software engineering research and indicates benefits in various application areas in that domain.

3 Quantum Software System Design

Based on theoretical considerations on quantum software and quantum computing, this part covers several contributions on quantum software system design. Quantum software is a multifaceted concept with several aspects. It covers algorithms, system software, application software, entire ecosystems, and hybrid systems, as well as suitable software and systems engineering concepts.

The fourth chapter, entitled "*QSandbox*: The Agile Quantum Software Sandbox," describes an *agile software sandbox* specifically designed for quantum software research and development. *QSandbox* is *itself modifiable* since its high-level modules are varied at will by quantum software developers. *QSandbox* has a series of unique features, to produce fast results when testing any recently modified quantum circuit. It uses high-level abstraction meaningful modules, instead of low-level quantum gates of conventional simulators. It has instantly synchronized dual views—high-level quantum circuit and density matrix. In addition, it has uniform quantum and classical representation, implying the innovative idea of quantum circuits for classical software.

The fifth chapter, entitled "Verification and Validation of Quantum Software," focuses on classical software testing approaches for quantum software. For that purpose, 16 quantum software testing techniques, which have been proposed for the IBM quantum framework Qiskit, are gathered and illustrated based on a running example. The chapter concludes that researchers should focus on delivering artifacts that are usable without much hindrance to the rest of the community, and the development of quantum benchmarks should be a priority to facilitate reproducibility, replicability, and comparison between different testing techniques.

The sixth chapter, entitled "Quantum Software Quality Metrics," defines and empirically assesses a set of metrics for assessing the understandability of quantum circuits. The provided metrics fall into the categories circuit size, circuit density, single-qubit gates, multi-qubit gates, all gates in the circuit, oracles, measurement gates, as well as other metrics. Furthermore, a tool prototype called QMetrics is provided for automated calculation of the proposed metrics.

The seventh chapter, entitled "Quantum Software Ecosystem Design," presents scientific considerations essential for building a quantum software ecosystem that makes quantum computing available for scientific and industrial problem-solving. It is based on the concept of hardware–software codesign, which fosters a bidirectional feedback loop from the application layer at the top of the software stack down to the hardware. The approach starts with compilers and low-level software that are specifically designed to align with the unique specifications and constraints of the quantum processor. Then, the chapter presents algorithms developed with a clear understanding of underlying hardware and computational model features, and extends to applications that effectively leverage the capabilities to achieve a quantum advantage. The chapter analyzes the ecosystem from a conceptual view, focusing on theoretical foundations, and the technical view, addressing practical implementations around real quantum devices necessary for a functional ecosystem. It offers a guide to the essential concepts and practical strategies necessary for developing a scientifically grounded quantum software ecosystem.

The eighth chapter, entitled "Development and Deployment of Quantum Services," emphasizes that new techniques and tools are needed to facilitate access to quantum computing technology provided by cloud providers like IBM, Amazon, Microsoft, or Google. This helps developers to increase the level of abstraction at which they work with this technology. The chapter performs a technical comparison between different quantum computing service providers using a case study by performing empirical tests based on the Traveling Salesman Problem. The study highlights the differences between the major providers. In order to address these differences and reduce the vendor lock-in effect, the chapter makes three proposals: an extension of the Quantum API Gateway to support the different vendors; a code generator making use of a modification of the OpenAPI specification; and a workflow to automate the continuous deployment of these services making use of GitHub Actions. This would allow programmers to deploy quantum code without specific knowledge of the major vendors, which would facilitate access and simplify the development of quantum applications.

The ninth chapter, entitled "Engineering Hybrid Software Systems," highlights that software modernization processes for transforming and migrating legacy software systems (which may include adding new existing quantum software) toward such hybrid software systems will be required. The chapter discusses the challenges of hybrid software and how software modernization (based on architecture-driven modernization) can be used as a reengineering solution for an effective evolution of classical and quantum software. This process makes it easier to combine both computing paradigms, quantum and classical. The modernization process consists of three phases, reverse engineering, restructuring, and forward engineering. The overall modernization process follows the Model-Driven Engineering (MDE) principles, and, therefore, it could be instantiated with different (meta)models. The main implication of the quantum software modernization process for practitioners is a set of challenges that may appear during the evolution of classical software systems toward hybrid software systems. Thus, software modernization helps companies to identify which components from their business models could be evolved, and how, or even to start new businesses following this new paradigm using techniques and standards which have been proved to be effective in solving such problems.

4 Quantum Software Laboratory and Applications

Based on the theoretical and software system design considerations, this part covers several contributions on quantum software laboratory and applications. It covers a concrete quantum computing technology, i.e., trapped-ion quantum computers, the application to quantum computer in the health domain, industrial application scenarios for quantum software engineering, as well as an empirical study to provide a comprehensive understanding of the current state of quantum software engineering.

The tenth chapter, entitled "Trapped-Ion Quantum Computing," presents trapped-ion quantum computing, which proves to be very suitable for the transition from tabletop, lab-based experiments to rack-mounted, on-premise systems that allow for operation in data center environments. However, several technical challenges need to be solved, and controlling many degrees of freedom needs to be optimized and automated before industrial applications can be successfully implemented on quantum computers situated within data centers. These necessary developments range from the architecture of an ion trap that fundamentally defines the supported instruction sets, over the control electronics and laser systems, which limit the quality of qubit operations, to the optimized compilation of quantum circuits based on qubit properties and gate fidelities. The chapter introduces the ion-trap quantum computing platform, presents the current technical state of the art of Alpine Quantum Technologies GmbH (AQT's) ion-trapping hardware and rack-based quantum computing systems, and highlights parts of the execution stack.

The eleventh chapter, entitled "Quantum Software Engineering and Programming Applied to Personalized Pharmacogenomics," applies upcoming best practices of quantum software engineering to the development of a hybrid quantum/classical software system in the context of personalized pharmacogenomics. It reports on results from the QHealth project. The chapter concludes that in order to achieve quantum software that can really be used in health information systems, it is necessary to build it in an engineering way and without forgetting the good practices of software engineering. In fact, in the QHealth project, tools for design, quality, testing, estimation, and process management were proposed to implement the project.

The twelfth chapter, entitled "Challenges for Quantum Software Engineering: An Industrial Application Scenario Perspective," analyzes three paradigmatic application scenarios for quantum software engineering from an industrial perspective. The use cases cover (1) optimization and quantum cloud services, (2) quantum simulation, and (3) embedded quantum computing. From the use case analysis, the chapter concludes that quantum programming today mostly means custom-tailoring a quantum solution to a very specific instruction set of a specifically developed special-purpose quantum computer. The tendency in software engineering today is, however, to abstract exactly from those low-level details and instead focus on requirements and design issues. Hence, recently outdated, former core disciplines of mainstream software engineering research like compiler construction and instruction set architecture design will become highly relevant again.

The thirteenth chapter, entitled "Quantum Software Engineering Issues and Challenges: Insights from Practitioners," presents an empirical study based on a survey and expert interviews. Its aim is to provide a comprehensive understanding of the current state of quantum software engineering. Results show that there is great enthusiasm and interest in quantum programming, with abundant educational and experimental repositories indicating a fertile ground for innovation. The potential applications of quantum computing, especially in fields like chemistry, physics, and cryptography, are promising, and this has led to a growing community of developers and researchers eager to explore and contribute to this emerging field. However, many challenges must be overcome before the full potential of quantum software engineering can be realized. These challenges include a steep learning curve, a lack of standardized frameworks, hardware limitations, and a nascent stage of community collaboration.

5   Conclusion and Acknowledgment

This chapter has discussed the importance of quantum software. It covers aspects of quantum software theory, quantum software systems, as well as quantum software laboratory. The editors of this book want to thank all chapter authors for their valuable contributions. Furthermore, the editors want to express their gratitude to all participants of the First Working Seminar on Quantum Software Engineering (WSQSE 22) [4] for the fruitful discussions. WSQSE 22 was held on December 15–16, 2022, in Innsbruck, and during that seminar, the idea for this book was born from the fruitful discussion.

References

1. Nielsen, M.A., Chuang, I.L.: Quantum Computation and Quantum Information. Cambridge University Press (2010)
2. SWEBOK V3.0. https://www.computer.org/education/bodies-of-knowledge/software-engineering/topics
3. Feynman, R.P.: simulating physics with computers. Int. J. Theor. Phys. **21**, 467 (1982)
4. Felderer, M., Taibi, D., Palomba, F., Epping, M., Lochau, M., Weder, B.: Software engineering challenges for quantum computing: Report from the First Working Seminar on Quantum Software Engineering (WSQSE 22). ACM SIGSOFT Softw. Eng. Notes. **48**(2), 29–32 (2023)

Part I
Aspects of Quantum Software Theory

Simulating Quantum Software with Density Matrices: Reading Feynman on Fast-Forward

Iaakov Exman (iD)

Abstract Richard P. Feynman's 1982 paper "Simulating Physics with Computers" is often recognized as a pioneer of quantum computing. However, careful reading between the lines finds further meaningful content. This work reinterprets the pioneering paper, as a precursor of Quantum Software. Feynman's proposal to represent the simulated system by a Density Matrix opens the way toward a mathematical Quantum Software systems theory.

Density Matrix modularization leads to *software modules* as high-level abstractions unifying conceptual software units and matrix basis kets, stimulating new software-related questions and novel quantum solutions. *Software modules* are building blocks for any imaginable Quantum Software computations in practice, such as software system evolution, measurement, compositionality, and future potential applications.

Keywords Quantum Software · Density Matrix · Software modules · Quantum Software theory · Computational applications

1 Introduction

Undoubtedly and rightly so, Richard P. Feynman's visionary 1982 article entitled "Simulating Physics with Computers" [1] is a pioneer in the field of Quantum Computing. This is due to Feynman's inimitable style and his extensive analysis of the difficulties of quantum simulation of nature.

But this characterization is not the whole story. Feynman also had a wide range of interests in very different computational issues, in particular how software works. As he stated, just before his paper discussion, it has been very challenging to make a computer able to understand human natural languages. Thus, computers

I. Exman (✉)
School of Computer Science, Faculty of Sciences, HIT – Holon Institute of Technology, Holon, Israel
e-mail: iaakov@hit.ac.il

© The Author(s) 2024
I. Exman et al. (eds.), *Quantum Software*,
https://doi.org/10.1007/978-3-031-64136-7_2

have stimulated new types of thinking. Feynman's paper, beyond being a quantum computing pioneer, is a precursor of *Quantum Software*. This is the thesis of this chapter.

This work offers a novel reinterpretation of Feynman's paper as a "Quantum Software" precursor for two reasons: first, the *language of software* in its highest level of abstraction is the human natural languages spoken and understood by human beings; second, Feynman's 1982 paper gave specific suggestions concerning the suitable way to simulate physical systems with computers: (a) to represent the simulated system by a *Density Matrix*; (b) to discretize space and time, and simulate time indirectly by state transitions. Indeed, Feynman's simulation suggestions perfectly fit *software systems*.

Density Matrices are a unique mathematical model with duality—*system state and operator*—perfectly fitting the duality of software systems—*structure and behavior*. A density Matrix, itself a projection operator, can be conceptually modularized by basis ket-bra projectors of its finite Hilbert space. This opens the horizon to a *Quantum Software* theory of systems, with deep and unexpected benefits. It stimulates new software-related questions and their solutions, in particular concerning software evolution and measurement. It offers *software modules* as the highest level of abstraction for Quantum Software, well above qubits and gates.

This chapter defines Quantum Software in terms of a conceptual software perspective and the Density Matrix as the rigorous bridge between concepts and qubits.

1.1   Feynman's Quantum Computing Pioneer Paper

It is interesting to follow Feynman's motivation and reasoning to reach simulation of physics—viz., our universal laws of nature—by means of computers. His main motivation was to acquire new knowledge about the laws of physics by performing experiments in a *computational laboratory*, by additional means other than experiments in a traditional physical laboratory or eventual "Gedanken" experiments.

Feynman starts asking about simulation of physics by means of a universal computer, i.e., equivalent to a Universal Turing Machine. Immediately, Feynman adds the importance of interactions locality (see also Lloyd [2]): no arbitrary numbers of interconnections within a huge computer. The desirable simulation, for a physical system of any size, would demand a quantity of computation units at most proportional to the enclosed volume of the system space-time.

Another desirable requirement is a simulation as exact as nature itself. Alternatively, one might think how to modify physical law, a central motivation for Feynman's interest in the simulation problem, for instance, instead of a continuous space, the usage of a lattice-like discrete space. An example of a problem in such a space is the dependence of speed of light on direction; other anisotropies could be *empirically discovered* through "experiments" in the *computational laboratory*.

But the hardest problem, instead of classical physics, is to simulate quantum mechanics, predicting probabilities. According to Feynman, probability prediction of an experiment amounts to repeating the "computational experiment" in each local region enough times to estimate the respective probability value and its accuracy. But if one has a very large number of particles, the only way to succeed in the calculations is to have the computer made of units themselves behaving according to quantum mechanics, viz., a universal quantum computing simulator (cf. Deutsch [3]). In particular, there is no way to store the numbers relevant to all particles along the quantum computation. One needs to generate correct probability results directly. A Density Matrix is the suitable entity, instead of wave functions.

Indeed, Feynman's 1982 article is considered a pioneer in the field of quantum computing. However, this is not the whole story, as described next.

1.2   Novel Insight: Feynman's Quantum Software

Feynman mentions in his 1982 paper [1] that computers triggered new ways of thinking relevant to various scientific fields. Among Feynman's wide range of interests, he had in mind computational issues, such as how software really works, reflected in the Feynman Lectures on Computation (see Preskill [4], Feynman and Hey [5]). Here we offer a novel reinterpretation of Feynman's paper: beyond being a quantum computing pioneer, it is a precursor of *Quantum Software*.

- Why Software?

A software system is essentially a set of natural language concepts, whose ultimate purpose is to be *understood by human beings*. Natural language concepts are first-class entities in the description of any software system. As stated by Feynman's 1982 paper, just before that paper's Discussion, one did not actually grasp how formidable a challenge it was to understand natural languages—certainly in his time—until the direct efforts to make computers able to "comprehend" language. Nowadays, with large language models (LLMs) we better appreciate both the difficulties and the surprising relationships between natural language and software.

- Why Quantum Software?

We propose to look at *Quantum Software* as an embodiment of a *runnable and verifiable theory* of software systems based upon *quantum computing*, and a *highest abstraction level simulation* in terms of conceptual software modules. In this view, *Quantum Software* subsumes all strictly Quantum Software systems, pure classical software systems, and hybrids of both kinds.

What is the starting point for Quantum Software simulation? Following the admirable precision, and surprising relevance to software systems, of Feynman's 1982 paper [1], suggestions include:

Density Matrix—describes the whole finite Hilbert *state space* of the quantum
software

Discretization—assumes discrete space (the finite number of Density Matrix elements) and discrete time (resembling a computer's clock period) fitting software
systems; simulates time indirectly by transitions between software system states

- How to Link Software Concepts to a Density Matrix?

Natural language software concepts of a given software system are not directly
manipulated in Density Matrix calculations for good reasons. They are indexed, and
the indices are in one-to-one correspondence with the Quantum Software system
Density Matrix columns and rows.

1.3   Quantum Software Is the Density Matrix

Quantum Software is the Density Matrix. All Quantum Software possible calculations and property measurements can use the Density Matrix mathematical model as
a highest abstraction level simulation, instead of a low-level implemented software
system, which may not be available.

Section 4.1 details a systematic approach to generate the Density Matrix of
Quantum Software systems. Once generated, one obtains from the Density Matrix
the Quantum Software modules, as described in Sect. 4.3. Then, one learns the
Quantum Software system properties and eventually improves its design. The whole
Density Matrix shows *structure and behavior* duality; likewise, each of the software
system *modules* also displays duality, being subspaces of the whole Density Matrix.

One may evolve the Density Matrix state from a certain module to the next
module by means of relevant unitary operators, in discrete time steps. This is a
simulated equivalent to the actual execution of the low-level runnable software.
One obtains Quantum Software properties by performing, upon the Density Matrix,
probabilistic projective measurements, as Feynman's computational experiments
suggested. Furthermore, one can compose the whole system Density Matrix using
direct sums of smaller matrices representing the Quantum Software modules.

1.4   Chapter Organization

The next sections of this chapter are organized as follows. Section 2 highlights
significant steps of the software history until just before one gets to Quantum
Software. Section 3 summarizes quantum computing ideas, which are essential
for the understanding of Quantum Software. Section 4 defines Quantum Software
based upon the ideas of the two previous sections. Section 5 illustrates the theory
by a few overviews of pure classical and strictly "Quantum" Software systems,

and hybrid composition of classical and quantum subsystems. Section 6 concisely refers to related work. This chapter is concluded in Sect. 7 with a discussion of its fundamental results.

2 What Is Software?

The relatively short history of software is a history of ideas. Our particular choice of milestones is not meant to be a comprehensive historical account. Nonetheless, one can clearly discern the evolving commonality of ideas which developed along software's history. It converges with the fundamental notion of "concepts," with the "structure and behavior" duality.

The first appearance of "software engineering" as a discipline was at a NATO conference in 1968 [6]. Our first software history milestone is the idea of "types": Dahl and Hoare's chapter with types embedded in "hierarchical structures" in 1972 [7] and Barbara Liskov's Substitution principle on *subtypes*' inheritance in 1974 [8].

The next milestone is Frederick Brooks' idea of "conceptual integrity," first formulated in his book *The Mythical Man-Month* [9] published in 1975. In the most recent milestone by Daniel Jackson, concepts are already visible in the title of his book, *The Essence of Software: Why Concepts Matter for Great Design* [10], published in 2021.

2.1 Liskov Types and Dahl and Hoare Hierarchical Structures

Original ideas by Barbara Liskov [8] and coworkers were published a few years after the proposal of the software engineering discipline, especially, the Liskov Substitution Principle, which tries to define the relation between *types* and their *subtypes*, i.e., the idea of inheritance.

Why is Liskov's Principle so interesting?

First, by what should have been obvious, the necessity of *structure and behavior* duality. Despite the fact that *types*—i.e., classes—are *structural* notions, inheritance by subtypes is surprisingly defined in terms of conservation of *behavior*.

Second, the audacity to generalize, motivated by the search for a *real theory of abstraction*. The Liskov Substitution Principle is formulated in terms of a certain *type* and its *subtype*. It refers to *all programs* containing such a type, despite the "all programs" generalization clearly being an obstacle to formal correctness verification of the principle for any particular case.

The "Hierarchical Program Structures" [7], written by Ole-Johan Dahl and C.A.R. Hoare, is the third monograph of the influential book entitled *Structured Programming* (published in 1972). It still uses the programs and programming notions, instead of software, although the term software engineering had already surfaced 4 years before.

The first sentence of Dahl and Hoare's monograph refers to exploration of program structure and its relation to concept modeling. *Concept modeling* is a central and recurrent theme of software. Basic examples refer to "type," which is a class of values. Associated with each *type concept*, there are a number of operations which apply to the type values. Thus, each of the types includes a data structure and a set of associated operations, again reflecting the *structure and behavior* duality.

The idea of *modularity* is expressed by concepts concerning limited aspects of the system, i.e., a subsystem obtained by decomposition of the whole system. Good design ensures system decomposition such that each module may be designed and revised virtually without implications for other modules of the system. An influential paper on modularity is that by Parnas in 1972 [11].

In modern terminology, Dahl and Hoare ([7], p. 179) state that a procedure originating block instances that survive its call is named a *class*. Its instances are coined *objects* of that class. A class also has variables and procedures local to the class body, named *attributes* of that class.

Conceptual hierarchies are built in which each layer is a conceptual level of understanding. A system is constructed and understood in terms of high-level concepts. These are in turn understood in terms of lower-level concepts and so on. The important construction principle (see [7] p. 209) is *abstraction*. One focuses on common features, abstracting away other features that are far removed from the relevant working conceptual level.

2.2   Brooks' Conceptual Integrity

Frederick P. Brooks, Jr. declared in his book *The Mythical Man-Month* in 1975 [9], and reiterated in his *The Design of Design* in 2010 [12], that "conceptual integrity is the most important consideration for Software system design."

Let us carefully analyze the implications of such a statement.

The first intriguing word is conceptual. *Concepts*, rather than programming language reserved words, are essential to human natural languages. The message conveyed is that instead of focusing on some formal or informal technique to avoid errors during the software system design, the important issue is clear understanding by humans of the final design product, viz., software systems.

The second intriguing word is *integrity*, which points to intimate relationships among concepts within a software system. Concepts are not arbitrary. Integrity means coherence. These relationships were already hinted at by Dahl and Hoare, in their abstracting away features that are irrelevant to the intended conceptual level.

The surprisingly far-fetched idea assigns the *most important design considera-tion* to conceptual integrity. Can this be justified in a deeper way? Brooks instead provides ([12], p. 143) design principles to answer another question: How to achieve conceptual integrity?

Brooks' *conceptual integrity* principles, slightly modified (see Perez De Rosso and Jackson [13], p. 39), are formulated as follows:

- *Propriety*—a software system should have only the concepts essential to its purpose and no more.
- *Orthogonality*—individual concepts should be independent of one another.

These principles—propriety and orthogonality—hint at linear algebra, the basis of quantum computing. Indeed, the deeper justification for Brooks' conceptual integrity principles is given in Sect. 4 of this chapter, where we define Quantum Software.

2.3 Jackson's Software Concepts

Daniel Jackson's book *The Essence of Software* [10] finally illustrates software concepts with many examples, once more emphasizing the *structure and behavior* duality.

One such concept, the "recycle bin" (cf. [10] p. 49), is ubiquitous on the computer operating system screen desktop. Our standard tabular concept, a variant of the format proposed by Jackson [10] with added structors, functionals, and modules, is shown in Fig. 1.

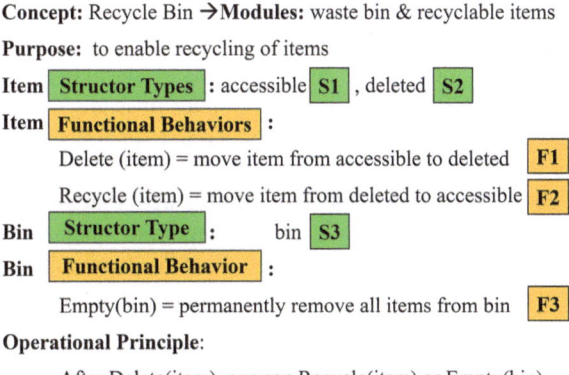

Fig. 1 Recycle Bin Quantum Software—tabular concept. Its two modules are a waste bin and recyclable items. It clearly shows, besides its purpose, the *structure and behavior* duality: its structor types (green) and its respective functional behaviors (orange). These are complemented by an explanatory operational principle

A few comments about Fig. 1 are in order:

- *Natural language concepts*—software concepts are always expressed in human natural language, providing suitable metaphors, which are very desirable.
- *Natural language richness*—concepts meaning is not necessarily linked to grammatical classification of a word; e.g., the word "empty" can be an adjective; in the recycle bin concept, empty is a verb. The word "accessible" is generally an adjective but has a multiplicity of meanings such as attainable, understandable, approachable, etc.
- *Structure and behavior*—at this stage, the *structure and behavior* duality should be familiar.

    Structors, as their name suggests, are related to *structure*, and *functionals* are related to *behavior*. More details are found in Sect. 4.
- *Structor types*—the *structor types* in the recycle bin refer to location. The bin itself is a possible location. The relevant metaphor is a waste basket. *Deleted* means inside the bin; *accessible* means outside the bin.
- *Concepts generality*—"recycle bin" does not fix the kind of item that can be recycled. One may use the concept whenever it is appropriate. Common usages are, for instance, a "file" or an "email message" that may be deleted or recycled.
- *Flexibility*—recycled means reusable, not necessarily for exactly the original usage.

3   What Is Quantum?

Assuming a potential chapter readership of both physicists and software researchers, we include in this section a very concise reminder of a few quantum computing ideas essential for understanding Quantum Software: superposition, entanglement, and the Density Matrix.[1]

We have already stated that Quantum Software is defined by its Density Matrix. Superposition and entanglement are important quantum properties, not found in classical computing, relevant to Density Matrix modularization and other calculations. The nature of Quantum Software is detailed in Sect. 4.

---

[1] The reader less familiar with these ideas is encouraged to read relevant sections of a quantum computing book (e.g., [14, 15]).

3.1 Superposition and Entanglement

In contrast to the two numerical values 0, 1 of classical bits, a qubit $|\psi\rangle$ may have any intermediate value between the ket state $|0\rangle$ and the ket state $|1\rangle$. It is said that $|\psi\rangle$ is in a *superposition*, as in Eq. (1):

$$|\psi\rangle = c_1{}^*|0\rangle + c_2{}^*|1\rangle \qquad (1)$$

where the coefficients c_1 and c_2 are complex numbers—probability amplitudes—obeying $c_1{}^2 + c_2{}^2 = 1$.

Assuming two particles a and b, each of them in a superposition state as in Eq. (1), their joint state is given by a tensor product $\otimes$:

$$|\psi\rangle = \left(a_1{}^* \ |0\rangle_a \ + a_2{}^* \ |1\rangle_a\right) \otimes \left(b_1{}^* \ |0\rangle_b \ + b_2{}^* \ |1\rangle_b\right) \qquad (2)$$

Actually performing the multiplication obtains

$$|\psi\rangle = \left(a_1{}^*b_1{}^* \ |00\rangle + a_1{}^*b_2{}^* \ |01\rangle + a_2{}^*b_1{}^* \ |10\rangle + a_2{}^*b_2{}^* \ |11\rangle\right) \qquad (3)$$

This is still a separable superposition: one easily reverts to Eq. (2) by extracting the coefficients a_1, a_2.

Now suppose one goes back to the laboratory and carefully prepares the particles a and b in the following joint state:

$$|\psi\rangle = \left(a_1{}^*b_1{}^* \ |00\rangle + a_2{}^*b_2{}^* \ |11\rangle\right) \qquad (4)$$

This is an example of *entanglement*. Whenever particle a is in a given state, say $|0\rangle$, particle b is in the same state, and they are not separable. There are no coefficients to be extracted.

3.2 Density Matrix

The Density Matrix—a Von Neumann concept [16]—is a mathematical model which describes the state of a whole quantum system, whose most elementary subspaces are ket states associated with the Density Matrix columns (see Sect. 4.1 and the examples in Sect. 5).

Strictly, the Density Matrix is the matrix representation of the density operator. Since the Density Matrix is itself an operator applicable to quantum vectors, interchanging the Density Matrix and density operator denominations is quite common. Thus, the Density Matrix duality, reflecting both the structure of a *state* and the behavior of an *operator*, nicely fits the *structure and behavior* software systems duality.

More formally, the Density Matrix associated with an n-dimensional Hilbert space is an n-by-n positive semi-definite, trace-one Hermitian matrix. Given a state-vector ψ describing the same pure quantum system, the fitting Density Matrix ρ is obtained as a ψ ket-bra, i.e., the operator is a projector:

$$\rho = |\psi\rangle\langle\psi| \tag{5}$$

A projector is an operator that projects its argument into a subspace of the whole space of the quantum system, justifying the relation between *projectors* and Quantum Software *modularization*.

4 What Is Quantum Software?

The next text box is a procedure from a tabular concept to a Quantum Software Density Matrix.

Procedure 1 – From Tabular Concept to Quantum Software Density Matrix

{   **Start from Tabular Concept** – with concepts possibly from Class Diagram or Quantum Circuit;

• **Translate Tabular Concept to Bipartite Graph** – with two indexed sets: Structors & Functionals;

• **Obtain Laplacian Matrix L** – from Bipartite Graph, using equation:

$$L = D - A$$

where D the Degree Matrix – whose elements are degrees of the Bipartite Graph vertices,

and A the Adjacency Matrix – whose non-zero elements are neighbors of each Bipartite Graph vertex;

• **Generate Density Matrix ρ** – by Laplacian normalization, dividing it by its *Trace(L)* as in

equation: $\rho = L / Trace(L)$ }

[more details in the text below]

This section describes the trajectory from a tabular concept—with concepts possibly extracted from a class diagram or a quantum circuit—until one reaches the Quantum Software Density Matrix. Its linear algebraic constraints, corresponding to Brooks' conceptual integrity principles, enable modularity. Finally, Quantum Software evolution and measurement are outlined.

4.1 From Tabular Concept to Its Quantum Software Density Matrix

Conceptualization, to decide what is the concepts' set of a specific software system defining its tabular concept is a very creative and nontrivial activity. The starting tabular concept of Procedure 1 can possibly be extracted from a suitable diagram:

	Modules		Providing Structors		Functionals	Consumed by Structors
M1	Item	**S1**	Accessible	**F1**	Delete-Item	**S2** Deleted
		S2	Deleted	**F2**	Recycle-Item	**S1** Accessible
M2	Waste Bin	**S3**	Bin	**F3**	Empty	

Fig. 2 Recycle bin software concept—explicit modules, structors, and functionals. Their assigned indices are shown in the bipartite graph, to be identifiers of rows and columns in the following matrices. For instance, the *S2* deleted structor provides the *F2* recycle-item functional, which is consumed by the *S1* accessible structor

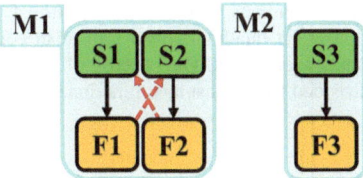

Fig. 3 Recycle bin software concept—bipartite graph. It has six vertices: structors have a green background; functionals are shown in orange. Arrows pointing downward (black) mark provided functionals. Arrows with dashed lines pointing upward (red) mark consumed functionals. Two modules are shown on a light blue background

class diagram for classical software system or quantum circuit for a quantum or hybrid software system. Once the tabular concept is obtained, the procedure is the same for all types of software systems.

The "recycle bin" tabular concept of Fig. 1 (shown in Sect. 2.3) serves to illustrate Procedure 1. Figure 2 details how to explicitly assign indices to the recycle bin concepts: structors indexed by *Sj* and functionals indexed by *Fk*. It also includes modules that in principle are seen only after Density Matrix modularization.

In order to allow software systems with conceptual hierarchies, where each conceptual level has its own Density Matrix, we generalize the notion of *class* to *structor*, and similarly generalize *class method* to *functional*, to be usable at any conceptual level.

The recycle bin tabular concept of Figs. 1 and 2 is translated to a bipartite graph shown in Fig. 3. According to the definition of any bipartite graph, it has two vertex sets, such that a vertex in a certain set is only linked to vertices in the other set.

One obtains a Laplacian Matrix *L* from the bipartite graph using Eq. (6):

$$L = D - A \tag{6}$$

where *D* is the *D*egree matrix, whose elements in the diagonal D_{mm} are the degree values of the vertex *m* of the bipartite graph. An element A_{mn} of the *A*djacency matrix *A* is nonzero when the vertex *n* is a neighbor of the vertex *m*, and zero otherwise.

	F1	F2	F3	S1	S2	S3
F1	3	0	0	-2	-1	0
F2	0	3	0	-1	-2	0
F3	0	0	2	0	0	-2
S1	-2	-1	0	3	0	0
S2	-1	-2	0	0	3	0
S3	0	0	-2	0	0	2

Fig. 4 Recycle bin software concept—Laplacian matrix. The degree matrix is diagonal (green background). The adjacency matrix upper-right quadrant provided functionals (blue background) with −2 values and consumed functionals (hatched blue) with −1 value elements are reflected around the diagonal to the lower-left quadrant. Each Laplacian column element sums to zero. The same is true for Laplacian row elements. The purpose of different nonzero adjacency values (−1, −2) is to differentiate provided from consumed functionals (compare the arrow colors in the bipartite graph)

The recycle bin Laplacian matrix in Fig. 4 is obtained from the bipartite graph in Fig. 3.

One generates the Density Matrix ρ by normalizing the Laplacian matrix L. This is given according to the Density Matrix definition (see Sect. 3.2 of this chapter) and following Braunstein et al. [17]. Dividing L by the Laplacian matrix $Trace(L)$ as in Eq. (7) obtains $Trace(\rho)=1$:

$$L = L/Trace\,(L) \tag{7}$$

In Quantum Software Density Matrices each column and each row represents a different elementary concept, indexed by Sj and Fk. Each module represents a new encompassing concept, subsuming its columns and rows in a software system sub-matrix.

The recycle bin Quantum Software Density Matrix in Fig. 5 is the result of normalizing the Laplacian in Fig. 4.

4.2 Linear Algebraic Constraints for Software Systems

Brooks' conceptual integrity principles (of Sect. 2.2)—*propriety* and *orthogonality*—are here, respectively, reexpressed in linear algebraic terms by means of inner products of column and row vectors of the adjacency matrix—within the density matrix:

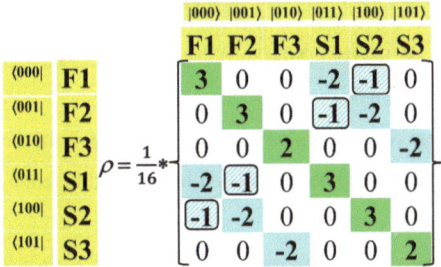

Fig. 5 Recycle bin Quantum Software—Density Matrix ρ. It is the Laplacian matrix of Fig. 4 normalized by *1/Trace(L)* of the Laplacian *L*, whose value is 1/16. Also added are the basis kets above the matrix columns, and corresponding basis bras to the left of matrix rows. See the explanation about modularity in Sect. 4.3

- *Vectors Linear Independence*—all adjacency matrix column vectors must be mutually linear independent, and the same must be true for all matrix row vectors, minimizing the number of Quantum Software system concepts. As a linear algebra consequence, each adjacency matrix quadrant, within the Density Matrix, is square.
- *Vectors Orthogonality*—all software system modules within the adjacency matrix should be mutually orthogonal because concepts in different modules have less in common than concepts in the same module. The adjacency matrix is block diagonal.

These linear algebraic constraints, within the Quantum Software context, are a deeper justification for Brooks' conceptual integrity idea, and also play a crucial role in Quantum Software modularization. On the other way round, these constraints are the beginning of the perception of Quantum Software as a verifiable theory of software systems.

4.3 Modularity

Modules are formally defined as subspaces of the whole Quantum Software Density matrix space. A Quantum Software formal modularization procedure is formulated in the next textbox.

Procedure 2 – Quantum Software <u>Density Matrix Modules</u>

{ **Start** – from Quantum Software Density Matrix;

- **Assign basis Kets & Bras** – Kets to Density Matrix columns, Bras to rows;
- **Apply Density Matrix to basis Kets** – obtaining the Density Matrix column corresponding to the respective Ket;
- **Express columns as algebraic sum of Kets** – each Ket fitting a non-zero matrix element of the obtained column;
- **Obtain basis Ket projector** – juxtapose fitting Bra at the end of sum of Kets;
- **Express the whole Density Matrix** – as a sum of basis Ket projectors;
- **Obtain Modules** – partition basis Ket projectors into disjoint sets of Kets/Bras }

The best clarification of this procedure is to illustrate it with an example, such as recycle bin. The assignment of the basis kets and bras to the Density Matrix columns and rows is already done in Fig. 5. Modularization results for the recycle bin software concept system are shown in Fig. 6.

Some relevant comments referring to Fig. 6 are:

- **Kets' columns and bras' rows**—it is easily checked that kets and bras in the projectors (middle column in Fig. 6) neatly fit to the Density Matrix columns and rows (in both quadrants of Fig. 5) indexed by the structors and functionals (r.h.s. column in Fig. 6).
- **Mathematical manipulation**—concepts are not directly manipulated in any procedure, due to the complex richness of natural language. Only their indices structors Sj and functionals Fk, kets and bras, which are clear-cut and unambigu-

	Module Concepts	Projectors	Structor & Functional Indices
M1	Item	$[\ 3*(\ \ |000\rangle*\langle000| + |001\rangle*\langle001| + |011\rangle*\langle011| + |100\rangle*\langle100|\ )\ ]$	S1 S2 F1 F2
M2	Bin	$2*[|010\rangle - |101\rangle] * [\langle010| - \langle101|]$	S3 F3

Fig. 6 Recycle bin Quantum Software—modules. These are obtained using Procedure 2. The bin module has a single projector shown in this figure. The item module has more projectors than the ones shown in this figure, but the displayed projectors are representative, since they contain all the kets and bras appearing in all other projectors. One clearly perceives that the item module projectors have kets and bras disjoint to those in the bin module projectors. For the sake of simplicity, the projectors do not include the Density Matrix normalizing factor

ous, are directly involved in any kind of calculation. The module concept names in the l.h.s. column of Fig. 6 are for illustration only.

- **Results confirmed by strict linear algebra**—the results in Fig. 6 are confirmed by a purely linear algebraic procedure: calculate Density Matrix eigenvectors and eigenvalues; modules are obtained from eigenvectors having eigenvalues equal to zero (see, e.g., [18]).
- **Absence of connectors**—*connectors* link modules allowing evolution (see Sect. 4.4). Here, the recycle bin Quantum Software does not have *connectors*, since there is no necessary linkage between the two modules, viz., *item* functionals and the *bin* "empty" functional. Items can be deleted or recycled, without the bin being emptied and vice versa, e.g., by an actuator external to the recycle bin system.

4.4 Evolution and Measurement

Density Matrix evolution means a highest-level simulated transition from state to state, in general from one module to the next one, equivalent to a low-level software run (see, e.g., Exman [19]).

Quantum Software Density Matrix evolution is done by means of unitary operators U and their adjoint, i.e., complex conjugate transpose $U^\dagger$ (U dagger) operators, defined in Eq. (8):

$$UU^\dagger = U^\dagger U = I \tag{8}$$

where I is the identity operator. Thus, $UU^\dagger$ is normalized.

Connectors are Density Matrix elements outside modules enabling evolution. Connectors serve as "cursors" defined by Feynman (see Feynman's 1985 paper [20], p. 15)—in analogy to a display movable indicator, pointing to a location where an evolution step may be selected. Unitary operators activate connectors: the simulation evolves by its focus moving from one module to the next one. This is indirect time simulation by state transitions, from module to module.

Quantum Software measurement upon its Density Matrix is actually done in a projective manner, again as Feynman previewed in his 1982 paper [1], by executing it several times until it converges to a stable value of the probabilistic result (see Exman and Zvulunov [21]).

5 Sample Quantum Software Concepts

This section offers a small set of Quantum Software concepts embodied in sample systems—one purely classical, some strictly quantum, and a hybrid combination of classical and quantum subsystems. The purpose is to illustrate the uniform approach to the variety of Quantum Software concepts, in the tabular concept and the corresponding Density Matrix for each case.

The emphasis is on *modules*, the essential highest abstraction level entities of Quantum Software. Modules obey linear algebraic constraints (from Sect. 4.2), especially *orthogonality*, and express conceptual meaning understood by human beings. We also point to specific modularity difficulties.

5.1   Reservation: A Purely Classical Concept

The *reservation* software concept ([10], p. 55) functionality is well known from everyday life: to make a *reservation* for a hotel room, a seat in a train or airplane, or a table at a restaurant. The goal, from the resource provider viewpoint, is to efficiently manage limited resources. It has two modules:

a) *Resource*—for instance, the rooms of a hotel; they may be provided to hotel guests after cleaning or retracted if the room needs periodic maintenance or repairs.
b) *User*—for example, hotel guests may make a reservation, use it as intended, or cancel it.

The reservation tabular concept is shown in Fig. 7.

The reservation Quantum Software Density Matrix in Fig. 8 fits the tabular concept in Fig. 7.

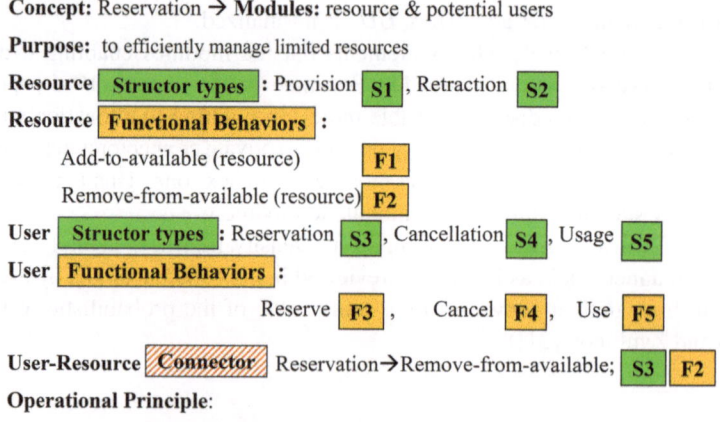

Fig. 7 Reservation Quantum Software—tabular concept. One sees two modules: *resource* with structors {S1, S2} and functionals {F1, F2}; *user* with structors {S3, S4, S5} and functionals {F3, F4, F5}, and one user-resource connector linking the two modules by means of a single matrix element {S3-F2}

		$\vert 0000\rangle$	$\vert 0001\rangle$	$\vert 0010\rangle$	$\vert 0011\rangle$	$\vert 0100\rangle$	$\vert 0101\rangle$	$\vert 0110\rangle$	$\vert 0111\rangle$	$\vert 1000\rangle$	$\vert 1001\rangle$
		F1	F2	F3	F4	F5	S1	S2	S3	S4	S5
$\langle 0000\vert$	F1	2	0	0	0	0	-2	0	0	0	0
$\langle 0001\vert$	F2	0	4	0	0	0	-1	-2	-1	0	0
$\langle 0010\vert$	F3	0	0	2	0	0	0	0	-2	0	0
$\langle 0011\vert$	F4	0	0	0	3	0	0	0	-1	-2	0
$\langle 0100\vert$	F5	0	0	0	0	3	0	0	-1	0	-2
$\langle 0101\vert$	S1	-2	-1	0	0	0	3	0	0	0	0
$\langle 0110\vert$	S2	0	-2	0	0	0	0	2	0	0	0
$\langle 0111\vert$	S3	0	-1	-2	-1	-1	0	0	5	0	0
$\langle 1000\vert$	S4	0	0	0	-2	0	0	0	0	2	0
$\langle 1001\vert$	S5	0	0	0	0	-2	0	0	0	0	2

$$\rho = \frac{1}{28} *$$

Fig. 8 Reservation Quantum Software—Density Matrix. In analogy to the recycle bin Density Matrix ρ in Fig. 5, one perceives the normalization factor whose value here is 1/28, the basis kets above the matrix columns, and fitting basis bras to the left of the matrix rows. Consumed functionals internal to the modules have a -1 value (hatched blue background). Please note the *connector* in the matrix element {S3-F2} (hatched brown background), also with a -1 value, linking the user 3-by-3 module to the resource 2-by-2 module

Comments on the reservation Quantum Software Density Matrix in Fig. 8 are:

- *Connector Evolution Step*—the specific purpose of this matrix in this chapter, with just one connector {S3-F2}, is to illustrate the very *connector* idea, as evolution enabler. The corresponding possible evolution step would be a transition from the *user* module making a reservation to the *resource* module removing the resource from the available ones.
- *Additional Connectors*—There could be additional connectors, not shown here; for example, Cancellation→Add-to-available could be added to the matrix element {S4-F1}.
- *Internally Consumed Functionals*—there are three consumed functionals inside their respective modules, whose meanings are: {S1-F2} a provided resource can be removed by the *resource* provision from the available ones, e.g., for maintenance or repairs; {S3-F4} a reservation can be cancelled by the *user*; {S3-F5} a reservation can be used by the respective *user*.
- *Modularization Confirmed by Strict Linear Algebra*—similar to the recycle bin (Fig. 6), the modularization in Fig. 8 is confirmed by a purely linear algebraic procedure based upon Density Matrix eigenvectors and eigenvalues [18]. Note that the highest degree values in the diagonal degree matrix are those referring to the *connector* matrix element. Excluding the connector from the Density Matrix leaves exactly two neat modules, *resource* and *user*.

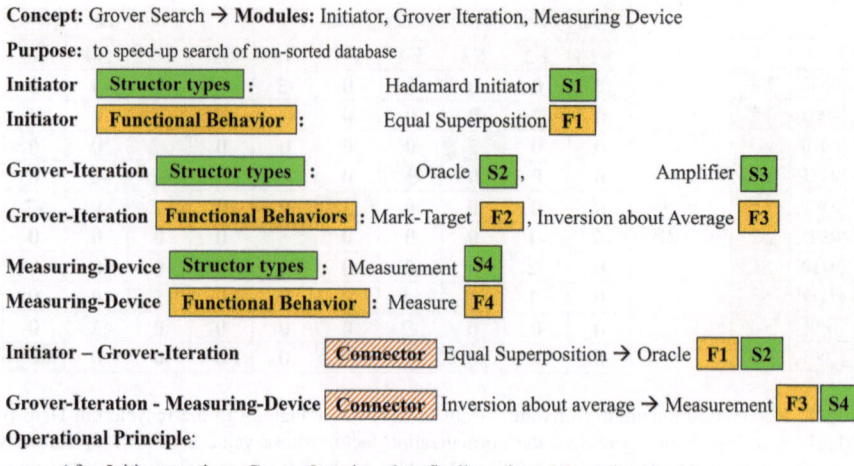

Concept: Grover Search → **Modules:** Initiator, Grover Iteration, Measuring Device

Purpose: to speed-up search of non-sorted database

Initiator   Structor types :   Hadamard Initiator S1

Initiator   Functional Behavior :   Equal Superposition F1

Grover-Iteration Structor types :   Oracle S2 ,   Amplifier S3

Grover-Iteration Functional Behaviors : Mark-Target F2 , Inversion about Average F3

Measuring-Device Structor types : Measurement S4

Measuring-Device Functional Behavior : Measure F4

Initiator – Grover-Iteration   Connector Equal Superposition → Oracle F1 S2

Grover-Iteration - Measuring-Device Connector Inversion about average → Measurement F3 S4

Operational Principle:

   After Initiator, activate Grover-Iteration, then finally activate Measuring-Device

Fig. 9 Grover search Quantum Software—tabular concept. It has three modules (initiator, Grover iteration, and measuring device) and two connectors linking the modules initiator to Grover iteration, and linking Grover iteration to measuring device

5.2   Grover Search: A Modular Quantum Concept

Grover search is a well-known quantum computing algorithm [22]. It speeds up search of a non-sorted database of N elements with a computational complexity of $O(\sqrt{N})$, compared to a classical algorithm with a complexity of $O(N)$. The Grover tabular concept, at the highest abstraction level, is shown in Fig. 9. The respective Quantum Software Density Matrix is shown in Fig. 10.

The obvious modularity of this Quantum Software concept is clearly perceived in the operational principle in Fig. 9. It corresponds to a quantum circuit strictly linear and sequential, widely described in literature sources (see, e.g., [14], page 251; [23] p. 168) with a single register of n qubits, where the number of search elements is $N=2^n$. There may be additional qubits internal to the oracle workspace. The Grover iteration is repeated $O(\sqrt{N})$ times.

Some comments about the Grover search Quantum Software concept in Fig. 9 are:

- *This is a highest-abstraction level model*—quantum gates implementation do not appear in the tabular concept or in the Density Matrix. For instance, one knows that Equal Superposition is performed by Hadamard Gates $H^{\otimes n}$ but they are not explicit here. The same is true for the threshold number of Grover cycle repetitions, which is absent.
- *Modules are orthogonal*—this is clearly seen by the Density Matrix element colors (blue and hatched blue); like in the reservation case, by eliminating *connectors*, one retains the neat modules.

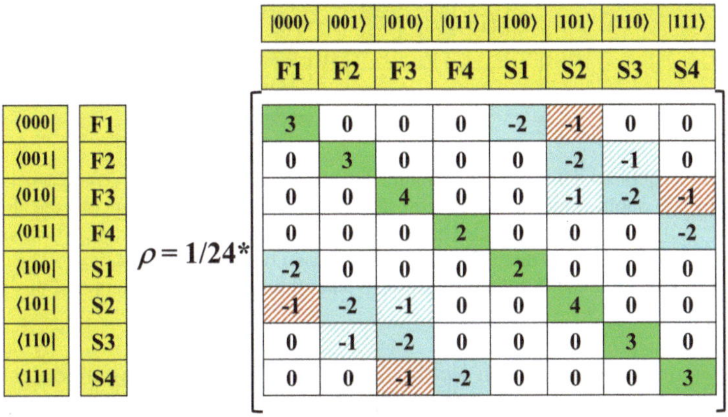

		|000⟩	|001⟩	|010⟩	|011⟩	|100⟩	|101⟩	|110⟩	|111⟩
		F1	**F2**	**F3**	**F4**	**S1**	**S2**	**S3**	**S4**
⟨000|	**F1**	3	0	0	0	-2	-1	0	0
⟨001|	**F2**	0	3	0	0	0	-2	-1	0
⟨010|	**F3**	0	0	4	0	0	-1	-2	-1
⟨011|	**F4**	0	0	0	2	0	0	0	-2
⟨100|	**S1**	-2	0	0	0	2	0	0	0
⟨101|	**S2**	-1	-2	-1	0	0	4	0	0
⟨110|	**S3**	0	-1	-2	0	0	0	3	0
⟨111|	**S4**	0	0	-1	-2	0	0	0	3

$\rho = 1/24*$

Fig. 10 Grover search Quantum Software—Density Matrix. It shows the three modules of Fig. 9, in descending order in the upper-right and lower-left quadrants: 1-by-1 initiator, 2-by-2 Grover iteration, and 1-by-1 measuring device (all three modules with blue matrix elements and the Grover iteration consumed functionals with hatched blue). One also sees the two connectors (F1, S2) and (F3, S4) (hatched brown), basis kets above the Density Matrix columns, basis bras to the left of the matrix rows, the diagonal degree matrix (green), and the normalization factor 1/24

- *Modules have meaning*—modules' meaning is given by their associated natural language concepts, found in general language dictionaries: initiator, iteration, and measuring device. Even structor and functional names have a long history (see the discussion in Sect. 7.3).

5.3 QFT and Order Finding: The Modularity Viewpoint

This section contrasts one of the simplest examples of QFT (quantum Fourier transform) with the order finding algorithm, which itself uses inverse QFT as one of its ingredients. It shows that such a simple QFT is *not* modular in the two senses that we have seen before:

- *No orthogonality*—one cannot easily compose its gates into a reduced number of most natural modules.
- *No meaning*—there is no natural language assignment to the potential modules.

To this end, we look at the well-known three qubits QFT quantum circuit in Fig. 11.

The $\mathbf{R_k}$ gates are unitary transformations defined in Eq. (9):

$$R_k \equiv \begin{pmatrix} 1 & 0 \\ 0 & e^{2\pi i /2^k} \end{pmatrix} \tag{9}$$

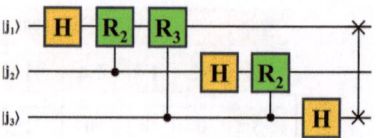

Fig. 11 Three qubits QFT—typical quantum circuit. Each horizontal line represents the time passing of each qubit. Time increases from left to right. The leftmost kets are the three input states $|j_1\rangle, \ldots, |j_3\rangle$. The quantum gates are **H** the Hadamard gate, and $\mathbf{R_k}$ gates, which are 2-by-2 matrices seen in Eq. (9). The three $\mathbf{R_k}$ boxes are each part of a **controlled-$\mathbf{R_k}$** gate. The rightmost symbol linking the first and third qubits is a swap gate. See below an explanation of this circuit

What is the essential reason for the three qubits QFT not being modular—in the above senses of orthogonality and meaning?

This is due to the nature of *controlled-gates*. Each of these gates involves two endpoints: one is the *controller*—graphically represented by a black dot—and the other is the *target* which is a single-qubit gate. The critical issue is that two endpoints sit on different qubits. The most common *controlled-gate* is the *controlled*-NOT, abbreviated CNOT. If the controller qubit value is $|1\rangle$, the target gate is activated; otherwise, if the controller value is $|0\rangle$, the target gate is not activated and there is no change of the target qubit value.

One can clearly see in Fig. 11 that controlled-gate endpoints link diverse pairs of qubits. For instance, counting from the left-hand side, the first *controlled*-R_2 links the upper qubit with the middle qubit, while the *controlled*-R_3 links the upper qubit with the lowest qubit. Moreover, these *controlled*-R_k gates are intermingled with Hadamard gates. The outcome of this situation is the difficulty of slicing the quantum circuit vertically—into *orthogonal* modules: there are no consecutive gate groups referring to the same qubits. Similarly, it is difficult to slice the quantum circuit horizontally—into coherent *meaning* modules: there are no consecutive gate groups performing the same functionality.

The conclusion is quite clear: this three qubits QFT is a circuit of too low abstraction level in order to afford meaningful modules. See the discussion in Sect. 7.1 on the definition of modules.

We significantly jump upward in abstraction level and deal with the order finding algorithm, used in Shor's ([14, 15, 24, 25]) quantum factorization algorithm. A quantum circuit is shown in Fig. 12.

The quantum circuit in Fig. 12 is not new; there are several variants in the quantum computing scientific literature (e.g., [14]), which the reader should be familiar with. Some clarifying comments are:

- *Definition of order*—assume a pair of positive integers $\mathbf{a} < \mathbf{N}$, which have no common factors; the order of $\mathbf{a} \bmod \mathbf{N}$ is formally defined as the least positive integer $\mathbf{x}$ such that $\mathbf{a^x} = 1 \ (\mathbf{mod\ N})$.
- *Order finding problem*—given a pair of positive integers, $\mathbf{a}$, $\mathbf{N}$, find the order $\mathbf{x}$. The function of relevance to the order finding problem, $\mathbf{f} = \mathbf{a^x} \bmod \mathbf{N}$, obtaining

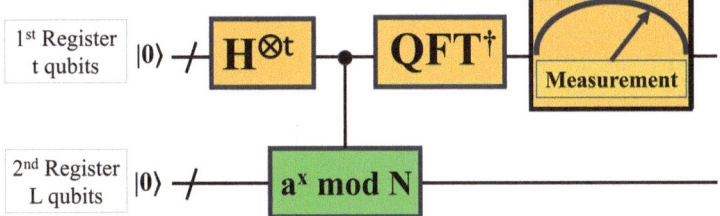

Fig. 12 Order finding algorithm—quantum circuit. Its entities, reminiscent of single quantum gates, actually stand for whole modules: from left to right, in the first register is the Hadamard *initiator*, a *controller* black dot, an *inverse QFT* (quantum Fourier transform—the dagger † here means "inverse"), and a *measurement* device. The module in the second register is a *modular exponentiation* represented by a term giving the "remainder after division of $\mathbf{a^x}$ by $\mathbf{N}$" (more details in the text below). The kets $|0\rangle$ at the left-side origin of both registers are computational initial states. The slash after the initial states is a conventional indication that each of these registers has a certain number of qubits, instead of just one

the remainder after division of $\mathbf{a^x}$ by $\mathbf{N}$, is periodic. The big numbers factoring problem reduces to finding the period of a function.

- *Do not confuse <u>module</u> with <u>modulo</u> or mod = <u>modulus</u>*—it is somewhat unfortunate that this chapter must refer to two (or three) well-established concepts with quite different meanings, and so similar writing. Even worse, the adjective "modular" is used with both meanings. *Module* is a separable component of a system; *modulus* (abbreviated *mod*) is a natural number used as a divisor in modular arithmetic; *modulo* means with respect to a specified modulus.
- *Modular exponentiation*—in this expression, "modular" refers to modulus and not to modules.

It is legitimate to still have a few reminders of quantum gates in the higher-level quantum circuit. This enables us to understand the ability to vertically slice the circuit into orthogonal modules. The obvious case is the *initiator* module whose gate implementation is a single Hadamard gate $\mathbf{H}$ to the tensor power of t. This is impossible in the three qubits QFT lower-level quantum circuit since there the Hadamard gates are intermingled with *controlled*-R_k gates.

The novel and important contribution of this Quantum Software concept example is the observation that going upward toward the modules highest abstraction level, one is well above the quantum gates and qubit registers implementation. These gates and registers are considered analogous to the lower machine language of classical software, whose history we do not wish to repeat.

In the tabular concept and its Quantum Software Density Matrix, we strictly avoid any reference to quantum gates implementation or to qubit registers. Thus, one regains modularity in the senses of *orthogonality* and *conceptual meaning*.

Figure 13 shows an order finding algorithm tabular concept, with modules, without referring to any quantum gates or qubit registers. See the discussion on proper names as concepts in Sect. 7.3.

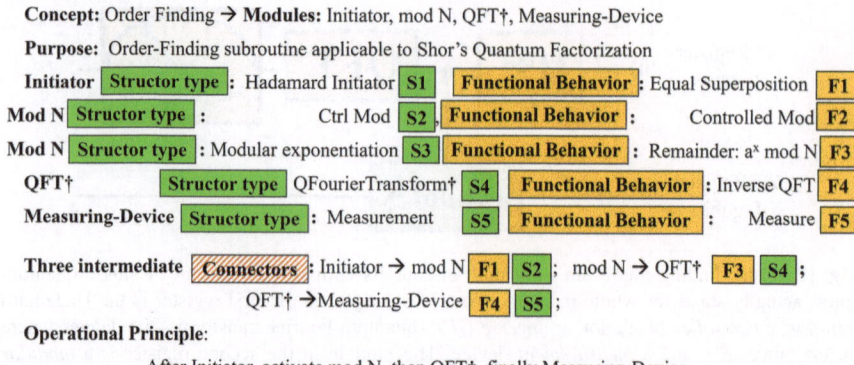

Concept: Order Finding → **Modules:** Initiator, mod N, QFT†, Measuring-Device

Purpose: Order-Finding subroutine applicable to Shor's Quantum Factorization

Fig. 13 Order finding algorithm Quantum Software—tabular concept With the same format as in previous tabular concepts, one sees four modules and respective structors and functionals. The number of connectors could in principle be changed (see the Density Matrix and its comments below)

		|0000⟩	|0001⟩	|0010⟩	|0011⟩	|0100⟩	|0101⟩	|0110⟩	|0111⟩	|1000⟩	|1001⟩
		F1	F2	F3	F4	F5	S1	S2	S3	S4	S5
⟨0000|	F1	3	0	0	0	0	-2	-1	0	0	0
⟨0001|	F2	0	3	0	0	0	0	-2	-1	0	0
⟨0010|	F3	0	0	3	0	0	0	0	-2	-1	0
⟨0011|	F4	0	0	0	3	0	0	0	0	-2	-1
⟨0100|	F5	0	0	0	0	2	0	0	0	0	-2
⟨0101|	S1	-2	0	0	0	0	2	0	0	0	0
⟨0110|	S2	-1	-2	0	0	0	0	3	0	0	0
⟨0111|	S3	0	-1	-2	0	0	0	0	3	0	0
⟨1000|	S4	0	0	-1	-2	0	0	0	0	3	0
⟨1001|	S5	0	0	0	-1	-2	0	0	0	0	3

$$\rho = \frac{1}{28} *$$

Fig. 14 Order finding algorithm Quantum Software—Density Matrix. One can see its four modules (blue background): all of them of 1-by-1 size, except the 2-by-2 **Mod N** module, with two structors {S2, S3} and two functionals {F2, F3}. The functional F2 (hatched blue) is internally consumed by the S3 structor. Transitions between pairs of modules are enabled by *connectors* (hatched brown). As usual, one also sees the diagonal degree matrix (green), the normalizing factor 1/28, the basis kets above columns, and basis bras to the left of the matrix rows

Figure 14 shows the order finding Density Matrix corresponding to the tabular concept in Fig. 13.

A comment on the Order Finding Density Matrix in Fig. 14 is:

- *Controlled Mod N*—the pragmatic Density Matrix solution to avoid explicit reference even to a generic so-to-speak controlled quantum gate seen in the quantum circuit in Fig. 12 has a 2-by-2 **Mod N** module, where the information transmitted from the controller structor S2 is conveyed by the internally consumed functional F2 to the target structor S3.

5.4   Modularity Within Hybrid Teleportation

The hybrid Quantum Software example is the teleportation protocol. Quantum circuits and detailed explanations of the teleportation protocol are widely found in the literature (e.g., [15] p. 82; [14] p. 26). Its purpose, based on entanglement of EPR (Einstein-Podolsky-Rosen [26]) pairs, is to teleport an unknown quantum state $|\phi\rangle$ from Alice's location A to Bob's other location B.

After a preliminary preparation in a joint Alice and Bob location A and B of an initial EPR pair, compare Eq. (4) in Sect. 3.1—in which Alice controls the first qubit "a" and Bob the second qubit "b":

$$|\textbf{EPR}_0\rangle = 1/\sqrt{2}^* \ (|0_a 0_b\rangle + |1_a 1_b\rangle) \tag{10}$$

Then Alice and Bob separate: Alice goes to location A, where she holds $|\phi\rangle$, and Bob goes to location B.

The teleportation hybrid character is characterized by three stages:

- *Initial quantum stage*—Alice's initial state in location A is $|\phi\rangle \otimes |\textbf{EPR}_0\rangle$; she performs *decoding*.
- *Classical stage*—Alice performs measurement of its two qubits in location A, projecting her state to Bob's state in B; then Alice does classical transmission of two bits.
- *Final quantum stage*—Bob receives two classical bits and does *encoding* by means of Pauli transforms, which are used to restore the original quantum state $|\phi\rangle$ in location B.

The teleportation protocol Quantum Software tabular concept is shown in Fig. 15. The corresponding Density Matrix is shown in Fig. 16.

A comment on the teleportation protocol Density Matrix is:

- *Classical communication message*—is represented in the Density Matrix, without any difference from purely quantum modules, by its structor and functional.

6   Related Work

The scientific literature dealing with relevant subjects is quite large, well beyond the reasonable scope of this chapter. We mention here a focused sample of references, among others covering the mutual interaction of programming, software, and physical systems.

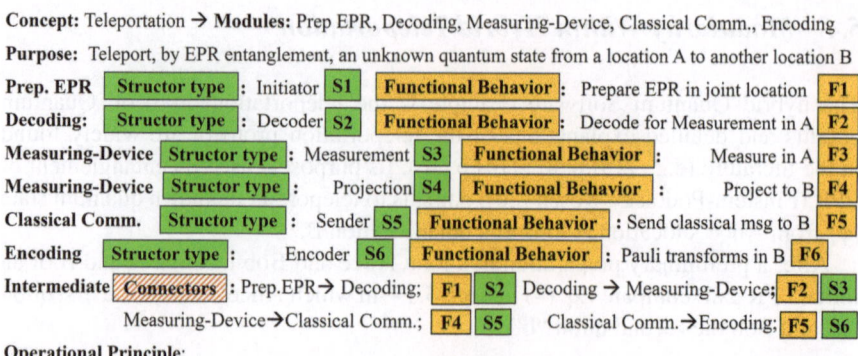

Fig. 15 Teleportation protocol Quantum Software—tabular concept. The teleportation protocol always triggers a surprise at first sight. Its causes are well exposed in this tabular concept. In particular, worthy of attention is the measuring device with two structors and their respective functionals: measurement in location A and projection to location B

		$\lvert 0000\rangle$	$\lvert 0001\rangle$	$\lvert 0010\rangle$	$\lvert 0011\rangle$	$\lvert 0100\rangle$	$\lvert 0101\rangle$	$\lvert 0110\rangle$	$\lvert 0111\rangle$	$\lvert 1000\rangle$	$\lvert 1001\rangle$	$\lvert 1010\rangle$	$\lvert 1011\rangle$
		F1	F2	F3	F4	F5	F6	S1	S2	S3	S4	S5	S6
$\langle 0000\rvert$	F1	3	0	0	0	0	0	-2	-1	0	0	0	0
$\langle 0001\rvert$	F2	0	3	0	0	0	0	0	-2	-1	0	0	0
$\langle 0010\rvert$	F3	0	0	3	0	0	0	0	0	-2	-1	0	0
$\langle 0011\rvert$	F4	0	0	0	3	0	0	0	0	0	-2	-1	0
$\langle 0100\rvert$	F5	0	0	0	0	3	0	0	0	0	0	-2	-1
$\langle 0101\rvert$	F6	0	0	0	0	0	2	0	0	0	0	0	-2
$\langle 0110\rvert$	S1	-2	0	0	0	0	0	2	0	0	0	0	0
$\langle 0111\rvert$	S2	-1	-2	0	0	0	0	0	3	0	0	0	0
$\langle 1000\rvert$	S3	0	-1	-2	0	0	0	0	0	3	0	0	0
$\langle 1001\rvert$	S4	0	0	-1	-2	0	0	0	0	0	3	0	0
$\langle 1010\rvert$	S5	0	0	0	-1	-2	0	0	0	0	0	3	0
$\langle 1011\rvert$	S6	0	0	0	0	-1	-2	0	0	0	0	0	3

$$\rho = \frac{1}{34} *$$

Fig. 16 Teleportation protocol Quantum Software—Density Matrix. Similar to its tabular concept in Fig. 15, the module worthy of attention is the 2-by-2 measuring device, whose structors are {S3, S4} with functionals {F3, F4}, as it represents both measurement in location A and projection to location B. The F3-S4 matrix element (hatched blue) is an internal functional F3 consumed by the structor S4, enabling transition from measurement to projection

6.1 Operators and Superoperators

A superoperator is a linear operator acting on a vector space of linear operators. Specifically, it may refer to a *TPCP* map, i.e., a trace-preserving completely positive map. This is especially the case for mappings of density operators to density operators (see, e.g., Preskill [27]).

Mauerer [28] presented a quantum programming language cQPL (an extended QPL), capable of quantum communication. This language has a denotational semantics based on a partial order of superoperators. In general, superoperators applied to Density Matrices describe quantum mechanical processes, being significant to this chapter's contents.

Javanainen [29] in his paper "The Software Atom" developed a set of C++ classes, abstracting concepts of quantum mechanics in a specific context of interactions between atom energy levels and light fields. The idea is to emphasize the possibility of such abstract software development and not to provide optimized end-user programs. Besides standard vector and matrix algebra, the abstract set of classes includes linear operators such as the density operator ρ and superoperators.

6.2 Extended UML

While the approach of this chapter is centered on the Quantum Software entity of Density Matrix, whose application is naturally extended to classical and hybrid kinds of software systems, one finds in the literature the opposite direction: to take existing classical sets of diagrams, mostly UML, the unified modeling language, and extend them to be applicable to Quantum Software systems.

Perez-Delgado [30] (pages 103–119, in Serrano et al. [31]) proposed Q-UML, a very preliminary extension of UML to model Quantum Software, with the goal of minimally changing the base UML. In other words, for a strictly classical software system, its modeling by Q-UML should be identical to the modeling by the original base UML. Q-UML diagrams—such as a class or sequence diagrams of a system—may contain together both quantum and classical elements. In Q-UML, quantum classes/objects are marked to distinguish them from the classical UML counterparts. This, in contrast to the Quantum Software Density Matrix of the current chapter which represents both quantum and classical modules in a uniform way, and purposefully avoids distinguishing quantum from classical systems.

Perez-Castillo, Jimenez-Navajas, and Piattini [32] in their paper "Modelling Quantum Circuits with UML" propose to define a UML profile for quantum modeling based upon UML metamodels. This is a lightweight extension of the UML Activity Diagram. The UML profile displays six stereotypes: *quantum circuit*, *qubit*, *quantum gate*, *controlled qubit*, *measure*, and *reset*. These stereotypes have their corresponding *metaclasses*. Once the metamodel is designed, one can use it to obtain specific quantum circuits represented with UML.

UML extensions have the advantage of being familiar to software developers, demanding a mild learning curve. On the other hand, UML and its extensions are informal, and do not offer the underlying theoretical richness of the Quantum Software Density Matrix of the current chapter.

6.3 Modules

Modularity is an important idea for classical computing, and indeed for any engineering discipline, as described in the Baldwin and Clark book *Design Rules*, whose volume 1 is entitled *The Power of Modularity* [33]. Their approach is from an economic perspective. The paper by Sullivan et al. on "The Structure and Value of Modularity in Software Design" [34] also refers to classical computing. Despite being more software oriented, it applies the economic approach of Baldwin and Clark. Newman and Girvan, in their paper "Finding and evaluating community structure in networks" [35], published in the physics literature, offers a widely used criterion for modularity.

There are many module definitions in the quantum computing literature. Here are two examples.

An interesting and quite recent (April 2023) paper by Kang and Oh [36] entitled "Modular Component-Based Quantum Circuit Synthesis" has some objectives similar to the current chapter. These authors observed that previous work (known as *unitary synthesis*) obtained quantum circuits which are nonintuitive, making their effects on data values difficult to comprehend. Kang and Oh's stated objectives are to generate human-readable, high-level circuits revealing the algorithm's inner workings. There is a subtle but significant difference between "readable" and *meaningful*. This follows from their assumptions and their procedures. They characterize as modules any arbitrary slicing of a quantum circuit. See the discussion in Sect. 7.1.

A thought-provoking paper by Thompson, Modi, Vedral, and Gu [37] entitled "Quantum Plug n' Play: Modular Computation in the Quantum Regime" was published in the *New Journal of Physics* in 2018. It enables usage of prefabricated circuits without knowing their construction. The lack of knowledge has many advantages, such as allowing partial outsourcing of quantum circuits, with exchange or upgrade of individual components. On the other hand, they prove a negative theorem: that it is not always possible to use quantum circuits without knowing their construction. They ask interesting questions such as: To what extent can a client invoke a server to automatically perform a computation $P(U)$, whenever one transforms an input $|\phi\rangle$ into $U|\phi\rangle$?

7 Discussion

This section is meant to coherently summarize this chapter with the following intentions:

- Sharpen central ideas of this work, such as modules and connectors.
- Clarify the importance of Quantum Software conceptualization.

- Offer Quantum Software practical applications, beyond the fundamental theoretical basis.
- Suggest Quantum Software's future potential roles.

7.1 Definition and Meaning of Quantum Software Modules

As stated at the beginning of Sect. 4.3, modules of Quantum Software are formally defined as subspaces of the whole Density Matrix space. These in turn have an essential conceptual meaning afforded by the subsumed structors and functionals, columns and rows, as assigned by their indices S_j, F_k.

To compare with alternatives in the scientific literature, mentioned in Sect. 6.3, we emphasize that our view of modules has two inseparable complementary aspects:

- *Tabular concept = modules have meaning*—natural language understood by humans
- *Density Matrix = modules are orthogonal*—subspaces of the whole Density Matrix

The already referred paper by Kang and Oh [36] defines modules in terms of quantum circuits, as consecutive slices of quantum gates. There is no notion of Density Matrix generated from a conceptual starting point. Contrasted with this chapter's modules, Kang and Oh's modules display two properties:

(a) *May have arbitrary size*—one can slice quantum circuits as desired: a single quantum circuit may have multiple modular representations.
(b) *Do not have intrinsic meaning*—human readability of quantum circuits does not necessarily imply modules with conceptual meaning.

A related issue demands high abstraction level of a Quantum Software system to attain modules with self-consistent meaning. The problem was illustrated by the intermingling of controlled-gates in the three qubits QFT counterexample (in Sect. 5.3). In this respect, the paper by Shende, Bullock, and Markov [38] on "Synthesis of Quantum Logic Circuits" states two relevant facts:

(a) *Quantum controlled-gates are considered "expensive gates"*—in particular, CNOTs which are often the standard two-qubit gate, up to the point that the cost of a quantum circuit can be realistically estimated by counting CNOT gates.
(b) *The number of CNOT gates is exponential on the number of qubits*—and there is a theoretical lower bound for the number of CNOT gates in any Quantum Software system. Moreover, if one insists in using the implementation technology with only nearest-neighbor gates, it significantly increases the number of gates.

7.2   Connector Roles Within the Quantum Software Density Matrix

In this chapter, connectors were defined in Sect. 4.4. *Connectors* are Density Matrix elements outside modules enabling evolution. Connectors serve as *cursors* as defined by Feynman (in his 1985 paper [20], on p. 15), pointing to a location where an evolution step may be selected.

Comparing the Quantum Software examples in Sect. 5, one perceives different connector roles, some of which may also be performed by internally consumed functionals:

- *Single connector between two modules*—is the simplest case. The presence of a connector does not imply its usage. In the middle of an evolution, in the absence of a connector, a transition between two modules is done automatically.
- *Two looping connectors*—in the example of the Grover search, in Figs. 9 and 10, instead of two connectors, the iteration is performed by a pair of internally consumed functionals.
- *Two connectors in opposite directions*—for instance, in the recycle bin, in Figs. 1 and 5, the delete functional F1 moves an item from accessible to deleted, while the recycle functional F2 moves an item back from deleted to accessible. These could be connectors, but in Fig. 5, they are performed by internally consumed functionals.

7.3   Conceptualization: Metaphors and Proper Names as Concepts

Conceptualization is a central activity for Quantum Software development, demanding significant amounts of creativity. The purpose of this short section is to characterize two deep conceptualization issues:

- *The unavoidable limitations of programming languages*—programming languages have a fixed number of reserved words defined by their syntax. They are inevitably restricted to low-level abstraction, insufficient for full range software development. This began to change with the ideas of abstract types and classes (described at the beginning of Sect. 2 of this chapter) but could never be liberated from their inherent limitations.
- *The complexity of natural languages*—natural languages seem to be the suitable linguistic tools for high-level abstraction software development, overcoming the programming limitations. Then a different difficulty appears: the richness and complexity of natural languages is an obstacle for a formal scientific theory of software, with a notion of verifiable correctness.

The proposed solution for the latter obstacle, offered in this chapter, is a complementary combination of two entities. Each Quantum Software system should be defined by a *tabular concept* freely expressed in natural language, together with the corresponding *Density Matrix* chosen as the necessary formal basis of a scientific theory. These two entities are supposed to be linked by a one-to-one relationship given by the indexing of the natural language concepts.

We emphasize that these two entities are essential since:

- Natural languages are indispensable and intrinsic to the meaning of software.
- On the other hand, natural languages are continuously evolving and apparently are too complex to be the basis of a foundational and stable scientific theory of software.

We conclude this short consideration of natural languages with a few observations. Most of the natural language concept meanings are adopted from everyday conversation: reservation, cancellation, recycle, and so on. But there are words with deeper cultural roots.

A wonderful example is the concept of an *oracle*—in the Grover search tabular concept. The huge contrast is notable between the underlying history, full of significant nuances—the oracle of Delphi, Greek mythology—and the clarity and conciseness of a software oracle, indeed, an excellent metaphor for software. How is this achieved?

A further example is proper names as common concepts. (Jacques) *Hadamard* is neither a quantum gate nor a transform. He was a prolific French mathematician, with a broader view of culture, who published a book on "The Psychology of Invention in the Mathematical Field" [39]. (Joseph) *Fourier* is not a high-level QFT gate, a transform, or a series. Another French mathematician and physicist, whose name has become synonymous with a concept with a relatively broad meaning, in the context of periodic phenomena, is found even in natural language dictionaries.

Perhaps in the conceptualization process we lose most of the original meaning of metaphors and proper names. Or do clarity and conciseness distill the essence of the original meaning?

7.4 Applications of Quantum Software

The main goal of this chapter is to delineate and open the way for a self-consistent theory of Quantum Software and emphasize its necessity and importance. Nonetheless, a strictly pure theory without testing it in practice against real applications is sterile.

This section is an intentional declaration that regardless of the possible calculations with Quantum Software Density Matrix, they should lead to practical applications of Quantum Software.

Modularization
Modules are the basic *sine qua non* for many applications of the Quantum Software Density Matrix. Modules are generated by this chapter's Procedure 2 in Sect. 4.3

(see Exman and Shmilovich [40]). It can be double-checked by a purely linear algebraic spectral approach, independent of any quantum theory considerations (Exman and Sakhnini [18], Fiedler [41], De Abreu [42]). Modularization leads to evolution, measurement, and compositionality applications.

Evolution

The evolution of a Quantum Software Density Matrix by means of unitary operators is the simulative equivalent of running an actual software system, which may not be available, among other reasons due to lack of its implementation.

The practical application in this situation is logical debugging (see Exman [19]), to check that (a) the Density Matrix faithfully reflects the tabular concept, and in the negative case to correct them and rerun the checking and (b) whether some basic concept is lacking; for instance, in the reservation tabular concept, by evolution running, one may notice that a second connector is lacking: *Cancellation→Add-to-available*, which also demands an addition to the Density Matrix.

Measurement

A practical application of measuring the Quantum Software Density Matrix is the efficiency improvement of quantum state tomography, by usage of "quantum modules tomography." The number of measurements to recover the whole software system Density Matrix is thereby significantly reduced (see Exman and Zvulunov [21]).

Compositionality

Compositionality means that the whole Quantum Software system Density Matrix can be decomposed into the component modules' smaller Density Matrices using a direct sum. This can be reversed, recomposing the whole system from its modules (see Exman and Nechaev [43]).

The practical application, in the "Plug n' Play" spirit of Thompson et al. [37], is to recompose a new Quantum Software system Density Matrix, by substituting one or more original modules with new versions or totally novel modules.

Open Issues

There are numerous potential applications of Quantum Software, beyond those mentioned above. We are systematically working on these new applications.

7.5   *Quantum Software's Potential Roles*

The potential roles of Quantum Software may be looked at from two quite general and different viewpoints: one qualitative and another quantitative.

The qualitative point of view refers to software system design, applications, and their improvements. Following the calculations and experiments referred to in the previous section, first of all, one obtains the software system modules. One then uses them to test design correctness and potential applications of the software system. The correctness is meant in conceptual terms.

The novelty of the quite different, quantitative point of view demands assignment to each module, and its component quantum gates, realistic run times which are proportional to run times of actual gates in a given common technology. The overall result should be a reliable simulation timing of the quantum computation in the spirit of Feynman, without having constructed a real quantum computing machine.

The proportional run-times assignment can be obtained from partial experimental data and/or estimates from computational complexity classes. These estimates should be carefully verified, before being used in actual simulations.

7.6 Main Contribution

The main contribution of this chapter is the reinterpretation of Feynman's "Simulating Physics with Computers" leading to a refined Quantum Software theory, based upon linear algebra, embodied in a *Density Matrix* generated from its *tabular concept* freely expressed in natural language.

Time will tell us whether Quantum Software theory already covers the full range of future software, or whether nonlinear algebra and more fundamental theoretical changes will be indispensable.

References

1. Feynman, R.P.: Simulating physics with computers. Int. J. Theor. Phys. **21**, 467 (1982)
2. Lloyd, S.: Universal quantum simulators. Science. **273**, 1073–1078 (1996)
3. Deutsch, D.: Quantum theory, the Church-Turing principle and the universal quantum computer. Proc. R. Soc. Lond. A. **400**, 97–117 (1985)
4. Preskill, J.: Quantum Computing 40 years Later. arXiv:2106.10522v3 [quant-ph] (2023)
5. Feynman, R.P.: Feynman Lectures on Computation, Anniversary edn. (Frontiers in Physics). Edited by Tony Hey. CRC Press, USA (2023)
6. Naur, P., Randell, B. (eds.): Software Engineering: Report of a Conference Sponsored by the NATO Science Committee, Garmisch, Germany, 7–11 Oct 1968. Scientific Affairs Division, NATO, Brussels (1969)
7. Dahl, O.-J., Hoare, C.A.R.: Hierarchical program structures. In: Dahl, O.-J., Dijkstra, E.W., Hoare, C.A.R. (eds.) Structured Programming, pp. 175–220. Academic Press, London (1972)
8. Liskov, B.H., Zilles, S.: Programming with abstract data types. Proc. ACM Conference on Very High Level Languages, SIGPLAN Notices 9, vol. 4, pp. 50–59 (1974)
9. Brooks Jr., F.P.: The Mythical Man-Month: Essays on Software Engineering, Anniversary edn. Addison-Wesley, Boston, MA (1995)
10. Jackson, D.: The Essence of Software – Why Concepts Matter for Great Design. Princeton University Press, Princeton, NJ (2021)
11. Parnas, D.L.: On the criteria to be used in decomposing systems into modules. Commun. ACM. **15**(12), 1053–1058 (1972). https://doi.org/10.1145/361598.361623

12. Brooks Jr., F.P.: The Design of Design – Essays from a Computer Scientist. Addison-Wesley, Boston, MA (2010)
13. De Rosso, S.P., Jackson, D.: What's wrong with Git? A conceptual design analysis. In: Proc. Onward! pp. 37–51, Indianapolis, IN (2013). https://doi.org/10.1145/2509578.2509584
14. Nielsen, M.A., Chuang, I.L.: Quantum Computation and Quantum Information. Cambridge University Press, Cambridge (2010)
15. Rieffel, E., Polak, W.: Quantum Computing – A Gentle Introduction. MIT Press, Cambridge, MA (2011)
16. Von Neumann, J.: Mathematical Foundations of Quantum Mechanics, New edn. Princeton University Press, Princeton, NJ (2018)
17. Braunstein, S., Ghosh, S., Severini, S.: The Laplacian of a graph as a density matrix: a basic combinatorial approach to separability in mixed states. arXiv:quant-ph/0405165 (2006)
18. Exman, I., Sakhnini, R.: Linear software models: bipartite isomorphism between Laplacian Eigenvectors and Modularity Matrix Eigenvectors. Int J Softw Eng Knowl Eng. 28(7), 897–935 (2018). https://doi.org/10.1142/S0218194018400107
19. Exman, I.: Quantum software evolution. (in Preparation), (2024)
20. Feynman, R.P.: Quantum mechanical computers. Optics News. 11, 11–20 (1985)
21. Exman, I., Zvulunov, A.: Quantum software models: quantum modules tomography and recovery theorem. In: Proc. SEKE'2023, San Francisco Bay Area, CA, pp. 91–96. https://doi.org/10.18293/SEKE2023-214
22. Grover, L.K.: A fast quantum mechanical algorithm for database search. In: Proc. 28th Annual ACM Symposium on Theory of Computation, pp. 212–219. ACM Press, New York, NY (1996)
23. Barenco, A.: Quantum computation: an introduction. In: Lo, H.K., Popescu, S., Spiller, T. (eds.) Introduction to Quantum Computation and Information, pp. 143–183. World Scientific, Singapore (1998)
24. Shor, P.W.: Algorithms for quantum computation: discrete logarithms and factoring. In: Proc. 35th Annual Symposium of Foundations of Computer Science. IEEE Press, Los Alamitos, CA (1994)
25. Shor, P.W.: Polynomial-time algorithms for prime factorization and discrete logarithms on a quantum computer. SIAM J. Comp. 26(5), 1484–1509 (1997)
26. Einstein, A., Podolsky, B., Rosen, N.: Can quantum-mechanical description of physical reality be considered complete? Phys. Rev. 47, 777–780 (1935)
27. Preskill, J.: Lecture Notes for Quantum Information Course Ph219/CS219, Chapter 3. California Institute of Technology, version of (2018)
28. Mauerer, W.: Semantics and Simulation of Communication in Quantum Programming. Diploma Thesis, University Erlangen-Nuremberg (2005)
29. Javanainen, J.: The Software Atom. arXiv:1610.00791 [physics.atom-ph] (2017)
30. Perez-Delgado, C.A.: A Quantum Software Modeling Language, Chapter 6, pp. 103–119, in Serrano et al. (2022)
31. Serrano, M.A., Perez-Castillo, R., Piattini, M. (eds.): Quantum Software Engineering. Springer-Nature, Cham (2022). https://doi.org/10.1007/978-3-031-05324-5
32. Ricardo Perez-Castillo, Luis Jimenez-Navajas and Mario Piattini, "Modelling Quantum Circuits with UML.", arXiv-2103.16169 (2021)
33. Baldwin, C.Y., Clark, K.B.: Design Rules The Power of Modularity, vol. 1. MIT Press (2000)
34. Sullivan, K., Griswold, W.G., Cai, Y., Hallen, B.: The structure and value of modularity in software design, pp. 99–108. Proc. ESEC/FSE Int. Conf., Vienna, Austria (2001)
35. Newman, M.E.J., Girvan, M.: Finding and evaluating community structure in networks. Phys. Rev. E. 69, 026113 (2004)
36. Kang, C.G., Oh, H.: Modular component-based quantum circuit synthesis. Proc. ACM Program. Lang. 7, OOPSLA1, Article 87 (2023). https://doi.org/10.1145/3586039
37. Thompson, J., Modi, K., Vedral, V., Mile, G.: Quantum plug n' play: modular computation in the quantum regime. N J Phys. 20, 013004 (2018). https://doi.org/10.1088/1367-2630/aa99b3

38. Shende, V.V., Bullock, S.S., Markov, I.L.: Synthesis of Quantum Logic Circuits, arXiv:quant-ph/0406176v5 April 2006. IEEE Trans. Computer-Aided Des. **25**, 1000–1010 (2006). https://doi.org/10.1109/TCAD.2005.855930
39. Hadamard, J.: The Psychology of Invention in the Mathematical Field. Dover, New York, NY (1954)
40. Exman, I., Shmilovich, A.T.: Quantum software models: the density matrix for classical and quantum software systems design. In: Proc. Q-SE 2nd Int. Workshop on Quantum Software Engineering, pp. 1–6 (2021) Also: arXiv:2103.13755 cs.SE quant-ph. https://doi.org/10.48550/arXiv.2103.13755
41. Fiedler, M.: Algebraic connectivity of graphs. Czech. Math. J. **23**(2), 298–305 (1973)
42. De Abreu, N.M.M.: Old and new results on algebraic connectivity of graphs. Linear Algebr. Appl. **423**, 53–73 (2007)
43. Exman, I., Nechaev, A.: Quantum software models: software density matrix is a perfect direct sum of module matrices. In: Proc. SEKE'2022, Virtual, Pittsburgh, PA, pp. 434–439. https://doi.org/10.18293/SEKE2022-158

Superoperators for Quantum Software Engineering

Wolfgang Mauerer

Abstract As implementations of quantum computers grow in size and maturity, the question of how to program this new class of machines is attracting increasing attention in the software engineering domain. Yet, many questions from how to design expressible quantum languages augmented with formal semantics via implementing appropriate optimizing compilers to abstracting details of machine properties in software systems remain challenging. Performing research at this intersection of quantum computing and software engineering requires sufficient knowledge of the physical processes underlying quantum computations, and how to model these. In this chapter, we review a superoperator-based approach to quantum dynamics, as it can provide means that are sufficiently abstract, yet concrete enough to be useful in quantum software and systems engineering, and outline how it is used in several important applications in the field.

Keywords Quantum computing · Software engineering · Quantum software engineering · Density operator · Superoperators · Formal semantics

1 Introduction

The actual and hypothesized capabilities of performing computational tasks based on the laws of quantum mechanics have made the implementation of quantum computers a target of interest to physics and engineering. Yet, producing software (and algorithms) for this class of machines has by far not reached the level of productivity and ease of handling that computer science has come to expect for classical machines following decades of development. This is likely because at the current level of abstraction, expressing algorithms resides close to the underlying

W. Mauerer (✉)
Technical University of Applied Sciences/Siemens AG, Regensburg, Germany
e-mail: wolfgang.mauerer@othr.de

© The Author(s) 2024
I. Exman et al. (eds.), *Quantum Software*,
https://doi.org/10.1007/978-3-031-64136-7_3

45

physical concepts. This necessitates strong inter-domain knowledge for researchers working in the field.

Detailed knowledge of alternative methods of describing the dynamics of quantum systems beyond applying unitary operators on finite-dimensional quantum states might not be universally spread in the software engineering community. This implies that appreciation of the usefulness of such descriptions for many open problems in quantum software engineering could be further fostered. Consequently, we provide an exposition of one particularly important such formalism—linear superoperators acting on density operators—in this chapter especially tailored toward software engineering research. We include a discussion of the possible benefits in various application areas in the domain.

Quantum circuits are the basis of many software engineering considerations, albeit at a low level of abstraction. Any typical introduction to quantum computing for computer scientists includes a discussion of circuits for the foundational set of algorithms like the ones invented by Grover, Shor, or Deutsch. In essence, a *quantum state* $|\psi\rangle$ (we provide precise formal definitions later) propagates through a quantum circuit in three phases—initialization, application of a sequence of quantum operations, and a measurement delivering stochastic results—that constitute a quantum program. The first two actions are described by so-called unitary operators U that capture possibilities (and limitations) of quantum operations, and exhibit peculiar properties that engineers are not accustomed to from classical programming. Keeping in mind that measurements, which are realized by other means than unitary transformations, are an important ingredient of quantum algorithms, the core part of any such algorithm can nonetheless be expressed as a unitary transformation of an appropriately initialized quantum state $|\psi\rangle$ by $|\psi\rangle \mapsto U|\psi\rangle = |\psi'\rangle$.

However, for most known algorithms, quantum circuits (or any other equivalent representation of operations on quantum states) only capture part of the overall computational sequence. Any required classical operations or the implementation of control flow is usually described (and handled) separately from the manipulation of purely quantum mechanical states. Variational algorithms that underlie many considerations of the current era of noisy, intermediate-scale quantum (NISQ) machines rely inherently on interleaved classical and quantum operations, and explicitly operate on quantum and classical data. Consequently, it is helpful to consider a mathematical formalism that can capture all these aspects in a unified description. Likewise, the unavoidable effects of noise and imperfections that exercise probabilistic influence on a quantum state, and thus directly concern any real-world analysis of algorithmic properties, must be taken into account. A good mathematical framework for this purpose is the *density operator* formalism, which generalizes quantum states $|\phi\rangle$ into density operators ϱ that can describe both quantum and classical aspects of a computational state. Instead of unitary operators U that act on states and describe operations, *superoperators* Λ map density operators to density operators (i.e., $\varrho \mapsto \Lambda(\varrho) = \varrho'$), and therefore generalize unitary quantum operations.[1]

In this chapter, we present an exposition of these concepts that targets the needs of software engineers working on the relatively new field of quantum software engineering, which necessitates gaining an understanding of quantum programming languages and possible approaches to equip them with formal semantics, or produce software with correctness by construction approaches. While we aim at using enough mathematical formalism to arrive at a precise and unambiguous presentation, we avoid the use of advanced mathematics, especially category theory, that is commonplace in research work on quantum programming language semantics, yet may act as an impediment to obtaining a higher-level view of the issues from a software engineering perspective.

This chapter nonetheless relies on some amount of formalism, and the particular mathematical topics might not be present in every computer science curriculum (and even if they are, it might have been a while since the reader had to deal with these topics). For those who are curious to hear the software engineering essentials short and crisp, if you trust us that

- a density operator ϱ can, compared to ket representations $|\psi\rangle$, describe quantum states that suffer from imperfections and intricacies of the real world;
- superoperators extend the role of quantum gates to this scenario; and
- the Kraus representation allows us to describe such operators in a form that is particularly convenient for computer science and software engineering purposes,

then you can skip directly to Sect. 5 that shows some of the most important software-centric applications for superoperators: formal semantics for and verification of quantum programs, communicating and distributed quantum systems, and dealing with imperfections in real-world NISQ machines.

1.1   Challenges in Quantum Software

Following the recent review by Garhwal et al. [5] and the textbook [34], currently established programming languages follow an either imperative paradigm (e.g., QCL [19], Silq [2], or Q# [27]) or functional paradigm (e.g., QPL [26], Quipper [7], or LIQUiD [31]). While they differ in their capabilities and degrees of abstraction, their quantum features center around generating quantum circuits that eventually apply lists of operators on quantum states. The same observations can be made for commercial approaches (e.g., Cirq, Ocean, or Qiskit) to the quantum

---

[1] The mathematical formalism of superoperators can handle more general operators than density operators, and we will see later how that can benefit software engineering when trace-decreasing operations come into play.

programming problem where instructions on how to generate quantum circuits are embedded into a host language, typically Python.

While software engineering research has established a multitude of methods, techniques, and processes aimed at systematically constructing high-quality software artifacts, some of the elementary developmental options like debugging, tracing, and some variants of testing are not directly applicable in a meaningful way in the quantum domain. Given the resulting reduction of engineering options, ascertaining the quality (or correctness) of quantum programs must focus more on other methods like formal verification. This, in turn, requires means of properly formalizing quantum programs. Starting with the seminal work [26], research on numerous approaches of equipping quantum programming languages with formal semantics, based on which verification efforts can take place, has been conducted. Yet, the current state of the art is still lagging behind the classical level of maturity.

While it should not be required to educate all software engineers working on quantum computing on the bells and whistles of quantum physics, a reasonable awareness of the underlying principles, methods, and formalisms is important for determining effective layers of abstraction. The situation is not unlike at the advent of software engineering as a discipline: then, the need for using structured engineering approaches to construct software became apparent, yet low-level details remained crucial—as embodied, for instance, by research topics like the construction of efficient compilers for expressive high-level languages that nonetheless catered to the very distinct hardware properties of then-current systems. We believe the superoperator-based view of quantum computing is an apt starting point for deriving such sound, practical, and useful abstractions using established methods of computer science for quantum programming and quantum software engineering.

2   Mathematical Foundations

In this and the following section, we introduce the necessary formalities to understand the superoperator-based view of quantum dynamics. We assume knowledge of the standard computer science curriculum of linear algebra, but try to give an otherwise self-contained exposition. All mathematical statements and facts that we refer to without providing an explicit rationale or proof sketch are part of the standard literature on quantum computing and quantum information theory, for instance [18, 28, 4, 22], to which we refer readers interested in a more in-depth formal treatment or explicit proofs.

2.1   The Need for Formalization

A quantum program enacts a transformation of a state (in the sense of computer science) comprised of quantum and classical input data to quantum and classical output data. While it is not possible to perform intermediate measurements on the quantum part of the state without influencing the state itself, this state nonetheless exists uniquely during the whole computation: after preparing required initial states based on classical input data, in each step of performing the computational sequence, and before performing any measurements. The latter, finally, reduce (parts of) the quantum data to classical information, usually in a stochastic way. A quantum program can, depending on the input data, lead to many possible intermediate states, and likewise to many possible different outputs, even when perfect machines are assumed for execution. This is similar to stochastic algorithms that find ample use in classical software, and mathematical frameworks that allow us to model such scenarios have been established.

Consequently, we need to deal with three different entities: the state of a system, a quantum program that acts on this state, and a transformation between the quantum program (specified in whatever programming language) and an appropriate collection of formal operations that represent the state transformations, and most importantly allow us to reason about properties of the quantum program with established and new methods. While the scenario in general is very similar to the approaches used in programming language semantics, a crucial difference is that the state is not open to direct inspection by observers, and is described by different mathematical objects than for classical computation. Also, the admissible transformations between states differ radically from classical approaches.

From a physical standpoint, there are different ways of viewing this scenario: a quantum program can be translated (and most of the contemporary compilers follow this approach) into a sequence of gates that are applied to a quantum state (together with a suitable formalization of the classical state), which can be expressed as the element of a Hilbert space. However, this formalism only applies to *perfect* underlying quantum computers that faithfully execute each gate, and are able to prepare initial quantum states that exactly represent the desired form without any stochastic uncertainties.

When machines are subject to noise and imperfections, gate operations, state preparation, readout, etc. are affected by uncontrolled influences that introduce stochasticity into the quantum state; straightforward kets cannot represent the arising statistical mixture of quantum states that requires an additional characterization of the associated classical distribution to be included in their description. This is, however, possible in the density operator formulation of quantum mechanics. As we have seen previously, superoperators extend the role of perfect gates in the bra-ket picture. We believe this formal representation is well suited to augmenting a quantum program with formal semantics, as it can capture a wider range of phenomena that cannot be ignored at the current state of hardware development, and will with some likelihood also be of interest in the long run. While the picture is solidly established in physics-centric research, this does not universally hold for computer science and software engineering. The aim of this chapter is to provide an introduction to the formalism tailored to the particular needs of software engineering researchers.

First, let us fix some notation conventions: a quantum register $|R\rangle$ is an element of a Hilbert space $\mathcal{H}$. This space is, in the finite-dimensional case relevant for quantum computing, a complex vector space with an inner product, which implies the existence of an orthonormal standard basis $\{|i\rangle\}$ (the infinite-dimensional case requires more care, but is only very rarely relevant for the computer science aspects of quantum computing). Operations on quantum registers are carried out using unitary (linear) operators U (satisfying $UU^{\dagger} = U^{\dagger}U = \mathbb{1}$, where the dagger operation $\dagger$ denotes taking the adjoint of a linear operator). $\langle R|$ is the co-vector from the dual space of $\mathcal{H}$ associated with $|R\rangle$. The inner product between two quantum registers is denoted by $\langle R_1 \mid R_2 \rangle$; recall that it satisfies, despite the somewhat different notation compared to inner products on vector spaces, (a) conjugate symmetry $\langle x \mid y \rangle = \overline{\langle y \mid x \rangle}$, (b) linearity in the second argument $\langle x|(\alpha|y_1\rangle + \beta|y_2\rangle) = \alpha\langle x \mid y_1 \rangle + \beta\langle y_2\rangle^2$, and (c) positive definiteness $\langle x \mid x \rangle > 0$. Since quantum states are normalized, the latter condition effectively reads $\langle x \mid x \rangle = 1$.

2.2 Linear and Hilbert-Schmid Operators

The notion of linearity is well established in physics and computer science, and linear maps find use in many domains. The concept of linearity can of course be easily applied to operators; for the sake of completeness, let us recall the exact definition of a *linear* operator on normed spaces, as it is the formal backbone of our considerations:

Definition 1 (Linear Operator) A *linear operator* T from a normed space X to another normed space Y is a linear map from $D(T) \subseteq X$ (the *domain* of T) to Y with the following property for $x, y \in D(T)$, $\alpha, \beta \in \mathbb{K}$, where $\mathbb{K}$ is an unspecified field:

$$T(\alpha x + \beta y) = \alpha T(x) + \beta T(y). \tag{1}$$

A particularly important class of operators in quantum computing (including, most importantly, density and unitary operators) is *bounded* as by the following definition:

Definition 2 (Bounded Operator) An operator is called *bounded* if $\exists C \geq 0, C \in \mathbb{R}$ such that

$$||Tx|| \leq C \cdot ||x|| \tag{2}$$

for all $x \in D(T)$.

---

[2] The standard scalar product on vector spaces requires linearity in the first argument.

We write $\mathcal{B}(\cdot)$ to denote the set of all bounded operators acting on an underlying space. Operators that map Hilbert spaces to Hilbert spaces are crucial for our considerations:

Definition 3 (Hilbert-Schmidt Operator) Let X, Y be Hilbert spaces. An operator $K \in \mathcal{B}(X, Y)$ is called *Hilbert-Schmidt operator* if there exists an orthonormal basis $\{e_\alpha : \alpha \in A\}$ (where A is some index set with $\sum_{\alpha \in A} ||Ke_\alpha||^2 < \infty$.

Using the trace of an operator M given by $\operatorname{tr} M = \sum_i \langle i|M|i\rangle$ for an orthonormal basis $\{|i\rangle\}$ of the Hilbert space $\mathcal{H}$, we can also express the latter condition in the above definition by $\operatorname{tr} K^\dagger K < \infty$, which is obviously fulfilled if $K \in \mathcal{B}(\mathcal{H})$ and $\dim(\mathcal{H}) < \infty$, and therefore for the finite-dimensional Hilbert spaces relevant for quantum computing.

Theorem 1 (Hilbert Space of Hilbert-Schmidt Operators) *For Hilbert-Schmidt operators K, L of a Hilbert space X to a Hilbert space Y, $||\cdot||_{HS}$ is a norm on this space induced by the scalar product*

$$\langle K, L \rangle_{HS} := \sum_\alpha \langle Ke_\alpha, Le_\alpha \rangle. \tag{3}$$

In the quantum computing literature (and more general expositions from quantum physics), this is usually expressed by using the trace operation:

$$\langle K, L \rangle_{HS} = \operatorname{tr} K^\dagger L. \tag{4}$$

Proof If K is a Hilbert-Schmidt operator, aK is a Hilbert-Schmidt operator as well for every $a \in \mathbb{K}$. If K, L are HS operators, then for every orthonormal basis $\{e_\alpha\}$, it holds that

$$\sum_\alpha ||(K + L)e_\alpha||^2 \leq 2 \cdot \sum_\alpha \left(||Ke_\alpha||^2 + ||Le_\alpha||^2 \right) < \infty, \tag{5}$$

which makes $K + L$ a Hilbert-Schmidt operator. By $\langle \cdot, \cdot \rangle$, we denote the scalar product in the space of Hilbert-Schmidt operators, and $||K||_{HS} = \langle K, K \rangle_{HS}^{1/2}$ (of course, the scalar product induces a metric). $\qquad\square$

A comparison of Hilbert spaces for quantum states and Hilbert spaces with a Hilbert-Schmidt operator basis that extend and generalize this concept is given in Table 1. The similarities between the two constructions that may seem very different at a first glance are particularly obvious when viewed in direct comparison.

Table 1 A comparison between standard Hilbert spaces used for quantum states and Hilbert spaces based on Hilbert-Schmidt operators.

Entity	Hilbert space	Hilbert space of Hilbert-Schmidt operators
State	$\lvert f\rangle \in \mathcal{H}$	$\hat{D}: \mathcal{H} \to \mathcal{H}$
Operator	$\mathcal{H} \to \mathcal{H}: \hat{D}\lvert x\rangle = \lvert x'\rangle$	$\Lambda: \hat{D} \to \hat{D} \equiv (\mathcal{H} \to \mathcal{H}) \to (\mathcal{H} \to \mathcal{H})$
Norm	$\lvert\lvert f\rangle\rvert = \sqrt{\langle f \vert f\rangle}$	$\lVert \hat{D}\rVert_{\mathrm{HS}} = \sqrt{\operatorname{tr} D^{\dagger}D}$
Operator norm[a]	$\lVert \hat{D}\rVert = \sup_{\substack{\lvert f\rangle \in \mathcal{H} \\ \lVert\lvert f\rangle\rVert \le 1}} \lvert \hat{D}\lvert f\rangle\rvert$	$\lVert \Lambda \rVert = \sup_{\substack{\hat{D}\in\mathcal{H} \\ \lVert\hat{D}\rVert \le 1}} \Lambda(\hat{D}) = \sup_{\substack{\hat{D}\in\mathcal{H} \\ \lVert\hat{D}\rVert \le 1}} \operatorname{tr} \Lambda(\hat{D})^{\dagger}\Lambda(\hat{D})$

[a] Other choices for the Hilbert space norm that fulfill the required properties are possible.

3 Modeling Hybrid Quantum-Classical Systems

Having laid out the mathematical preliminaries, we commence with discussing how to apply the formalism to model hybrid quantum-classical systems, as they form the basis of essentially all known quantum algorithms.

3.1 States and Effects

Ideally, an experiment resulting in a probability distribution can be carried out by repeating the following two processes until a a meaningful level of statistical significance is reached.

- *Preparation* of a (quantum mechanical) state according to some fixed procedure that can be repeated a sufficient number of times.
- *Measurement* of some *observable* quantity (e.g., spin, energy, . . .). *Effects* are a special class of measurement that can result in either the answer "yes" or "no" according to some probability distribution.

It is important to note that quantum measurements do not correspond to a passive acquisition of information that is common in classical computing. While it is a physical process, it is described by a different set of mathematical tools in the standard formalism of quantum computing based on states and operators. This unsatisfactory difference can be mostly mended by the use of superoperators.

Since quantum computing does not only deal with pure quantum states (and, at least in the NISQ era, statistical mixtures), but needs to handle classical and quantum data, the formalism must be able to account for such settings. Resulting systems are usually termed *hybrid* systems. It is obvious that any measurement results obtained from quantum systems fall into the classical category since measurement gauges that materialize in the macroscopic world are used to infer them from the quantum system, whatever their exact mechanism of performing the measurement is; this requires providing mechanisms that reduce quantum to classical data.[3]

Every quantum system can be completely characterized by its observable quantities which in turn are characterized by self-adjoint operators. These operators form an algebra $\mathcal{A}$; since we only deal with finite-dimensional Hilbert spaces here, we can restrict ourselves to sub-algebras of $\mathcal{B}(\mathcal{H})$ (i.e., $\mathcal{A} \subset \mathcal{B}(\mathcal{H})$). $\mathcal{A}$ is called the *observable algebra* of the system and is often identified with the system itself because it is possible to deduce all properties of the system from its observable algebra. The *dual algebra* of $\mathcal{A}$ is denoted by $\mathcal{A}^*$ and is the algebra defined on the dual space.

To capture the notions of *state* and *effect* mathematically, two sets ($\mathcal{S}$ representing all states, and $\mathcal{E}$ containing all effects) are defined as follows:

$$\mathcal{S}(\mathcal{A}) = \{\varrho \in \mathcal{A}^* \mid \varrho \geq 0 \wedge \varrho(\mathbb{1}) = 1\}, \tag{6}$$

$$\mathcal{E}(\mathcal{A}) = \{A \in \mathcal{A} \mid A \geq 0 \wedge A \leq \mathbb{1}\}. \tag{7}$$

For every tuple $(\varrho, A) \in \mathcal{S} \times \mathcal{E}$, there exists a map $(\varrho, A) \rightarrow \varrho(A) \in [0, 1]$ which gives the probability $p = \varrho(A)$ that measuring an effect A on a (system prepared in the) state ϱ results in the answer "yes." Accordingly, the probability for the answer "no' is given by $1 - p$. $\varrho(A)$ is called the *expectation value* of an effect A; states are thus defined as expectation value functionals from an abstract point of view. These expectation value functionals can be uniquely connected with a normalized trace-class operator (for which the value of the trace operation is independent of the basis chosen to evaluate the trace) ϱ such that $\varrho(A) = \mathrm{tr}(\varrho A)$. In principle, it would be necessary to introduce two different symbols for the expectation value functional and the operator, but for simplicity, we omit this complication.

We need to distinguish between two different kinds of states: *pure* and *mixed* ones. This is a consequence of both $\mathcal{S}$ and $\mathcal{E}$ being convex spaces: for two states $\varrho_1, \varrho_2 \in \mathcal{S}(\mathcal{A})$ and $\lambda \in \mathbb{R}, 0 \leq \lambda \leq 1$, the convex combination $\lambda \varrho_1 + (1 - \lambda)\varrho_2$ is also an element of $\mathcal{S}(\mathcal{A})$. The same statement holds for the elements of $\mathcal{E}(\mathcal{A})$. This decomposition provides a nice insight into the structure of both spaces: extremal points cannot be written as a proper convex decomposition, that is, for $x = \lambda y + (1 - \lambda)z$ it follows that $\lambda = 1$, or $\lambda = 0$, or $x = y = z$. They can be interpreted as follows:

- For $\mathcal{S}(\mathcal{A})$, extremal points are *pure states* with no associated classical uncertainty.
- For $\mathcal{E}(\mathcal{A})$, extremal points describe measurements which do not allow any fuzziness as is, for instance, introduced by a detector which detects some property

---

[3] The problem of how measurements of a quantum system are to be interpreted (or even how the whole process can be described consistently) has been and still is one of the fundamental philosophical problems of quantum mechanics [1]. Fortunately, choosing an interpretation (or answering the question if an interpretation is necessary at all) is not relevant for any of the formalisms discussed in this chapter.

not with certainty, but only up to some finite error (alas, this applies to all real-world detectors used in NISQ machines to read the result of a computation).

It can be shown that the density matrix $\varrho = |\phi\rangle\langle\phi|$ of pure states fulfills the property $\text{tr}(\varrho^2) = 1$, whereas for mixed states, $\text{tr}(\varrho^2) < 1$. Consequently, it is possible to distinguish between pure and mixed states when a physical tomography of the resulting state (or any intermediate state of a computation) is available. While this is not within the usual functionalities offered by NISQ machines, it can be implemented with some effort, and it is important to know from a software point of view (especially in terms of result reliability and quality) that the approach is available.

3.2 Observables

Until now, we have only considered effects, that is, measurements resulting in a binary answer that is either "yes" or "no." We also need to cover measurements with a more complicated result range; this is necessary to describe general *observables*. Although we would have to consider an infinite (even uncountable) number of possible outcomes for a general description of quantum mechanics, it is sufficient to consider only observables with a finite range for the purposes of quantum computing.[4] Such observables are represented by maps which connect elements x of a finite set R to some effect $E_x \in \mathcal{E}(\mathcal{A})$; this in turn gives rise to a probability distribution $p_x = \varrho(E_x)$. More formally, we can put it as in the following:

Definition 4 (Positive Operator-Valued Measurement) A family $E = \{E_x\}, x \in R$ of effects $E_x \in \mathcal{A}$ is called a *positive operator valued measurement* (POVM) on R if $\sum_{x \in R} E_x = \mathbb{1}$.

Note that the E_x need *not* necessarily be projectors, that is, they must *not* necessarily satisfy the identity $E_x^2 = E_x$. Should this be the case for all x, the measurement is called a *projective measurement*, which is the type of measurement used in most canonical quantum algorithms and variational approaches when a projection onto the binary basis is performed.

Observables of this kind can be described by self-adjoint operators of the underlying Hilbert space $\mathcal{H}$ which can be seen as follows: every self-adjoint operator A on a Hilbert space $\mathcal{H}$ of finite dimension can (owing to the spectral theorem for normal matrices) be decomposed as $A = \sum_{\lambda \in \sigma(A)} \lambda P_\lambda$. Here $\sigma(A)$ denotes the

---

[4] This is justified because quantum computers process states of the type $(|0\rangle, |1\rangle)^{\otimes n}$. Although quantum computers can possess an arbitrary number of qubits, it is still a fixed and (which is most important) finite number; additionally, we are not concerned with any continuous quantum properties of these objects. Note that special types of computations like analogue quantum simulation of molecules of chemical compounds that are seen as possible use-cases for quantum computers are not included in the framework discussed here.

spectrum of A, while P_λ provide projectors onto the corresponding eigenspace. The expectation value $\sum_\lambda \lambda \varrho(P_\lambda)$ of A for a given state ϱ can equivalently be calculated by $\varrho(A) = \text{tr}(\varrho A)$. Since this is the standard way of formulating the expectation value of an operator, both points of view coincide.

3.3 Classical Components

Systems consisting solely of quantum components are generally not to be found: at the latest after a measurement has been performed, classical probabilities need to be accounted for. Therefore, we need to pay attention to hybrid systems composed from quantum and classical parts as well. Obviously, we have to orient ourselves along the lines of Sect. 3.1 to provide proper grounding for both possibilities. Consider a finite set X of elementary events, that is, all possible outcomes of an experiment. Again, $\mathcal{S}(\mathcal{A})$ and $\mathcal{E}(\mathcal{A})$ define the set of states and effects, respectively, but this time, the observable algebra is given by all complex valued functions from the set X to $\mathbb{C}$ as defined by

$$\mathcal{A} = \mathcal{C}(X) = \{f : X \to \mathbb{C}\}. \tag{8}$$

By identifying the function f with the operator $\hat{f}$ given by

$$\hat{f} = \sum_{x \in X} f_x |x\rangle\langle x| \tag{9}$$

where $|x\rangle$ denotes a fixed orthonormal basis, the probability distribution can be interpreted as an operator algebra similar to the quantum mechanical case because $\hat{f}$ is an element of $\mathcal{B}(\mathcal{H})$. Thus, $\mathcal{C}(X)$ can be used as an observable algebra $\mathcal{A}$ along any other quantum mechanical or classical constituent of a multi-partite composite system.

3.4 Composite and Hybrid Systems

Since quantum mechanical and classical systems can be described with very similar structures, the presented formalism is well suited for the presentation of composite systems, as becomes necessary when quantum computations are subjected to a classical control flow, or when hybrid quantum-classical calculations are performed, as is the case for variational algorithms. Let $\mathcal{A} \subset \mathcal{B}(\mathcal{H})$ and $\mathcal{A}' \subset \mathcal{B}(\mathcal{K})$ be systems given in terms of their observable algebras; the composite system is then given by

$$\mathcal{A} \otimes \mathcal{A}' \equiv \text{span}\{A \otimes B | A \in \mathcal{A}, B \in \mathcal{A}'\}. \tag{10}$$

Three cases for the choice of $\mathcal{H}, \mathcal{K}$ can be distinguished:

- If both systems are quantum, then $\mathcal{A} \otimes \mathcal{A}' = \mathcal{B}(\mathcal{H} \otimes \mathcal{K})$.
- If both systems are classical, then $\mathcal{A} \otimes \mathcal{A}' = \mathcal{C}(X \times Y)$ with $\mathcal{C}$ as defined by Eq. (8)
- If $\mathcal{A}$ is classical and $\mathcal{A}'$ is quantum mechanical, we have a *hybrid* system; the composite observable algebra is then given by $\mathcal{C}(X) \otimes \mathcal{B}(\mathcal{H})$, which cannot be simplified any further. Observables are operator-valued functions in this case, as expected.

4 Completely Positive Maps and Their Representation

In quantum mechanics, time evolution is described by transformations of density matrices with an operator Λ that is called a *superoperator*.[5] Before we can proceed to formally define superoperators, let us fix some terminology: an operator O acting on a Hilbert space is positive definite if $\langle \psi | O | \psi \rangle > 0$ for all elements $|\psi\rangle$ of the Hilbert space, and positive semidefinite if $\langle \psi | O | \psi \rangle$ is non-negative. Physical density operators are Hermitian and positive semidefinite, which implies they have real non-negative eigenvalues. A positive map Λ transforms positive operators into positive operators. If $\Lambda \otimes \mathbb{1}$ is semidefinite positive ($\forall n \in \mathbb{N} : \Lambda \otimes \mathbb{1}_n \geq 0$), then Λ is called a completely positive map.

Definition 5 (Superoperator) A superoperator $\Lambda : \mathcal{B}(\mathcal{H}) \rightarrow \mathcal{B}(\mathcal{H})$ has the following properties for all density operators ϱ with $\varrho' = \Lambda(\varrho)$:

1. Λ is linear.
2. If $\varrho^\dagger = \varrho$, then $\varrho'^\dagger = \varrho'$ (Hermiticity preservation).
3. If $\operatorname{tr} \varrho = 1$, then $\operatorname{tr} \varrho' = 1$ (trace preservation).
4. Λ is a completely positive map.

Superoperators share the convenient property of linearity with many other objects in computer science. Since physical density operators are Hermitian, the preservation of Hermiticity in property (2) means this important characteristic of a density operator is not changed by any superoperator. Specifically, it implies that eigenvalues of the operator remain real-valued after transformations. Property (3) means that statistical mixtures of quantum states are mapped to other valid

---

[5] The Schrödinger equation $i\hbar \frac{\partial}{\partial t} |\psi(t)\rangle = H |\psi(t)\rangle$ governs, given a Hamilton operator H (whose meaning is extensively discussed in the quantum software engineering chapter of this book) the time evolution of a closed quantum system. The Liouville–von Neumann equation $i\hbar \frac{\partial \varrho}{\partial t} = [H, \varrho] = H\varrho - \varrho H$ generalizes the Schrödinger equation to density operators. For a time-independent system (which we take as a simple illustration, albeit the consideration would also apply to time-dependent interactions), the density operator at time t, $\varrho(t)$, can be obtained as $\varrho(t) = \exp(-iHt/\hbar)\varrho(t = 0)\exp(iHt/\hbar)$, which is nothing other than a mapping $\varrho(t = 0) \mapsto \varrho(t) = \Lambda(\varrho)$ using a superoperator Λ.

statistical mixtures of quantum states, and we cannot produce "invalid" objects by executing transformations described by superoperators. Note that if dissipative processes are considered, the second condition must be loosened to $\text{tr}(\varrho') \leq 1$; we will see later that relaxing this physically motivated condition is reasonable for the computer science domain. Finally, property (4) is of physical importance: Λ is not only positive semidefinite (i.e., ϱ' is non-negative if ϱ is non-negative) on $\mathcal{H}_A$, but also on any possible extension $\mathcal{H}_A \otimes \mathcal{H}_B$. This ensures that Λ maps a density operator to another valid density operator even when the system under consideration is entangled with some outside entity.

4.1 Operator-Sum Representation

Kraus [11] provides a seminal result about the decomposability of completely positive maps that allows us to specify concrete, operational representations for superoperators:

Theorem 2 (Kraus Representation Theorem) *A superoperator Λ as defined in Definition 5 can be written as a partition of $\mathbb{1} = \sum_{k=1}^{N} A_k^{\dagger} A_k$ where A_k are linear operators acting on the Hilbert space of the system such that*

$$\varrho' = \Lambda(\varrho) = \sum_{k=1}^{N} A_k \varrho A_k^{\dagger} \tag{11}$$

for any density matrix ϱ that represents a mixed or a pure state.[6]

This representation is also known by the illustrative name *operator-sum representation*.

A unitary operator U that is applied to a (possibly mixed) density operator ϱ is a Kraus representation with a single element ($k = 1$) for the underlying transformation, as $\varrho' = U\varrho U^{\dagger}$, and $U^{\dagger}U = \mathbb{1}$. Superoperators, in that sense, generalize unitary transformations as they allow for expressing more complex transformations than can be provided by $\varrho \mapsto U\varrho U^{\dagger}$.

To further illustrate the Kraus representation, consider the situation that the system is in contact with a (larger) environment, which is a common situation not only for more general physical experiments, but especially for quantum computers: the processing unit (QPU) where quantum effects take place is surrounded by multiple levels of cooling, the laboratory room in an experimental facility (or a

---

[6] Note that while Kraus published his representation theorem relatively late compared to the advent of quantum mechanics, and coincidentally around the time when Feynman first considered the computational power of quantum mechanics, the concept of density operators goes back much further in history. Both concept and representation find widespread use outside quantum computing in the dynamical description of general dissipative systems.

data center), and ultimately, the rest of the universe. All of these can perturb and therefore influence the QPU, which must be shielded from the influence of this environment. Even setting aside engineering issues, a perfect shielding that eliminates the influence of the environment is impossible to achieve, as this would make it impossible to prepare initial states, apply transformations on them, and read out the result.

If the environment is modeled sufficiently large, both systems form a closed quantum system. Transformations in the combined system can be described by a unitary transformation $U \in U(\dim(\mathcal{H}) \cdot \dim(\mathcal{H}_{\text{env}}))$ where $\mathcal{H}$ denotes the Hilbert space of the system under consideration and $\mathcal{H}_{\text{env}}$ the Hilbert space of the environment. Assume that the environment is in a pure state $|e_0\rangle\langle e_0|$.[7] The density operator of the system under consideration *after* the unitary operation was applied to the total system can be recovered by tracing out the environment:

$$\varrho' = \Lambda(\varrho) = \text{tr}_{\text{env}}(U\varrho \otimes |e_0\rangle\langle e_0|U^\dagger) \tag{12}$$

$$= \sum_k \langle e_k|U(\varrho \otimes |e_0\rangle\langle e_0|)U^\dagger|e_k\rangle \tag{13}$$

$$= \sum_k \langle e_k|U|e_0\rangle\varrho\langle e_0|U^\dagger|e_k\rangle \tag{14}$$

$$= \sum_k A_k\varrho A_k^\dagger. \tag{15}$$

In the last step, we define A_k by $A_k \equiv \langle e_k|U|e_0\rangle$. A set of Kraus operators $\{A_k\}$ *implements* a completely positive Λ if $\forall \varrho \in \mathcal{D} : \sum_k A_k\varrho A_k^\dagger = \Lambda(\varrho)$.

Theorem 3 *The operation elements of a given superoperator Λ are not unique: if $\{E_j\}$ is a set of Kraus operators, then a different set of Kraus operators $\{F_k\}$ describes the same operation if and only if there exists a unitary matrix $U \in U(n)$ with $n = \text{card}(\{E_k\})$ (where $\text{card}(X)$ is the cardinality of the set X) such that*

$$F_k = \sum_j U_{kj}E_j. \tag{16}$$

Note that the shorter set may be padded with zero elements until the cardinality of both matches.

Let $\{A_k\}$ be a set of Kraus operators that represents the cp-map Λ. Note that if any number of elements A_i is taken from $\{A_k\}$, the set still remains a completely positive map, but is not trace preserving any more.

---

[7] This assumption holds without loss of generality because it can be shown that a system can be purified by introducing extra dimensions which do not have any physical consequences.

Superoperators are elements of $\mathcal{B}(\mathcal{H})$, which makes it possible to apply many theorems of linear operator algebra to superoperators. As we have seen above, superoperators can themselves be used as elements of a Hilbert space, which implies that from a structural point of view, any distinction between operators and superoperators is mathematically irrelevant. However, we believe this is an argument in favor of using superoperators to describe quantum programming languages, as insights and techniques from linear operator theory can be immediately applied. Finally, note that the number of Kraus elements needed to express any arbitrary completely positive map $T : \mathcal{B}(\mathcal{H}_1) \rightarrow \mathcal{B}(\mathcal{H}_2)$ is bounded by $\dim(\mathcal{H}_1) \cdot \dim(\mathcal{H}_2)$.

5 Applications in Quantum Software and Systems Engineering

In this section, we provide concrete examples for the use of superoperators in problems related to software engineering, embedding a brief discussion of seminal and recent results.

5.1 Formal Semantics and Verification

Several semantic domains based on various mathematical formalisms of the underlying quantum physics have been used to provide semantics for quantum programs: unitary operations or probabilistic functions on pure quantum states, admissible transformations [21], or completely positive maps on density operators, for which [26] initiated a series of follow-up results that established connections between the physical framework outlined in this chapter and established approaches to (denotational) semantics in computer science, in particular based on category theory.

Following [16], it is known that modeling classical computational effects like assignments or exceptions is possible using the category theoretical concept of monads that have received considerable attention in computer science as abstract data types in functional programming languages. Likewise, quantum computing based on states and linear operators is known to be almost a monad [17]; by extending the physical model to density operators and superoperators [29], it is possible to formalize the computational semantics by the category theoretical construct of arrows, which generalize monads. Importantly, such approaches do not need to distinguish between computation and measurement, as the underlying superoperator formalism unifies both aspects. As stated earlier, establishing connections between quantum computations (in terms of the superoperator formalism) and monads and arrows enables embeddings in current classical languages, and exposes connections to well-understood concepts from the semantics of (classical) programming languages.

Earlier seminal work [26] defines a functional programming language that can establish various compile-time guarantees, and is equipped with a denotational semantics based on complete partial orders of superoperators: the established Löwner partial order, in which $A \sqsubseteq B$ holds if and only if $B - A$ is positive semidefinite, is slightly extended to apply on matrix tuples. The approach also offers a formal category theoretic treatment based on so-called complete partial order-enriched traced monadial categories, for which categorical operations like composition and tensor are Scott-continuous (i.e., they preserve least upper bounds of increasing sequences), which allows for using the guaranteed existence of fix-points of Scott-continuous endofunctions on pointed (i.e., equipped with a least element) complete partial orders to deal with loops and recursion.

An additional recent approach, QUnity, [30] provides a type system based on algebraic data types, and allows for combining (and nesting) the use of unitary transformations and superoperators. Denotational semantics are provided in the form of pure and mixed semantics, building upon unitary transformation of quantum states and superoperators applied to density operators, respectively. Finally, let us mention the review of formal verification [12] that summarizes further approaches to quantum semantics, not limited to superoperator-based constructions.

Given the multitude of existing approaches, it is interesting to observe that actual software containing quantum code [24] and patterns for quantum software [13] are almost exclusively expressed in languages that are not equipped with advanced formal semantics, while languages that enjoy this quality find popularity restricted to within academic circles. This leaves important gaps to be filled, given that it is textbook knowledge in software engineering how software quality and reliability of systems can be considerably improved by formal verification, static analysis, or correctness by construction. First results along this line for the quantum domain have appeared recently (albeit also based, as is customary in this line of research, on toy languages that expose only the most salient features without syntactic sugar) [20, 35]; interestingly, both approaches revolve around denotational semantics [25] for a "while" language $[\![C]\!] : \mathcal{B}(\mathcal{H}) \to \mathcal{B}(\mathcal{H})$ as denotation of program (fragment) C. To convey the flavor of how the approaches relate to superoperators, consider the following (incomplete) fragment of a language similar to what is used by Peduri et al. and Zhou et al.:

$$S := \textbf{skip} \mid \textbf{abort} \mid \vec{q} := \hat{U}(\vec{q}) \mid S_1; S_2 \mid \textbf{repeat } N \textbf{ do } S \textbf{ end} \mid$$
$$\textbf{while meas } \vec{q} \textbf{ with } B \textbf{ do } S \textbf{ end}$$

Here, S_i denote quantum program fragments obtained from the production S, $\vec{q}$ allows us to select quantum bits from the overall quantum register, and $\hat{U}$ is a unitary operator, as usual. An application of the operator on a subset of the available quantum bits is given by $\hat{U}(\vec{q})$. A denotational semantics, again similar to the variants used in the cited approaches, can be defined as follows:

$[\![\mathbf{skip}]\!] = 1$; that is, $[\![\mathbf{skip}]\!](\varrho) = 1\varrho 1^{\dagger} = \varrho$

$[\![\mathbf{abort}]\!] = 0$; that is, $[\![\mathbf{abort}]\!](\varrho) = 0$

$[\![\vec{q} := \hat{U}(\vec{q})]\!] = \hat{U}_{\vec{q}}$; that is, $[\![\vec{q} := \hat{U}(\vec{q})]\!](\varrho) = \hat{U}_{\vec{q}} \rho \hat{U}_{\vec{q}}^{\dagger}$

$[\![S_1; S_2]\!] = [\![S_2]\!] \circ [\![S_1]\!]$

$[\![\mathbf{repeat}\ N\ \mathbf{do}\ S\ \mathbf{end}]\!] = \underbrace{[\![S]\!] \circ [\![S]\!] \circ \cdots \circ [\![S]\!]}_{N\ \text{times}}$

$[\![\mathbf{while\ meas}\ \vec{q}\ \mathbf{with}\ B\ \mathbf{do}\ S\ \mathbf{end}]\!] = \sum_{k=0}^{\infty} \left(\mathcal{B}_{0,\vec{q}} \circ \left([\![S]\!] \circ \mathcal{B}_{1,\vec{q}} \right)^k \right)$

The definitions for the skip statement and unitary operator application on (a list of) quantum states $\vec{q}$ defined in the first two lines make it clear that the denotations for the fragments are superoperators that can be applied on concrete density matrices ϱ; however, a density matrix is not required to define the actual denotation. The while statement uses two binary projective measurement operations that can also be represented by superoperators that define the transformation: $\mathcal{B}_i(\varrho) = B_i \varrho B_i^{\dagger}$ for $B_i = |i\rangle\langle i|$ in the computational standard basis.

Multiple approaches can establish that the while statement is well defined; Peduri et al. base their consideration on an increasing sequence (in terms of the Löwner partial order as defined above) of density operators obtained for termination within an increasing number of iterations. To allow for modeling non-termination, their considerations are based on sub-normalized density operators, that is, positive semidefinite operators with trace *at most* one instead of exactly one, which is satisfied for physical density operators. It is immediately clear that the **abort** is non-trace preserving, and the **while** loop can be non-trace preserving if it does not terminate after a finite number of iterations.

However, despite recent progress and compared to the substantial body of literature on classical programming language semantics, the field is still very much in its early stages. Apt mathematical models to describe foundational semantics that attract researchers from both fields, together with a common understanding of necessities, can hopefully lead to fruitful progress in the future, possibly also eventually benefiting classical software engineering. As many of the approaches are implicitly or explicitly based on superoperators, it is not unlikely that this formalization of quantum computing will play an important role in the further development of quantum software semantics.

5.2 Communicating and Distributed Systems

Quantum communicating systems [10] can be seen as an example of restricted, distributed quantum computers; while they are not intended for general-purpose computing, they share some characteristics with quantum computers in that they prepare, manipulate, and measure quantum states. In contrast to NISQ machines and future fault-tolerant quantum computers, quantum communication systems have reached commercial maturity. In view of future distributed quantum computers that will also face how to distribute quantum states over spatial distances, insights into quantum communication systems can therefore benefit future quantum software engineering. Again, superoperators play a pronounced role in this domain.

Let, for example, ϱ_{AB} denote the density matrix of the state shared by Alice and Bob, the two customary virtual representative parties of distributed (communication) systems. The information available for each of them can be inferred by calculating the partial trace: $\varrho_A = \text{tr}_B\,\varrho_{AB}$ and $\varrho_B = \text{tr}_A(\varrho_{AB})$. The bipartite density matrix can never be recovered from these partial density matrices because, as is known in general, many bipartite density matrices give rise to the same partial density matrices . It is also obvious that a density operator representing an entangled state cannot be represented by a direct tensor product of unrelated partial density operators by the very definition of entanglement. One of the goals of denotational semantics as exemplified for the quantum case in the previous section is, essentially, to assign sufficient information to every edge of a flow graph such that the complete semantics of a program can be reconstructed by combining only the information given by the edges constituting the program. The denotation of a statement composed of several sub-statements must be completely determined only by a function of the denotations of the sub-statements.

This is impossible when transformations between explicit density matrices are considered. Since a combination of the partial density matrices ϱ_A, ϱ_B which were manipulated by Alice and Bob does not restore the total bipartite state ϱ_{AB}, a description that relies on a single density operator would obviously not comply with the physical state afterwards.

A possible solution would be to annotate the complete flow graph, that is, of both paths representing the control flow for Alice and Bob. In this case, the operations performed by Alice and Bob would be written as tensor products of the type $A \otimes \mathbb{1}_B$ and $\mathbb{1}_A \otimes B$ that act on the combined density matrix ϱ_{AB}. This way, we could assign semantics to the program as a whole, but would lose the ability to construct the denotation of a phrase from the denotations of its sub-phrases. This means that the semantics of the complete program could not be constructed from the denotation of Alice's and Bob's programs (each running on a separate computational entity) alone, which contrasts the key idea of denotational semantics.

Therefore, we need to seek a solution that does not characterize quantum operations by showing transformations of explicit density matrices (or provide superoperators that operate on the overall density operator), but instead captures the notion of a transformation in a more abstract sense. Completely positive maps (as explicitly represented by a set of Kraus operators) obviously fulfill this need, and we consequently deem them a good choice to describe quantum communication processes, and more general quantum computations that involve communication [15], or distributed computations [3]. While this requires some additional care in making sure that the definition of denotations does not carry an implicit dependence on an actual density operator, this is possible with the Kraus representation of superoperators as introduced above.

5.3 Noise and Imperfection Modeling

At the time of writing, all physically available quantum computers fall into the class of noisy, intermediate-scale quantum (NISQ) machines that are not fully fault-tolerant. This means that there is a difference between the *intended* transformation of quantum states (and measurements) described by a quantum program and the *actual* transformation performed by the hardware. While no physical obstacles prevent the building of perfect machines that reduce error rates to arbitrary low levels by using error-correcting codes, this comes at the expense of substantial overhead in the amount of required qubits and other resources that are currently much beyond experimental reach. Therefore, any formal and semantic considerations that implicitly assume perfect quantum computers will be in disagreement with experimental and practical reality, which is counter to their crucial point as they are supposed to improve software quality and correctness, which is a strongly practical desideratum.

However, even if this problem will disappear with the advent of perfect quantum computers, there are reasons to believe that NISQ machines of sufficient quality will be able to perform advantageous computations, and it cannot be ruled out that this class of machines—given that it will likely be possible to manufacture them at substantially reduced cost and effort in comparison to fault-tolerant machines with application-specific co-design techniques [32, 23]—will be of long-term or even permanent relevance. Considering the effects of imperfections is, consequently, not only worthwhile in the NISQ area, but might also display benefits beyond, and software engineering research should consider the respective implications: we believe it is important to understand the scalability, performance, quality, and reliability of quantum software on NISQ machines beyond empirical measurements, as these are also core considerations for classical software executing on classical hardware.

As NISQ systems can be seen as open quantum systems, superoperators are again well suited to modeling their properties and behavior (other techniques like Lindbladian dynamics [22] could model such scenarios, but are outside the scope of our considerations).

Current software-centric research deals with effectively adapting noise models to real machines [6] or the efficient learning of quantum noise [9], as characterizing noise from first physical principles or even measuring the actual characteristics on machines can be computationally prohibitive. The (non-)resilience against noise of variational algorithms like the quantum alternating operator approach (QAOA), an optimization algorithm targeted at NISQ machines, has been studied [14, 33]. From the software engineering point of view, [8] provide a didactic exposition to modeling imperfections of quantum computers with a focus on consequences for non-functional properties; we partly follow their presentation below.

To model such imperfections, consider that while the evolution of a closed quantum system is described by unitary operations, NISQ machines do not enjoy a complete isolation against their environment. Until fully error-corrected systems that mitigate this deficiency are available, the arising consequences will penetrate into the quantum software and programming language layers. A noisy system is subject to the influence of an external, uncontrolled environment that must be included in any model of the system, eventually ending up with a larger, but closed quantum system.

Similar to the earlier illustration of the Kraus representation theorem, ϱ denotes the open quantum system under consideration. It is combined with an uncontrolled environment ϱ_{env}, equating to a larger, closed system $\varrho \otimes \varrho_{env}$ subject to evolution $U(\varrho \otimes \varrho_{env})U^{\dagger}$. This *overall* evolution is described by a unitary operator $U^{\dagger}$. By eliminating the uncontrolled environment using a partial trace operation, the effective (and usually non-unitary) evolution of ϱ under noise is given by $\mathcal{E}(\varrho) = \mathrm{tr}_{env}(U(\varrho \otimes \varrho_{env})U^{\dagger})$.

Let $\mathcal{B}_e = \{|e_k\rangle\}_k$ be a basis of the environment. If the environment is measured in $\mathcal{B}_e$ after the time evolution, then the outcome determines the state of the principal system. We end up with a random distribution of states for the principal system depending on the measurement. The effect the environment had on ϱ when the outcome k occurred can be described by an operator E_k, leading to a mixed state description

$$\varrho \mapsto \sum_k E_k \varrho E_k^{\dagger}. \tag{17}$$

This Kraus representation can be used to describe effects that occur in *imperfect*, NISQ-era quantum systems. One canonical example of a probabilistic qubit flip that randomly with probability p (i.e., by the influence of external factors like energy dissipation, or the imperfect operation of quantum gates) negates a quantum bit can be described by

$$\varrho \mapsto (1 - p)\mathbb{1}\varrho\mathbb{1}^{\dagger} + pX\varrho X^{\dagger}. \tag{18}$$

The Pauli X gate is a unitary operator that, in state-based notation, flips a quantum bit: $X|0\rangle = |1\rangle$, and $X|1\rangle = |0\rangle$. The operator can be applied as usual in a quantum circuit to *deterministically* negate a quantum bit. In the above formulation of Eq. (18), however, the gate is applied to the one qubit system ϱ with probability p, and otherwise leaves the state as is. When the source of corresponding errors is unclear in a NISQ system, probability p is an effective (classical) parameter of the system whose magnitude can be determined by testing the system. By comparing the structure of Eq. (17) with the above equation, it can be seen that this delivers operators E_k. Similarly, randomly occurring phase flip errors (described in the state formulation by a Pauli Z gate) or a combination of bit and phase flip error (described in the state formulation by a Pauli Y gate) can be constructed by replacing X by Z or Y in Eq. (18). In each case, the interpretation of the operation is that the quantum state is left intact with probability $1 - p$ by applying an identity transformation, and affected by the error with probability p, resulting in a convex combination of density operators that includes *classical, stochastic* uncertainty: while the actual quantum system is in each of possibly multiple computational runs either in state ϱ (when no error occurred) *or* state $X\varrho X$ (in case an error occurred), an observer does not know *if* a stochastic error occurred, and must therefore include this lack of knowledge in the description of the quantum state. Note that while the initial state may be a pure state that does not contain any lack of knowledge before the operation induced by Eq. (18) is performed, it is also possible that a density operator already featuring classical lack of knowledge enters the quantum operation, which then in turn (usually) increases the lack of knowledge even further.

Generalizing from the binary error model use for bit, phase, and phase-bit flips, the formalism also allows us to model more complex imperfections as they occur in realistic systems, for instance with the commonly employed completely depolarizing operator: one qubit is randomly subjected to one of the Pauli operators X, Y, Z by

$$\varrho \mapsto (1 - p)\mathbb{1}\varrho\mathbb{1}^{\dagger} + \\ p\frac{1}{4}\left(\mathbb{1}\varrho\mathbb{1}^{\dagger} + X\varrho X^{\dagger} + Y\varrho Y^{\dagger} + Z\varrho Z^{\dagger}\right), \tag{19}$$

with a certain probability, and otherwise leaves the qubit as is. A quick calculation reveals that (19) equals $\varrho \mapsto (1 - p)\varrho + p\frac{1}{2}\mathbb{1}$, where $\frac{1}{2}\mathbb{1}$ is the density representing the state of a system being in every basis state with equal probability. Hence, the system either stays intact or all information gets destroyed with probability p. For an n qubit system, we obtain

$$\varrho \mapsto (1 - p)\varrho + p\frac{1}{2^n}\mathbb{1} \tag{20}$$

following a textbook calculation.

6   Summary and Conclusion

Superoperators provide a rigorous mathematical representation of quantum operations that go beyond unitary transformations, as they allow us to model measurements and imperfections. In this chapter, we have provided an introductory exposition to the concept tailored toward the domain of software engineering, and have elaborated on existing and possible use-cases for the concept, including to equip quantum programs with formal semantics, and how to handle communication and imperfection in current and future quantum computers.

While constructing practical software and algorithms for NISQ machines is likely to differ substantially from approaches geared toward scalable and fault-tolerant quantum computing, the superoperator formalism may provide a unified and consistent representation that caters well to both scenarios. We expect that with an increasing interest in quantum computing in software engineering, more uses of the concept will appear in future literature, which makes it important for software engineering researchers to be aware of the necessary structures and methods.

Acknowledgments This work is partly supported by the German Federal Ministry of Education and Research within the funding program Quantum technologies—from basic research to market, contract numbers 13N15647 and 13NI6092, and by the high-tech agenda of the Free State of Bavaria. The author would like to thank Felix Greiwe, Tom Krüger, and four semi-anonymous reviewers for helpful comments on a draft of this chapter that helped to substantially improve presentation.

References

1. Auletta, G., Fortunato, M., Parisi, G.: Quantum Mechanics. Cambridge University Press, Cambridge (2009). https://doi.org/10.1017/CBO9780511813955
2. Bichsel, B., et al. (June 2020) Silq: A High-Level Quantum Language with Safe Uncomputation and Intuitive Semantics. In: Proc. 41st ACM SIGPLAN, pp. 286–300. ACM. ISBN: 978-1-4503-7613-6. https://doi.org/10.1145/3385412.3386007 (visited on 24/04/2023)
3. Cirac, J.I. et al.: Distributed quantum computation over noisy channels. Phys. Rev. A **59**(6), 4249–4254 (1999). https://doi.org/10.1103/PhysRevA.59.4249 https://link.aps.org/doi/10.1103/PhysRevA.59.4249
4. Ekert, A., Hosgold, T.: Introduction to Quantum Information Science (2022). https://qubit.guide/qubit_guide.pdf
5. Garhwal, S., Ghorani, M., Ahmad, A.: Quantum programming language: a systematic review of research topic and top cited languages. Arch. Comput. Methods Eng. **28**(2), 289–310 (Mar. 2021). ISSN: 1134-3060, 1886-1784. https://doi.org/10.1007/s11831-019-09372-6
6. Georgopoulos, K., Emary, C., Zuliani, P.: Modeling and simulating the noisy behavior of near-term quantum computers. Phys. Rev. A **104**(6), 062432 (Dec. 2021). https://doi.org/10.1103/PhysRevA.104.062432. https://link.aps.org/doi/10.1103/PhysRevA.104.062432
7. Green, A.S. et al.: Quipper: a scalable quantum programming language. SIGPLAN Not. **48**(6), 333–342 (2013). ISSN: 0362-1340. https://doi.org/10.1145/2499370.2462177
8. Greiwe, F., Krüger, T., Mauerer, W.: Effects of Imperfections on Quantum Algorithms: A Software Engineering Perspective. In: 2023 IEEE International Conference on Quantum Software (QSW), pp. 31–42. https://doi.org/10.1109/QSW59989.2023.00014
9. Harper, R., Flammia, S.T., Wallman, J.J.: Efficient learning of quantum noise. Nature Phys. **16**(12), 1184–1188 (2020). https://doi.org/10.1038/s41567-020-0992-8
10. Khatri, S., Wilde, M.M.: Principles of quantum communication theory: A modern approach. Preprint (2020). arXiv:2011.04672. https://doi.org/10.48550/arXiv.2011.04672
11. Kraus, K.: States, Effects, and Operations Fundamental Notions of Quantum Theory, vol. 190. In: Lecture Notes in Physics. Springer, Berlin, Heidelberg (1983). ISBN: 9783540127321. https://doi.org/10.1007/3-540-12732-1. http://link.springer.com/10.1007/3-540-12732-1
12. Lewis, M., Soudjani, S., Zuliani, P.: Formal verification of quantum programs: theory, tools and challenges. ACM Trans. Quantum Comput. (2023). https://doi.org/10.1145/3624483
13. Leymann, F.: Towards a Pattern Language for Quantum Algorithms. Quantum Technology and Optimization Problems, vol. 11413. In: Lecture Notes in Computer Science (LNCS), pp.

218–230. Springer International Publishing, Cham (2019). https://doi.org/10.1007/978-3-030-14082-3_19

14. Marshall, J. et al.: Characterizing local noise in QAOA circuits. IOP SciNotes **1**(2), 025208 (2020). https://doi.org/10.1088/2633-1357/abb0d7

15. Mauerer, W.: Semantics and Simulation of Communication in Quantum Programming (2005). https://doi.org/10.48550/ARXIV.QUANT-PH/0511145. https://arxiv.org/abs/quant-ph/0511145

16. Moggi, E.: Notions of computation and monads. Inf. Comput. **93**(1), (1991). Selections from 1989 IEEE Symposium on Logic in Computer Science, pp. 55–92. ISSN: 0890-5401. https://doi.org/10.1016/0890-5401(91)90052-4. https://www.sciencedirect.com/science/article/pii/0890540191900524

17. Mu, S.-C., Bird, R.: Functional Quantum Programming. In: Asian Workshop on Programming Languages and Systems KAIST, Dajeaon, Korea (Dec. 2001). http://www.cs.ox.ac.uk/people/richard.bird/online/MuBird2001Functional.pdf

18. Nielsen, M.A., Chuang, I.L.: Quantum Computation and Quantum Information: 10th Anniversary Edition. Cambridge University Press, Cambridge (2010). https://doi.org/10.1017/CBO9780511976667

19. Ömer, B.: Procedural quantum programming. AIP Confer. Proc. **627**(1), 276–285 (Sept. 2002). ISSN: 0094-243X. https://doi.org/10.1063/1.1503695. eprint: https://pubs.aip.org/aip/acp/article-pdf/627/1/276/11571870/276_1_online.pdf

20. Peduri, A., Schaefer, I., Walter, M.: QbC: Quantum Correctness by Construction (2023). arXiv: 2307.15641 [quant-ph]

21. Perdrix, S.: A hierarchy of quantum semantics. Electron. Notes Theor. Comput. Sci. **192**(3), 71–83 (Nov. 2008). ISSN: 1571-0661. https://doi.org/10.1016/j.entcs.2008.10.028

22. Preskill, J.: Lecture Notes for Physics 229:Quantum Information and Computation. CreateSpace Independent Publishing Platform (2015). ISBN: 9781506189918. https://books.google.de/books?id=MIv8rQEACAAJ

23. Safi, H., Winterspergerm, K., Mauerer, W.: Influence of HW-SW-Co-Design on Quantum Computing Scalability. In: 2023 IEEE International Conference on Quantum Software (QSW), pp. 104–115 (2023). https://doi.org/10.1109/QSW59989.2023.00022

24. Schönberger, M., et al.: Peel — Pile? Cross-Framework Portability of Quantum Software. In: 2022 IEEE 19th International Conference on Software Architecture Companion (ICSA-C), pp. 164–169 (2022). https://doi.org/10.1109/ICSA-C54293.2022.00039

25. Scott, D., Strachey, C.: Toward a Mathematical Semantics for Computer Languages. Technical Monograph PRG-6. Programming Research Group. Oxford Univ. Computing Lab., Oxford (1971)

26. Selinger, P.: Towards a quantum programming language. Math. Struct. Comput. Sci. **14**(4), 527–586 (Aug. 2004). ISSN: 0960-1295, 1469-8072. https://doi.org/10.1017/S0960129504004256

27. Svore, K., et al.: Q#: Enabling Scalable Quantum Computing and Development with a High-level DSL. In: Proceedings of the Real World Domain Specific Languages Workshop 2018, pp. 1–10. ACM, (Feb. 2018). ISBN: 978-1-4503-6355-6. https://doi.org/10.1145/3183895.3183901 (visited on 24/08/2023)

28. Vedral, V.: Introduction to Quantum Information Science (Oxford Graduate Texts). Oxford University Press, USA (2006). ISBN: 0199215707

29. Vizotto, J., Altenkirch, T., Sabry, A.: Structuring quantum effects: superoperators as arrows. Math. Struct. Comput. Sci. **16**(3), 453–468 (2006). https://doi.org/10.1017/S0960129506005287

30. Voichick, F., et al.: Qunity: a unified language for quantum and classical computing. Proc. ACM Program. Lang. **7**(POPL), (2023). https://doi.org/10.1145/357122510.1145/3571225

31. Wecker, D., Svore, K.M.: LIQUi|>: A Software Design Architecture and Domain-Specific Language for Quantum Computing (Feb. 2014). CoRR abs/1402.4467. https://doi.org/10.48550/arXiv.1402.4467

32. Wintersperger, K., Safi, H., Mauerer, W.: QPU-System Co-Design for Quantum HPC Accelerators. In: Schulz, M., et al. (eds.) Proceedings of the 35th GI/ITG International Conference on the Architecture of Computing Systems. Gesellschaft für Informatik, pp. 100–114 (Aug. 2022). ISBN: 978-3-031-21867-5. https://doi.org/10.1007/978-3-031-21867-5_7
33. Xue, C., et al.: Effects of quantum noise on quantum approximate optimization algorithm. Chin. Phys. Lett. **38**(3), 030302 (2021). https://dx.doi.org/10.1088/0256-307X/38/3/030302
34. Ying, M., Zhou, L., Li, Y.: Reasoning about Parallel Quantum Programs (Aug. 2019). https://doi.org/10.48550/arXiv.1810.11334. http://arxiv.org/abs/1810.11334
35. Zhou, L., et al.: CoqQ: Foundational verification of quantum programs. Proc. ACM Program. Lang. **7**(POPL), (Jan. 2023). https://doi.org/10.1145/3571222

Part II
Quantum Software System Design

QSandbox: The Agile Quantum Software Sandbox

Iaakov Exman (ID)

Abstract *QSandbox* is an *agile software sandbox* specifically designed for Quantum Software research and development. *QSandbox* agility goes beyond the System Under Development within the sandbox. *QSandbox* agility is *itself modifiable* since its high-level modules are varied at will by Quantum Software developers.

QSandbox has a series of unique features suitable for agile development. It uses high-level abstraction meaningful modules, instead of low-level quantum gates of conventional simulators. It has instantly synchronized dual views—high-level quantum circuit and density matrix. It has uniform quantum and classical representation, implying the innovative idea of quantum circuits for classical software.

Keywords Quantum Software · Agile *QSandbox* · High-level quantum circuit · Density matrix · Abstraction · Meaningful modules · Quantum circuits for classical software

1 Introduction

The relatively young Quantum Software discipline should adopt classic software techniques that have demonstrated great advantages in software development (e.g., Kent Beck [1], Fox and Patterson [2]), to enable an *agile* approach to Quantum Software systems.

A generic sandbox is *a safe and isolated environment* to test software, which has been used for agile software development (e.g. [3]). The *agile Quantum Software sandbox*—in short *QSandbox*—is specifically designed for Quantum Software. *QSandbox* agility goes beyond the System Under Development (SUD) within the sandbox. *QSandbox* agility is *itself modifiable* by Quantum Software developers and researchers, as an experimental substrate. Therefore, it preserves exactly what

I. Exman (✉)
HIT Holon Institute of Technology, School of Computer Science, Holon, Israel
e-mail: iaakov@hit.ac.il

© The Author(s) 2024
I. Exman et al. (eds.), *Quantum Software*,
https://doi.org/10.1007/978-3-031-64136-7_4

71

the Quantum Software professionals think are *meaningful modules* for their own work. We use high-level abstraction modules, instead of low-level quantum gates of conventional simulators.

The current chapter's purpose is to characterize *QSandbox* as a theoretical based but useful system in practice. It aims to be a concrete implementation of the ideas exposed by Exman [4], enabling actual testing of those ideas.

1.1 Concise QSandbox Characterization

QSandbox is a software development environment specifically designed for Quantum Software, either pure quantum or hybrid systems composed of quantum and classical subsystems. *QSandbox* is useful for pure classical systems, as we believe these are limiting cases of more general Quantum Software systems.

An essential *QSandbox* characteristic is ease of "modify and keep it meaningful" or even "modify and sharpen its meaning." Thus, it displays the following properties:

1. *Dual views*—consisting of instantly synchronized high-level "quantum circuit" and its "density matrix": if the quantum circuit is changed, the density matrix is concurrently modified; if the density matrix is changed, the quantum circuit is instantly modified as well. If a developer chooses to add an optional view, this view is also automatically synchronized. Instant views synchronization avoids special synchronization commands, shortening development time.
2. *Modular perspective*—*QSandbox* enables *whole modules* to be inserted/removed from each of its dual views, for example, a module containing a complete set of gates needed for the oracle recognition of the correct answer of a Grover search. One should be able to easily substitute a module for another one.

Why the Insistence on Modules?

Modules must have *meaning*, due to the higher abstraction level of Quantum Software systems, in which they are embedded.

The dual views and the modular approach, due to their theoretical basis, should afford a significantly higher perspective to Quantum Software development and immediate response by *QSandbox*.

1.2 Chapter Organization

This chapter is organized as follows. Section 2 presents a set of *QSandbox* focused ideas. Section 3 overviews the *QSandbox* software architecture. Section 4 contains an explanation of the dual views from a theoretical perspective. Section 5 presents the novel idea of a quantum circuit for classical software. Section 6 displays agile compressed views with a Quantum Software system case study. Section 7 refers to related work. Section 8 concludes the chapter with an in-depth discussion of *QSandbox*, including open issues and future work.

2   *QSandbox* Focused Ideas

QSandbox is based upon a set of focused ideas, aiming at fundamentally changing how a Quantum Software system is perceived by developers and researchers.

2.1   *High Abstraction Level Interface: First Idea*

An important goal of *QSandbox* is to *hide any underlying low-level details* that are not essential for agile Quantum Software system development and understanding. It is analogous to an operating system which hides the underlying computing machine, be it real or virtual, or to the memory hierarchy—cache, RAM, virtual memory— hiding the various hierarchy levels, to give an illusion that memory is almost always very fast.

The high abstraction level interface deals with high-level modules, each one having a well-understood meaning in natural language. Its advantages are:

(a) One avoids repeating mistakes of the history of classical computing. Low-level quantum gates would be analogous to a return to classical machine language.
(b) Low-level quantum gates refer to specific problem solutions, e.g., a specific number of qubits; high abstraction module level focuses on perceiving generic solutions.

2.2   *Modular Perspective: Second Idea*

A unique trait of the *QSandbox* is the particular set of Quantum Software modules available within a specific copy of *QSandbox*, at a certain development time and place.

The set of high-level modules is *varied at will by developers or researchers*, in contrast to the fixed set of simple quantum gates permanently available in conventional simulators.

When first acquired, *QSandbox* offers a useful initial repertoire of modules. An example of a high-level module has a variable number n of Hadamard gates $H^{\otimes n}$ frequently necessary to attain equal superposition. Another example is a set of measurement devices. These, despite not strictly being a kind of quantum gate, often appear in quantum circuits, as the way to acquire specific information about a quantum subsystem by measuring its variables. A slightly different kind of "modules" offers localized types of control, for instance, a loop with a variable number of cycles, easily inserted/removed around a desired set of modules.

Additional modules are expected to be collected by developer or researcher teams along the lifetime of a given copy of *QSandbox*. Specific modules may also be discarded if rarely used, or if deemed irrelevant by the software developers. Finally, similar module versions may be preserved if they are frequently applied modules by these teams.

2.3 Uniform Quantum and Classical System Representations: Third Idea

The module representations in both views—high-level quantum circuit and density matrix—are uniform and independent of the type of software system, whether pure quantum, pure classical, or hybrid systems, composed of quantum and classical subsystems.

The representation uniformity facilitates immediate recognition of modules during research and development activities. Moreover, it stimulates innovative ideas such as quantum circuits for classical software.

3 *QSandbox* Software Architecture Overview

This section describes the initial *QSandbox* from the following points of view:

1. Its software architecture, components, and their interrelations
2. The user interface as seen from the outside
3. The most important user commands and their purposes

3.1 *QSandbox* Software Architecture

The initial *QSandbox* software architecture has the following groups of components:

Active Components

- *Views generator*—generating and synchronizing the available views, either the dual standard (quantum circuit and density matrix) or additional optional ones (such as particular quantum computing languages)
- *Simulator*—to run and test any System Under Development (SUD), either upon the quantum circuit or upon the density matrix
- *Modulaser* [5]—an internal software program designed to manipulate matrices, in particular for density matrix modularization

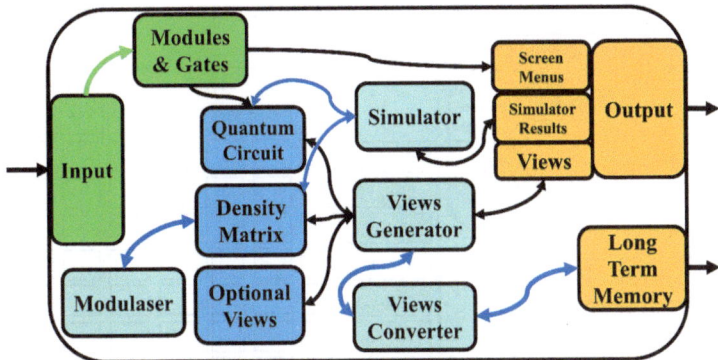

Fig. 1 Schematic diagram of the *QSandbox* software architecture—component types are grouped with distinct colors: active components (light blue), internal views implementation (dark blue), input (green), and output (orange)

- *Views converter*—to convert back and forth display representations to efficiently save formats internally or exportable to external long-term memory devices

System Input/Output

- *Input*—to add new kinds of modules and possibly quantum gates.
- *Output*—views, menus, and simulator results on a computer/mobile phone screen; the long-term memory contents may be exported to external memory devices.

The *QSandbox* software architecture is summarized in Fig. 1. Component types are grouped with distinct colors. The *QSandbox* center of gravity is the *views generator* (light blue), linking internal views (dark blue), the views converter, and their output. On the left-hand side, the *input* gets *modules and gates*. On the right-hand side is the *output* to a screen.

Now, suppose that the developer wishes to make additions to the initial *overall software architecture*. From Fig. 1, one can clearly see an essentially modular architecture based on the idea that the components are grouped by component types, which in Fig. 1 have distinct colors. This idea should be cautiously preserved in every addition.

One may add a single component to an existing group, for instance, a new optional view. A concrete example could be to add a view of a previously absent quantum computing language. In this particular case, one essentially needs to link the new optional view to the views generator.

Alternatively, one may add a whole new group. For example, in the future, a system developer may wish to add a series of noise models, to allow one to test various such models. In such a case, one needs to add a new group, with a number of components as the number of models, and link all these models to the simulator.

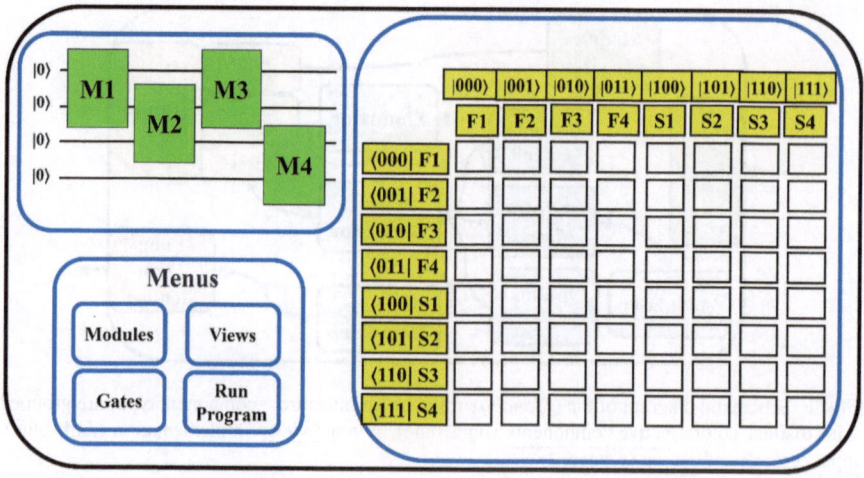

Fig. 2 *QSandbox* default user interface—schematic diagram. The upper left-hand side shows the default quantum circuit. On the right-hand side, one sees a default density matrix. The lower left-hand side shows the four-button menus

3.2   User Interface

The *QSandbox* user interface, consistent with the purposeful approach—to hide superfluous low-level details—is as neat and sharp as possible:

- *The dual views*—a *quantum circuit* with a schematic initial default diagram; a *density matrix* with suggestive default values
- *A concise menu*—with four buttons: (1) quantum modules; (2) simple quantum gates; (3) views; and (4) run program. Each of these buttons when clicked will open a more detailed menu offering a choice of the respective items.

The default user interface view is shown in Fig. 2. In detail, the default *quantum circuit* has a single register, four qubits with initial state values $|0\rangle$, and four empty modules.

The default *density matrix* values, illustrated later on in Sects. 5 and 6, are eight columns and eight rows, whose respective indices are four functionals followed by four structors, with empty initial values; upon the columns, there are kets with values from $|000\rangle$ to $|111\rangle$, and to the left of the rows, there are bras with values from $\langle 000|$ to $\langle 111|$; these default values are only for the sake of illustration.

The quantum modules detailed menu when opened offers the available modules to add them to the quantum circuit, similar to the simple quantum gates.

The opened views menu shows six items:

- Optional views
- Restart view
- Save view and retrieve view
- Compress and decompress view

Most views items are self-explanatory. Compress view reduces the internal module details displayed in a view; it is defined in Sect. 4.3 and further illustrated in Sect. 6.

The run program menu shows two items:

- Simulator
- Modulaser

Additions to the initial user interface are simpler than those to the overall architecture. Looking at Fig. 2, possible additions can be made to the menus. One may add a single component to an existing menu button, or one may need to add a whole new button, containing a submenu with several possible alternatives.

3.3 User Commands' Set

The *QSandbox* user commands' set follows from the neat approach of the user interface:

- *Modules and Gates*—one simply drags and drops the chosen module or gate icon on the quantum circuit.
- *Views*—one chooses the desired command—save, retrieve, restart, compress, decompress—and puts the pointer (say a mouse) on the view to which the command should be applied. In case of an optional view, one should choose it, move it out of the menu, and release it outside the menu to be usable.
- *Run Program*—for the simulator upon the quantum circuit, one can run *one-step-forward*, *run-to-the-end* of the circuit, *one-step-backward*, or *return-to-the-beginning* of the circuit. For the simulator upon the density matrix, one chooses the desired initial matrix element and applies the relevant unitary operator. For the modulaser, one should choose the desired matrix operation, e.g., modularization.

There will also be trivial commands of practical value, for instance, to extend a view to cover the whole screen, to reduce the view to its original size, and so on.

This is only a brief overview. For effective use of *QSandbox*, one will need a self-explanatory interface and, to be on the safe side, a more detailed user's guide.

4 Dual Views in Depth

This section explains and justifies the dual views by deep theoretical considerations. The relatively abstract terms in this section are clarified in Sects. 5 and 6 by case studies with concrete examples. The theory [4] defines Quantum Software modules by two complementary aspects of high-level modules:

- *Modules have meaning*—meaning is afforded by natural language concepts understood by humans. Concepts are the essence of Quantum Software systems.
- *Modules are orthogonal*—modularization implies algebraic constraints, enabling correctness verification; the purpose of a real software theory is to check whether the software is correctly built as a self-consistent system.

For instance, a car *braking system* has no relation whatsoever with the car *air-conditioner*. These are orthogonal modules; thus, the car is a self-consistent system. It would be strange if in order to <u>brake</u> (reduce the car speed), one needed to *turn on the air-conditioner*. This is inconsistent; these subsystems do not belong to a single module.

But the meaning and orthogonality of high-level modules by themselves are not enough to constitute a software theory useful in practice. One needs computable entities. The computable entities corresponding to meaning and orthogonality are, respectively, the high-level quantum circuit and its fitting density matrix, explained in the next sections.

4.1 High-Level Quantum Circuit

How do we represent module concepts in a high-level quantum circuit of a Quantum Software system?

First, by the high-level modules themselves named by concepts, which are understood by human developers and researchers.

Second, the high-level modules contain indices of two types: structors {**S1, S2, . . . Sj**}, a term reminding one that this deals with structures), and functionals {**F1, F2, . . . Fk**}, reminding one that these are "functions" performing computations. The necessity for indices is discussed in Sect. 4.4 describing the density matrix.

High-level modules enable understanding the nature of computations but are not themselves computing entities. To perform computations, one inserts low-level modules with computing quantum gates into the high-level modules. Then computation is feasible.

4.2 Computations with High-Level Quantum Circuits

What is the nature of the computations with a high-level quantum circuit?

Assume low-level modules were previously input in *QSandbox*. A run is a sequential application of modules on the Quantum Software system states, summarized in the next text box.

Procedure 1—Computation with a High-Level Quantum Circuit

{ Given that high-level quantum circuits (QC) are composed with generic modules, which are not computing entities by themselves:

Modules choice—for each generic module in the QC, choose a specific low-level module composed of simple quantum gates from the long-term memory. Specific modules are recognized by the number of qubits n and a serial number for module type.

Substitute generic with specific modules—drag and drop specific modules on the high-level quantum circuit with generic modules.

Loop: until the desired state, eventually doing steps-forward or steps-backward

{ *Run the QC upon the software system current state*—starting from the initial state, say $|0\rangle$, chose a command, e.g., *one-step-forward*, and apply it by the relevant module upon the current state. }

}

4.3 Compressed Views

Compressed views is an additional agility tool, to shorten development time.

Suppose that computation results with one or more modules belonging to a given Quantum Software system are already satisfactory, and there is no current need for further detailed computations with these modules. Then one can *compress* its internal structors and continue working only with the remaining modules. This is the general idea of a compressed higher-level quantum circuit.

Compressing a set of modules is done as follows:

- *Save Original Quantum Circuit*—save the original high-level quantum circuit to allow decompression, after all remaining modules have satisfactory computations.
- *Modules Substitution*—substitute the whole set of modules to be compressed by just one compressed module.
- *Compressed Module Contents*—the compressed module should have just a single structor and a single functional, with names provided by the developer.
- *Coalesced Structor and Functional Indices*—the structor index is a pair of coalesced juxtaposed indices of the first and the last compressed modules, for instance, "S3S5," and corresponding functional index, "F3F5," where the first compressed module is M3 and the last one is M5. Coalesced indices tell *QSandbox* that the marked structor is inside a compressed module.
- *Decompression*—is done by restoring the saved original quantum circuit.

4.4 Density Matrix

A density matrix,[1] usually designated by ρ (the Greek letter "rho"), is one of the ways to describe the state of a quantum system. Formally, it is defined as a square positive semi-definite trace-one Hermitian matrix. Trace-one means that the matrix *trace*—the sum of the diagonal matrix elements—equals one. The density matrix in this chapter serves to describe the overall state of a Quantum Software system.

What are the relationships between structors, functionals, modules, and a density matrix?

We first observe that structors are a generalization of classes in object-oriented design (OOD). Functionals generalize class methods in OOD. The generalizations are needed since to describe a very complex system, one would use not just a single density matrix but a hierarchy of density matrices, for example, a density matrix for the whole car, other matrices for the subsystems—one for the air-conditioner, another for the braking subsystem, etc. Each matrix has its structor and functional sets.

For example, the air-conditioner could have three structors {S1=heater; S2=cooler; S3=fan} and three functionals {F1=heating function; F2=cooling; F3=ventilating}. One can say that a structor provides a functional. For instance, the heater provides the heating function. The number of functionals per structor is not necessarily one to one. One could have two functionals (heating and warming) for the same structor (the heater). The same functional provided by two structors is also possible: this is OOD "inheritance."

Each structor *Sj* and each functional *Fk* index should always and consistently represent each respective concept. The necessity for *Sj* and *Fk* indices is that matrices do not perform computations directly with concepts but rather with their respective index values.

A matrix with structors represented by columns and functionals represented by rows is called an *adjacency matrix*, whose nonzero matrix elements stand for "neighbors," marking which functionals are provided by their respective structors.

In order to minimize the structors and functionals number of a system, the adjacency matrix set of columns must be linear independent. The same is true for the set of rows of this matrix. Then, by linear algebra considerations, the adjacency matrix must be square.

Modules are sub-matrices of the adjacency matrix, containing a consistent subset of structors and functionals, with related meaning. An air-conditioner module should have a set of columns (structors) as seen above: heater, cooler, and fan. The braking system module should have a different set of columns (structors) such as brake, handbrake, brake fluid, etc., in order to be self-consistent. The same is true for matrix rows. There must not be mixing of concepts belonging to diverse modules. The outcome is that modules are orthogonal. Thus, an adjacency matrix

---

[1] Readers not familiar with quantum computing terms are encouraged to read relevant sections of a quantum computing book (e.g., [6–9]).

correctly modularized must be block-diagonal. This is the real Quantum Software theory enabling modularity correctness verification.

Finally, any Quantum Software density matrix is composed of the diagonal with trace equals one, an upper-right quadrant adjacency matrix above the diagonal, and its reflection in the lower left below the diagonal. This is illustrated by case studies in Sects. 5 and 6.

4.5   Computations with a Density Matrix

This section does not explain the nature of the computations with a density matrix in detail. But these computations are so important that we provide here concise descriptions of these computations and references to the relevant literature where one can find these detailed descriptions.

- *Modularization*—this means a procedure to find the modules of a Quantum Software system, given a density matrix. If the software developer or researcher is not satisfied with the resulting modularization, one can reconceptualize the system, obtaining a slightly different density matrix.

  There are two ways to modularize a Quantum Software density matrix. One is purely linear algebraic, based upon the fact that the density matrix inherits properties of the Laplacian matrix (see, e.g., Braunstein et al. [10]). Modules correspond to zero-valued matrix eigenvalues, whose size is given by the corresponding eigenvectors (see, e.g., Exman and Sakhnini [11] and references therein; see also von Luxburg [12]).

  Another modularization method is by representing the density matrix as sums of projectors. In this case, modules are given by disjoint sets of projectors (see Exman and Shmilovich [13]).

- *Projective Measurements*—projective measurements are one of the well-known kinds of quantum measurements, which may be used for several applications. One possible application is to reduce the number of measurements in a quantum tomography process. This reduction of the number of measurements is due to the use of "modules" in a so-called modules tomography (see Exman and Zvulunov [14] and references therein).

- *System Simulation*—instead of actually running a Quantum Software System, whose code may not be available, one can perform evolution of the matrix state, which is a very high-level simulation of running the Quantum Software system represented by the density matrix.

4.6 Optional Views

As discussed in the previous subsections, there are well-funded theoretical arguments linking the high-level quantum circuit with the density matrix of a given
Quantum Software system, jointly consisting of the basic mandatory dual views
of *QSandbox*.

Besides the standard dual views, one can use optional views. A common optional
view is a translation of the high-level quantum circuit to a quantum computing
programming language, such as Qiskit [15], QWIRE [16], or Cirq [17] (see also
Serrano et al. [18]).

If optional views are available in a given *QSandbox* version, the basic dual views
mechanisms are applicable to the optional views. These mechanisms are instant
automatic views synchronization, views appearance in the views submenus, and
their preservation in the *QSandbox* long-term memory. The decision as to whether
to actually use optional views is left to the developer or researcher using his specific
QSandbox version.

5 Quantum Circuit for Classical Software: The Recycle Bin Case Study

This case study offers plenty of challenges. The novelty is a quantum circuit for pure
classical software systems. It is legitimate as the latter are viewed as limiting cases
of quantum systems. The open question is the possibility of designing high-level
quantum circuits in general for classical software. A fitting density matrix is also
obtained.

5.1 Recycle Bin Overview and High-Level Quantum Circuit

What is a recycle bin? Any computer user is familiar with the waste basket in a
computer screen corner, where deleted files are pictorially thrown. A recycle bin
enables recycling of a file or an email message, previously deleted. Deleting and
then recycling can be done many times, until one empties the waste basket, and
recycling is not possible anymore.

A recycle bin (see Jackson [19], [20] p. 49) high-level quantum circuit is shown
in Fig. 3.

We start the high-level quantum circuit top-to-bottom description with *modules*:

- M1 = Item—that can be deleted and recycled, such as a file or an email message
- M2 = Waste bin—location that can be emptied, and then items are permanently
  unusable

Fig. 3 Recycle bin—high-level quantum circuit. Time increases from left to right. It has two *modules* (light blue); three *structors* (green); three *functionals* (orange); and one connector. This is a first example of a quantum circuit for classical software

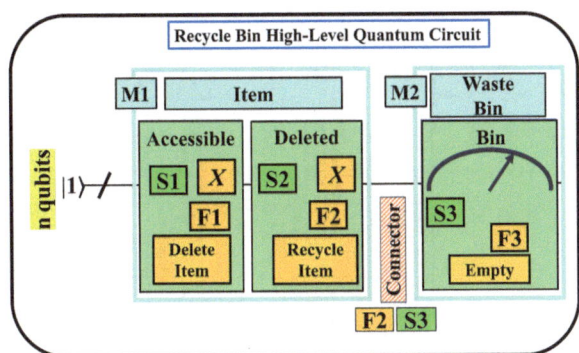

Modules contain *structors*:

- S1 = Accessible—structor with items that can be used.
- S2 = Deleted—structor with items that cannot be used.
- S3 = Bin—this is the only structor within the waste bin.

Structors provide *functionals*:

- F1 = Delete—move item from accessible to deleted.
- F2 = Recycle—move item from deleted to accessible.
- F3 = Empty—permanently remove all items from bin.

When *connector* is activated, it removes all deleted items, emptying the waste bin.

Now we describe the quantum entities, which seem quite interesting:

- **Number of qubits**—is left unspecified as **n**; each qubit represents one item; but there is just one qubit timeline; a *slash* in the beginning of the qubit line is a conventional way to state that there are multiple qubits.
- **Initial qubit value**—it is $|1\rangle$ because an item is initially accessible.
- **The operator Pauli X**—is the quantum not, transforming $|1\rangle$ into $|0\rangle$ and back; $|0\rangle$ represents a deleted item. Thus, delete and recycle are reversible, as they should be.
- **The empty operator is a measurement**—since it should be irreversible.
- **The connector is needed**—emptying is a voluntary decision and not automatically performed.

An exercise left for the reader is the following question: What is a reasonable value for the result of the (empty) measurement? How is this function implemented?

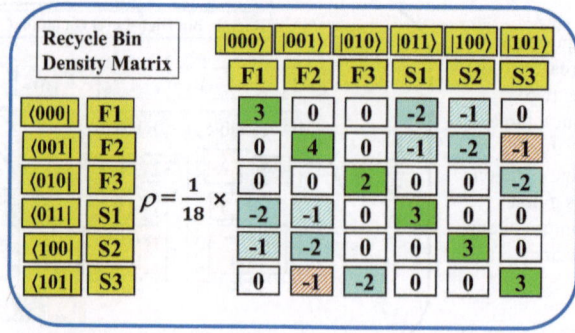

Fig. 4 Recycle bin Quantum Software density matrix—one sees diagonal matrix elements (green). Above and below the diagonal is the square adjacency matrix with two modules in descending order: a 2-by-2 item module (plain and hatched light blue) and a 1-by-1 waste bin module (plain light blue). The connector is shown in {F2, S3}

5.2 Recycle Bin: Density Matrix

The density matrix fitting the high-level quantum circuit in Fig. 3 is shown in Fig. 4.

The recycle bin density matrix in Fig. 4 perfectly corresponds to the high-level quantum circuit in Fig. 3. For instance, the item module is located in the density matrix elements {S1, S2, F1, F2} fitting structors and functionals of the quantum circuit.

6 Compressed Dual Views of Quantum Software: Grover Search Case Study

Grover search is a well-known quantum computing algorithm. Here it concretely illustrates usage facets of *QSandbox*, focusing on the user interface and modules.

After a concise Grover overview, we separate the two Grover search dual views, to examine each of them in more detail. First, we have a look at the high-level quantum circuit and its compressed version. Then, we look at the compressed density matrix.

6.1 Grover Search Concise Overview

Grover's overall idea [21] is, for an unsorted database of size N, to search a desired database item. Assume a telephone directory sorted by subscriber names; asking for a phone number given a subscriber's name, there are efficient classical search algorithms.

But, given a telephone number and asking for the subscriber's name, the same telephone directory is unstructured for this request: a classical algorithm takes $O(N)$ search function evaluations, while Grover quantum search takes only $O\left(\sqrt{N}\right)$, a quadratic speed-up. The number of qubits necessary for Grover search is a register of $n = \log_2 N$ qubits.

The algorithm initiates by an equal superposition of all states. Next, a Grover iteration is performed where an "oracle" recognizes and marks the solution, followed by an amplification of the marked solution, gradually increasing the probability of finding the solution. A final measurement obtains the solution. The iteration cycles number is $O\left(\sqrt{N}\right)$.

6.2   Grover: High-Level Quantum Circuit

A high-level quantum circuit of the Grover Quantum Software system is shown in Fig. 5.

The high-level quantum circuit in Fig. 5 is consistent with the *QSandbox* approach in two senses: (a) there are only high-level modules, no explicit simple quantum gates or registers; (b) all module names are natural language concepts, understood by developers.

Hadamard, Grover, and Fourier for that matter are not "quantum gates" or transforms; these are proper person names, scientists that became common natural language concepts, for their contribution to science (see Discussion in [4]).

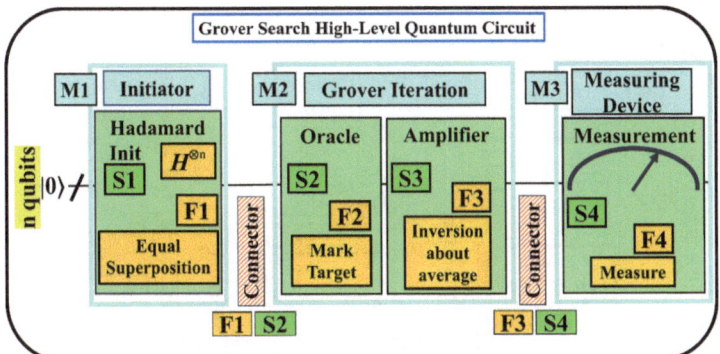

Fig. 5 Grover search—high-level quantum circuit. Time increases left to right. It has three *modules* {M1, M2, M3} (light blue), four *structors* {S1, Hadamard init; S2, oracle; S3, amplifier; S4, measurement} (green), four *Functionals* {F1, equal superposition; F2, mark target; F3, inversion about average; F4, measure} (orange), and two connectors

Below the *connectors*, between consecutive modules in the circuit of Fig. 5, there are linking points: from the preceding module *functional* to the next module first *structor*.

An important *connectors*' role in this system is to delimit the beginning and end of the Grover iteration cycles. One probably needs a better way to demarcate the components of iterations, as suggested above in Sect. 2.2. The number of Grover iteration cycles is not shown in this kind of quantum circuit: one wishes to keep it as general as possible.

The number of qubits **n** is also unspecified, by the same generality consideration. Similar to the recycle bin (in Fig. 3), there is just one qubit timeline, with a *slash* right in the beginning, meaning multiple qubits. Here the initial state is $|0\rangle$.

QSandbox simulator computations apply the Hadamard init structor on the initial $|0\rangle$ state, passing by the connector, to the next module, as described in Procedure 1 Sect. 4.2.

6.3 Grover: Compressed Higher-Level Quantum Circuit

The Grover quantum circuit obtained from Fig. 5, by compressing the intermediate Grover iteration module M2, is shown in Fig. 6.

6.4 Grover: Compressed Density Matrix

The respective Grover Quantum Software system compressed density matrix is shown in Fig. 7.

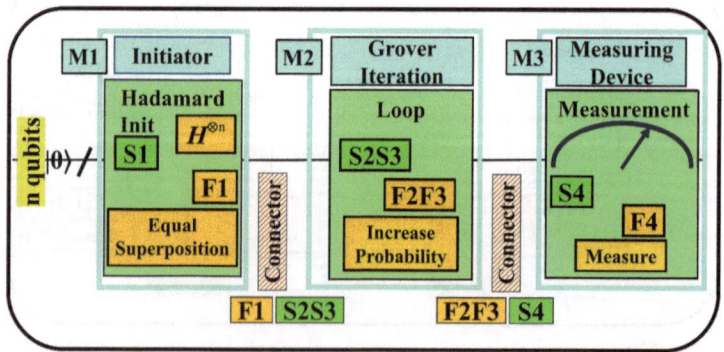

Fig. 6 Grover search compressed higher-level quantum circuit—the "Grover iteration" module M2 is compressed. Its two structors coalesced into a single "loop" structor and a single "increase probability" functional. The original structor and functional indices coalesced into double indices, "S2S3" and "F2F3." The other modules were not changed

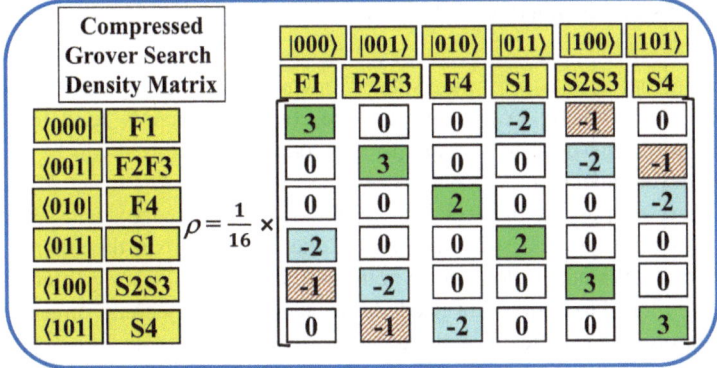

Fig. 7 Grover search compressed density matrix ρ—the 3-by-3 adjacency matrix (upper-right and lower-left quadrant) has 1-by-1 *modules* (light blue), in descending order: M, initiator {S1,F1}; M2, compressed Grover iteration {S2S3, F2F3}; M3, measuring device {S4,F4}. *Connectors* (hatched brown) are in {F1, S2S3} and {F2F3, S4}

The exact correspondence of the compressed density matrix in Fig. 7 with the compressed higher-level quantum circuit modules of Fig. 6 is clearly seen. For instance, the *initiator module M1* in the quantum circuit contains the structor S1 and its functional F1; the corresponding initiator module M1 in the density matrix is the matrix element {S1, F1}. The next module in both views is the compressed *Grover iterator M2* with just a single matrix element {S2S3, F2F3}. In between, one sees the *connector* located in {F1, S2S3}.

All the density matrix columns sum to zero, and the same is true for all its rows, a property inherited from the Laplacian matrix (see, e.g., [11]), being a further checking of its correctness. The reason for not normalizing the density matrix—actually dividing its matrix elements by the trace, whose value is 16—is that algebraically adding some of these division outcomes gives results equaling very close to but not exactly zero, due to rounding errors.

The kets above the density matrix columns and bras at the left of the density matrix rows are relevant to the density matrix modularization, described elsewhere (e.g., [13, 22]). A linear algebraic modularization can be performed by the modu-laser [5] accessible within *QSandbox* (in Fig. 1).

7 Related Work

In this section, one can find a concise review of the scientific literature relevant to the material in this chapter. It includes classical sandbox examples, such as the Java sandbox.

7.1   Classical Software Sandbox

Sandboxing operates a safe and isolated environment, decoupled from the surrounding infrastructure, to test and analyze code. It is mainly used for security considerations. But once it is usable to test code, in principle it can be applied to software development.

The main purpose of the well-known classical Java sandbox is a secure environment to run untrusted software code. Coker et al. [23] in their paper carried out an empirical study to test the hypothesis that the Java security model affords developers more flexibility than needed, i.e., its complexity compromises security without improving practical functionality.

Herzog and Shahmehri [24] refer to the secure Java sandbox, with a slightly different purpose. They investigate if the Java permission syntax can be used to formulate policies for resource management of high-level resources. These resources are, e.g., the file system, I/O device APIs (application programmer interfaces), threads, sockets, or properties.

Wilcox et al. [3] take a very different approach to sandboxing. Their paper's focus is agile development, using many sandboxes to enable parallel development. Their sandbox is a complete clone of the source code, including continuous integration and deployment capabilities. They aggressively use sandboxes for all changes beyond what has been completed in a day. The sandbox, apart from code, has a running application instance. The book containing the Wilcox et al. paper (see Book ref. [25]) is a potentially good source of ideas.

The classical software usage of sandboxes referred to above had a serious and useful technological basis, mainly for security and software development.

In contrast, searching for references to quantum sandboxes for software applications, we found many papers using very liberally the sandbox terminology, but the technological aspects are very disappointing. We decided not to include references to those papers.

8   Discussion

This section discusses central assumptions behind *QSandbox*, speculating somewhat about open issues and future work, and concludes with the main contribution of this chapter.

8.1　Main QSandbox Assumptions

Here are the most important *QSandbox* assumptions:

- *Two complementary and inseparable views*—the high-level quantum circuit with modules named by natural language understood by humans and the density matrix enabling exact computations with Quantum Software.
- *The usage of abstract and generic high-level modules*—the deeper reason for *high-level quantum modules*, instead of low-level quantum gates, is the ability to compose *abstract and generic* quantum circuits from concrete specific modules.

8.2　Open Issues: Quantum Circuit for Classical Software

The quantum circuit of the recycle bin—a quantum circuit for a pure classical software (Sect. 5.2)—opens wider and very interesting questions: Why and how should one make routine use of quantum circuits for classical software?

Concerning the "why" question: What have we learned from the quantum circuit of the recycle bin? The remarkable answer is that it is so obvious, because the recycle bin quantum circuit is readable and understandable, like any other quantum circuit of an actual Quantum Software, that we would not have asked such a question.

Concerning the "how" question explicitly formulated: How to systematically generate a quantum circuit for classical software? This seems more challenging, deserving further consideration.

We have justified quantum circuits for classical software, claiming that classical software is a limiting case of quantum systems. This needs a deeper argumentation.

8.3　Quantum Agile Software?

Classical agile software development as expressed as the four rules of simple design (see Kent Beck [1, 26], Bekkers [27], Fowler [28], Haines [29]) tells us two things:

1. *Learn from experience in the laboratory*—it is an *objective test* indifferent to our chaotic thoughts.
2. *The importance of theory*—theory is also an *objective test*: theories are checked again and again, accumulating knowledge independent of capricious decisions; they are expressed in mathematical terms, the language of science.

To attain the "four rules" of quantum agility, one needs an acceptable theory and/or laboratory experience. But while quantum computing theory is well developed, quantum laboratory experience is still at a very far level from agile software.

8.4   Future Work

The *QSandbox* feasibility test in practice, and the proof of the expected *QSandbox* efficiency is the full *QSandbox* implementation as described in this chapter, and subsequent performance of experiments with a variety of Quantum Software systems, under diverse conditions.

8.5   Main Contribution

The main chapter contribution is the software architecture and the user interface of the *QSandbox*, based upon the theoretical basis of the dual views—the high-level quantum circuit and a fitting density matrix—specifically designed to be applicable to any Quantum Software system.

References

1. Beck, K., et al.: Manifesto for Agile Software Development. agilealliance.org (2001)
2. Armando Fox and David Patterson, Engineering Software as a Service – An Agile Approach Using Cloud Computing, 2nd Beta edn (2013)
3. Wilcox, E., Nusser, S., Schoudt, J., Cerruti, J., Badenes, H.: Agile development meets strategic design in the enterprise. In: Concas, G., et al. (eds.) XP 2007, LNCS 4536, pp. 208–212. Springer, Berlin (2007)
4. Exman, I.: Simulating quantum software with density matrices: reading Feynman on fast forward, Chapter 2. In: Exman, I., Perez-Castillo, R., Piattini, M., Felderer, M. (eds.) Quantum Software – Aspects of Theory and System Design. Springer, Cham (2024)
5. Exman, I., Katz, P.: Modulaser: a tool for conceptual analysis of software systems. In: Proc. SKY 7th Int. Workshop on Software Knowledge, pp. 19–26. ScitePress, Portugal (2016)
6. Barenco, A.: Quantum computing: an introduction. In: Lo, H.-K., Popescu, S., Spiller, T. (eds.) Introduction to Quantum Computation and Information, pp. 143–183. World Scientific, Singapore (1998)
7. Lo, H.-K., Popescu, S., Spiller, T. (eds.): Introduction to Quantum Computation and Information. World Scientific, Singapore (1998)
8. Nielsen, M.A., Chuang, I.L.: Quantum Computation and Quantum Information. Cambridge University Press, Cambridge (2000)
9. Rieffel, E., Polak, W.: Quantum Computing – A Gentle Introduction. MIT Press, Cambridge, MA (2011)
10. Braunstein, S., Ghosh, S., Severini, S.: The Laplacian of a Graph as a Density Matrix: A Basic Combinatorial Approach to Separability in Mixed States. arXiv:quant-ph/0405165 (2006)
11. Exman, I., Sakhnini, R.: Linear software models: bipartite isomorphism between Laplacian Eigenvectors and Modularity Matrix Eigenvectors. Int J Softw Eng Knowl Eng. **28**(7), 897–935 (2018). https://doi.org/10.1142/S0218194018400107
12. von Luxburg, U.: A tutorial on spectral clustering. Stat Computing. **17**(4), 395–416 (2007). https://doi.org/10.1007/s11222-007-9033-z
13. Exman, I., Shmilovich, A.T.: Quantum software models: the density matrix for classical and quantum software systems design. In: Proc. Q-SE 2nd Int. Workshop on Quantum Software Engineering, pp. 1–6 (2021)

14. Exman, I., Zvulunov, A.: Quantum software models: quantum modules tomography and recovery theorem. In: Proc. SEKE'2023, San Francisco Bay Area, CA, pp. 91–96. https://doi.org/10.18293/SEKE2023-214
15. Qiskit Community: Qiskit: An Open-Source Framework for Quantum Computing. https://github.com/Qiskit/qiskit (2017)
16. Paykin, J., Rand, R., Zdancewic, S.: QWIRE: a core language for quantum circuits. In: Proc. of the 44th ACM SIGPLAN Symposium on Principles of Programming Languages, POPL '17, pp. 846–858. New York, NY. https://jpaykin.github.io/papers/prz qwire 2017.pdf (2017)
17. Cirq Developers: Cirq. https://github.com/quantumlib/Cirq (2018)
18. Serrano, M.A., Cruz-Lemus, J.A., Pérez-Castillo, R., Piattini, M.: Quantum software components and platforms: overview and quality assessment. ACM Comput. Surv. **55**(8), 164:1–164:31 (2023)
19. Jackson, D.: Towards a theory of conceptual design for software. In: Proc. Onward! ACM Int. Symposium on New Ideas, New Paradigms and Reflections on Programming and Software, pp. 282–296 (2015). https://doi.org/10.1145/2814228.2814248
20. Jackson, D.: The Essence of Software – Why Concepts Matter for Great Design. Princeton University Press, Princeton, NJ (2021)
21. Grover, L.: Quantum mechanics helps in searching for a needle in a haystack. Phys. Rev. Lett. **79**(2), 325 (1997) Also arXiv qunt-ph/9706033
22. Exman, I., Shmilovich, A.T.: Quantum software models: density matrix for universal software design, Chapter 7. In: Serrano, M.A., Perez-Castillo, R., Piattini, M. (eds.) Quantum Software Engineering, pp. 121–148. Springer-Nature, Cham (2022). https://doi.org/10.1007/978-3-031-05324-5
23. Coker, Z., Maass, M., Ding, T., Le Goues, C., Sunshine, J.: Evaluating the flexibility of the Java sandbox. In: Proc. ACSAC '15, Los Angeles, CA (2015). https://doi.org/10.1145/2818000.2818003
24. Herzog, A., Shahmehri, N.: Using the Java sandbox for resource control. In: 7th Nordic Workshop on Secure IT Systems (NordSec) (2002)
25. Concas, G., Damiani, E., Scotto, M., Succi, G.: Agile processes in software engineering and extreme programming: Proc. 8th International Conference, XP 2007, Como, Italy, June 18–22, (2007), LNCS 4536, Springer, Heidelberg, Germany
26. Beck, K., Fowler, M.: Planning Extreme Programming. Addison-Wesley, Boston, MA (2000)
27. Bekkers, N.: 4 Rules of Simple Design. https://www.theguild.nl/4-rules-of-simple-design/ (2016)
28. Fowler, M.: Beck Design Rules. Blog. https://martinfowler.com/bliki/BeckDesignRules.html (2015)
29. Haines, C.: Understanding the Four Rules of Simple Design. Leanpub (2014)

Verification and Validation of Quantum Software

Daniel Fortunato, Luis Jiménez-Navajas, José Campos, and Rui Abreu

Abstract Quantum software—like classic software—needs to be designed, specified, developed, and, most importantly, tested by developers. Writing tests is a complex, error-prone, and time-consuming task. Due to the particular properties of quantum physics (e.g., superposition), quantum software is inherently more complex to develop and effectively test than classical software. Nevertheless, some preliminary works have tried to bring commonly used classical testing practices for quantum computing to assess and improve the quality of quantum programs. In this chapter, we first gather 16 quantum software testing techniques that have been proposed for the IBM quantum framework, Qiskit. Then, whenever possible, we illustrate the usage of each technique (through the proposed tool that implements it, if available) on a given running example. We showcase that although several works have been proposed to ease the burn of testing quantum software, we are still in the early stages of testing in the quantum world. Researchers should focus on delivering artifacts that are usable without much hindrance to the rest of the

D. Fortunato (✉)
Faculty of Engineering of University of Porto, Porto, Portugal

LIACC—Artificial Intelligence and Computer Science Laboratory (member of LASI LA), Porto, Portugal
e-mail: dabf@fe.up.pt

L. Jiménez-Navajas
aQuantum, Faculty of Social Sciences & IT, University of Castilla-La Mancha, Talavera de la Reina, Toledo, Spain
e-mail: Luis.JimenezNavajas@uclm.es

J. Campos
Faculty of Engineering of University of Porto, Porto, Portugal

LASIGE, Faculdade de Ciências, Universidade de Lisboa, Lisboa, Portugal
e-mail: jcmc@fe.up.pt

R. Abreu
Faculty of Engineering of University of Porto, Porto, Portugal

INESC-ID, Lisboa, Portugal
e-mail: rui@computer.org

© The Author(s) 2024
I. Exman et al. (eds.), *Quantum Software*,
https://doi.org/10.1007/978-3-031-64136-7_5

community, and the development of quantum benchmarks should be a priority to facilitate reproducibility, replicability, and comparison between different testing techniques.

Keywords Quantum software · Verification and validation · Software testing

1 Introduction

In the last few years, quantum computing has evolved enormously in many aspects. It was not until 2019 that IBM unveiled its first commercial quantum computer with 20 qubits [1] and, in 2022, the same company developed a quantum computer with 433 qubits [2]. In addition, these hardware breakthroughs have been accompanied by software, where the largest companies in the world have created quantum programming languages [3] (such as Microsoft with Q# or IBM with OpenQASM), libraries to develop quantum software (such as Google with Cirq or IBM with Qiskit), or services to run and design quantum software (such as Amazon with Braket).

The entire ecosystem that quantum computing vendors have built allows users and organizations to develop and run quantum software in a straightforward manner [4]. This implies that, at some point, organizations that can take advantage of the potential benefits of this new technology will design and develop quantum components that can provide them with speedup. In other words, quantum software will be developed in a large-scale industrial context in the same way that classic software is nowadays produced [5].

Quantum software, as classical software, will, at some point in its development life cycle, need to be tested [6]. Apart from the evaluation of the functionality of the quantum software, concerns related to security vulnerabilities can also appear in this new programming domain [7].

However, we face three main challenges when testing quantum software [8]. First, unlike classical computing, with quantum computing, we cannot read the state of qubits at any time. If a qubit in superposition is measured, its state collapses. Second, the inherent nature of this new paradigm is non-deterministic. This implies that we will likely get a different result every time we run the quantum software. Third, the fact that current quantum computers are sensitive to noise and are fault-tolerant implies that when we run a quantum program and the result is different than expected, we cannot be sure whether the failure is caused by noise or by natural randomness.

Over the past few years, several approaches have been developed to alleviate the challenges associated with quantum testing. Regarding the verification of quantum programs, one can find works based on Hoare logic [9, 10, 11] or static analysis of source code [12, 13, 14, 15]. Concerning the validation of quantum programs, there are works related to the generation of data inputs aiming at detecting faults [16, 17,

18], oracle generation [19, 20], and a combination of both techniques [21, 22, 23, 24, 25, 26].

This chapter details current testing approaches used to help developers verify and validate their quantum software. More specifically, we focus our analysis on testing approaches designed to test quantum circuits since most quantum software is written through the application of quantum gates to quantum circuits. Consequently, we only present techniques and tools designed for circuit-based techniques. For instance, testing techniques for quantum annealing [27] are not included. Additionally, given that Qiskit [28], the circuit-based IBM framework, is one of the most popular quantum software development frameworks, we focus our analysis on works that use it.

This chapter is organized as follows. We present some concepts and definitions in Sect. 2. In Sect. 3, we discuss techniques that have been proposed for quantum software testing. Section 4 discusses current quantum fault benchmarks. We discuss some limitations of quantum software testing in Sect. 5 and conclude the chapter in Sect. 6.

2 Concepts and Definitions

2.1 Quantum Computing

Given that quantum computing is an emerging field, the definition of certain key concepts is warranted.

Qubit Unlike classical computers that use bits, quantum computers use the quantum bit (qubit for short) as their fundamental unit of memory. A qubit, just like the bit, has a state that can be $|0\rangle$ or $|1\rangle$, but contrary to the bit, those are just two possible states. The Dyrac notation, '$|\rangle$', is used to represent states in quantum mechanics. The difference between classic states and quantum states is that quantum states can be in superposition [29], meaning that it is possible to form linear combinations of states. A qubit can be expressed as $|\Psi\rangle = \alpha|0\rangle + \beta|1\rangle$.

Unlike the classical bit, in which we can easily determine whether it is in state 0 or 1, we cannot determine a qubit's state [29]. We can only measure a qubit, and when we do, we obtain either 0 with $|\alpha|^2$ probability or 1 with $|\beta|^2$ probability. Another important qubit property is entanglement. Entanglement is, at the moment, still an ill-defined concept currently being subjected to heavy research, but its main idea is that the state of a qubit affects the state of other qubits in the system, meaning that there is a correlation between them.

Quantum Circuits A classical computer is built from electrical circuits containing wires and logic gates. Similarly, some quantum computers are built from quantum circuits (there are other types of quantum computers, although these are out of the scope of this chapter) containing wires and quantum gates that carry around and operate on qubits. One of the quantum gates used throughout this chapter is the Not gate. Classically, this gate brings a bit from 0 to 1 and from 1 to 0. The quantum Not gate [29] interchanges the weights on α and β. It is represented by the following X matrix:

$$X \equiv \begin{bmatrix} 0 & 1 \\ 1 & 0 \end{bmatrix} \tag{1}$$

If we have the following quantum state $\alpha|0\rangle + \beta|1\rangle$, its vector notation would be

$$\begin{bmatrix} \alpha \\ \beta \end{bmatrix}, \tag{2}$$

and applying the Not gate to this state would yield the following output:

$$X \begin{bmatrix} \alpha \\ \beta \end{bmatrix} = \begin{bmatrix} \beta \\ \alpha \end{bmatrix}. \tag{3}$$

This is how gates are applied to qubits and how we can alter their state.

Quantum Programs A program is considered to be *quantum* when it initializes qubits and performs some operations that alter their state through the application of quantum gates. Quantum programs can be hybrid (i.e., they combine classical and quantum operations), the more common option, or pure (i.e., they only use quantum operations), the less common option.

2.2 Software Testing

As described by the IEEE Std. 610.12-1990, "Software testing is the process of operating a system or component under specified conditions, observing and recording the results, and making an evaluation." In other words, in software testing, a *test case* sets up a testing scenario that exercises software behavior and assesses whether the observed behavior matches the expected one; if not, a *fault* has been found. These faults, also known as *bugs* or *defects*, can cause failures in software systems.

Although a simple idea, it is far from easy—recent studies estimate that 20% to 80% of the total cost and time to develop a classical software system is fully dedicated to software testing and debugging [30], mostly because

(i) Assessing whether a piece of software performs correctly could be extremely complex due to the extremely large or even infinite number of possible tests that exist for any non-trivial system.
(ii) Software testing is traditionally a manual and tedious process that is subject to incompleteness and further errors.

The usage of some testing concepts throughout this chapter justifies their clarification.

Mutation Testing This testing technique refers to the change/mutation of statements in the source code (Fig. 1 is an example of a mutant) to check if tests can find errors in the source code. Mutation testing aims to ensure the quality of the source code's test suite. This is measured through the source code's mutation score, the number of killed mutants divided by the number of total mutants generated.

Coverage This is a testing metric that measures how thoroughly tests cover a given program. A test suite's coverage is the percentage of lines, branches, or paths of the code covered by at least one test case.

3 Automatic Verification and Validation of Quantum Software

Verifying and validating code is laborious, error-prone, and time-consuming in the classical realm. Given the added complexity of quantum programs, this endeavor is even more challenging in the quantum world [31, 5, 32]. Additionally, not all technologies are fully tailored to this new paradigm, and neither are the developers who would have to understand quantum physics/mechanics.

Nevertheless, some preliminary works are bringing commonly used classical testing practices for quantum computing [5] to assess and improve the quality of quantum programs. Regarding verification, there are works on the application of Hoare Logic [9, 10] and static code analysis [12, 14, 15, 11, 33]. And regarding validation, there are also techniques designed to automatically generate test inputs and/or full test cases based on mutation [34, 35, 36, 37, 18], metamorphic [19, 20], fuzzing [16], differential [17], projection [38], search-based [24, 23, 25, 26], and combinatorial testing [22, 21].

Table 1 shows the details of the collected research papers. These papers present tools that are 'Available' and can be used and experimented with, tools that are 'Unavailable' and do not provide any artifact with their paper, and tools that we considered 'Unusable' since they are not easily available or capable of testing any other program than the ones used in the empirical study of the tool. For instance, although LintQ's [33] source code is available online, it is stored in an anonymous repository that does not allow its download or cloning. QDiff [17] and Abreu et al. [19]'s tool only allows one to reproduce the experiments described in the paper, i.e., in order to run the proposed tool on any program, its source code would have to be adapted (which is out of the scope of this chapter). We discuss the "Available" tools in detail in the following subsections. It is also worth pointing out that there are several other works on verification and validation of quantum software applied on different quantum frameworks, test levels, or issues related to quantum software testing that are not included in this study as they target different quantum

Table 1 Details of the collected research papers

ID	Topic	Paper title	Tool	Year	Reference
Verification					
1	Hoare Logic	Floyd–Hoare Logic for Quantum Programs	Unavailable	2012	[9]
2	Hoare Logic	An Applied Quantum Hoare Logic	Unavailable	2019	[10]
3	Static analysis	QChecker: Detecting Bugs in Quantum Programs via Static Analysis	Available	2023	[12]
4	Static/Dynamic analysis	The Smelly Eight: An Empirical Study on the Prevalence of Code Smells in Quantum Computing	Available	2023	[51]
5	Static analysis	Quantum abstract interpretation	Unavailable	2021	[13]
6	Static analysis	Static Entanglement Analysis of Quantum Programs	Unavailable	2023	[14]
7	Static analysis	A Uniform Representation of Classical and Quantum Source Code for Static Code Analysis	Unavailable	2023	[15]
8	Static analysis	LintQ: A Static Analysis Framework for Qiskit Quantum Programs	Unusable	2023	[33]
Validation					
9	Data generation	QuanFuzz: Fuzz Testing of Quantum Program	Unavailable	2018	[16]
10	Data generation	QDiff: Differential Testing of Quantum Software Stacks	Unusable	2021	[17]
11	Data generation	Mutation-Based Test Generation for Quantum Programs with Multi-Objective Search	Unavailable	2022	[18]
12	Oracle generation	Metamorphic testing of oracle quantum programs	Unusable	2022	[19]
13	Oracle generation	MorphQ: Metamorphic Testing of Quantum Computing Platforms	Available	2022	[20]
14	Data/Oracle generation	Application of Combinatorial Testing To Quantum Programs	Available	2021	[21, 22]
15	Data/Oracle generation	Generating Failing Test Suites for Quantum Programs With Search	Available	2021	[23, 24]
16	Data/Oracle generation	Assessing the Effectiveness of Input and Output Coverage Criteria for Testing Quantum Programs	Available	2021	[25, 26]

frameworks or used quantum physics knowledge that cannot be applied directly to software. The following paragraph briefly mentions them.

Muqeet et al. [39] propose a testing technique aware of the inherent problem of quantum computing related to noise. Zhang et al. [40] examine whether flaky tests (i.e., intermittently failing tests) affect quantum software development. They identify flaky tests in 12 out of 14 quantum software projects and note that quantum programmers need to start using flaky test countermeasures developed by software engineers. Long and Zhao [41, 42] address specific testing requirements of multi-subroutine quantum programs in their work. They present a systematic testing process tailored to the intricacies of quantum programming. They cover unit and integration testing, focusing on IO analysis, quantum relation checking, structural testing, behavior testing, and test case generation for Q#. Honarvar et al. [11] present a property-based framework applied for Q# derived from Hoare logic [43]. They review various aspects of design concerning property specification, test case generation, and test result analysis. Xia and Zhao [14] present a static analysis tool that constructs an interprocedural control flow graph for Q# programs and gathers the entanglement information within quantum programs. A similar tool is proposed by Yamaguchi et al. [44] for Qiskit; we detail it in Sect. 3.2. de la Barrera et al. [45] propose QuMU, a quantum mutation tool based on the Quirk[1] quantum circuit simulator. QuMU exports quantum circuits as JSON objects from Quirk and creates a circuit representation that shows the quantum operations of a quantum program. Mutation operators defined in QuMU can mutate the circuit representation of a quantum program, and their tool can then execute these mutants in Quirk.

3.1   Running Example

Let us introduce a running example for the remainder of this section. The quantum program in Fig. 1 implements a Bell state [46], the simplest example of quantum entanglement. Bell states are four entangled two-qubit states. We obtain a Bell state by applying the Hadamard gate to qubit 1 (line 13) and the Control-Not with qubit 1 as the control qubit and qubit 2 as the target qubit (line 16). This means that when the quantum program is executed, the qubits are dependent on each other, and one will obtain either 00 or 11 as a result, with a 50% chance of getting either one. Note that Qiskit initializes qubits as zero.

The quantum program listed in Fig. 1 follows the specification reported in Table 2. Note that although inputs 01 and 11 **do not** produce a Bell state, we still list them in the table to have the full program specification.

Suppose we introduce a fault in the program's source code to create a faulty version of the program. For instance, swap the Hadamard gate (h) in line 13 for the Not gate (x) in line 13. Note that this is a change (i.e., mutation) that a tool

---

[1] https://algassert.com/quirk, visited October 2023.

```
1   # Bell State quantum program example
2   from qiskit import *
3
4   def BellState(input='00'):
5       # Create a Quantum Circuit object acting on a quantum and classical
6       # register of two qubits/bits
7       qr = QuantumRegister(2)
8       cr = ClassicalRegister(2)
9       circ = QuantumCircuit(qr, cr)
10      circ.initialize(input, circ.qubits)
11
12      # Add a H gate on qubit 0, putting this qubit in superposition
13  -   circ.h(qr[0])
13  +   circ.x(qr[0]) // Introduce a FAULT, swaped Hadamard gate for the Not gate
14      # Add a CX (CNOT) gate on control qubit 0 and target qubit 1, putting the
15      # qubits in a Bell state
16      circ.cx(qr[0], qr[1])
17      # Add measurement to the circuit
18      circ.measure(qr, cr)
19
20      # Execute the circuit
21      backend = BasicAer.get_backend('qasm_simulator')
22      job = execute(circ, backend, shots=1000)
23      counts = job.result().get_counts()
24
25      return counts
```

Fig. 1 Fault-free and faulty Bell state quantum program

Table 2 Specification of the Bell state quantum program in Fig. 1

Input	Output	Output Probability
00	00	50%
00	11	50%
01	00	50%
01	11	50%
10	10	50%
10	01	50%
11	01	50%
11	10	50%

like Muskit [37] or QMutPy [34, 35, 36] (described in Sect. 3.3.4) can produce. We then apply different verification and validation techniques on this faulty version of the running example in the following subsections to understand to what extent techniques can detect this fault. Note that if a tool of a specific technique is not available or usable, we do not apply it.

3.2 Automatic Verification of Quantum Software

Verification aims to assess whether developers have built the software correctly, i.e., it answers the question: *Does the software correctly do what has been specified?*

3.2.1 Hoare Logic

The Hoare logic testing [43] is a formal system with a set of logical rules for formal verification of the correctness of an algorithm against a formal specification. This logic is based on the idea of a specification as a contract between the implementation of a function and its client. To prove the correctness of a specification, it provides a mathematical framework using logical assertions, a pre- and post-condition, for describing the desired behavior of a program before and after its execution.

The central component of the Hoare logic is the Hoare triple. A Hoare triple is a notation used to express the relationship between a pre-condition, a program or program segment, and a post-condition. It is written as $\{P\}S\{Q\}$ where P is the pre-condition (predicate describing the condition the function relies on for correct operation), Q is the post-condition (predicate describing the condition the function establishes after correctly running), and S the statement implementing the function. The Hoare logic also provides a set of axioms and rules of inference that can be used in proofs of the properties of computer programs.

Regarding quantum software testing, Ying [9] derives from Hoare logic the Quantum Hoare Logic (QHL) for verifying the correctness of quantum programs. The correctness formula of QHL is also written as $\{P\}S\{Q\}$, but S is a quantum program, and both P and Q are quantum predicates on $\mathcal{H}_{all}$, which is the tensor product of the state spaces of all quantum variables.

Zhou et al. [10] further develop the work of Ying [9]. They propose aQHL, a new class of Hermitian operators (i.e., an operator that is equal to its conjugate transpose, e.g., $A = A\dagger$), which are used in the pre- and post-conditions and allow a simplification of the inference rules in case statements, and loops and computation of ranking functions in QHL. The authors prove that with aQHL they can verify the correctness of a well-known quantum algorithm for linear systems of equations, the HHL (Harrow-Hassidim-Lloyd) [47] algorithm. Zhou et al. [10] also propose several rules for reasoning about the robustness of quantum programs, i.e., error bounds of the output software programs, to prove that the outputs of a quantum program approximately satisfy a post-condition. They use these new rules to verify the quantum Principal Component Analysis (PCA) [48], a machine learning algorithm.

3.2.2 Static Analysis

Zhao et al. [12] propose QChecker,[2] a static analysis tool that generates warning messages to assist developers in pinpointing potential *faults* in their quantum programs. QChecker starts by extracting the abstract syntactic tree of a quantum program and parses it through a detection module equipped with a catalog of quantum faults patterns [49]. If the source code of a quantum program matches any

---

[2] https://github.com/Z-928/QChecker, visited October 2023.

of the patterns, a *true* fault might have been identified. The authors evaluate their tool on 20 real faults[3] from open-source quantum programs written in Qiskit [50] and their results attest to the efficiency and effectiveness of QChecker—all faults were detected.

Applying QChecker to our faulty running example (Fig. 1) we obtained two warnings (that might be *true* faults):

1. Incorrect initial state in lines 7 and 8. To fix it, one would have to create a variable n = 2 and then reuse n in lines 7 and 8, i.e.,

```
7   -   qr = QuantumRegister(2)
8   -   cr = ClassicalRegister(2)
7   +   n = 2; qr = QuantumRegister(n)
8   +   cr = ClassicalRegister(n)
```

   The rationale is that one might initialize the `QuantumRegister` with a number of qubits and/or the `ClassicalRegister` with a different number of bits. This potential error is mitigated with a variable that defines the number of bits.

2. Parameter error in line 21. To fix it, one would have to hard code line 21 as the second parameter of the *execute* function in line 22, i.e.,

```
21  -   backend = BasicAer.get_backend('qasm_simulator')
22  -   job = execute(circ, backend, shots=1000)
21  +   job = execute(circ, BasicAer.get_backend('qasm_simulator'), shots=1000)
```

   We could not find any rationale for this QChecker warning and were inclined to label it as a false positive. Note that if we apply QChecker suggestion and the `execute` call starts to fail, we will not know whether the failure is due to `execute` or `get_backend`. This would make debugging more difficult.

It is worth noting that QChecker did not produce any warning regarding the fault we introduced in line 13 (in Fig. 1).

Chen et al. [51] define, for Qiskit programs, eight quantum-specific smells (which might lead to a fault) inspired by the best coding practices suggested by Google Cirq's team.[4] For example, LC (Long circuit) smell—the wider the circuit, the higher the probability of quantum noise affecting a quantum circuit's intended behavior. They also developed a tool named QSmell[5] that supports the proposed quantum-specific smells and empirically evaluated its effectiveness at detecting the smells in 15 quantum programs. Their results show that most quantum programs (73%) have at least one smell and, on average, a program has three smells; LC is the most common smell.

---

[3] Although the first version of the catalog proposed by Zhao et al. [49] is composed by only 36 real faults, Zhao et al. [12] used an augmented version of the catalog with 42 real faults of which only 22 can be detected by running the quantum program. Thus, Zhao et al. [12] only consider the remaining 20 in the evaluation conducted with QChecker.

[4] https://quantumai.google/cirq/google/best_practices, visited October 2023.

[5] https://github.com/jose/qsmell, visited October 2023.

Fig. 2 Quantum circuit of the faulty Bell state quantum program

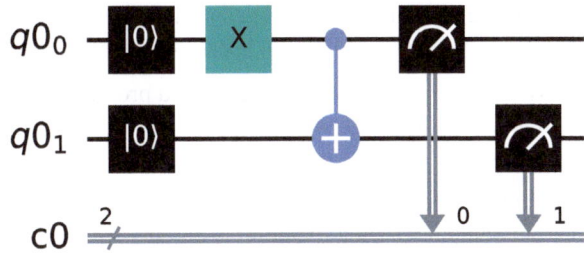

When we apply QSmell to our faulty running example (Fig. 1), one smell is reported by the tool, IdQ (Idle Qubits). With current quantum computers, it is only possible to ensure the correctness of a qubit's state for very short periods of time. This means that having idle qubits for too long enhances the loss of quantum information and might jeopardize the results of the running quantum programs. In a nutshell, QSmell reports that qubit 1 is idle between lines 10 and 16 (in Fig. 1) or between the first and third operations (Fig. 2), which might indicate a fault. In this case, and to the best of our knowledge, there is no other way to write the quantum circuit to avoid that. Thus, we consider this a false positive.

Yu and Palsberg [13] propose an abstract interpretation of quantum programs and use it to automatically verify whether a program might behave as expected in polynomial time. To achieve this, the authors take the density matrix of a quantum program and divide it into parts (i.e., reduced density matrixes). Then, they approximate each reduced matrix by a projection. Recall that a projection is the closest point/vector in a subspace to a given point in the space. This enables them to define abstract states to be a tuple of projections. To transition from abstract state to abstract state, the authors present a new abstract interpretation of quantum programs with new abstractions and concretization functions that form a Galois connection, and they use them to define abstract operations. Yu and Palsberg [13] evaluate their approach on three quantum programs. They first run the abstract interpretation, which produces an abstraction of the state of each quantum program. Then, they abstract the assertion (i.e., the circuit output desired) to the same format as the abstract states, and finally, they check that the abstract state satisfies the abstracted assertion. If the check succeeds, then the assertion is correct. For all three programs, the authors successfully verified their assertions.

Applying this technique would detect the fault in our running example. Starting with qubit state $|00\rangle$ and successfully generating the abstract states to be a tuple of projections through the application of the Not and Controlled-Not would not result in a successful assertion with our desired output, i.e., $\{|00\rangle, |11\rangle\}$. However, our correct running example would.

Paltenghi and Pradel [33] propose LintQ, a static analysis framework for detecting faults in quantum programs. LintQ receives a quantum program as input and extracts general information about Python code, such as control flow paths, data flow facts, and how to resolve imports. Then it represents the behavior of the quantum program using a set of reusable quantum programming abstractions, such as qubits, gates, and circuits. Finally, LintQ contains a set of nine quantum analyses that detect potential faults. LinQ performs three main types of analysis:

1. Measurement-related and gate-related problems
2. Resource allocation problems
3. Implicit API constraints

The authors perform an empirical study applying LintQ to a quantum program dataset containing 7568 quantum programs where LintQ found multiple true positives with a precision of 80.5%. The authors also tried LintQ with the Bugs4Q [50] benchmark of real faults and obtained a recall of only 4.8%. The authors argue that the low recall achieved in the Bugs4Q benchmark programs is mainly due to the incomplete code snippets gathered from issues and forum questions provided by the benchmark.

Kaul et al. [15] extend the Code Property Graph (CPG) static code analysis technique [44] used in classical computing to quantum computing. CPG is a computer program representation that captures syntactic structure, control flow, and data dependencies in a language-independent property graph model. The authors extended this concept to quantum computing by modeling the memory and operations as well as dependencies between qubits and quantum registers. Their prototype supports Qiskit [28] and QASM [52] programs. It also includes information from the quantum realm in the graph (i.e., qubits, gates, gates arguments) and demonstrates CPG's ability to analyze classical and quantum source code. By combining all relevant information into a single detailed analysis, this tool can facilitate quantum source code analysis. To that end, the authors propose a series of eight queries that return specific information about the quantum program to the user, such as the quantum/classical parts of the program, constant conditions, or the result bits. This allows users to have a clearer picture of the implementation of the program.

3.3   Automatic Validation of Quantum Software

Validation aims to assess whether developers have built the correct software according to the user requirements, i.e., it answers the question: *Does the software do what it is supposed to do?*

To improve the effectiveness of software testing and to reduce its cost, researchers have devised approaches (in both the classical and quantum realm) to automate the generation of test cases and validate quantum software. Automating the creation of test cases offers several benefits over manually writing the test cases. In classical computing, it is computationally cheap to automatically generate test cases, and they are often more complete as they are generated systematically; there is no evidence that it would be otherwise for the automatic generation of test cases for quantum programs. Automatic test generation is a two-step process: (1) generation of *test data*, i.e., inputs to exercise the software, and (2) generation of *test oracles* (also known as assertions) to verify whether the execution of the test data reveals any fault.

3.3.1 Test Data Generation

Wang et al. [17] propose QDiff, a differential testing approach for quantum programs, which can be used with three quantum frameworks: Qiskit, Cirq, and Pyquil. QDiff takes as input a quantum program and derives equivalent programs from it (i.e., programs that are supposed to produce identical behavior) that trigger unexpected behavior on the target quantum framework. To speed up their analysis, QDiff analyzes static program characteristics such as circuit depth (i.e., the longest sequence of applied gates to the circuit), the number of two-qubit gates, and known error rates. Finally, QDiff performs a statistical comparison between the measurements of the equivalent circuits. The empirical evaluation of QDiff found six sources of instability in the three quantum frameworks and managed to reduce compute-intensive simulation.

Fuzz testing [53, 54, 55, 56, 57, 58]—a set of software testing techniques implying the generation of a set of inputs aiming at finding errors/crashes and identifying security flaws—is gaining relevance in quantum software testing [16]. Wang et al. [16] adapt this technique to the quantum realm and present QuanFuzz, a search-based test input generator for quantum programs. In a nutshell, it can automatically find the input that triggers the quantum-sensitive branches. QuanFuzz was evaluated with seven programs and outperformed a random technique, increasing branch coverage by 20% to 60%.

Wang et al. [18] propose MutTG, a multi-objective and search-based approach to generate the minimum number of test cases that kill as many mutants as possible. The authors introduce a *discount factor* to tackle the equivalent mutants problem [59, 60, 61, 62, 63] ever-present in mutation testing (i.e., mutants that are equivalent to the source code and do not alter its result) to prevent their approach from repeatedly trying to kill those non-killable mutants. The authors employ NSGA-II as the multi-objective search algorithm and use five quantum programs for which they created 20 different versions (four mutants per program) with three distinct difficulty levels of killing mutants (easy, medium, difficult) to evaluate their approach. Results from their experimental evaluation show that NSGA-II [64] significantly outperforms the random search technique employed as a baseline for all the difficult benchmarks composed of subtle mutants (i.e., mutants that are killed by few inputs). Also, they show that their discount factor is effective in avoiding spending meaningless effort trying to kill non-killable mutants.

3.3.2 Test Oracle Generation

The well-known oracle problem [65] for classical testing becomes even more complex in this new programming paradigm. Test oracle automation is essential to remove the bottleneck that inhibits greater overall test automation. In other words, without a formal specification of how software should behave, it is impossible to generate effective fault-revealing test oracles. Thus, techniques that generate tests usually generate regression tests.

To the best of our knowledge, two metamorphic approaches [19, 20] have attempted to address the oracle problem by substituting conventional oracles with mutated versions of the quantum program under test. Recall that metamorphic testing consists of injecting small mutations to the code that do not alter a program's execution (e.g., in classical computing, adding zero to a number; in quantum computing, introducing the identity gate to a circuit).

The approaches that Abreu et al. [19] and Paltenghi and Pradel [20] propose are similar in nature and define oracle quantum programs which validate a source quantum program's properties by doing mutations to its source code that do not alter the program output. Both of these approaches define a set of metamorphic rules and assert whether their mutated program behaves when executed. They empirically evaluate their metamorphic rules on quantum programs (i.e., they create a mutated version of a quantum program that is expected to produce the same result) and find that metamorphic rules are effective at finding crashes and incorrect outputs in quantum programs.

3.3.3   Test Data and Oracle Generation

Wang et al. [26] propose QUITO[6] (QUantum InpuT Output testing) consisting of three coverage criteria defined by the inputs and outputs of a quantum program:

1. Input coverage: checks that for a valid input, the quantum program produces a valid output. Only one execution of the program is necessary for this criterion. This is the least expensive (i.e., runs the smallest number of tests).
2. Output coverage: checks that all valid outputs are covered, iterating over all valid inputs until a wrong output value is detected or time runs out. This is the second most expensive criterion.
3. Input-Output coverage: checks that all possible output values are covered for all valid inputs, iterating over all valid inputs until a wrong output value is detected or time runs out. This is the most expensive criterion.

It also consists of two oracle generation strategies:

1. Wrong Output Oracle (WOO), which asserts whether the quantum program produced expected output values
2. Output Probability Oracle (OPO), which asserts whether the quantum program produced an expected output with its corresponding expected probability

To assess the effectiveness of the three coverage criteria, the authors perform an empirical study on 78 mutated versions of four quantum programs. They generate

---

[6] https://github.com/Simula-COMPLEX/quito, visited October 2023.

```
1   def run(circ):
2       # Add (incorrectly) a X gate on qubit 0
3       circ.x(0)
4       # Add a CX (CNOT) gate on control qubit 0 and target qubit 1, putting the
5       # qubits in a bell state
6       circ.cx(0, 1)
7       # Add measurement to the circuit
8       circ.measure([0,1], [0,1])
```

Fig. 3 Faulty Bell state program adapted to be executed with QuCAT [21], QUITO [26], and QuSBT [23]

```
1   [program]
2   ;The absolute root of your quantum program file.
3   root=bell_state.py
4   ;The total number of qubits of your quantum program.
5   num_qubit=2
6   ;The ID of input qubits.
7   inputID=0,1
8   ;The ID of output qubits which are the qubits to be measured.
9   outputID=0,1
10
11  [program_specification_category]
12  ;The category of your program specification. Choice: full/partial/no
13  ps_category=full
14
15  [quito_configuration]
16  ;The coverage criterion you choose. Choice: IC/OC/IOC
17  coverage_criterion=IC
18
19  [program_specification]
20  ;The program specification. Format: <input,output=probability>
21  00,00=0.5
22  00,11=0.5
23  01,00=0.5
24  01,11=0.5
25  10,10=0.5
26  10,01=0.5
27  11,01=0.5
28  11,10=0.5
```

Fig. 4 Configuration for the QUITO tool. In this figure, we only list the required parameters and which values we used. Other parameters were left with their default values. Consult QUITO's documentation (https://github.com/Simula-COMPLEX/quito/blob/main/README.md, visited October 2023) for more information

these mutants with the Muskit [37] tool. After generating a set of test cases for each mutant using the three coverage criteria, the authors evaluate them with WOO, stopping the testing if a failure occurs, and then the OPO. Results indicate that input coverage is more effective than the others.

We run QUITO with our faulty running example in Fig. 1. To test our example, we had to adapt it to the tool's requirements (Fig. 3) and create a configuration file where we define the number of input and output qubits our program would have, in our case, two input qubits and two output qubits (see Fig. 4). We also set input coverage (line 17 in Fig. 4) as the coverage criterion as it is the most effective according to QUITO's authors. Finally, we also detail the program specification (lines 21–29 in Fig. 4) for our example as shown in Table 2. QUITO generates 800 tests (total number of test suites, i.e., 200 by default × number of possible input states, i.e., four). For our example, all of our eight input/output qubit combinations fail with the OPO oracle.

Wang et al. [21, 22] proposed QuCAT[7] (QUantum CombinAtorial Testing), which attempts to trigger faults by particular input combinations of a given strength. These faults are found through the two oracles previously defined in QUITO (i.e., WOO and OPO). The strength of a combination is the number of input qubits used, meaning that two input qubits are a combination of strength two, three input qubits are a combination of strength three, and so on. QuCAT supports two test generation scenarios:

1. The generation of combinatorial test cases of a given strength
2. The incremental generation of combinatorial test cases of increasing strengths

The authors performed an empirical study on six Qiskit quantum programs, in which they manually introduced three faults in each. They found that their combinatorial technique of strength four (highest strength attempted) always detects the faults, tests of strength three have more difficulty in detecting all faults, and strength two only detects one fault consistently. Thus, with increased cost, this combinatorial technique increases in effectiveness. Also, results showed that combinatorial testing is always more effective than random testing in terms of generating test cases that expose program failure and performs better in 88% of the faulty programs.

Trying QuCAT was similar to QUITO. We include in its configuration file the same qubit and specification information as before. However, we also define the strength of the input combination as two as our program has two input qubits (see Fig. 5). This means that we execute QuCAT with the first test generation scenario (i.e., we generated combinatorial test cases of strength two). The tool generates four tests in a Python file and the results of the oracles in a separate text file, these bundled together in Fig. 6 for reading convenience. As we can see, the generated tests perform a print of the execution of the program with certain inputs. Although no explicit oracle (e.g., assert) exists in any test, all reveal the fault. If one compares the tests' output and the program's specification, one will notice that each output has only one result with 100% probability instead of two results with 50% each. To have fully automated tests, QuCAT should have generated the test oracles in Fig. 7 for `test_bell_state_0` (line 3 in Fig. 6). These test oracles would fail in lines 6 (as we obtained one pair of bits as output and not two), 7 (as there were no 00 results), 9 (since the probability of obtaining 11 is 100% which is superior to 55%), and 10 (because the probability of obtaining 00 is 0%, which is inferior to 45%). Line 8 does not fail; there are results of state 11.

Wang et al. [23, 24] propose QuSBT[8] (Quantum Search-Based Testing), a test generation tool for quantum programs that uses an evolutionary algorithm to search for the maximum set of tests that reveal the fault. The authors also use the WOO and

---

[7] https://github.com/Simula-COMPLEX/qucat-tool, visited October 2023.

[8] https://github.com/Simula-COMPLEX/qusbt-tool, visited October 2023.

```
 1  [program]
 2  ;The absolute root of your quantum program file.
 3  root=bell_state.py
 4  ;The total number of qubit of your quantum program.
 5  num_qubit=2
 6  ;The IDs of input qubits.
 7  inputID=0,1
 8  ;The IDs of output qubits which are the qubits to be measured.
 9  outputID=0,1
10
11  [qucat_configuration]
12  ;The maximum value of strength of a combination as the number of inputs used.
13  k=2
14
15  [program_specification]
16  ;The program specification. Format: <input,output=probability>
17  00,00=0.5
18  00,11=0.5
19  01,00=0.5
20  01,11=0.5
21  10,10=0.5
22  10,01=0.5
23  11,01=0.5
24  11,10=0.5
```

Fig. 5 Configuration for the QuCAT tool. In this figure, we only list the required parameters and which values we use. We left all other parameters with their default values. Consult QuCAT's documentation (https://github.com/Simula-COMPLEX/qucat-tool/blob/main/README.md, visited October 2023) for more information

```
 1  class bell_stateFun1K2Test(unittest.TestCase):
 2
 3    def test_bell_state_0(self):
 4      input = '00'
 5      print(execute_quantum_program([0,1], [0,1], 2, input, "bell_state", 200))
 6      # output '11' | result OPO
 7
 8    def test_bell_state_1(self):
 9      input = '01'
10      print(execute_quantum_program([0,1], [0,1], 2, input, "bell_state", 200))
11      # output '00' | result OPO
12
13    def test_bell_state_2(self):
14      input = '10'
15      print(execute_quantum_program([0,1], [0,1], 2, input, "bell_state", 200))
16      # output '01' | result OPO
17
18    def test_bell_state_3(self):
19      input = '11'
20      print(execute_quantum_program([0,1], [0,1], 2, input, "bell_state", 200))
21      # output '10' | result OPO
```

Fig. 6 Tests generated by the QuCAT tool [21, 22] for the faulty Bell state quantum program

OPO oracles in QuSBT. The authors evaluate QuSBT on six quantum programs, in which they manually introduce five faults in each and compare QuSBT's results with a random search strategy. The authors find that for the majority of the faulty programs (87%), QuSBT performs significantly better than the random approach. For the remainder of the faulty programs, no significant differences are detected.

```
5  -  print(execute_quantum_program([0,1], [0,1], 2, input, "bell_state", 200))
5  +  counts = execute_quantum_program([0,1], [0,1], 2, input, "bell_state", 200)
6  +  self.assertTrue(len(counts) == 2)
7  +  self.assertTrue('00' in counts)
8  +  self.assertTrue('11' in counts) // nao falha
9  +  self.assertTrue(0.45 < counts['00']/200 < 0.55)
10 +  self.assertTrue(0.45 < counts['11']/200 < 0.55)
```

Fig. 7 Ideal set of test oracles for the test_bell_state_0 test (in Fig. 6)

```
1   [program]
2   ;The absolute root of your quantum program file.
3   root=bell_state.py
4   ;The total number of qubit of your quantum program.
5   num_qubit=2
6   ;The IDs of input qubits.
7   inputID=0,1
8   ;The IDs of output qubits which are the qubits to be measured.
9   outputID=0,1
10
11  [qusbt_configuration]
12  ;A percentage of the inputs as the number of generated tests, 0.05 by default.
13  beta=1.0
14  ;The confidence level for the statistical test, 0.01 by default.
15  ;Although it is not required according to the official documentation, it is
16  ;required at runtime.
17  confidence_level=0.01
18
19  [program_specification]
20  ;The program specification. Format: <input,output=probability>
21  00,00=0.5
22  00,11=0.5
23  01,00=0.5
24  01,11=0.5
25  10,10=0.5
26  10,01=0.5
27  11,01=0.5
28  11,10=0.5
```

Fig. 8 Configuration for the QuSBT tool. In this figure, we only list the required parameters and the values we use. Other parameters are left with their default values. Consult QuSBT's documentation (https://github.com/Simula-COMPLEX/qusbt-tool/blob/main/README.md, visited October 2023) for more information

Running QuSBT requires the same initial configurations as QUITO and QuCAT (i.e., number of input and output qubits, program specification). Additionally, we set the beta parameter, a percentage of the inputs, as the number of generated tests, so that all possible tests are generated (see Fig. 8). The default value of beta is 0.05, which would mean, for our example, that only one test would have been generated. QuSBT generates two tests (similar to the first and third tests generated by QuCAT; see Fig. 9) that also fail with the OPO oracle. Note that extending QuSBT tests as we did for QuCAT in Fig. 7 would pass and fail for the same assertions.

```
1   class Bell_StateTest(unittest.TestCase):
2
3     def test_bell_State_0(self):
4       #Input: 00
5       print(execute_quantum_program([0, 1], [0, 1], 2, 0, "bell_state", 200))
6
7     def test_bell_State_1(self):
8       #Input: 10
9       print(execute_quantum_program([0, 1], [0, 1], 2, 2, "bell_state", 200))
```

Fig. 9 Tests generated by the QuSBT tool [23, 24] for the faulty Bell state quantum program

3.3.4   Test Adequacy Measurements

In the quantum realm, a few approaches and tools (based on the ideas borrowed from the classical realm) have been proposed to measure the effectiveness of manually written or automatically generated tests of quantum programs.

Structural Coverage

Code coverage and other source-code metrics used for classical software have not been adopted for quantum programs [66]. This may be because the differences in the importance between quantum code and classical code have not yet been fully explored. Also, thresholds for source code metrics and their significance as predictors of defects [67] cannot be used as a starting point for quantum programs since quantum programmers and their knowledge of this new programming paradigm are likely to be completely different.

Thus, recent studies propose other metrics besides traditional coverage. For instance, Kumar [68] proposes single-, two-, and three-qubit gate coverage and multiple controlled qubit gate coverage, which are defined by the total number of times test cases would execute these types of gates divided by the number of instances that gate is used in the code. Ali et al. [25] also propose three new types of coverage criteria previously discussed in Sect. 3.3.3: input coverage, output coverage, and input-output coverage.

Nevertheless, other studies still use classical coverage. For instance, the previously discussed work of Wang et al. [16] empirically evaluates whether their input generation technique increases coverage compared to random input generation (see Sect. 3.3.1). Also, Fortunato et al. [34] measure the coverage of 24 real Qiskit programs and find that tests covered on average 90% of the lines of code of a quantum program.

Fault Detection

Classically, mutation testing is often used as a practical substitute for real faults since mutant detection is positively correlated with fault detection [69]. Current

```
1  from qiskit import *
2
3  # Create a Quantum Circuit object acting on a quantum and classical
4  # register of two qubits/bits
5  qr = QuantumRegister(2)
6  cr = ClassicalRegister(2)
7  circ = QuantumCircuit(qr, cr)
8  circ.initialize('00', circ.qubits)
9
10 # Add a H gate on qubit 0, putting this qubit in superposition
11 circ.h(qr[0])
12 # Add a CX (CNOT) gate on control qubit 0 and target qubit 1, putting the
13 # qubits in a Bell state
14 circ.cx(qr[0], qr[1])
```

Fig. 10 Fault-free Bell state program implementation for Muskit

research in quantum testing uses mutants to artificially generate faults in programs and evaluate the effectiveness of their approaches at detecting the mutant, as seen in Sect. 3.3.3. Mendiluze et al. [37] propose Muskit[9] and Fortunato et al. [34, 36, 35] propose QMutPy[10] to perform mutation analysis. These tools are similar in nature since they perform mutations (i.e., artificial faults) to the input source program.

On the one hand, Muskit requires the raw circuit of a program to be able to execute. This means that real programs such as our running example in Fig. 1 would need to be transformed to the one in Fig. 10. Then to use Muskit, we have to:

- Create a configuration file to specify what we are going to mutate (i.e., which gates, which types of gates (1-qubit, 2-qubit, etc.), the maximum number of mutants to generate, what mutation operators we are going to use (Muskit mutation operators are Add, Remove, and Replace Gate), and the location of where to Add a new gate if the Add operator is selected).
- Create the executor file to specify the number of times we want to execute the circuit, if we are going to use all possible input values (in the case of Fig. 10, those would be 00, 01, 10, or 11) or not, and if we want to specify our input values we would need to create another custom test file where we specify which ones we want to use.
- Create an analyzer file to specify the number of qubits our program has that we want to measure (in our case, we have two qubits and want to measure both of them) and what is the significance level (p-value) for our tests.

To determine whether a mutant was detected, Muskit uses two oracles already explained in Sect. 3.3.3: the WOO (i.e., if the program output is wrong, the mutant is detected) and the OPO (i.e., if our p-value is lower than the chosen significance level the mutant is detected). Suppose we apply the Remove gate operator to both our gates with input values 00 (the default Qiskit qubit initialization value) to our running example (Fig. 1). After setting up all of the necessary files described above

---

[9] https://github.com/Simula-COMPLEX/muskit, visited October 2023.

[10] https://github.com/danielfobooss/mutpy, visited October 2023.

```
1   from unittest import TestCase
2
3   class BellStateTest(TestCase):
4
5     def test(self):
6       counts = BellState()
7       self.assertTrue(len(counts) == 2)
8       self.assertTrue('00' in counts)
9       self.assertTrue('11' in counts)
10      self.assertTrue(0.45 < counts['00']/1000 < 0.55)
11      self.assertTrue(0.45 < counts['11']/1000 < 0.55)
```

Fig. 11 Manually written test for the Bell state quantum program

and running the tool, Muskit reports that two mutants were generated and that both were detected by the WOO. This is expected as the output value of our example without the Hadamard gate will always be 00 (i.e., only one correct output instead of two), and without the Controlled-Not gate, it will always be 00 with 50% probability, which is a correct output, and 10 with 50% probability, which is an incorrect output.

On the other hand, QMutPy only requires a Qiskit program and its set of test cases (either written in unittest[11] or pytest[12]). QMutPy allows us to select from five quantum mutation operators:

- QGD—Quantum Gate Deletion (equivalent to the Remove operator from Muskit)
- QGI—Quantum Gate Insertion (equivalent to the Add operator from Muskit)
- QGR—Quantum Gate Replacement (equivalent to the Replace operator from Muskit)
- QMD—Quantum Measurement Deletion
- QMI—Quantum Measurement Insertion

To run QMutPy, we simply execute a command where we select the target program file (i.e., the fault-free version in Fig. 1) and the target test file (Fig. 11) and select which operators we want to use. If we perform the same experiment (i.e., select the QGD operator), QMutPy will also report that both mutants were detected.

The empirical results from both studies [37, 34] show that both Muskit and QMutPy tools are efficient and effective at assessing the performance of programs' specifications or test cases. However, as we can see, QMutPy is far simpler to set up than Muskit since it does not require a formal specification of each quantum program. It only requires the program's source code and its corresponding tests. Also, in case we wish to re-run our experiment with different setups, we would have to manually alter our program specification files for Muskit, while for QMutPy we would only need to select additional or fewer operators to use. It is worth pointing out that Muskit could run a mutation analysis with different inputs, and for QMutPy to do this, it would be necessary to create more tests for the quantum program under

---

[11] https://docs.python.org/3/library/unittest.html, visited October 2023.

[12] https://docs.pytest.org, visited October 2023.

test. However, the QMutPy's authors left for future work the addition of an input mutation operator to the tool.

4 Benchmarks of Real Faults in Open-Source Quantum Programs

Although several techniques and tools have been proposed to verify and validate quantum programs (see Sect. 3), reproducing[13] previous studies or evaluating/-comparing new techniques is still challenging. The lack of widely accepted and easy-to-use databases of *real* quantum faults (i.e., faults that have occurred in *real* quantum projects) is one of the main challenges. For instance, Fortunato et al. [34] and Mendiluze et al. [37] proposed a similar tool for mutation analysis, but both conducted an empirical evaluation on a different set of Qiskit quantum programs. Hence, it is not possible to answer the question: Which tool performs better?

In classical computing, many databases of *real* faults have been proposed, e.g., Defects4J [70] for Java, BugsJS [71] for JavaScript, and BugsInPy [72] for Python. These benchmarks have allowed researchers to conduct empirical studies on *real* faults on different research topics, e.g., automatic test generation [73, 74], test prioritization [75, 76], fault localization [77, 78, 79, 80, 81], automatic program repair [82], on whether *artificial* faults might be a practical substitute for *real* faults [69], etc.

In quantum computing, to the best of our knowledge, only three benchmarks (not yet widely accepted or easy to use) have been proposed in quantum computing [83, 50, 84].

Campos and Souto [83] propose QBugs, a framework that includes a catalog of reproducible faults of real quantum programs and an infrastructure to enable empirical and controlled experiments in quantum software testing and debugging. QBugs is not available at the time of writing this chapter.

Zhao et al. [50] propose Bugs4Q,[14] a benchmark of 36 real and manually validated faults on programs written in Qiskit.[15] These faulty programs are not accompanied by, for example, any test that reproduces and reveals the faulty behavior (as, for example, in the Defects4J [70] benchmark). Furthermore, Bugs4Q

---

[13] ACM defines *reproducibility* as the measurement obtained with stated precision by a different team using the same measurement procedure, the same measuring system, under the same operating conditions, in the same or a different location on multiple trials for the same artifact. For computational experiments, this means that an independent group can obtain the same result as the author using the author's artifacts. https://www.acm.org/publications/policies/artifact-review-and-badging-current, visited October 2023.

[14] https://github.com/Z-928/Bugs4Q, visited October 2023.

[15] Since its release, Bugs4Q has been augmented with seven more faults on programs written in Qiskit, two faults on programs written in Q#, and seven faults on programs written in Cirq (October 2023).

only provides (for each fault) the faulty and fixed files. In other words, it does not provide fully faulty programs (i.e., including configuration files, build files, documentation, commit history, etc.) that might be relevant to some tools or other research venues. For instance, Paltenghi and Pradel [33] pointed out that the low precision of the LintQ tool in the Bugs4Q benchmark was due to incomplete faulty programs. Other research venues, for example, fault predictors that require the commit history of a program to predict which components (e.g., functions) are likely faulty [85, 86, 87, 88, 89, 75], might also perform poorly or not work at all due to the lack of such information.

Paltenghi and Pradel [84][16] present a catalog of 223 real-world faults mined from 18 open-source quantum computing platforms (including Qiskit, Cirq, and Q#) and perform an in-depth analysis of the types of faults most frequently found in quantum software. The authors make available the faults as a catalog, the type of faults found, and their fixes. Similar to the Bugs4Q benchmark, there is no interface to interact with the catalog of faults.

To the best of our knowledge, QChecker [12] and LintQ [33] are the only tools evaluated on *real* faults, i.e., that considered the Bugs4Q benchmark.

5   Discussion

Despite the many advances in the verification and validation of quantum programs, most approaches remain to be adopted or perfected. Based on our observations, we have compiled a list of limitations that researchers (Sect. 5.1), tool developers (Sect. 5.2), and benchmark developers (Sect. 5.3) should try to address in the future.

5.1   For Researchers

The approaches presented in Sect. 3 do not exercise to their full extent the underlying idiosyncrasies of the quantum programs under test [31, 5, 32], for example, the number of independent paths generated due to the superposition of each qubit [68].

5.2   For Developers of Testing Tools

Developing a quantum testing tool is not an easy endeavor. We highlight four key aspects for developers of testing tools to keep in mind.

---

[16] https://github.com/MattePalte/Bugs-Quantum-Computing-Platforms, visited October 2023.

- **Setup:** The installation and configuration of each tool require a huge amount of time to perform correctly. For instance, QuSBT [24], QuCAT [22], QUITO [26], and Muskit [37] require that we clone the tool from GitHub, set up the correct environment with the right packages and the right packages' versions, manually create a configuration file and set some parameters, execute a Python file, and then select options from a menu on the command line at runtime. All of these requirements and steps might discourage users from using these tools. Even tools like QMutPy [34] or QChecker [12] that only require the cloning, the environment setup, and the execution of a single command can be inconvenient and frustrating.
- **Usage:** Developers of tools should aim to, for example, integrate their tools with common Integrated Development Environments (IDEs) such as Visual Studio or IntelliJ IDEA to ease their usage. Tools such as EvoSuite [90] (a test generation automation tool for Java programs) increase their usability when integrated with an IDE. It should be no different for quantum tools.
- **Produce test suites source code:** Tools like QUITO [26] do not generate tests source code (i.e., written in Python) and therefore do not use any of the common testing frameworks (unittest[17] and pytest[18]). Without such functionalities, tests cannot be executed or integrated into any project. Thus, tests could not be used to, for example, (i) detect regressions in future versions of the quantum program or (ii) assist developers in localizing [91, 77] and repairing faults [82], as has been proposed in classical computing.
- **Produce test suites with an oracle:** Tools like QuCAT [22] and QuSBT [24] do generate tests source code (i.e., written in Python), but they do not generate an explicit oracle (i.e., assertion). Oracleless tests hold down the adoption of automatically generated tests as they would not be able to detect any fault in the program under test.

5.3   For Developers of Quantum Faults Benchmarks

Benchmarks, which are a pillar of reproducibility and applicability, allow one to compare the performance of different techniques with the same datasets. Currently, benchmarks are lacking in quantum software testing, and in regard to our focus of interest, more specifically, quantum faults benchmarks. This is mainly due to the fact that there are still few quantum programs to analyze, and fault patterns are still being extracted from real faulty quantum programs. As pointed out in Sect. 4, to support different venues of research in quantum software testing, benchmarks for quantum software testing should (1) provide an interface to interact with the fixed and faulty version of a quantum program, (2) provide fully fixed and faulty

---

[17] https://docs.python.org/3/library/unittest.html, visited October 2023.

[18] https://docs.pytest.org, visited October 2023.

programs, and (3) provide fault-revealing test cases (either manually written or automatically generated).

6 Conclusion

The field of quantum computing is developing at a very fast pace. Therefore, the development of tools to ensure the correctness of quantum programs is of the utmost importance. In this chapter, we presented and detailed novel techniques and tools researchers have proposed to verify and validate quantum programs. Based on our exploration of the many techniques, tools, and benchmarks that have been proposed in quantum verification and validation, we highlighted key aspects of what is still lacking in the field and offered suggestions for future work. In short, researchers should focus on further exploring the properties of quantum programs. Developers should work on delivering tools and quantum fault benchmarks in ways that promote their adoption and usefulness to the scientific community.

References

1. Russell, J.: IBM Quantum Update: Q System One Launch, New Collaborators, and QC Center Plans. HPC Wire
2. Collins, H., Nay, C.: IBM Unveils 400 Qubit-Plus Quantum Processor and Next-Generation IBM Quantum. IBM Newsroom
3. Ferreira, F.: An Exploratory Study on the Usage of Quantum Programming Languages. Available at http://hdl.handle.net/10451/56751
4. Hevia, J.L., Peterssen, G., Ebert, C., Piattini, M.: Quantum computing. IEEE Software **38**(5), 7–15 (2021). https://doi.org/10.1109/MS.2021.3087755
5. Barrera, A., Guzmán, I., Polo, M., Piattini, M.: Quantum software testing: state of the art. J. Software Evol. Process **35**(4), 2419 (2023). https://doi.org/10.1002/smr.2419
6. Weder, B., Barzen, J., Leymann, F., Salm, M., Vietz, D.: The Quantum Software Lifecycle. In: Proceedings of the 1st ACM SIGSOFT International Workshop on Architectures and Paradigms for Engineering Quantum Software. APEQS 2020, pp. 2–9. Association for Computing Machinery, New York, NY, USA (2020). https://doi.org/10.1145/3412451.3428497
7. Arias, D., García Rodríguez de Guzmán, I., Rodríguez, M., Terres, E.B., Sanz, B., Gaviria de la Puerta, J., Pastor, I., Zubillaga, A., García Bringas, P.: Let's do it right the first time: Survey on security concerns in the way to quantum software engineering. Neurocomputing **538**, 126199 (2023). https://doi.org/10.1016/j.neucom.2023.03.060
8. Tao Yue, P.A., Ali, S.: Quantum Software Testing: Challenges, Early Achievements, and Opportunities. ERCIM News
9. Ying, M.: Floyd–Hoare logic for quantum programs. ACM Trans. Program. Lang. Syst. **33**(6) (2012). https://doi.org/10.1145/2049706.2049708
10. Zhou, L., Yu, N., Ying, M.: An Applied Quantum Hoare Logic. In: Proceedings of the 40th ACM SIGPLAN Conference on Programming Language Design and Implementation. PLDI 2019, pp. 1149–1162. Association for Computing Machinery, New York, NY, USA (2019). https://doi.org/10.1145/3314221.3314584

11. Honarvar, S., Mousavi, M.R., Nagarajan, R.: Property-Based Testing of Quantum Programs in q#. In: Proceedings of the IEEE/ACM 42nd International Conference on Software Engineering Workshops, pp. 430–435 (2020)
12. Zhao, P., Wu, X., Li, Z., Zhao, J.: QChecker: Detecting Bugs in Quantum Programs via Static Analysis (2023)
13. Yu, N., Palsberg, J.: Quantum Abstract Interpretation. In: Proceedings of the 42nd ACM SIGPLAN International Conference on Programming Language Design and Implementation, pp. 542–558. ACM, Virtual Canada (2021). https://doi.org/10.1145/3453483.3454061. https://dl.acm.org/doi/10.1145/3453483.3454061
14. Xia, S., Zhao, J.: Static Entanglement Analysis of Quantum Programs (2023). https://doi.org/10.48550/arXiv.2304.05049. arXiv:2304.05049 [quant-ph]
15. Kaul, M., Küchler, A., Banse, C.: A Uniform Representation of Classical and Quantum Source Code for Static Code Analysis (2023). https://doi.org/10.48550/arXiv.2308.06113. arXiv:2308.06113 [cs]
16. Wang, J., Gao, M., Jiang, Y., Lou, J., Gao, Y., Zhang, D., Sun, J.: QuanFuzz: Fuzz Testing of Quantum Program (2018). arXiv:1810.10310 [cs]
17. Wang, J., Zhang, Q., Xu, G.H., Kim, M.: QDiff: Differential Testing of Quantum Software Stacks. In: 2021 36th IEEE/ACM International Conference on Automated Software Engineering (ASE), pp. 692–704 (2021). https://doi.org/10.1109/ASE51524.2021.9678792
18. Wang, X., Yu, T., Arcaini, P., Yue, T., Ali, S.: Mutation-Based Test Generation for Quantum Programs with Multi-Objective Search. In: Proceedings of the Genetic and Evolutionary Computation Conference, pp. 1345–1353. ACM, Boston Massachusetts (2022). https://doi.org/10.1145/3512290.3528869. https://dl.acm.org/doi/10.1145/3512290.3528869
19. Abreu, R., Fernandes, J.P., Llana, L., Tavares, G.: Metamorphic Testing of Oracle Quantum Programs. In: Proceedings of the 3rd International Workshop on Quantum Software Engineering, pp. 16–23. ACM, Pittsburgh Pennsylvania (2022). https://doi.org/10.1145/3528230.3529189. https://dl.acm.org/doi/10.1145/3528230.3529189
20. Paltenghi, M., Pradel, M.: MorphQ: Metamorphic Testing of Quantum Computing Platforms (2022). https://doi.org/10.48550/arXiv.2206.01111. arXiv:2206.01111 [cs]
21. Wang, X., Arcaini, P., Yue, T., Ali, S.: Application of Combinatorial Testing to Quantum Programs. In: 2021 IEEE 21st International Conference on Software Quality, Reliability and Security (QRS), pp. 179–188 (2021). https://doi.org/10.1109/QRS54544.2021.00029
22. Wang, X., Arcaini, P., Yue, T., Ali, S.: QuCAT: A Combinatorial Testing Tool for Quantum Software (2023). https://arxiv.org/abs/2309.00119v1
23. Wang, X., Arcaini, P., Yue, T., Ali, S.: Generating Failing Test Suites for Quantum Programs With Search. In: O'Reilly, U.-M., Devroey, X. (eds.) Search-Based Software Engineering. Lecture Notes in Computer Science, pp. 9–25. Springer, Cham (2021). https://doi.org/10.1007/978-3-030-88106-1_2
24. Wang, X., Arcaini, P., Yue, T., Ali, S.: QuSBT: Search-Based Testing of Quantum Programs. In: Proceedings of the ACM/IEEE 44th International Conference on Software Engineering: Companion Proceedings, pp. 173–177 (2022)
25. Ali, S., Arcaini, P., Wang, X., Yue, T.: Assessing the Effectiveness of Input and Output Coverage Criteria for Testing Quantum Programs. In: 2021 14th IEEE Conference on Software Testing, Verification and Validation (ICST), pp. 13–23 (2021). https://doi.org/10.1109/ICST49551.2021.00014
26. Wang, X., Arcaini, P., Yue, T., Ali, S.: Quito: A Coverage-Guided Test Generator for Quantum Programs. In: 2021 36th IEEE/ACM International Conference on Automated Software Engineering (ASE), pp. 1237–1241 (2021). https://doi.org/10.1109/ASE51524.2021.9678798
27. Rajak, A., Suzuki, S., Dutta, A., Chakrabarti, B.K.: Quantum annealing: an overview. Phil. Trans. Roy. Soc. A Math. Phys. Eng. Sci. **381**(2241), 20210417 (2023). https://doi.org/10.1098/rsta.2021.0417. https://royalsocietypublishing.org/doi/pdf/10.1098/rsta.2021.0417
28. Aleksandrowicz, G., Alexander, T., Barkoutsos, P., Bello, L., Ben-Haim, Y., Bucher, D., Cabrera-Hernández, F.J., Carballo-Franquis, J., Chen, A., Chen, C.-F., Chow, J.M., Córcoles-Gonzales, A.D., Cross, A.J., Cross, A., Cruz-Benito, J., Culver, C., González, S.D.L.P., Torre,

E.D.L., Ding, D., Dumitrescu, E., Duran, I., Eendebak, P., Everitt, M., Sertage, I.F., Frisch, A., Fuhrer, A., Gambetta, J., Gago, B.G., Gomez-Mosquera, J., Greenberg, D., Hamamura, I., Havlicek, V., Hellmers, J., Herok, Horii, H., Hu, S., Imamichi, T., Itoko, T., Javadi-Abhari, A., Kanazawa, N., Karazeev, A., Krsulich, K., Liu, P., Luh, Y., Maeng, Y., Marques, M., Martín-Fernández, F.J., McClure, D.T., McKay, D., Meesala, S., Mezzacapo, A., Moll, N., Rodríguez, D.M., Nannicini, G., Nation, P., Ollitrault, P., O'Riordan, L.J., Paik, H., Pérez, J., Phan, A., Pistoia, M., Prutyanov, V., Reuter, M., Rice, J., Davila, A.R., Rudy, R.H.P., Ryu, M., Sathaye, N., Schnabel, C., Schoute, E., Setia, K., Shi, Y., Silva, A., Siraichi, Y., Sivarajah, S., Smolin, J.A., Soeken, M., Takahashi, H., Tavernelli, I., Taylor, C., Taylour, P., Trabing, K., Treinish, M., Turner, W., Vogt-Lee, D., Vuillot, C., Wildstrom, J.A., Wilson, J., Winston, E., Wood, C., Wood, S., Wörner, S., Akhalwaya, I.Y., Zoufal, C.: Qiskit: An Open-source Framework for Quantum Computing. Zenodo (2019). https://doi.org/10.5281/zenodo.2562111

29. Nielsen, M.A., Chuang, I.L.: Quantum Computation and Quantum Information: 10th Anniversary Edition. Cambridge University Press, Cambridge (2010). https://doi.org/10.1017/CBO9780511976667
30. Alaqail, H., Ahmed, S.: Overview of software testing standard iso/iec/ieee 29119. Int. J. Comput. Sci. Network Secur. (IJCSNS) **18**(2), 112–116 (2018)
31. Miranskyy, A., Zhang, L.: On Testing Quantum Programs. In: 2019 IEEE/ACM 41st International Conference on Software Engineering: New Ideas and Emerging Results (ICSE-NIER), pp. 57–60 (2019). https://doi.org/10.1109/ICSE-NIER.2019.00023. http://arxiv.org/abs/1812.09261
32. De Stefano, M., Pecorelli, F., Di Nucci, D., Palomba, F., De Lucia, A.: Software engineering for quantum programming: How far are we? J. Syst. Software **190**, 111326 (2022). https://doi.org/10.1016/j.jss.2022.111326
33. Paltenghi, M., Pradel, M.: LintQ: A Static Analysis Framework for Qiskit Quantum Programs (2023). arXiv:2310.00718 [cs]
34. Fortunato, D., Campos, J., Abreu, R.: Mutation testing of quantum programs: a case study with Qiskit. IEEE Trans. Quant. Eng. **3**, 1–17 (2022). https://doi.org/10.1109/TQE.2022.3195061
35. Fortunato, D., Campos, J., Abreu, R.: Mutation Testing of Quantum Programs Written in QISKit. In: 2022 IEEE/ACM 44th International Conference on Software Engineering: Companion Proceedings (ICSE-Companion), pp. 358–359 (2022). https://doi.org/10.1145/3510454.3528649
36. Fortunato, D., Campos, J., Abreu, R.: QMutPy: A Mutation Testing tool for Quantum algorithms and Applications in Qiskit. In: Proceedings of the 31st ACM SIGSOFT International Symposium on Software Testing and Analysis, pp. 797–800. ACM, Virtual South Korea (2022). https://doi.org/10.1145/3533767.3543296 . https://dl.acm.org/doi/10.1145/3533767.3543296
37. Mendiluze, E., Ali, S., Arcaini, P., Yue, T.: Muskit: A Mutation Analysis Tool for Quantum Software Testing. In: 2021 36th IEEE/ACM International Conference on Automated Software Engineering (ASE), pp. 1266–1270 (2021). https://doi.org/10.1109/ASE51524.2021.9678563
38. Li, G., Zhou, L., Yu, N., Ding, Y., Ying, M., Xie, Y.: Projection-based runtime assertions for testing and debugging quantum programs (2020). Accepted: 2021-03-14T22:46:19Z
39. Muqeet, A., Yue, T., Ali, S., Arcaini, P.: Noise-Aware Quantum Software Testing (2023)
40. Zhang, L., Radnejad, M., Miranskyy, A.: Identifying Flakiness in Quantum Programs. Preprint (2023). arXiv:2302.03256
41. Long, P., Zhao, J.: Testing multi-subroutine quantum programs: From unit testing to integration testing (2023). arXiv:2306.17407 [quant-ph]
42. Long, P., Zhao, J.: Testing quantum programs with multiple subroutines (2023). arXiv:2208.09206 [cs]
43. Hoare, C.A.R.: An axiomatic basis for computer programming. Commun. ACM **12**(10), 576–580 (1969). https://doi.org/10.1145/363235.363259
44. Yamaguchi, F., Golde, N., Arp, D., Rieck, K.: Modeling and Discovering Vulnerabilities with Code Property Graphs. In: 2014 IEEE Symposium on Security and Privacy, pp. 590–604 (2014). https://doi.org/10.1109/SP.2014.44

45. Barrera, A.G., Guzmán, I.G.-R., Polo, M., Cruz-Lemus, J.A.: In: Serrano, M.A., Pérez-Castillo, R., Piattini, M. (eds.) Quantum Software Testing: Current Trends and Emerging Proposals, pp. 167–191. Springer, Cham (2022). https://doi.org/10.1007/978-3-031-05324-5_9

46. Sych, D., Leuchs, G.: A complete basis of generalized bell states. New J. Phys. **11**(1), 013006 (2009). https://doi.org/10.1088/1367-2630/11/1/013006

47. Harrow, A.W., Hassidim, A., Lloyd, S.: Quantum algorithm for linear systems of equations. Phys. Rev. Lett. **103**(15), (2009). https://doi.org/10.1103/physrevlett.103.150502

48. Lloyd, S., Mohseni, M., Rebentrost, P.: Quantum principal component analysis. Nature Phys. **10**(9), 631–633 (2014) https://doi.org/10.1038/nphys3029

49. Zhao, P., Zhao, J., Ma, L.: Identifying Bug Patterns in Quantum Programs. In: 2021 IEEE/ACM 2nd International Workshop on Quantum Software Engineering (Q-SE), pp. 16–21. IEEE, Madrid, Spain (2021). https://doi.org/10.1109/Q-SE52541.2021.00011. https://ieeexplore.ieee.org/document/9474564/

50. Zhao, P., Zhao, J., Miao, Z., Lan, S.: Bugs4Q: A Benchmark of Real Bugs for Quantum Programs. In: 2021 36th IEEE/ACM International Conference on Automated Software Engineering (ASE), pp. 1373–1376 (2021). https://doi.org/10.1109/ASE51524.2021.9678908

51. Chen, Q., Câmara, R., Campos, J., Souto, A., Ahmed, I.: The Smelly Eight: An Empirical Study on the Prevalence of Code Smells in Quantum Computing. In: 2023 IEEE/ACM 45th International Conference on Software Engineering (ICSE), pp. 358–370 (2023). https://doi.org/10.1109/ICSE48619.2023.00041

52. Cross, A.W., Bishop, L.S., Smolin, J.A., Gambetta, J.M.: Open Quantum Assembly Language (2017)

53. Liang, H., Pei, X., Jia, X., Shen, W., Zhang, J.: Fuzzing: state of the art. IEEE Trans. Reliab. **67**(3), 1199–1218 (2018). https://doi.org/10.1109/TR.2018.2834476

54. Zhu, X., Wen, S., Camtepe, S., Xiang, Y.: Fuzzing: A survey for roadmap. ACM Comput. Surv. **54**(11s), (2022). https://doi.org/10.1145/3512345

55. Manès, V.J.M., Han, H., Han, C., Cha, S.K., Egele, M., Schwartz, E.J., Woo, M.: The art, science, and engineering of fuzzing: A survey. IEEE Trans. Software Eng. **47**(11), 2312–2331 (2021). https://doi.org/10.1109/TSE.2019.2946563

56. Li, J., Zhao, B., Zhang, C.: Fuzzing: a survey. Cybersecurity **1**(1), 1–13 (2018)

57. Godefroid, P.: Fuzzing: Hack, art, and science. Commun. ACM **63**(2), 70–76 (2020)

58. Wang, Y., Jia, P., Liu, L., Huang, C., Liu, Z.: A systematic review of fuzzing based on machine learning techniques. PLOS ONE **15**(8), 1–37 (2020). https://doi.org/10.1371/journal.pone.0237749

59. Offutt, A.J., Pan, J.: Automatically detecting equivalent mutants and infeasible paths. Software Test. Verif. Reliab. **7**(3), 165–192 (1997). https://doi.org/10.1002/(SICI)1099-1689(199709)7:3<165::AID-STVR143>3.0.CO;2-U

60. Just, R., Kapfhammer, G.M., Schweiggert, F.: Do Redundant Mutants Affect the Effectiveness and Efficiency of Mutation Analysis? In: 2012 IEEE Fifth International Conference on Software Testing, Verification and Validation, pp. 720–725 (2012). https://doi.org/10.1109/ICST.2012.162

61. Madeyski, L., Orzeszyna, W., Torkar, R., Józala, M.: Overcoming the equivalent mutant problem: a systematic literature review and a comparative experiment of second order mutation. IEEE Trans. Software Eng. **40**(1), 23–42 (2014). https://doi.org/10.1109/TSE.2013.44

62. Just, R., Kapfhammer, G.M., Schweiggert, F.: Using Non-redundant Mutation Operators and Test Suite Prioritization to Achieve Efficient and Scalable Mutation Analysis. In: 2012 IEEE 23rd International Symposium on Software Reliability Engineering, pp. 11–20 (2012). https://doi.org/10.1109/ISSRE.2012.31

63. Just, R., Schweiggert, F.: Higher accuracy and lower run time: efficient mutation analysis using non-redundant mutation operators. Software Test. Verif. Reliab. **25**(5-7), 490–507 (2015). https://doi.org/10.1002/stvr.1561

64. Deb, K., Pratap, A., Agarwal, S., Meyarivan, T.: A fast and elitist multiobjective genetic algorithm: Nsga-ii. IEEE Trans. Evol. Comput. **6**(2), 182–197 (2002). https://doi.org/10.1109/4235.996017
65. Barr, E.T., Harman, M., McMinn, P., Shahbaz, M., Yoo, S.: The Oracle problem in software testing: a survey. IEEE Trans. Software Eng. **41**(5), 507–525 (2015). https://doi.org/10.1109/TSE.2014.2372785
66. Sicilia, M.-A., Sánchez-Alonso, S., Mora-Cantallops, M., García-Barriocanal, E.: On the Source Code Structure of Quantum Code: Insights from Q# and QDK. In: Shepperd, M., Abreu, F., Silva, A., Pérez-Castillo, R. (eds.) Quality of Information and Communications Technology. Communications in Computer and Information Science, pp. 292–299. Springer, Cham (2020). https://doi.org/10.1007/978-3-030-58793-2_24
67. Yamashita, K., Huang, C., Nagappan, M., Kamei, Y., Mockus, A., Hassan, A.E., Ubayashi, N.: Thresholds for Size and Complexity Metrics: A Case Study from the Perspective of Defect Density. In: 2016 IEEE International Conference on Software Quality, Reliability and Security (QRS), pp. 191–201 (2016). https://doi.org/10.1109/QRS.2016.31
68. Kumar, A.: Formalization of structural test cases coverage criteria for quantum software testing. Int. J. Theor. Phys. **62**, (2023). https://doi.org/10.1007/s10773-022-05271-y
69. Just, R., Jalali, D., Inozemtseva, L., Ernst, M.D., Holmes, R., Fraser, G.: Are Mutants a Valid Substitute for Real Faults in Software Testing? In: Proceedings of the 22nd ACM SIGSOFT International Symposium on Foundations of Software Engineering, pp. 654–665. ACM, Hong Kong China (2014). https://doi.org/10.1145/2635868.2635929. https://dl.acm.org/doi/10.1145/2635868.2635929
70. Just, R., Jalali, D., Ernst, M.D.: Defects4j: A Database of Existing Faults to Enable Controlled Testing Studies for Java Programs. In: Proceedings of the 2014 International Symposium on Software Testing and Analysis, pp. 437–440. ACM, San Jose, CA, USA (2014). https://doi.org/10.1145/2610384.2628055. https://dl.acm.org/doi/10.1145/2610384.2628055
71. Gyimesi, P., Vancsics, B., Stocco, A., Mazinanian, D., Beszédes, A., Ferenc, R., Mesbah, A.: BugsJS: A Benchmark of JavaScript Bugs. In: 2019 12th IEEE Conference on Software Testing, Validation and Verification (ICST), pp. 90–101 (2019). https://doi.org/10.1109/ICST.2019.00019
72. Widyasari, R., Sim, S.Q., Lok, C., Qi, H., Phan, J., Tay, Q., Tan, C., Wee, F., Tan, J.E., Yieh, Y., Goh, B., Thung, F., Kang, H.J., Hoang, T., Lo, D., Ouh, E.L.: BugsInPy: A Database of Existing Bugs in Python Programs to Enable Controlled Testing and Debugging Studies. In: Proceedings of the 28th ACM Joint Meeting on European Software Engineering Conference and Symposium on the Foundations of Software Engineering. ESEC/FSE 2020, pp. 1556–1560. Association for Computing Machinery, New York, NY, USA (2020). https://doi.org/10.1145/3368089.3417943
73. Shamshiri, S., Just, R., Rojas, J.M., Fraser, G., McMinn, P., Arcuri, A.: Do Automatically Generated Unit Tests Find Real Faults? An Empirical Study of Effectiveness and Challenges. In: 2015 30th IEEE/ACM International Conference on Automated Software Engineering (ASE), pp. 201–211 (2015). https://doi.org/10.1109/ASE.2015.86
74. Lukasczyk, S., Kroiß, F., Fraser, G.: An empirical study of automated unit test generation for Python. Empirical Software Eng. **28**(2), 36 (2023)
75. Paterson, D., Campos, J., Abreu, R., Kapfhammer, G.M., Fraser, G., McMinn, P.: An Empirical Study on the Use of Defect Prediction for Test Case Prioritization. In: 2019 12th IEEE Conference on Software Testing, Validation and Verification (ICST), pp. 346–357 (2019). https://doi.org/10.1109/ICST.2019.00041
76. Miranda, B., Cruciani, E., Verdecchia, R., Bertolino, A.: FAST Approaches to Scalable Similarity-Based Test Case Prioritization. In: Proceedings of the 40th International Conference on Software Engineering. ICSE '18, pp. 222–232. Association for Computing Machinery, New York, NY, USA (2018). https://doi.org/10.1145/3180155.3180210

77. Pearson, S., Campos, J., Just, R., Fraser, G., Abreu, R., Ernst, M.D., Pang, D., Keller, B.: Evaluating and Improving Fault Localization. In: 2017 IEEE/ACM 39th International Conference on Software Engineering (ICSE), pp. 609–620 (2017). https://doi.org/10.1109/ICSE.2017.62

78. Li, X., Li, W., Zhang, Y., Zhang, L.: DeepFL: Integrating Multiple Fault Diagnosis Dimensions for Deep Fault Localization. In: Proceedings of the 28th ACM SIGSOFT International Symposium on Software Testing and Analysis. ISSTA 2019, pp. 169–180. Association for Computing Machinery, New York, NY, USA (2019). https://doi.org/10.1145/3293882.3330574

79. Zou, D., Liang, J., Xiong, Y., Ernst, M.D., Zhang, L.: An empirical study of fault localization families and their combinations. IEEE Trans. Software Eng. **47**(2), 332–347 (2021). https://doi.org/10.1109/TSE.2019.2892102

80. Sarhan, Q.I., Beszédes, A.: A survey of challenges in spectrum-based software fault localization. IEEE Access **10**, 10618–10639 (2022). https://doi.org/10.1109/ACCESS.2022.3144079

81. Widyasari, R., Prana, G.A.A., Haryono, S.A., Wang, S., Lo, D.: Real world projects, real faults: evaluating spectrum based fault localization techniques on Python projects. Empirical Software Eng. **27**(6), 147 (2022)

82. Durieux, T., Madeiral, F., Martinez, M., Abreu, R.: Empirical Review of Java Program Repair Tools: A Large-Scale Experiment on 2,141 Bugs and 23,551 Repair Attempts. In: Proceedings of the 2019 27th ACM Joint Meeting on European Software Engineering Conference and Symposium on the Foundations of Software Engineering. ESEC/FSE 2019, pp. 302–313. Association for Computing Machinery, New York, NY, USA (2019). https://doi.org/10.1145/3338906.3338911

83. Campos, J., Souto, A.: QBugs: A Collection of Reproducible Bugs in Quantum Algorithms and a Supporting Infrastructure to Enable Controlled Quantum Software Testing and Debugging Experiments (2021)

84. Paltenghi, M., Pradel, M.: Bugs in quantum computing platforms: an empirical study. Proc. ACM Program. Lang. **6**(OOPSLA1), (2022). https://doi.org/10.1145/3527330

85. Lewis, C., Lin, Z., Sadowski, C., Zhu, X., Ou, R., Whitehead Jr., E.J.: Does Bug Prediction Support Human Developers? Findings from a Google Case Study. In: Proceedings of the 2013 International Conference on Software Engineering. ICSE '13, pp. 372–381. IEEE Press, San Francisco, CA, USA (2013)

86. Freitas, P.A.F.: Software repository mining analytics to estimate software component reliability (2015)

87. D'Ambros, M., Lanza, M., Robbes, R.: Evaluating defect prediction approaches: a benchmark and an extensive comparison. Empirical Software Eng. **17**(4–5), 531–577 (2012). https://doi.org/10.1007/s10664-011-9173-9

88. Catal, C., Diri, B.: A systematic review of software fault prediction studies. Expert Syst. Appl. **36**(4), 7346–7354 (2009). https://doi.org/10.1016/j.eswa.2008.10.027

89. Ostrand, T.J., Weyuker, E.J., Bell, R.M.: Predicting the location and number of faults in large software systems. IEEE Trans. Software Eng. **31**(4), 340–355 (2005). https://doi.org/10.1109/TSE.2005.49

90. Arcuri, A., Campos, J., Fraser, G.: Unit Test Generation During Software Development: EvoSuite Plugins for Maven, IntelliJ and Jenkins. In: 2016 IEEE International Conference on Software Testing, Verification and Validation (ICST), pp. 401–408 (2016). https://doi.org/10.1109/ICST.2016.44

91. Campos, J., Riboira, A., Perez, A., Abreu, R.: Gzoltar: An Eclipse Plug-in for Testing and Debugging. In: Proceedings of the 27th IEEE/ACM International Conference on Automated Software Engineering. ASE '12, pp. 378–381. Association for Computing Machinery, New York, NY, USA (2012). https://doi.org/10.1145/2351676.2351752

Quantum Software Quality Metrics

José A. Cruz-Lemus, Moisés Rodríguez, Raúl Barba-Rojas,
and Mario Piattini

Abstract Until now, the quality problems of quantum software have been largely ignored. This chapter analyzes the applicability of models and metrics for quantum software and, to mitigate this lack of attention to quality issues, presents a set of metrics that have been proposed and empirically validated to characterize the complexity of quantum circuits in terms of their understandability. The validation experiment design, execution, and results are reported. In addition, the main functionalities of a prototype tool that has been created for the automatic computation of the metrics are briefly presented.

Keywords Quantum computing · Quantum software engineering · Quantum circuits understandability · Metrics validation

1 Introduction

To drive the large-scale production of quantum software, an adequate level of quality is required [20] so that society can truly benefit from the promising quantum applications that exist in different domains. In a quantum information system, there are several factors that influence the quality of the results: the quality of the quantum hardware, the quality of the quantum software platform (development and operational), and the quality of the quantum software itself. Regarding the first factor, there are different types of simulators and quantum computers (adiabatic, gate-based, measurement-based, etc.); however, to date, most of them are still flawed, and hence their name: noisy intermediate-scale quantum (NISQ) [21].

J. A. Cruz-Lemus (✉) · M. Rodríguez · R. Barba-Rojas · M. Piattini
Escuela Superior de Informática de Ciudad Real, University of Castilla-La Mancha, Spain
e-mail: joseantonio.cruz@uclm.es; moises.rodriguez@uclm.es; mario.piattini@uclm.es

© The Author(s) 2024
I. Exman et al. (eds.), *Quantum Software*,
https://doi.org/10.1007/978-3-031-64136-7_6

As far as platform quality is concerned, an analysis of how quantum computing affects the most relevant software quality characteristics is proposed in [19]. However, quantum hardware and platforms are not the only important issues in achieving *high-quality* quantum information systems; software quality is also essential. In fact, quantum software engineering (QSE) is an essential contribution to the success of quantum computing. One of the tenets of the Talavera Manifesto for Quantum Software Engineering and Programming [19] states that "QSE must ensure the quality of quantum software. Quality management of both processes and products is essential if quantum software is to be produced at the expected quality levels."

In fact, it would be necessary to adapt the quality models as specified in ISO/IEC 25010 [16], as some quality characteristics should be redefined and perhaps others incorporated to take into account the peculiarities of quantum software. In any case, there are characteristics such as understandability that are still fundamental, since quantum software that cannot be understood is not quantum software.

Unfortunately, until now, the quality problems of quantum software have been largely ignored, and hence this chapter aims to alleviate this situation. First, we will focus on defining and empirically validating a set of metrics for assessing the understandability of quantum circuits. As interesting as it is, quantum annealing is out of the scope of this research, although the quality of this quantum computing approach will eventually be dealt with in the future.

The remainder of this chapter is organized as follows. In Sect. 2, the proposals that have been found in the literature are detailed. In Sect. 2.2 a proposal of metrics for quantum circuits is presented. An empirical validation of these metrics is briefly explained in Sect. 4, while Sect. 5 presents a prototype of a tool that has been developed to calculate these metrics automatically. Finally, in Sect. 6 the most important conclusions of this chapter are detailed.

2   State-of-the-Art

2.1   Quality in Quantum Computing Software

Sodhi and Kapur [28] published an analysis of the main quantum programming platforms, examining how they affect the most relevant software quality characteristics: availability, interoperability, maintainability, manageability, performance, reliability, scalability, security, testability, and usability. In their study, some of the characteristics that most affect the quality attributes are:

1. Lower level of programming abstractions, which increases the complexity of the code impacting maintainability, testability, reliability, and availability
2. Platform heterogeneity, which impairs software cohesion, affecting maintainability, reliability, robustness, reusability, and system manageability and testability

3. Remote software development and deployment, which slows programming, testing, and debugging of quantum programs, affecting maintainability and testability
4. Dependence on known quantum algorithms, which affects the ability to perform enhancements and corrective maintenance, as well as testability and interoperability (with classical software)
5. Limited software portability, resulting in a lack of standardization in several areas, affecting availability, interoperability, maintainability, and scalability
6. Lack of a native quantum operating system, which decreases performance, manageability, reliability, scalability, and security
7. Fundamentally different programming models, which can increase code complexity and affect maintainability, interoperability, security, and testability

As for other related work, most of the existing research efforts related to quantum software quality have generally focused on quantum program verification [23] and specifically on verified compilation [22], verification protocols [15], relational verification of quantum programs [1], formal description of quantum programs [6], formal verification and certification of programs [7], and equivalence checking for quantum circuits [5]. But, as in classical computer science, formal verification is not a realistic solution since it is only useful for very specific programs of small size and requires mathematical knowledge that is foreign to most computer scientists. This is why it is much more convenient to have a set of metrics that can guide the work of quantum software designers and programmers.

2.2 Metrics for Quantum Computing Software

It is important to adapt software quality metrics to the characteristics of quantum systems. In fact, on the one hand, there is a lot of research on metrics for classical conceptual models [8, 10, 12, 26], but very little for quantum software.

On the other hand, for quantum circuits, there is the "quantum volume" metric, which summarizes performance as a function of a few factors: number of physical qubits, number of gates, device connectivity, and number of operations that can be executed in parallel [2]. But it is intended as a hardware performance metric measuring the useful amount of quantum computation performed by a device in space and time, or as an alternative means of formalizing the complexity of quantum algorithms [25].

Different "quantum circuit performance measures" are collected in [29]: cubic cost (total number of qubits required to design the quantum circuit), gate count (total number of gates used in the quantum circuit), "junk" gates (all gates that exist to preserve reversibility but are not primary inputs or useful outputs), ancillae (all constant inputs to the quantum circuit), and depth (the number of layers of gates in the circuit).

In [18], QUANTIFY, an open source framework for quantitative analysis of quantum circuits, is proposed, which uses the number of physical qubits and the amount of time to operate the physical qubits, which influence the total energy consumed to perform the computation.

Finally, some other proposals can be found in [17, 27, 31].

3   Metrics for Quantum Circuits

We are aware that the easier it is to understand a quantum circuit, as with any modeling artifact, the easier the tasks of debugging, testing, and, in general, maintenance of quantum software will be, and we will be able to achieve quality quantum applications. Hence a set of metrics has been defined to measure the understandability of quantum circuits. Thus, this section presents a set of metrics [9] to evaluate the understandability of quantum circuits, which can influence the time and resources required for their development, their testability, and their maintainability. For better understanding, the metrics have been grouped according to their measurement objective.

3.1   Circuit Size

Intuitively, the larger the circuit, the more complex it must also be to understand. The metrics in this group are:

- **Width**: Number of qubits in the circuit
- **Depth**: Maximum number of operations applied to a qubit in the circuit

3.2   Circuit Density

This group of metrics refers to the number of gates applied to each qubit in the circuit. We can find several equivalent circuits in which the gates are deployed differently (see Fig. 1). The density of these two circuits, i.e., the number of steps needed in the quantum circuit to perform the same number of operations, is different. This group contains the following metrics:

- **MaxDens**: Maximum number of operations applied to the qubits
- **AvgDens**: Average number of operations applied to the qubits

Fig. 1 Two equivalent quantum circuits with different densities

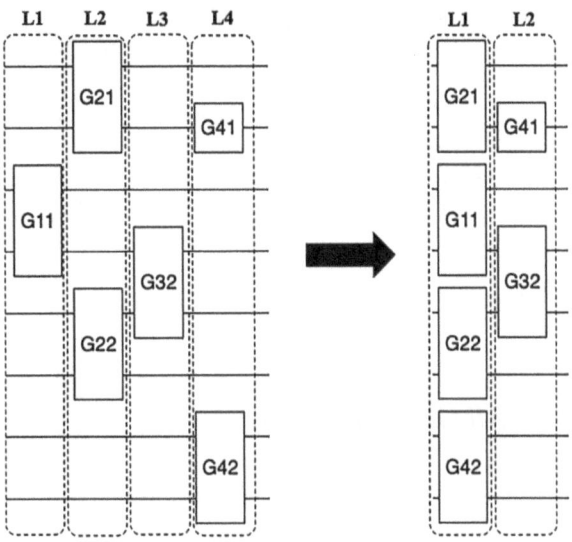

3.3 Single-Qubit Gates

This group contains the gates most commonly used in quantum circuits:

- **NoP-X**: Number of Pauli-X gates (NOT)
- **NoP-Y**: Number of Pauli-Y gates
- **NoP-Z**: Number of Pauli-Z gates
- **TNo-P**: Total number of Pauli gates in the circuit (calculated as the sum of the previous three)
- **NoH**: Number of Hadamard gates
- **%SpposQ**: Ratio of qubits with a Hadamard gate as an initial gate (qubits in superposition state)
- **NoOtherSG**: Number of other single-qubit gates in the circuit
- **TNoSQG**: Total number of single-qubit gates
- **TNoCSQG**: Total number of controlled single-qubit gates

3.4 Multi-Qubit Gates

This group includes gates involving several qubits as input and output:

- **NoCAnyG**: Number of controlled gates (any).
- **NoSWAP**: Number of exchange gates.
- **NoCNOT**: Number of NOT controlled gates (CNOT).

- **%QinCNOT**: Ratio of qubits affected by CNOT gates. Both the controlled qubit and the target qubit in a CNOT will be considered affected for the calculation of this metric.
- **AvgCNOT**: Average number of CNOT gates directed to any qubit in a circuit.
- **MaxCNOT**: Maximum number of CNOT gates directed to any qubit of a circuit.
- **NoToff**: Number of Toffoli gates.
- **%QinToff**: Ratio of qubits affected by Toffoli gates. The calculation will take into account the controlled qubit and the target qubits as affected.
- **AvgToff**: Average number of Toffoli gates targeting any qubit of a circuit.
- **MaxToff**: Maximum number of Toffoli gates targeting any qubit of a circuit.

3.5 All Gates in the Circuit

- **NoGates**: Total number of gates in the circuit
- **NoCGates**: Total number of controlled gates in the circuit
- **NoGates**: Ratio of single gates to total gates

3.6 Oracles

We are aware that there are certain features regarding the use of oracles in quantum circuits that could affect their understandability but, because they behave as "black boxes," it is not possible to compute them. However, a comprehensive study of how oracles affect the understandability of quantum circuits is planned for future work.

- **NoOr**: Number of oracles in the circuit.
- **NoCOr**: Number of controlled oracles in the circuit.
- **%QinOr**: Proportion of qubits affected by the oracles. For the calculation of this metric, only the oracle input qubits will be considered affected.
- **%QinCOr**: Ratio of qubits affected by controlled oracles. The controlled qubit and the oracle input qubits will be considered affected for the calculation of this metric.
- **AvgOrD**: Average depth of an oracle in the circuit.
- **MaxOrD**: Maximum depth of an oracle in the circuit.

3.7 Measurement Gates

- **NoQM**: Number of measured qubits
- **%QM**: Ratio of measured qubits

3.8   Other Metrics

- **%Anc**: Ratio of ancilla (auxiliary) qubits in the circuit

3.9   Metrics for Quantum Circuits Calculation Examples

In this section, a couple of examples (Figs. 2 and 3) are used to illustrate the calculation of the metrics proposed in the previous section. Table 1 shows these calculations when applied to the examples.

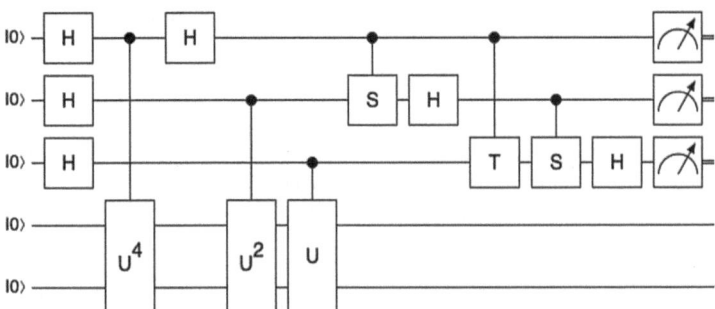

Fig. 2 An example (A) of a quantum circuit

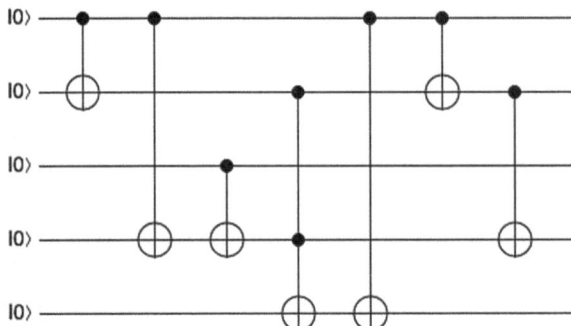

Fig. 3 Another example (B) of a quantum circuit

Table 1 Metrics calculation for the given examples

Metric	Example A	Example B	Metric	Example A	Example B
Width	5	5	MaxCNOT	0	3
Depth	10	7	NoToff	0	1
MaxDens	3	1	%QinCNOT	0	0.60
AvgDens	1.20	1	AvgToff(q)	0	0.20
NoP-X	0	0	MaxToff(q)	0	1
NoP-Y	0	0	NoGates	12	7
NoP-Z	0	0	NoCGates	6	7
TNo-P	0	0	%SGates	0.75	1.00
NoH	6	0	NoOr	3	0
%SpposQ	0.60	0	NoCOr	3	0
NoOtherSG	3	0	%QinOr	0.40	0
TNoSQG	9	0	%QinCOr	1.00	0
TNoCSQG	3	0	AvgOrD	2.00	0
NoCAnyG	6	7	MaxOrD	2	0
NoSWAP	0	0	NoQM	3	0
NoCNOT	0	6	%QM	0.60	0
%QinCNOT	0	1.00	%Anc	0.40	0
AvgCNOT	0	1.20			

4 Validation of Quantum Circuits Metrics

This section briefly describes an experiment performed to empirically validate the metrics proposed in Sect. 3. In different subsections, its design, execution, results, conclusions, and limitations will be explained.

4.1 Experiment Design

The whole experimental process is based on the methodology proposed in [30].

First, the main goal of the experiment was to validate the set of metrics presented in Sect. 3. The experimental null hypothesis (H_0) was defined as the quantum circuit aspects measured by each of the metrics under study do not have an impact on the understandability of the quantum circuit .

The experiment was carried out online from mid-April until the end of May of 2023 and, as for the experimental subjects, over 600 quantum software researchers and professionals were sent an invitation to participate in the experiment, but finally, only 32 of them filled out the online materials, consisting of a set of questionnaires with a quantum circuit on each of them and questions about that circuit, state change when some gates were added or removed, results on several qubits, etc. Part of one

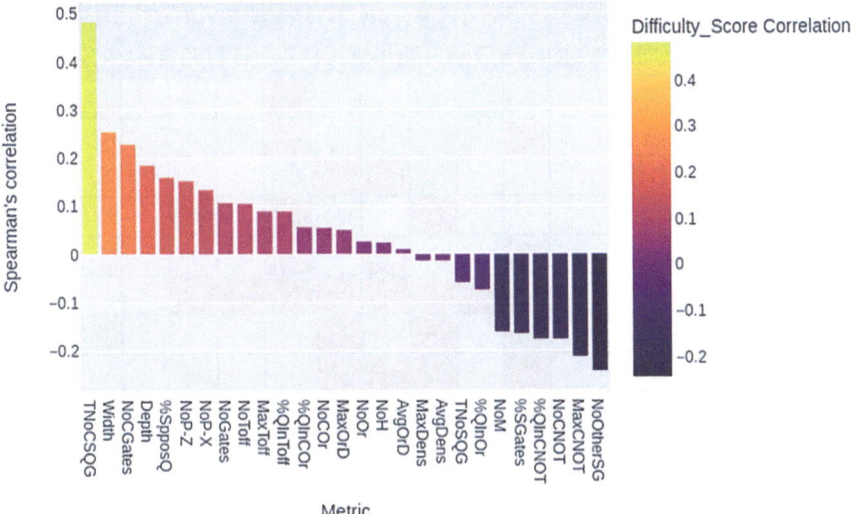

Fig. 4 Spearman's correlation coefficient results

of the questionnaires can be found as an example in the appendix at the end of the chapter (see Fig. 12).

4.2 Experiment Results

When trying to apply the typical correlation analyses, we obtained that Pearson's coefficient could not be applied as the data did not meet the conditions required to do so. On the other hand, we could apply Spearman's correlation coefficient to the obtained data. When doing so, only one metric showed a statistically significant result (see Fig. 4). It was the metric **TNoCSQG** that, as mentioned in Sect. 3.3, counts the total number of controlled single-qubit gates.

As these results had been quite discouraging so far, because only one of the whole set of metrics had been validated, we decided to use several machine learning (ML) techniques, such as decision trees [3] and random forests [4], on a discretized and a non-discretized version of the dataset.

The color code in Fig. 5 puts a green square where a certain metric had a feature relevance higher than the third quartile related to a certain technique. This implies that the metric is affecting how the quantum circuit has been understood by the subjects. It also puts a red square when the feature relevance was lower than the first quartile and, finally, leaves a white square on the other cases.

Thus, it can be observed that there is a subset of metrics with green squares in several techniques, which means that they have been validated as good indicators for assessing the understandability of quantum circuits. These metrics are **Depth**,

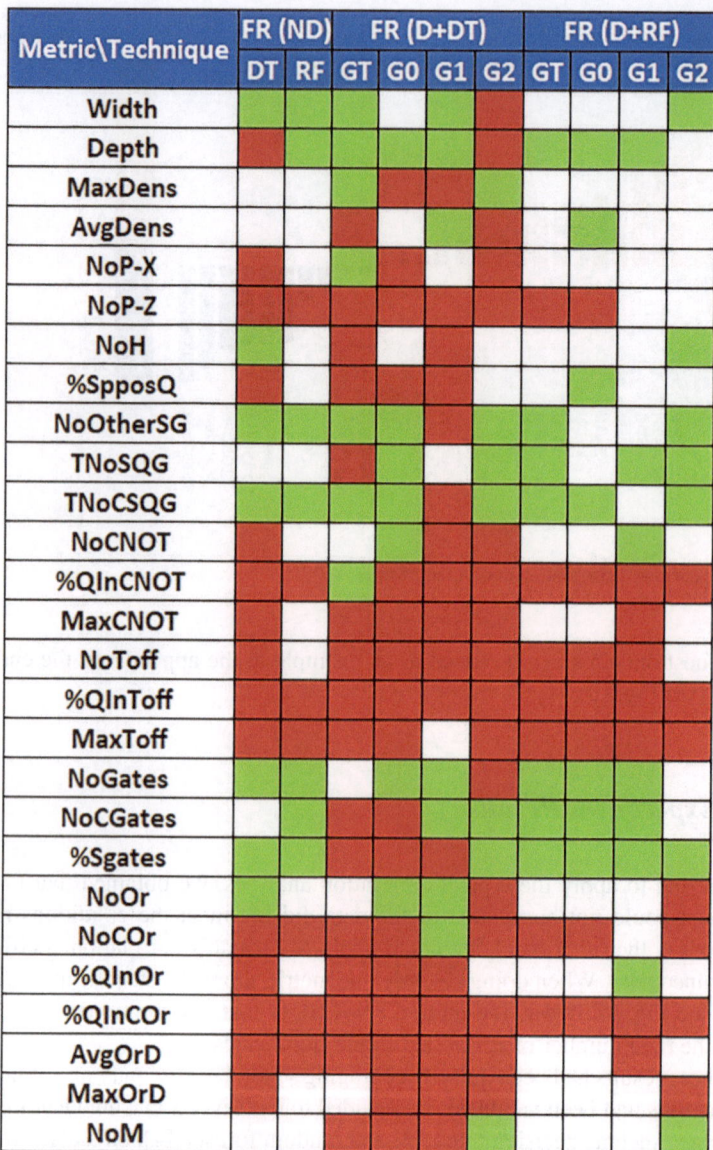

Fig. 5 Machine learning techniques results

NoOtherSG, **TNoCSQG** (confirming the results of the Spearman's correlation), **Width**, and **%SGates**.

4.3 Experiment Limitations

This experiment has a set of limitations that need to be taken into account. First, the use of ML techniques for validating the metrics is a different approach from other metrics validation processes [11]. In this case, several ML techniques were used, and metrics are validated when they are located in the highest quartile in a relevant number of cases. Also, the number of experimental subjects (32) is quite low. Unfortunately, the quantum computing community is still growing, and it is hoped that we will have more experimental subjects in future replication studies. Finally, although a methodological approach has been undertaken for the design, execution, and analysis of the data collected by this experiment, further replication studies should be conducted to confirm the strength of the conclusions achieved in this experiment.

5 QMetrics

A tool prototype called *QMetrics* was created for the automatic calculation of the proposed metrics. Essentially, it is a Web application that allows for automatically calculating each of the metrics proposed over a quantum circuit provided by the user. An example of use is presented in this section, to highlight its main functionalities, which will be commented on next:

1. **Adding a new quantum circuit** (optional): The first step to perform the calculation of the metrics for a given quantum circuit is to add such a circuit, provided the quantum circuit is not already loaded on the tool. To insert the quantum circuit, the user must specify its code, generated by *QPainter*, another tool that allows the graphical designing of quantum circuits, similar to other tools such as IBM Composer[1] or Quirk.[2] The name of the circuit has to be added too (see Fig. 6).
2. **Selecting the circuit**: In the following step, the circuit on which the metrics will be calculated can be selected from the list of quantum circuits loaded on the tool (see Fig. 7).

---

[1] https://quantum-computing.ibm.com/composer/.

[2] https://algassert.com/quirk.

2. Your circuit ▼

Here is the JSON code of your circuit:

[["_","_","_",{"CONTROL":1},"H","MEASURE","_","_",{"CONTROL":2}],["H",
{"CONTROL":2},"X","_","_","MEASURE",{"CONTROL":2}],
["_","X","_","_","_","_","X","Z"]]

Do you want to save a new circuit? If you do, simply copy and paste the code of your circuit into the text area, put a name of your choice and click the "Save my circuit" button.

Circuit name: [Quantum Teleportation]   [Save my circuit]

Fig. 6 Adding a quantum circuit in QMetrics

1. Introduce your circuit ▼

You can either select a circuit from the list of circuits, or you can introduce a new circuit in the next section.

Available Circuits: [Quantum Teleportation   ∨]

Fig. 7 Selecting a quantum circuit in QMetrics

3. Visualize your circuit ▼

If you want to visualize the introduced circuit, you can visualize it (as it is displayed in QPainter) by simply clicking the "Draw my circuit" button.

[Draw my circuit]

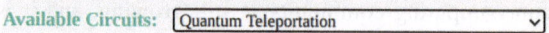

Fig. 8 Visualizing a quantum circuit in QMetrics

3. **Visualizing the circuit**: The tool provides a component for the visualization of quantum circuits, using the *QPainter* interface. Once a quantum circuit is selected and loaded, it is graphically shown (see Fig. 8).
4. **Selecting the metrics to be calculated**: After that, the metrics to be computed can be selected. The user can decide to compute all the metrics or only a subset of them (see Fig. 9).
5. **Calculating the metrics**: In order to compute the metrics for the selected circuit, a "Calculate Metrics" is clicked, obtaining a table with the metrics values, as shown in Fig. 10. The table can be exported to several file formats, such as PDF or CSV.
6. **Visualizing the results**: Finally, *QMetrics* offers some charts to visualize the calculated metrics (see Fig. 11).

4. Metric Selector ▼

Use this section to select the metrics that will be calculated for your circuit.

Validated metrics	Circuit density	Single qubit gates	Multiple qubit gates	All gates	Oracles	Measurement gates
Toggle selection	Toggle selection	Toggle selection	Toggle selection	Toggle selection	Toggle selection	Toggle selection
☑ Width	☑ MaxDens	☑ NoP-X	☑ NoSWAP	☑ NoGates	☑ NoOr	☑ NoM
☑ Depth	☑ AvgDens	☑ NoP-Y	☑ NoCNOT	☑ NoCGates	☑ NoCOr	☑ %QM
☑ NoOtherSG		☑ NoP-Z	☑ %QInCNOT		☑ %QInOr	
☑ TNoCSQG		☑ TNo-P	☑ AvgCNOT		☑ %QInCOr	
☑ %SGates		☑ NoH	☑ MaxCNOT		☑ AvgOrD	
		☑ %SpposQ	☑ NoToff		☑ MaxOrD	
		☑ TNoSQG	☑ %QInToff			
			☑ AvgToff			
			☑ MaxToff			

Fig. 9 Selecting metrics in QMetrics

5. Metric Calculator ▼

If you want to calculate the metrics for the selected circuit, then click the button "Calculate Metrics".

You can also download the table with the metrics corresponding to the selected circuit by selecting a file format and clicking the "Download" button.
Note: If the table style is not being displayed properly when downloading as "PDF" format, make sure to check the option "Background graphics" in the "More Settings" section of the Download Window.

[Calculate Metrics] Export to: [CSV ▼] [Download]

Metric Type	Metric Name	Metric Value	Metric Description
Validated metrics	Width	3	Number of qubits in the circuit
	Depth	7	Maximum number of operations applied to a qubit in the circuit
	NoOtherSG	2	Number of other single-qubit gates in the circuit
	TNoCSQG	1	Total number of controlled single-qubit gates
	%SGates	0.5000	Ratio single vs total gates
Circuit density	MaxDens	2	Maximum number of operations applied to the circuit qubits in parallel
	AvgDens	1.1429	Average of the number of operations applied to the circuit qubits in parallel
Single qubit gates	NoP-X	0	Number of Pauli-X (NOT) gates
	NoP-Y	0	Number of Pauli-Y gates
	NoP-Z	0	Number of Pauli-Z gates
	TNo-P	0	Total number of Pauli gates in the circuit (calculated as the addition of the previous three)
	NoH	2	Number of Hadamard gates
	%SpposQ	0.3333	Ratio of qubits with a Hadamard gate as initial gate (qubits in superposition state)
	TNoSQG	4	Total number of single-qubit gates
Multiple qubit gates	NoSWAP	0	Number of swap gates
	NoCNOT	3	Number of Controlled NOT (CNOT) gates
	%QInCNOT	1	Ratio of qubits affected by CNOT gates (both the controlled and the target qubit in a CNOT will be considered as affected for the calculation of this metric)
	AvgCNOT	1	Average number of CNOT gates targeting any qubit of a circuit
	MaxCNOT	2	Maximum number of CNOT gates targeting any qubit of a circuit
	NoToff	0	Number of Toffoli gates
	%QInToff	0	Ratio of qubits affected by Toffoli gates (the controlled qubit and the target qubits will be taken into account as affected for the calculation)
	AvgToff	0	Average number of Toffoli gates targeting any qubit of a circuit
	MaxToff	0	Maximum number of Toffoli gates targeting any qubit of a circuit
All gates	NoGates	8	Total number of gates in the circuit
	NoCGates	4	Total number of controlled gates in the circuit
Oracles	NoOr	0	Number of oracles in the circuit
	NoCOr	0	Number of controlled oracles in the circuit
	%QInOr	0	Ratio of qubits affected by oracles. Only the non-controlled qubits of the oracle will be considered as affected for this metric.
	%QInCOr	0	Ratio of qubits affected by controlled oracles
	AvgOrD	0	Average depth of an oracle in the circuit
	MaxOrD	0	Maximum depth of an oracle in the circuit
Measurement gates	NoM	2	Number of measurement gates
	%QM	0.6667	Ratio of qubits measured

Fig. 10 Calculating metrics in QMetrics

6. Metric Analyzer ▼

In this section you will be able to understand, graphically, the metrics that were computed before. You can download the charts by blicking the "Download as PDF" button

Click the "Analyze Metrics" button if you want to refresh the chart regarding the current calculation.
Note: If you want a specific metric to not appear in the chart, you must make sure it is deselected before analyzing the metrics.

`Analyze Metrics` `Download as PDF`

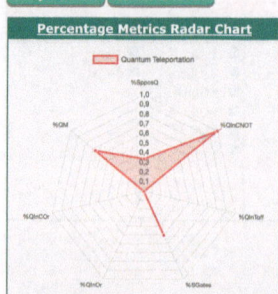
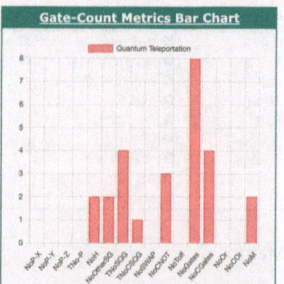
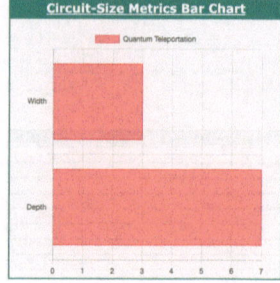
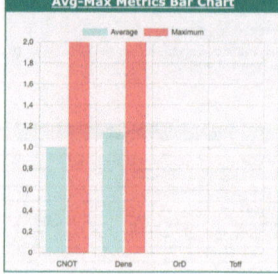

Fig. 11 Visualizing the calculated metrics in QMetrics

6 Conclusions

Establishing solid foundations is crucial when creating new disciplines, such as quantum software engineering (QSE). One of the fundamental principles of this new area is the establishment of a QSE that is agnostic with respect to quantum programming languages and technologies to ensure the quality of quantum software. The quality characteristics of classical software are still valid in quantum software, but it is essential to have a set of appropriate metrics, adapted to the peculiarities of these systems, that are able to accurately measure quantum circuits.

In this chapter, a set of metrics has been defined to measure the understandability of quantum circuits. In addition, a first empirical study has been presented in which a subset of these metrics have been validated as indicators of the understandability of quantum circuits. Finally, a prototype tool capable of automatically calculating the proposed metrics has been described.

After this first step, there are several challenges on which we will focus our efforts. The first will obviously consist of future experimental replications to endorse the conclusions obtained.

Also in the future, it is considered interesting to develop refactoring techniques for quantum circuits that will allow us to improve their understandability in any new improved and equivalent version that maintains all the original functionality.

Finally, as stated in the introduction, we consider it crucial to carry out an in-depth study of the quality of quantum annealing systems.

Acknowledgments The authors want to sincerely thank Sergio Jiménez Fernández, who gave crucial feedback for improving the experimental materials.

This work was partially funded by the QHealth: Quantum Pharmacogenomics Applied to Aging project (EXP 00135977/MIG-20201059) by the 2020 CDTI Missions Program (Center for the Development of Industrial Technology of the Ministry of Science and Innovation of Spain), the AETHER-UCLM project: A smart data holistic approach for context-aware data analytics focused on Quality and Security project (Ministry of Science and Innovation of Spain, PID2020-112540RB-C42), and the QSERV project: Quantum Software Quality Assurance and Testing (Ministry of Science and Innovation of Spain & FEDER, PID2021-124054OB-C32).

Appendix. Example of Experimental Material

See Fig. 12.

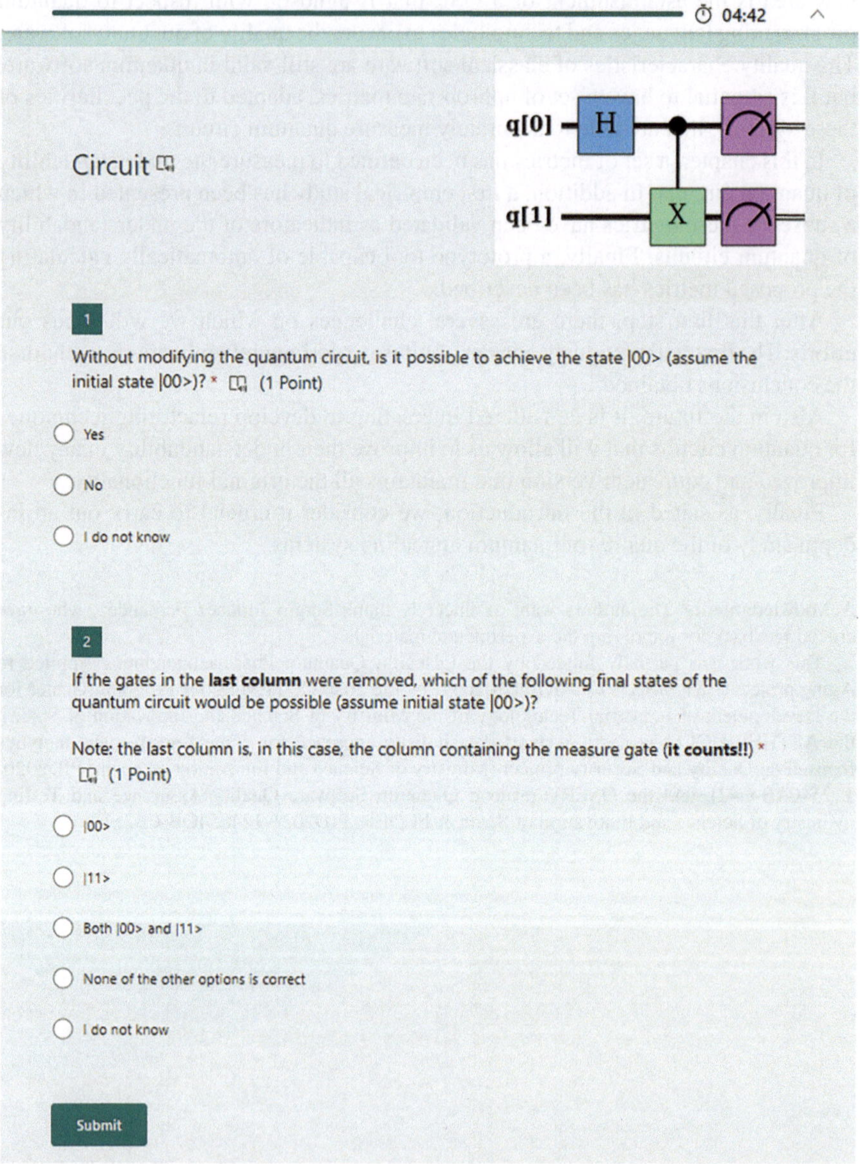

04:42

Circuit

q[0] H

q[1] X

1

Without modifying the quantum circuit, is it possible to achieve the state |00> (assume the initial state |00>)? * (1 Point)

- Yes
- No
- I do not know

2

If the gates in the **last column** were removed, which of the following final states of the quantum circuit would be possible (assume initial state |00>)?

Note: the last column is, in this case, the column containing the measure gate (**it counts!!**) * (1 Point)

- |00>
- |11>
- Both |00> and |11>
- None of the other options is correct
- I do not know

Submit

Fig. 12 Experimental materials: Part of a questionnaire

References

1. Barthe, G., Hsu, J., Ying, M., Yu, N., Zhou, L.: Relational proofs for quantum programs. POPL (2020). https://doi.org/10.1145/3371089
2. Bishop, L., Bravyi, S., Cross, A., Gambetta, J., Smolin, J.: Quantum volume (2017). https://storageconsortium.de/content/sites/default/files/quantum-volumehp08co1vbo0cc8fr.pdf
3. Breiman, L., Friedman, J., Stone, C.J., Olshen, R.A.: Classification and Regression Trees. Taylor & Francis (1984). https://doi.org/10.1201/9781315139470
4. Breiman, L.: Random forests. Mach. Learn. (2001). https://doi.org/10.1023/A:1010933404324
5. Burgholzer, L., Wille, R.: Advanced Equivalence Checking for Quantum Circuits (2020). https://doi.org/10.48550/arXiv.2004.08420
6. Cartiere, C.R.: Formal Quantum Software Engineering: Introducing the Formal Methods of Software Engineering to Quantum Computing. QSET (2021). https://doi.org/10.13140/RG.2.2.26157.10725/2
7. Chareton, C., Bardin, S., Bobot, F., Perrelle, V., Valiron, B.: Toward certified quantum programming (2020). https://doi.org/10.48550/arXiv.2003.05841
8. Cruz-Lemus, J.A., Maes, A., Genero, M., Poels, G., Piattini, M.: The impact of structural complexity on the understandability of UML statechart diagrams. Inf. Sci. (2010). https://doi.org/10.1016/j.ins.2010.01.026
9. Cruz-Lemus, J.A., Marcelo, L.A., Piattini, M.: Towards a set of metrics for quantum circuits understandability. QUATIC (2021). https://doi.org/10.1007/978-3-030-85347-1_18
10. Genero, M., Piattini, M., Calero, C. A survey of metrics for UML class diagrams. J. Object Technol. (2005). https://doi.org/10.5381/jot.2005.4.9.a1
11. Genero, M., Piattini, M., Calero, C.: Metrics for Software Conceptual Models. Imperial College Press (2005). https://doi.org/10.1142/P359
12. Genero, M., Piattini, M., Chaudron, M.: Quality of UML models. Inf. Soft. Technol (2009). https://doi.org/10.1016/j.infsof.2009.04.006
13. Grumbling, E., Horowitz, M.: Quantum Computing Progress and Prospects. The National Academies Press, Washington DC (2019)
14. EQF.: Strategic Research Agenda. European Quantum Flagship. February (2020)
15. Gheorghiu, A., Kapourniotis, T., Kashefi, E.: Verification of quantum computation: An overview of existing approaches. Theory Comput. Sys. (2018). https://doi.org/10.48550/arXiv.1709.06984
16. ISO/IEC 25010.: Software Engineering - Systems and Software Quality Requirements and Evaluation (SQuaRE) – System and Software quality models. International Organization for Standardization, Geneva (2011)
17. Maslov, D., Miller, M.: Comparison of the cost metrics through investigation of the relation between optimal NCV and optimal NCT three-qubit reversible circuits. IET Comput. Digit. Tech. (2007). https://doi.org/10.1049/iet-cdt:20060070
18. Pérez-Delgado, C., Perez-Gonzalez, H.: Towards a quantum software modeling language. Q-SE (2020). https://doi.org/10.48550/arXiv.2006.16690
19. Piattini, M., Peterssen, G., Pérez-Castillo, R., Hevia, J.L., et al.: The Talavera Manifesto for Quantum Software Engineering and Programming. QANSWER (2020). http://ceur-ws.org/Vol-2561/paper0.pdf
20. Piattini, M., Serrano, M., Pérez-Castillo, R., Peterssen, G., Hevia J.L.: Towards a Quantum Software Engineering. IT Prof. (2021). https://doi.org/10.1109/MITP.2020.3019522
21. Preskill, J.: Quantum Computing in the NISQ era and beyond. Quantum (2018). https://doi.org/10.22331/q-2018-08-06-79
22. Rand, R., Paykin, J., Zdancewic, S.: QWIRE practice: formal verification of quantum circuits. EPTCS **266**, (2018). https://doi.org/10.4204/EPTCS.266.8
23. Rand, R.: Research Statement: Languages, Verification and Compilation for the Quantum Era (2020). http://www.cs.umd.edu/~rrand/Research_Statement.pdf

24. Resch, S., Karpuzcu, U.R.: Quantum Computing: An Overview Across the System. Stack (2019). https://doi.org/10.48550/arXiv.1905.07240

25. Rieffel, E., Polak, W.: Quantum Computing: A Gentle Introduction. The MIT Press (2014)

26. Serrano, M., Trujillo, J., Calero, C., Piattini, M.: Metrics for data warehouse conceptual models understandability. Inf. Soft. Technol. (2007). https://doi.org/10.1016/j.infsof.2006.09.008

27. Sicilia, M., Sánchez-Alonso, S., Mora-Cantallops, M., García-Barriocanal, E.: On the source code structure of quantum code: Insights from q# and qdk. QUATIC (2020). https://doi.org/10.1007/978-3-030-58793-2_24

28. Sodhi, B., Kapur, R.: Quantum Computing Platforms: Assessing Impact on Quality Attributes and SDLC Activities. ICSA (2021). https://doi.org/10.48550/arXiv.2104.14261

29. Thapliyal, H., Muñoz-Coreas, E.: Design of Quantum Computing Circuits. IT Prof. (2019). https://doi.org/10.1109/MITP.2019.2943134

30. Wohlin, C., Runeson, P., Höst, M., Ohlsson, M.C., Regnell, B.: Experimentation in Software Engineering. Springer (2012). https://doi.org/10.1007/978-3-642-29044-2

31. Zhao, J.: Some size and structure metrics for quantum software. Q-SE (2020). https://doi.org/10.48550/arXiv.2103.08815

Quantum Software Ecosystem Design

Achim Basermann ⓘ, Michael Epping ⓘ, Benedikt Fauseweh ⓘ,
Michael Felderer ⓘ, Elisabeth Lobe ⓘ, Melven Röhrig-Zöllner ⓘ,
Gary Schmiedinghoff ⓘ, Peter K. Schuhmacher ⓘ, Yoshinta Setyawati ⓘ,
and Alexander Weinert ⓘ

Abstract The rapid advancements in quantum computing necessitate a scientific
and rigorous approach to the construction of a corresponding software ecosystem,
a topic underexplored and primed for systematic investigation. This chapter takes
an important step in this direction. It presents scientific considerations essential for
building a quantum software ecosystem that makes quantum computing available
for scientific and industrial problem-solving. Central to this discourse is the concept
of hardware–software co-design, which fosters a bidirectional feedback loop from
the application layer at the top of the software stack down to the hardware.
This approach begins with compilers and low-level software that are specifically
designed to align with the unique specifications and constraints of the quantum
processor, proceeds with algorithms developed with a clear understanding of
underlying hardware and computational model features, and extends to applications that effectively leverage the capabilities to achieve a quantum advantage.
We analyze the ecosystem from two critical perspectives: the conceptual view,
focusing on theoretical foundations, and the technical infrastructure, addressing
practical implementations around real quantum devices necessary for a functional
ecosystem. This approach ensures that the focus is toward promising applications
with optimized algorithm–circuit synergy, while ensuring a user-friendly design, an
effective data management, and an overall orchestration. This chapter thus offers a
guide to the essential concepts and practical strategies necessary for developing a
scientifically grounded quantum software ecosystem.

Keywords Quantum computing · Software ecosystem · Hardware–software
co-design · Software engineering

A. Basermann · M. Epping · B. Fauseweh · M. Felderer · E. Lobe (✉) · M. Röhrig-Zöllner · G.
Schmiedinghoff · P. K. Schuhmacher · Y. Setyawati · A. Weinert
Institute of Software Technology, German Aerospace Center (DLR), Cologne, Germany
e-mail: elisabeth.lobe@dlr.de

I. Exman et al. (eds.), *Quantum Software*,
https://doi.org/10.1007/978-3-031-64136-7_7

143

1 Introduction

Over the past few decades, quantum computing has steadily garnered attention owing to its potentially transformative applications in various fields including cryptography [1], material science [2], linear algebra [3], and combinatorial optimization [4], among others. The possibility to vastly improve computational efficiencies in solving certain classes of problems, compared to classical computers, has driven significant interest and investment in quantum computing technologies from both the scientific community and industry.

In recent years the field has reached a new level of maturity, characterized by the development of more stable qubit systems and increased gate fidelities [5]. The emergence of quantum hardware platforms from academia and industry has underlined the significant strides made in this direction, creating a foundation for more advanced research and practical explorations in quantum computing [6]. However, it must be acknowledged that while substantial, these advancements are but the precursors to a fully fault-tolerant quantum computing potential.

Despite the progress, the current era of noisy intermediate-scale quantum (NISQ) devices [7] presents significant challenges, including limited qubit connectivity, low coherence times, and gate cross-talk. Moreover, the reliable physical fabrication of these devices, especially on an industrial scale, involves considerable hurdles: ensuring the purity of materials, achieving the precise alignment of nanostructures, and maintaining the ultra-low temperatures necessary for operation present ongoing challenges. Another problem is our limited understanding concerning the underlying principles of quantum algorithms, with a yet limited selection of algorithmic building blocks available, like the quantum Fourier transformation and the amplitude amplification. The development of a diverse and comprehensive portfolio of high-level algorithms is central to advancing the quantum computing field.

These factors naturally lead to the question: What is necessary to advance the field of quantum algorithms and how can we obtain meaningful results from these near-term quantum devices given the existing limitations? It is evident that, in the NISQ era, the fruitful utilization of quantum devices necessitates approaches that can effectively navigate the noise and errors inherent to current hardware.

In answer to this central question, we propose the necessity of creating an ecosystem that uses an interdisciplinary approach grounded in the principle of hardware–software co-design. This ecosystem requires the systematic development in software encompassing applications, algorithms, and compilers, and a robust technical infrastructure that is precisely aligned with the intricacies of existing and swiftly advancing quantum hardware. By establishing a framework where software development is intricately linked with hardware evolution, we aim to maximize the utility of quantum computing in its current NISQ stage and beyond. This approach does not exclude but rather complements hardware-agnostic abstractions that allow for more generic software development independently of the specific hardware.

In our view, a quantum software ecosystem comprehends all aspects in and around software designed for quantum computers, e.g., novel quantum algorithms designed for specific devices, optimized compilers, pre- and post-processing tools for results from quantum computations, and the technical integration into existing high-performance computing (HPC) environments. It includes the whole path from user perspective over access to actual hardware and, reversely, from the embedded hardware access to the general availability for different end users.

In this review we first describe a potential vision, how such a quantum software ecosystem interfaces with the potential end users and with the quantum hardware, in Sect. 2. We then analyze the requirements for an efficient ecosystem from the conceptual view, focusing on abstract requirements and methods, in Sect. 3. In Sect. 4 we are concerned with the technical implementation of such an ecosystem, and finally in Sect. 5 we give a concise conclusion and an outlook for the potential of such a scientifically constructed software ecosystem.

2 Quantum Computing Perspective

Future applications of quantum algorithms have the potential to provide novel efficient solutions in various sectors. This includes breakthroughs in material science, such as new superconductors or ultrafast memory, solutions for industrial size planning problems, applications in cryptography, or the design of new and more efficient drugs. In the following section we describe how a quantum software ecosystem supports these aims, by interfacing the applications with the quantum devices in a comprehensive and user-centered way.

2.1 Achieving the Vision Through the Quantum Software Ecosystem

As quantum computers continue to develop, it is plausible to predict a scenario where stakeholders, from academic researchers to industrial partners, gain access to quantum computational capabilities through cloud platforms. While such cloud access to quantum devices is already available for a limited number of platforms, the process is not yet streamlined and has various drawbacks due to the quantum device imperfections. However, such cloud-based access simplifies the challenges associated with operating and using quantum hardware, making it more feasible for a wider range of users.

At the heart of such a scenario, specialized quantum algorithms, devised by algorithmic developers, will be processed. In order to make these algorithms compatible with quantum hardware, specialized compilers, developed by experts in quantum software, will be crucial. These compilers will be responsible for translating high-level quantum logic into specific instructions, tailored for the distinct hardware platforms created by quantum hardware designers. Facilitating this process is the core responsibility of the quantum software ecosystem.

Furthermore, an integral component of this ecosystem will be the integration of quantum computers with classical systems. Fast embedded classical computers will process quantum-classical feedback algorithms within the coherence time of the quantum computer, especially those related to error correction. Additionally, HPC frameworks will be instrumental for algorithms that use parameterized quantum circuits, as these often require intensive computations to optimize parameters in tandem with quantum processors.

Another component shaping this ecosystem is the principle of hardware–software co-design. In this paradigm, not only is software adapted to optimally exploit the capabilities of the underlying quantum hardware, but the design of future quantum processors is also influenced by application-driven requirements. This bidirectional feedback ensures that hardware evolution remains attuned to the practical needs and challenges posed by real-world quantum applications. By closely intertwining the development processes of both hardware and software, the co-design approach seeks to accelerate the maturation and optimization of the quantum computing landscape.

After the computations are completed, users will receive their results via the same cloud interface. This closed-loop system aims to streamline the process of quantum computing, from input to result retrieval, while maximizing efficiency and user accessibility. The sustainability and success of this vision are inherently tied to the collaborative effort between quantum algorithm developers, compiler specialists, hardware builders, software engineers, and the users themselves.

2.2 Interested Parties and Their Requirements

Research and development in Quantum computing (QC) have accelerated dramatically in recent years. Due to its potential, efforts in QC have attracted different parties. They are classified as primary and secondary stakeholders. Primary stakeholders are stakeholders that directly contribute to the development of quantum computing as shown in Fig. 1.

1. End users: End users are individuals or organizations from different fields that use or adopt QC for various purposes, e.g., to speed up simulations for electric car batteries, to predict financial risk in insurance companies, or to optimize antenna patterns in radar technology. They are influenced by design and functionality features provided by the QC software researchers and the QC hardware developers. End users' expectations, values, and requirements must be considered to guarantee that the technology is effective and benefits them. The end users may not know how to write the algorithm and formulate the problem as a quantum program, but they can express it mathematically and are capable of post-processing the result of the computation as shown on the left panel of Fig. 1.

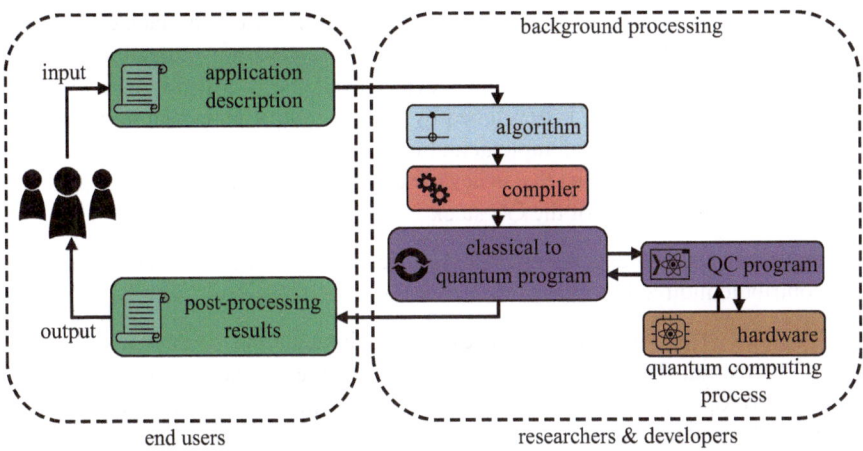

Fig. 1 Schematic diagram of the workflow and the stakeholders that directly use and develop quantum computing technologies

2. Researchers and developers: They are individuals and organizations that are directly involved in the development of and research on QC. Currently, research institutes and universities are the primary sources of this group, but also more and more large companies and start-ups participate in the development of QC. These vendors contribute significantly to the advancement of QC, for example, by developing hardware and software packages for industry and research institutions. Their role is shown on the right panel of Fig. 1 and includes algorithmic problem descriptions, compilation, software, and hardware development, such that the produced results can be post-processed and returned back to the end users. Hence, their work influences the design and development of technology; at the same time they must align with the goals of other stakeholders.

   (a) Software developers: These include private companies or research institutions that develop novel quantum algorithms, compilation schemes, and software interfaces between algorithmic solutions and hardware for QC. They also explore novel quantum computing architectures and investigate promising use cases for QC. Due to the noisy nature of current devices, the development has to take the low-level hardware properties into account to ensure optimal algorithm execution leading to unique design paradigms. In this context, it is important to have a clear and precise understanding of the performance of components and of the impact of physical quantum noise, which can be characterized by low-level benchmarks.

   (b) Hardware designers: The development of physical quantum computers is crucial. In many cases, hardware advancement is the bottleneck in the field of QC. Quantum computers are particularly sensitive to noise and errors caused by interactions with their surroundings. This can lead to an accumulation of errors, lowering computation quality. Thus, improving the fidelity of the hardware operations is critical, even though noise can be tackled to some extent in software as well (see Sect. 3.7). Hardware manufacturers have a natural interest in making their devices available to a wide range of users. Some QC hardware is developed by private companies which might restrict information about the implementation details and restrict access to low-level control features, a fact that needs to be considered when developing software at the lower layers of the QC stack.

Secondary stakeholders are interested parties who can influence the future of QC but contribute indirectly to the workflow in Fig. 1.

1. Suppliers: They provide the necessary equipment and spare parts to build QC hardware. These stakeholders should consider requests from researchers and developers, whose involvement can shape the design and availability of technology. Semiconductor and chip manufacturers are two examples of this stakeholder group. The term "enabling technologies" is used in the context of QC to denote the development of products and enhanced manufacturing techniques that are not directly related to QC itself but will facilitate breakthroughs in QC and other fields. Therefore the suppliers play a crucial role in advancing the ecosystem.

2. Regulators and policymakers: They are responsible for the community's well-being and ensure that the developed technology boosts innovation. These governmental entities are also responsible for ensuring that QC aligns with society's values and needs, for example by motivating the development of QC to strengthen the economy and industrial advancement. Hence, they create laws and regulations for the development and use of QC. In many situations, they provide state funding for research and development and encourage enterprises to foster the growth of QC.

3. Investors: These are private funding sources that support research and development of QC. Investors are interested in the development of QC and expect a return on investment in the future. Investment in QC has increased significantly from US$93.5 million in 2015 to US$1.02 billion in 2021 globally [8]. Most investments are made for hardware, but there are also deals for software promising potential applications in the future.

4. Media: Media also play a significant role in the advancement of QC technology. They shape public opinion, hence raising awareness of QC development and its impact on society. They also convey the basic principles of this technology to the general public. Not only the potential, but also the growth of research, technology, startups, and investment is communicated through media.

Only the collaborative effort between all of these stakeholders will enable quantum computing to be established as a well-founded technology, where the quantum software ecosystem should support the communication and form the baseline for further advancements.

Fig. 2 Conceptual stack of the components necessary to solve problems using QC

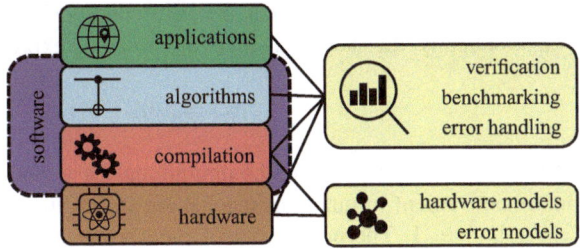

3   Conceptual View

In this section, we examine the quantum software ecosystem from a more theoretical viewpoint, focusing on conceptually important ideas and abstracted QC concepts, which are the main area of scientific research on QC. This conceptual view includes various topics, as shown in Fig. 2.

At the top of this "stack," i.e., on the side of the user, is the application or problem that needs to be solved, and on the bottom of the stack lies the hardware that executes the necessary QC steps. Those ends are connected by the software, including various algorithms and compilation schemes. In order to attain the correct results, it is necessary to handle the noise-induced errors emerging during the computation, which requires accurate error models for the hardware. One major challenge is the verification of the various parts of this stack. In the following, we look at each part of this stack and its role in the quantum software ecosystem.

3.1   Computational Paradigms

The development of a functional quantum computer is a central research goal these days. There exist different paradigms on how such a machine could look even on a conceptual level. In this section, we first review the basic principles of quantum mechanics on which all these quantum computing paradigms rely. Afterwards, we discuss the most prominent ones, namely the gate-based model and adiabatic quantum computation. Finally, we briefly mention a few alternatives.

3.1.1   Foundations of Quantum Computing

In this section, we outline the phenomenology that builds the foundation of QC without elucidating the rich mathematical framework of quantum mechanics that can be found in many textbooks [9, 10].

A quantum bit, or qubit for short, is a direct generalization of a classical bit with two additional, inherently quantum-mechanical properties: superposition and entanglement with other qubits. While a classical bit can only take one of the two states 0 and 1, a qubit can be in a superposition of both at the same time. Mathematically, the state of a single qubit can be expressed as

$$|\psi\rangle = a|0\rangle + b|1\rangle, \tag{1}$$

where $|0\rangle$ and $|1\rangle$ denote the computational basis states written in Dirac notation that is convenient in quantum mechanics and a and b are complex numbers with $|a|^2 + |b|^2 = 1$. The probability of measuring the state $|0\rangle$, i.e., a bit 0, is given by $|a|^2$ and analogously for $|1\rangle$ by $|b|^2$. After measurement, the state of the qubit collapses to only the parts in agreement with the measurement outcome, i.e., $|\psi_0\rangle = |0\rangle$ or $|\psi_1\rangle = |1\rangle$.

Since a and b are complex numbers, they each contain a phase ($a = |a|e^{i\varphi_a}$). In quantum mechanics, only the phase difference $\varphi = \varphi_b - \varphi_a$ is relevant; hence the single-qubit state can be fully expressed by one probability and the relative phase, or equally by two angles. Thus, any single-qubit state can be visualized as a unit vector

$$|\psi\rangle = \begin{pmatrix} \sin(\theta)\cos(\varphi) \\ \sin(\theta)\sin(\varphi) \\ \cos(\theta) \end{pmatrix} \tag{2}$$

on the Bloch sphere, which is depicted in Fig. 3. This visualization is also useful to understand the concept of the computational basis: any two opposite points on the Bloch sphere can be chosen as the computational basis states $|0\rangle$ and $|1\rangle$ and changing the basis is equivalent to rotating the qubit state.

A superposition state needs to be initialized using classical information and after performing a measurement collapses to one of these two states, i.e., back to a classical bit. Therefore, the input and output are always restricted to classical bits, but during the computation the full space of superpositions can be exploited. It needs to be stressed that while a register of N classical bits can describe one of 2^N different states at a time, an N-qubit register can describe any state in a

Fig. 3 Visualization of an arbitrary qubit state called the Bloch sphere. The computational basis states $|0\rangle$ and $|1\rangle$ are mapped to the north pole and the south pole respectively. A general state $|\psi\rangle$ is fully determined by the angles θ and φ. Any quantum gate on a single qubit corresponds to a rotation of the state on that sphere. Graphic taken from [11]

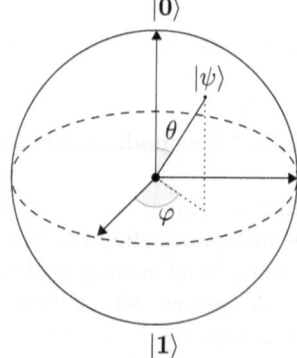

continuous region of a 2^N-dimensional vector space. As a consequence, qubits are tremendously more expressive than bits. Since each measurement can change the qubit state $|\psi\rangle$, consecutive measurements of the same qubit in different bases do not yield additional information, unless one prepares $|\psi\rangle$ anew for each measurement.

The second important property of qubits, quantum entanglement, is the ability of multiple qubits to interfere with one another such that their probabilities become correlated in a way that is not possible for classical bits. For instance, two qubits can be entangled in the state $|\psi\rangle = a|00\rangle + b|11\rangle$. When measuring the state of one of the qubits, the result automatically determines the state of the other qubit in the same computational basis, since, e.g., finding $|0\rangle$ for the first qubit collapses the full state to $|\psi_0\rangle = |00\rangle$.

It is noteworthy that any computation on the full qubit state $|\psi\rangle$ acts on all superposed states at the same time, e.g., on both $|00\rangle$ and $|11\rangle$. This is utilized by many powerful quantum algorithms that perform computations using precisely choreographed patterns of interference between superpositions of bit strings, which together with quantum entanglement realize the quantum computational efficiency. One needs to remember that measuring all qubits in a register collapses the carefully computed quantum state to a classical bit string, so care must be taken to prepare the final quantum state in a way that maximizes the probability of measuring the bit string that contains the relevant computational result.

Any natural or artificial quantum mechanical two-level system could in principle serve as a qubit, making the number of possible realizations incredible large. However, for fault tolerance a hardware platform needs at least to satisfy the DiVincenzo criteria [12]. It is necessary to have

1. A scalable physical system with well-characterized qubits
2. The ability to initialize the state of the qubits to a simple state
3. Long relevant coherence times
4. A universal set of gates
5. A qubit-specific measurement capability

These qualitative criteria point out immediately why building a functional quantum computer remains a challenge to date: on the one hand, satisfying criterion 3 requires decoupling the quantum system from any environmental disturbances. On the other hand, criteria 2, 4, and 5 demand direct physical access to the system and, therefore it is necessary to couple it at least to its measurement apparatus and some control electronics. This ambivalence makes quantum computers inherently error prone. As of now, no quantum system exists that fulfills all criteria equally, but recent quantum hardware has reached a level of maturity that allows for small-scale quantum computations. Platforms that have reached this level are dubbed NISQ devices.

3.1.2 Gate-Based Quantum Computing

In this section, we review the paradigm of gate-based quantum computing, which was the first quantum computing paradigm to be proposed [10]. Here, a quantum gate denotes the analog of a logical gate in classical computing. In the latter, there are only two possible gates on a single bit, namely the identity and the negation. By contrast, any operation corresponding to a rotation on the Bloch sphere, shown in Fig. 3, represents a valid quantum gate on a single qubit. Therefore, the set of valid quantum gates is uncountable even for that single qubit.

In order to realize an actually useful quantum computer, it does not suffice to consider single-qubit rotations. Instead, we need an N-qubit register, and we need to be able to apply multi-qubit gates on any set of qubits. Fortuitously, it turns out to be sufficient to have access to just a single maximally entangling two-qubit gate and to arbitrary single-qubit rotations to achieve universality [13]. In other words, any quantum gate applied to the N-qubit register can be realized as a sequence of these elementary gates. There are multiple universal gate sets. In many cases the QC hardware provides a basic set of gates, which ideally is universal.

One important consequence of quantum mechanical dynamics is that valid quantum gates must be unitary, i.e., the gate operations are represented by unitary matrices, which are reversible. Therefore, classical logic gates like the AND-gate, which has two input bits and one output bit, cannot be implemented directly on qubits without a second output qubit to ensure reversibility. Another consequence is that it is not possible to fully clone arbitrary qubit states, turning error correction by redundancy into a challenging prospect.

A sequence of quantum gates that solves a computational task composes a quantum algorithm. Quantum circuit diagrams have become established as a mode of representation, where the individual qubits usually correspond to horizontal lines on which gate operations are drawn (time runs from left to right) [10]. An example can be seen in Fig. 4.

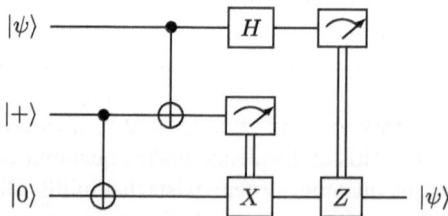

Fig. 4 An example of a circuit diagram, the most common way to represent quantum programs today. Horizontal lines correspond to qubits. Gates are represented by special symbols or boxes with labels. Double lines indicate classical information, which can represent results of the circuit. But they can also be used to condition the application of gates on measurement results, a technique called feed-forward

3.1.3   Adiabatic Quantum Computation and Quantum Annealing

Around 2000, a new computational concept based on quantum mechanical principles was developed, the adiabatic quantum computation (AQC) [14]. The underlying adiabatic theorem is a fundamental result in quantum mechanics, originally formulated in [15]. The AQC paradigm is different to the "conventional" quantum computing in the way that it does not provide a universal programmability straightforwardly in terms of implementing quantum gates to form quantum circuits. It rather represents a single algorithm whose input data can be varied. Nevertheless, the authors of [16] and [17] have shown that QC and AQC are equivalent in the sense that each can efficiently simulate the other. We briefly summarize the main background of AQC here, but for a more detailed review, we refer the reader to [18].

Given two related quantum systems, the rapid transfer from one to another might cause the system to change its state from their lowest-energy state, i.e., the ground state. However, by applying an adiabatic evolution process instead, which means a sufficiently slow transformation according to the adiabatic theorem, the system can remain in its instantaneous ground state with high probability. By encoding a mathematical optimization problem in the target quantum system, where the energy states represent the feasible solutions, we could thus obtain the minimal solution to the problem.

The first company that strived to build quantum systems based on AQC and made them commercially available was D-Wave Systems Inc. They implement the transverse field Ising model [19, 20], established by Ernst Ising, using superconducting loops to form qubits in a quantum system [21]. A current flow induces a magnetic flux in these loops, pointing either up or down or being in a superposition of both. Due to couplings of the loops by joints, the qubits interact with each other pairwise, where the strengths of the interactions can be adjusted with external magnetic fields. This way we can encode a quadratic function over binary variables, with linear and quadratic terms weighted according to the magnetic field strength. Finding the solution for such a quadratic unconstrained binary optimization (QUBO) problem is hard on classical computers. More precisely, its corresponding decision problem belongs to the class of NP-hard problems. This also means it relates to a large number of other problems, which can easily be transferred into a QUBO and therefore solved with these machines, at least in theory.

Although empirical studies like [22] provide hints that the output of the devices is in general close to the optimal solution, it is, however, not guaranteed to be achieved, nor is the success probability known in advance. Several physical restrictions prevent the realization of the theoretical concept of the adiabatic theorem, which only applies if ideal conditions prevail. One obstacle is, for instance, the shielding against environmental noise, which is never entirely achieved. Therefore, the term quantum annealing (QA) has been established, in reference to the classical heuristic simulated annealing, to distinguish the theoretical concept from the heuristic process performed by the corresponding devices [23]. In general, quantum annealing is repeated several times with the same configuration to obtain a sample set of solutions, and from those the best one is extracted.

3.1.4 Others

The gate-based model and quantum annealing are without question the leading quantum computing paradigms. However, there exist alternative paradigms that turn out to be computationally equivalent to these mainstream approaches. For example, a paradigm called one-way quantum computing is pursued in the context of photonic quantum computers [24]. As photons hardly interact in nature, they can have enormous coherence times (one detects coherent photons from other stars regularly), but it is a challenge to perform two-qubit gates between them for the same reason. In order to circumvent this issue, an elegant idea that relies on the Knill-Laflamme-Milburn proposal [25] is to prepare all entanglement non-deterministically first. If successful, then the computation is proceeded by measurements and single-qubit rotations only, i.e., by avoiding any further interaction [26]. However, functional one-way quantum computing has not been demonstrated yet.

Another universal approach for quantum computation is quantum random walks, or short quantum walks, a quantum mechanical analog to the classical random walk [27, 28, 29, 30, 31]. They can either be discrete-time [32] or continuous-time [33], and they are studied in the context of machine learning [34, 35] and photosynthesis [36]. Both versions can again be extended to non-unitary evolution by a joint generalization of quantum and classical random walks, called quantum stochastic walks [37, 38, 39]. In contrast to the completely coherent quantum walk, quantum stochastic walks give rise to a directed evolution.

3.2 Hardware

In 1936, Alan Turing proposed a conceptual blueprint for a universally programmable computer [40]. This event became the child birth of modern computer science. However, as the direct physical implementation of the "Turing machine" would be impractical, a huge variety of different hardware platforms were used to realize different computational models. This early time of modern computer science came to a sudden end with the invention of the transistor [41]. Since then, the development of classical computers has relied on the same key building blocks but miniaturizing them.

In close analogy to these early days of classical computing, there exists a huge variety of candidates for quantum computing hardware—the current status of quantum computer development resembles the construction of the Z3 by Konrad Zuse rather than building modern HPC systems. A rather broad overview of hardware platforms, including a classification with respect to the state of development,[1] can be found in [42]. In the following, we focus on the most developed platforms according to this study, which are depicted in Fig. 5.

---

[1] Due to the status of the year 2020.

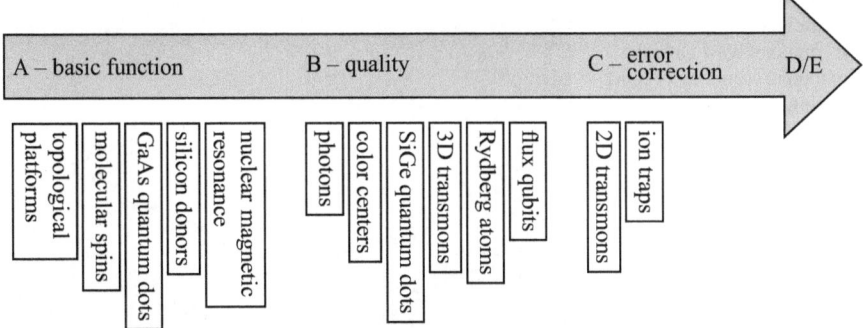

Fig. 5 State of development of different hardware platforms according to [42]. In this study, the platforms are classified into five different levels from satisfying the DiVincenco criteria (level A), to demonstration of high fidelities (level B), to the demonstration of quantum error correction (level C). The levels D (execution of fault-tolerant operations) and E (running fault-tolerant algorithms) have not been achieved by any platform so far

Generally speaking, there are two different classes of qubit candidates: natural quantum systems like neutral atoms, ions, or photons [25, 43, 44, 45], and artificial quantum systems like superconducting circuits or other solid state architectures [46, 47, 48, 49]. The state-of-the-art leading hardware platforms are based on trapped ions and planar transmons; the latter is a specific version of superconducting circuits. These platforms achieved the level of development C in Fig. 5, i.e., they allow for the demonstration of quantum error correction.

Superconducting integrated circuits are viewed as one of the most promising hardware candidates [50]. These circuits are put onto a chip that needs to be cooled to cryogenic temperatures, i.e., a few tens of mK, and they are controlled with electromagnetic fields in the microwave range. Even for this specific architecture, there is a variety of different qubit designs. However, all these designs share the same key ingredient, namely the Josephson junction [51]. This is a nonlinear element leading to a non-equidistant energy spectrum of the circuit. This property is crucial to address two quantum states as the computational states individually.

There are two mainstream types of superconducting qubits, i.e., charge qubit-[52, 53, 54] and flux qubit [55, 56, 57]-derived designs. To date, the primary representative of charge-derived qubits is the planar transmon, due to its suppressed sensitivity against charge noise at the cost of small anharmonicities in the level splittings [54, 58]. It operates at a sweet spot with rather long coherence times and a good reproducability of the qubits. The main benefit of planar transmons is their rather straightforward scaling in qubit numbers; the challenge here is to maintain the controllability of the individual qubits and to keep high-fidelity operations when scaling up. Transmons are typically considered for implementing gate-based quantum computing. One draft of a corresponding chip is shown in Fig. 6, where the planar transmons are arranged in a two-dimensional square lattice with nearest-

Fig. 6 Sketch of the
KQCircuits chip design by
the company IQM Quantum
Computers (courtesy of IQM
Quantum Computers)

neighbor interactions. Control and readout lines are connected to the qubits from
below.

Flux qubits consist of superconducting loops that are interrupted by an (effectively) odd number of Josephson junctions. Their computational states are encoded
in the magnetic fluxes that are induced by clockwise and anticlockwise circulating
currents. By design, they share a lot of similarities to superconducting quantum
interference devices (SQUIDs) [59]. Flux qubits can be coupled easily via mutual
induction with coupling constants up to ultra-strong coupling if needed. This makes
them an auspicious candidate for quantum annealing, and possibly for specific
quantum simulation applications. In comparison to planar transmons, flux qubits
are easier to couple, but it is harder to reproduce them reliably.

Apart from technical challenges, one of the main drawbacks of superconducting
qubits is their limited connectivity: only nearest neighbors are directly coupled and
hence two-qubit gates can only be applied between them directly. If a gate-based
quantum algorithm needs gates between qubits that are not physically connected,
one needs to perform the desired logical gate by swapping the qubit state through the
intermediate qubits. This process produces a serious overhead in circuit depth. For
quantum annealing, the limited connectivity becomes even more serious, because
general optimization problems require strongly connected problem Hamiltonians.
Therefore, embedding the desired problem Hamiltonian on the actual hardware
becomes a nontrivial task [60]. Moreover, as superconducting qubits are artificially
made, every single qubit has slightly different parameters than the others, an issue
that needs to be tackled by optimal control theory [61].

With up to about 20 qubits, the best performing quantum computer is a chain
of isotopically pure ions in a linear Paul trap.[2] The ions are trapped in an ultrahigh
vacuum using electromagnetic fields in a quadrupole geometry such that they form
a one-dimensional crystal [62, 63]. No cryogenics are needed; the trap operates
at room temperature. In contrast to superconducting qubits, the ions in the trap

---

[2] Named after Nobel laureate Wolfgang Paul.

are coupled via the long-range Coulomb interaction, leading to a natural all-to-all connectivity of the qubits. In comparison to other hardware platforms, the relevant coherence times are high, and the gate quality is excellent.

Unfortunately, the design of the linear Paul trap does not allow for a scaling to large qubit numbers for two reasons. On the one hand, adding more and more ions into the trap deforms their arrangement; the ions start to form two-dimensional structures instead of a well-controlled chain. On the other hand, an effect called frequency crowding becomes more and more dominant, such that the system becomes uncontrollable [64]. Therefore, the main challenge for trap ion-based quantum computing is the scaling to larger qubit numbers. One ansatz is to combine several linear Paul traps via photonic links [65]. Here, the quantum information needs to be converted from the ions in the trap to photons that are transmitted through a fiber, and then it is converted back to the ions in another trap. This process makes quantum computing with trapped ions enormously slow, because every single conversion only succeeds with limited probability. A different strategy is to use two-dimensional surface traps instead of linear Paul traps [66]. Here, the second dimension is used to shuttle the ions during the computation to different zones on the chip, depending on their current purpose (performing a gate, readout, etc). In the gate zone, the surface trap mimics the linear Paul trap with its advantages locally. A photograph of such a surface trap is shown in Fig. 7. However, surface traps have not yet been able to demonstrate the same quality as linear Paul traps.

In this section, we discussed the benefits and drawbacks of the furthest developed hardware platforms to date, namely superconducting circuits and ion traps. However, as the field develops rapidly, other platforms may take over in the future. But even in this case, the substantial challenges to build functional quantum computers will probably remain during the coming decades [7]. Therefore, any near-term quantum software ecosystem needs to incorporate the specific hardware restrictions that are present or that are expected to remain in the near future. For example, one requires additional compilation techniques to run a desired quantum

Fig. 7 Photograph of the surface trap chip design by the company eleQtron (courtesy of eleQtron)

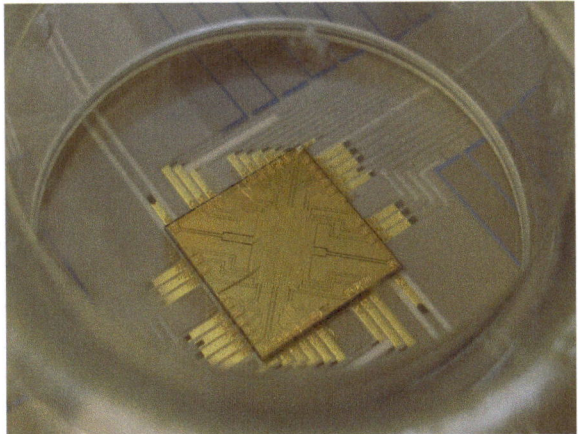

algorithm on a superconducting qubit platform due to its limited connectivity, as on ion-trap platforms with natural all-to-all connectivity. Conversely, if a given quantum algorithm can be easily embedded on the connectivity graph of the superconducting chip, then this platform might be preferential because of the larger qubit numbers that can be achieved. In the long term, as soon as universal fault-tolerant quantum computers are realized, the necessity to keep track of the specific hardware limitations by designing a quantum software ecosystem will become less and less important.

3.3 Applications

Quantum computers have enabled advancements in a range of applications, starting with well-established domains such as database search and factorization using Grover's and Shor's algorithms. These have a proven potential in enhancing search capabilities and disrupting traditional cryptographic methods, respectively, but require a level of fault tolerance not yet reached on quantum devices.

Beyond these utilities, quantum machine learning is emerging as a noteworthy area of application [67, 68], enabling advancements in categorization, learning tasks, and the solution for partial differential equations. However, it is on the intermediate timeline where quantum simulation and optimization are drawing heightened attention. Quantum simulation facilitates the study of quantum systems, promising more accurate modeling of atomic and chemical processes, with applications in material science, quantum chemistry, and drug design. In parallel, quantum optimization provides avenues for solving complex problems more efficiently, finding its relevance in logistics, finance, and more.

In the forthcoming sections, we narrow our focus on quantum simulation and optimization, as these represent the realms where quantum computing is expected to offer significant advantages in the near term.

3.3.1 Simulation

Digital quantum simulation (DQS) represents a notable application for future quantum computers, focusing on simulating quantum systems with universal quantum computers. Richard P. Feynman originally suggested this application [69], later formalized by Lloyd [2]. DQS is of particular significance for studying quantum materials like superconductors and topological insulators, which prove challenging for classical simulations.

Emergence, described as the rise of new system properties from the fundamental interactions of its components, has been evident in quantum phases and is directly connected to the existence of strong quantum fluctuations and entanglement. Traditionally, the examination of such phenomena relied on resource-intensive experiments, which explored only a limited range of parameters, including material composition and external electromagnetic fields. Theoretical modeling and simulation can significantly conserve resources and is pivotal for advancing material science. Yet, simulations of quantum models on conventional computers face challenges due to the exponential scaling with system size. Classical simulations on modern HPC hardware are capable of describing non-equilibrium dynamics in quantum dots [70], of 1D quantum systems [71], as well as 2D systems [72, 73], but with strong limitations in the simulatable system size.

DQS employs quantum computers to efficiently simulate quantum systems. However, the current state of DQS struggles to match the capabilities of conventional HPC. Advancements in the present NISQ hardware require innovative quantum algorithms like the variational quantum eigensolvers (VQEs) [74], which capitalize on the increased expressiveness of quantum computers [75]. Ongoing research is centered on assessing the strengths and weaknesses of various hardware platforms concerning their potential DQS applications [76].

3.3.2 Optimization

Optimization problems appear in all fields where resources are limited, for instance in engineering, economics, computer science, and many others. The development of efficient solution methods and answering the question as to whether these actually exist is the essential part of the research in mathematical optimization and complexity theory. A very important and well-studied class of problems are the NP-hard ones, which are, loosely speaking, those problems that cannot be solved efficiently using classical computation. This situation cannot be alleviated simply by increasing the computational resources of classical computers. This naturally calls for the exploration of different, more powerful computational models. And the hope is that quantum computation steps into the breach due to properties of superposition, entanglement, and quantum parallelism.

As explained in Sect. 3.1.3, quantum annealing is a tailored method to solve discrete optimization problems. Several studies have shown the practical feasibility of this approach in different research areas, e.g., for the optimization of flight routes [77], flight gate assignments [78], and satellite scheduling [79]. However, due to their heuristic nature, the actual practical advantage of the quantum annealers over dedicated classical approaches, including approximation algorithms and heuristics, is still under discussion.

Besides the optimization-tailored QA, also algorithms for the gate-based quantum computing concept have been developed, like quantum approximate optimization algorithm (QAOA) or Grover search, which we elaborate in the next section. However, due to currently too limited available resources, their performance on interesting industrial applications still needs to be evaluated in the future [80]. To investigate the capabilities of all such approaches systematically, they need to be integrated into a full software environment that allows for quickly formulating different applications and for benchmarking the results of the quantum devices against several classical approaches.

3.4   Algorithms

The application cases described in Sect. 3.3 can also, in principle, be solved on classical computers. In order to gain a speedup over these classical approaches by using quantum computers, efficient quantum algorithms are necessary. While many promising algorithms already exist, there is active work on expanding the existing toolbox. A quantum software ecosystem must provide a library of algorithms that end users can access and must also support the development of new algorithms for domain and quantum experts.

The development of novel quantum algorithms faces two main challenges: Currently, there is much less experience in realizing quantum algorithms as software than for classical algorithms, and in order for quantum algorithms to be viable, they need to provide a significant asymptotic speedup over existing classical algorithms. The following section provides a selection of important quantum algorithms, many of which provide super-polynomial speedup. A more extensive overview can be found in [81].

3.4.1   Powerful Algorithms for Fault-Tolerant Devices

Table 1 lists some of the most promising quantum algorithms [82], which are expected to provide a quantum advantage on fully fault-tolerant QC. One such algorithm is Shor's algorithm for the prime factorization of large integers with super-polynomial speedup compared to the classical counterpart. Shor's algorithm is based on the quantum Fourier transformation and connected to the more general class of hidden subgroup problems, which include e.g., discrete logarithms and Gauss sums. Grover's algorithm searches through an unsorted list with a polynomial speedup. The quantum phase estimation algorithm approximates eigenvalues of a given Hamiltonian. Furthermore, a quantum computer can efficiently perform quantum time evolutions and SLE can be solved with the algorithm by Harrow et al. [3]. A variety of other quantum algorithms, such as the Deutsch-Jozsa algorithm [83], the

Table 1 Examples of promising quantum algorithms for fault-tolerant QC

Algorithm	Application case	Complexity	Classical complexity
Shor	Prime factorization of integer with N bits	$\mathcal{O}(N^2 \log N)$	$\mathcal{O}(\exp(1.9N^{1/3} \times (\log N)^{2/3}))$
Quantum Fourier Transform	Fourier transform with N amplitudes	$\mathcal{O}((\log N)^2)$	$\mathcal{O}(N \log N)$
Grover	Unsorted search on N items	$\mathcal{O}(\sqrt{N})$	$\mathcal{O}(N)$
Quantum Phase Estimation	Eigenvalues of unitaries up to error ϵ	$\mathcal{O}(1/\epsilon)$	$\mathcal{O}(N^2)$
Harrow-Hassidim-Lloyd	Solving SLE with N eq. and condition number κ	$\mathcal{O}(\kappa^2 \log N)$	$\mathcal{O}(\kappa N)$

Table 2 Examples of promising quantum algorithms for NISQ devices

Algorithm	Application case	Complexity	Classical
VQE	Eigenenergies and -states	Heuristic, often $\mathcal{O}(N^p)$	$\mathcal{O}(e^N)$
QITE	Ground state preparation	For highly local Hamiltonians $\mathcal{O}(N^p)$	$\mathcal{O}(e^N)$
QAOA	Combinatorial optimization	Heuristic, potentially $\mathcal{O}(N^p)$	$\mathcal{O}(e^N)$

Bernstein-Vazirani algorithm [84], and the Simon algorithm [85], have been found as well, but won't be discussed here in detail.

3.4.2 Hybrid Algorithms for Noisy Intermediate Scale Devices

Fully fault-tolerant quantum computers are not expected to be built in the near future. Therefore, great effort is put into researching efficient algorithms for NISQ devices, where the focus lies more on achieving quantum advantage over classical devices than on the best asymptotic performance. Many of these algorithms are heuristic and an asymptotic speedup is expected in special cases [86]. Some promising approaches in this area are listed in Table 2.

One general strategy to bring useful quantum algorithms on NISQ devices is hybrid computation, where only the part of the problem that gains most from quantum hardware is solved on such, while the remaining problem is solved on a classical device. One example of this is variational quantum algorithms (VQAs), most famously VQEs [87]. The idea of VQAs is to use a parameterized circuit on the quantum processor to prepare highly entangled states in the exponentially large Hilbert space and perform measurements on them. The classical processor evaluates the measurement results and adapts the parameters of the quantum circuit in order to improve the result. For instance, VQEs minimize the energy to find the ground state. Various adaptions of this approach are being researched at the moment, such as searching for excited states by optimizing the energy to be in a certain range or by enforcing orthogonality to the ground state. Furthermore, ground states can be prepared efficiently for highly local Hamiltonians by using quantum imaginary time evolution (QITE) [88].

The QAOA [89] is used to solve combinatorial problems by encoding them as a Hamiltonian with bit strings as representations of the possible solutions. The QAOA applies time evolution of a mixer Hamiltonian and problem Hamiltonian in alternation to find the bit string that minimizes the problem Hamiltonian expectation value.

A central challenge with performing these optimization algorithms in polynomial time is the risk of converging to local minima. It is important to extend the scope of these algorithms and facilitate an infrastructure where a hybrid compiler (see Sect. 3.6) can efficiently select which parts of a given problem to solve on the quantum device with quantum speedup.

3.5 Software Engineering

The goal of software engineering is the efficient development of high-quality software through scientific methods and precise processes. In this context, we understand software to be a structured collection of program code, documentation, quality assurance measures, artifacts, and, where applicable, other data required to execute the programs. All software is written to perform specific tasks that can be described in the form of user stories: A user wants to achieve a goal with the software. The value of the software therefore lies in the efficient and reliable achievement of these goals.

Quantum software fits the above scheme just as well [90]. At this level of abstraction, the only difference is that quantum software contains parts that are executed on a quantum computer. As described above, quantum computers are particularly suitable for difficult problems, and the applications institutions, such as the German Aerospace Center (DLR),[3] are particularly interested in having a strong interdisciplinary character and will have a large scope. An efficient, structured approach and an integrated quality assurance strategy will therefore be essential in the near future.

In the following, we take a closer look at the aspects of software engineering where we recognize specific requirements of quantum computing or which, in our view, are particularly important in this context.

3.5.1 Requirements

A particular challenge in the development of software for quantum computers is the collection and specification of requirements [91]. It can differ significantly from classical software requirement engineering [92].

The first step is to describe the primary requirements. In our experience, this is done in collaboration with domain experts who often have little experience with quantum computers. Finding a common understanding of the problem to be solved is tedious, but always worthwhile. Subsequently, a precise mathematical formulation must be worked out that allows the mapping of the application to an existing quantum algorithm or the development of a new one.

The joint elaboration not only helps the software engineer to find a solution approach, but also gives insights into quantum computing to a wider circle of interested people. This experience building within the organization, but also within the ecosystem as a whole, is something we have recognized as having its own value [93, 94].

Secondary requirements arise from the primary ones, e.g., requirements on the size of the system via the input data. The requirements must be considered together

---

[3] www.dlr.de

with the expected limitations of the hardware, a step that admittedly often leads to disillusionment and requires several iterations at this point. For instance, at DLR there is a huge gap between the problem sizes that quantum computers can handle and the massive computing tasks that arise in engineering questions. However, we must and can already set the course for future advantages in our fields of application. Despite or precisely because of the current hardware-related limitations, scalability must always be considered in quantum software development. There is great value today in demonstrating an algorithm that can solve small instances of difficult problems if it "only" needs to be scaled in the future; see [95, 96, 97] for the example of Shor's algorithm [1]. In contrast, it seems questionable to implement a highly optimized algorithm that does not even theoretically scale to large instances.

3.5.2 Software Design

Software design is always about defining the architecture, components, and their interfaces. In the design of quantum software, a dimension is added that is very important. It is necessary to decide which parts of the program are to be calculated on a conventional computer and which on a quantum computer. In this context, one also speaks of a quantum processing unit (QPU), which can take over specific tasks. Not every task is well suited for a QPU, and it does not currently look as if quantum computers will completely replace conventional processors.

Once it has been determined what is to be computed where (which includes in particular the choice of a quantum algorithm as discussed above), a specification of the data exchanged between the conventional and quantum parts must be made. A hardware-aware concept is required in order to feed data of a certain accuracy from a classical computer system reliably and accurately into a specific quantum circuit. Speed requirements here depend on the integration of the quantum hardware with the classical hardware and on the algorithm to be executed. Some hybrid algorithms require communication between the classical and the quantum systems within the coherence time. The challenge here is to define abstract layers in the software design so that software solutions for reliable and accurate data communication between classical and quantum system are at least partially reusable.

A conceptual separation of software into hardware-specific and -agnostic parts increases the reusability of the software we develop. It is important to understand that, although we use very low-level methods to get the most out of our quantum computers, we aim to develop software and methods that are useful in the long term. Therefore, reusability is an important criterion.

Interfaces must be defined for the transfer of data. At present, there is practically no distinction between program code and data on the quantum computer. Input data is transferred via program code for preparing the data [98], which can be very hardware-specific; see [99, 100] for examples on ion traps. We expect that future abstractions will facilitate data transmission.

The development of suitable data types on quantum computers is still in its infancy. A lot of research and standardization is still needed here. However, it is already apparent that, even for integers, the type of encoding has a major influence on the performance of quantum computers [101]. Possible choices are amplitude encoding or basis encodings like binary encoding, one hot encoding, and domain wall encoding [102]. More ways to encode classical data into quantum states are considered in the context of machine learning; see, e.g., [103]. They affect the performance mainly due to the strong noise of current models, so any form of resource optimization can help a lot.

In many engineering applications, decimal fractions are of course required, which, depending on the required resolution, generate a very high resource requirement by today's standards (measured in number of qubits). It can therefore be worthwhile to choose an algorithm that is formulated in data types that fit well with a quantum computer.

Finally, a good design process for quantum software includes simulations of the program and, if possible, test runs on available hardware. It allows challenges to be identified and the design to be adapted if necessary. A rigid approach here is even more doomed to failure than in conventional software design.

3.5.3 Models and Representation

Let's take a look at current ways of representing quantum software, or rather program code for quantum computers. At the moment, mainly low-level descriptions are used. Even in most recent publications we are still on a level where quantum algorithms are described via elementary gates and quantum circuits. Internally, these circuits can be represented as a list of gates, directed acyclic graphs (DAGs), path integrals/phase polynomials, or decision diagrams. Low-level languages such as OpenQASM [104], cirq [105], and qiskit [106] have become established as descriptions by a user and as interfaces between tools. Despite some attempts to create more high-level quantum programming languages, e.g., Q# [107], Silq [108], or qrisp [109], none of these is currently widely used (for various reasons). In the long term, however, there is no way around the introduction of more powerful language constructs in our view. It will be crucial that these find a natural way to represent the special capabilities of quantum computers. Although perhaps only years of programming experience will make natural programming languages for quantum computers possible, we want to support developments in this direction at an early stage.

In the context of compilers in particular, intermediate representations (IR) are also introduced as an intermediate level between the abstraction layers of the programming language and the machine language. Examples are QIR [110] and QSSA [111]. The formulation of quantum-specific optimization steps on this level is a subject of current research, which we will discuss in Sect. 3.6. We should also mention that other established tools of conventional software design are currently translated to and tried in the context of quantum computing, e.g., the unified modeling language (UML) [112].

3.5.4   Software Testing

Software testing is part of the software development process that aims to ensure the quality and reliability of the software. There are different types of tests, and common categories are unit tests (testing small components), integration tests, functional tests, and acceptance tests (checking fulfilment of requirements). Tests are artifacts (code or instructions) that are executed automatically or manually. In contrast, verification relies on formal proofs which employ static code analysis, and benchmarking is concerned with the quantification of the performance of software and hardware. We look at verification and benchmarking in more detail in Sect. 3.8. We emphasize that testing is about finding programming bugs, not hardware errors, whose treatment we discuss in Sect. 3.7. However, we investigate how the methods developed for handling hardware errors can also be adapted to testing.

Given the above definition of testing it is clear that future software for powerful quantum computers will also need to be tested. It is important to do basic preliminary work already now, before the hardware allows complex software to run. And research in this direction has indeed started [113, 114, 115, 90]. This ensures that the reliability of software does not become a bottleneck in future developments of QC. It is particularly important because in QC the transition from low-level circuits to high-level programs mostly still lies ahead of us. And testing is an exciting research topic in the field of quantum software engineering because quantum-specific phenomena have to be taken into account.

It is obvious that facts like the no-cloning theorem [116] are obstacles in testing programs. Classical approaches that often use copying implicitly need to be adapted in order to apply them to quantum software. The fact that in general measurements in quantum theory disturb the observed system also complicates state monitoring. This severely affects the possibilities for runtime tests on quantum computers (see e.g., [117, 118]), and further research in this direction will be necessary.

Furthermore, what constitutes a typical error is quite different between classical and quantum programming. Due to the difference in the computational model there are even programming errors that are not meaningful in classical programming, e.g., when they affect only the phase of the state. It is therefore necessary to conduct studies on what bugs are typical in quantum programs [119, 120]. Such studies can be very programming language-specific, i.e., tailored toward Q# [121]. Only with knowledge about typical bugs is it possible to then develop good tests that detect as many of them as possible. A useful tool here is the creation of benchmark collections, as well as the automatic generation of test cases.

It is necessary to define tests that circumvent the abovementioned quantum-specific challenges, and are still meaningful. And this leads to further research questions, such as the definition of meaningful measures for the significance of tests. Once more and more quantum software is written, guidelines for writing reliable code and informative tests which are based on the above research will be very useful.

3.6   Compiling

3.6.1   Gate-Based Quantum Computing

Like conventional computers, quantum computers also implement a finite set of elementary basic operations, the gates already mentioned above. Different sets of gates have become accepted for the description of quantum circuits [122, 123, 10]. If a gate set enables an efficient approximation of any unitary operation, we call it a universal gate set. By efficient here we mean that the new length of the circuit scales polynomially with the original circuit length when switching from any other gate set.

On the one hand, convenient gate sets are used for the theoretical description of quantum algorithms. These sets in general contain significantly more gates than necessary, are useful in the context of fault tolerance, and might also contain larger, undecomposed blocks. On the other hand, each hardware platform implements different, sometimes very limited, gate sets. A major restriction results, for example, from limited connectivity, which means that the two-qubit operations provided are not possible for every pair of qubits. However, some hardware platforms, in particular ion traps, provide native multi-qubit gates that allow this issue to be circumvented; see also Sect. 3.2.

The transition from one description of the quantum circuit to another is called *transpiling*. Specifically, the transition from a general unitary to a set of elementary gates is called *synthesis*. Both transitions are core tasks of a compiler. Furthermore, the compiler, just like its conventional analog, has the task of customizing the output to the specific hardware as best as possible. In summary, the requirement of a compiler is producing correct, efficient, and hardware-compatible output, as explained in more detail below.

The typical compiler architecture can be divided into individual steps (passes), which are connected in series as a pipeline where each step transforms the quantum circuit. The best order is not obvious and passes can also be repeated at a later point in the compilation. Typical transformation steps include:

- **Synthesis**. Larger operations need to be decomposed into a universal set of basic gates. Small operations can be decomposed optimally with regard to a certain cost function, while synthesis of larger operations will not yield optimal solutions in general.
- **Routing**. The circuit needs to be rewritten in a way that contains only gates that are natively supported by the hardware. In particular, multi-qubit gates can only act on qubits that can interact physically. Even qubits that might not be part of a calculation can mediate the interaction.
- **Optimization**. The overall circuit can be optimized with regard to some cost function as well. Here the input and the output are both decomposed circuits. We discuss this point in more detail in the following.

Various objective functions for circuit optimization are conceivable and are used. For example, the number of certain gates (e.g., controlled-Not gate, T gate), the depth of the circuit (related but not identical to the runtime), or the expected noise on the final state can be minimized. Of course, one can also try to maximize algorithm-specific performance, e.g., the probability of success. The problem of optimizing a circuit with respect to a particular objective is generally very difficult [124, 125, 126], such that there is no efficient algorithm to find the global minimum except for small circuits. Some approaches are based on meet-in-the-middle [127] or satisfiability (SAT) solvers [128]. For larger circuits only heuristic algorithms are feasible; see, e.g., [129]. For the optimization passes there are promising research approaches to transfer the conventionally established methods based on IR to quantum compilers.

Deciding whether the result of the compilation is indeed efficient on actual devices is not obvious. Since the global optimum is generally not known, one can only compare the result with other reference compilers. However, this comparison depends strongly on the circuits. It is important to use balanced benchmark suites, for example, the Arline Benchmark suite [130]. Further developments in this direction are foreseeable.

The development of compilers of hybrid programs has a major impact on the possibilities for optimization. Such hybrid compilers are compilers that do not generate pure quantum circuits, but executable code on conventional computers that contains calls to a QPU [131]. This results in strong optimization potential because the compiler can automatically decide whether the calculations are better computed on the QPU or on a conventional computer. Furthermore, it is even possible to apply hybrid simplification rules, which, e.g., move individual operations from the quantum circuit to conventional pre- or post-processing [132], where they can be combined and simplified with established methods. The goal is to leave only the essence of the quantum algorithm in the quantum circuit. These hybrid simplification rules in particular can benefit from the established concept of IR.

Another motivation for hybrid compilers is a closer coupling of the central processing unit (CPU) and the QPU. In particular, hybrid quantum algorithms such as VQAs [87] benefit greatly from an efficient coupling of conventional and quantum systems. Here, experience in GPU programming (e.g., CUDA [133]) can be built upon. In the future, abstract language constructs should simplify and unify the use of different hardware architectures. QPU and CPU codes are developed in a common project folder, where calls to the QPU are controlled via synchronous and asynchronous commands. Efficient interfaces and protocols must be developed for uploading data and code to the QPU and downloading measurement results. The QPU code may not only contain quantum operations but also increasingly complex dynamic operations that directly process measurement results and influence subsequent quantum operations. This feed-forward approach opens up exciting possibilities for new experiments, and it is essential in the measurement-based model of quantum computation [134]. The close coupling of a CPU and a QPU is flanked by development work aimed at integrating quantum computers into HPC environments; see [135, 136]. The experience with these prototypes will influence the necessary standards.

As mentioned, we require the correctness of the compiler, i.e., a proof that the output corresponds in functionality to the original input, possibly in human-readable form. However, it is known that the general equivalence test problem for quantum circuits is not efficiently solvable, as it is in the class of QMA-complete problems [137], which are, loosely speaking, those problems that are hard to solve for quantum computers. This means that we have little hope of proving the correctness of the final result. What we can do instead is to prove the correctness of the process. The compiler is correct if it only applies correct transformations. And for each individual transformation, it is possible to show correctness. When we speak of heuristics in the compiler pipeline, we mean procedures that do not necessarily lead to improved circuits but which nevertheless output a correct circuit in every case.

In addition to the described methodology, some approaches attempt to prove the equivalence of circuits. Although they suffer from an exponential increase in resources (time or memory), they can still deliver results for "simple" circuits. We refer the interested reader here to the literature [138, 139, 140].

3.6.2 Quantum Annealing

Although quantum annealing (QA) is a different computational model and therefore poses its own challenges, compiling in a certain sense is also needed here: quantum annealers can only process a very specific optimization problem, in case of D-Wave, a restricted version of the Ising problem [60]. Programming such devices essentially means providing the problem-defining parameters. However, exemplary applications from industry and research, cf. Sect. 3.3.2, show that there is in general no trivial way of obtaining these parameters. Several transformation steps from the original problem formulation to the native one of the device are required. A compiler handling these different abstraction layers would make the technology available for various users with different levels of expertise in QA.

From a mathematical point of view, the step from an arbitrary discrete optimization problem to a general Ising problem is solved and can be done using a set of standard methods. However, a complete software suite implementing this is not yet available. Nevertheless, toolboxes like the D-Wave Ocean SDK [141] or quark [142] already support users with utility methods. But further expansion of the software suites and conceptual advances are necessary. For instance, the recent research on the reduction of combinatorial optimization problems has mainly focused on any kind of (polynomial) reduction and not on the optimal one in a certain sense, e.g., in the number of resulting variables, which would be advantageous regarding the limited resources of current quantum computational devices. Furthermore, the actually implemented Ising problem is not a general one but faces further restrictions, such as a specific non-complete hardware graph and a limited parameter precision. This causes the reformulation of the original problem to be a nontrivial task and demands that a "compiler" implement all the necessary steps and hide the complexity from the application-focused users.

The two main transformation steps are the graph embedding and the parameter setting. Unfortunately, the first step, the embedding of the original problem graph into the hardware graph, has appeared to be a computationally hard problem, in particular, as hard as the problem D-Wave's annealers are capable of solving [143]. Therefore, in practice, heuristic methods need to be applied to circumvent this bottleneck [144, 145]. In the second step, the hardware-native Ising problem has to be formulated based on the found embedding. If this step is not done correctly, we will not be able to analyze the actual performance of the quantum device itself, because the success probability might be suppressed due to a wrongly formulated problem. Recently, a new formulation has been developed that provides an embedded Ising problem which provably corresponds to the original problem and meanwhile optimizes its parameters with respect to the machine precision [146]. Based on this recent and future theoretical work, the compilation software has to be steadily improved and extended, and the full software ecosystem has to be able to adapt to these changes.

3.7 Error Handling

It is essential that errors caused by imperfect hardware are considered in the software stack, because the amplitudes and phases of the qubits are not discrete. Additional steps or layers are necessary to protect the information against this unavoidable noise introduced by the hardware. This section briefly sketches the main concepts in this field of research and provides references to more in-depth introductions.

We distinguish three categories of error-handling strategies. First, techniques that start directly at the hardware level and attempt to reduce the noise level [147]. This includes, for example, dynamical decoupling [148], where special control pulse sequences are used to eliminate the disturbing influence of the environment. Second, techniques that encode the quantum information into subspaces that do not couple to the environment and are therefore not affected by decoherence introduced by the environment [149]. Third, taking the noise of the quantum computer into account for the compilation can lead to circuits that are less prone to noise. For example, we investigated which decompositions of a common multi-qubit gate introduce the least amount of noise [150].

Furthermore, some post-processing steps on the classical measurement data are aimed at removing the noise [151, 152]. For example, zero-noise extrapolation [153] and readout error mitigation [154] have proven effective in some applications. The term error mitigation has come to refer to these types of techniques. We emphasize that they do not avoid errors, but try to eliminate the errors afterwards. Finally, methods on the error correction codes are aimed to suppress the noise to any degree [155, 156, 157]. We explain error mitigation and error correction in more detail in the following sections.

3.7.1 Error Models

Simple models for describing noise on quantum computers may only depend on a single parameter or a few parameters. They can be found in any textbook on quantum information, e.g., [10]. The depolarizing noise model is often used and can be interpreted in such a way that with a certain probability (the parameter of the model) the state of the system is replaced by white noise. Of course, this is a poor representation of the real experiment. However, we have found that it is often very suitable for a first qualitative picture of the effect of noise. Other simple models are the bit-flip, phase-flip, and amplitude damping channels.

A more precise description of the noise is possible with a Pauli channel [10], where every tensor product of Pauli operators can appear as an error. These errors can occur with different probabilities. A complete description of the error channel via Kraus operators [10] is also possible. The free parameters of this model can be determined via process tomography in the experiment [158, 159]. It is a complex procedure that does not scale well with the system size but obtains complete information. It is worthwhile, for example, if one wants to obtain a very precise picture of a single gate of a quantum computer. Instead of determining the parameters experimentally, one can also use "realistic" noise models. In this case, one tries to understand and model the physics of the process as well as possible. Often the parameters of the model have a physical interpretation. This approach is very hardware-specific and requires an exact fit of the model to the experiment. However, it also offers the chance to draw conclusions about necessary hardware improvements from model calculations, which is very helpful in the paradigm of hardware–software co-design.

We follow yet another approach in which the noisy process is largely considered as a black box, with few assumptions to be made about the noise [160]. In this context, the assumption of Pauli noise and the assumption that the noise of a circuit block are independent of the context. This means that the same gate causes the same noise at different positions in the circuit. Of course, these assumptions might not be fully satisfied in a real experiment. Instead of a description that is as complete as possible, we obtain information regarding errors that affect operators in the stabilizer elements, which we will discuss below.

3.7.2 Error Mitigation

Error mitigation is a form of post-processing in which one tries to infer the ideal result from the noisy result [151, 152]. The techniques of error mitigation use additional measurements to extract information about the noise, which can be partially removed from the outcome. They go beyond simply improving the measurement statistics by increasing the number of runs. However, they are interesting for NISQ computers because they do not require additional quantum resources. Prominent examples are zero-noise extrapolation [153] and readout error mitigation [154].

Furthermore, the method of [160] to model the noise above can be used as an error mitigation technique. The parameters of the error model are determined via a calibration measurement. It allows us to infer the ideal expected values from the noisy ones of the stabilizer elements. The results are comparable to readout error mitigation, while the method generates significantly less effort.

3.7.3 Error Correction

The topic of quantum error correction is vast and plays an important role. In this subsection, we briefly sketch the relevant concepts and refer interested readers to excellent introductions in [155, 156, 157]. Generally speaking, it is the extension of classical error correction codes to correct not only bit-flip but also phase-flip errors, and thus also general errors on a quantum system.

Quantum error correction codes encode k logical qubits into n physical qubits. Many codes can be described via the stabilizer of this code space, i.e., via a subgroup of the Pauli group whose elements leave the code words invariant. Small size examples are the nine-qubit Shor code [161], the seven-qubit Steane code [162], and the five-qubit code [163, 164]. A family of widely used codes is the surface code [165]. The layout of the qubits follows a lattice structure with the stabilizer generators acting locally, a fact that makes these codes a natural choice for hardware platforms with a matching architecture, e.g., those based on superconducting qubits.

The capacity of a code to correct errors is described by distance d, the minimum Hamming distance between two code words. The information about an error in the system is determined via the *syndrome measurements*. Here, one measures a set of observables that yield enough information to inform the correction operation. This measurement result is called a *syndrome*.

The concept of fault tolerance is crucial in quantum computing [155]. It is possible, with the help of quantum error correction codes and clever design of circuits, to perform arbitrarily long calculations despite the noisy operations. One can simply choose an arbitrarily large code, if it does not introduce too much noise due to the overhead of the additional operations, and the existing faults cannot propagate badly. It allows us to push the noise down to a desired level. The required quality of operations that achieves this scaling is called the threshold of the error correction scheme [166]. The additional complexity can be hidden in an abstract layer of the stack, e.g., when focusing on higher layers. It allows us to develop an ideal QC without having to consider the additional complexity of error correction at all times.

3.8 Verification and Benchmarking

Verification aims to ensure that software fulfills its requirements, e.g., that the output is correct under certain preconditions for given inputs. Similar to conventional non-deterministic software, the stochastic nature of most quantum algorithms poses a challenge to verification. That is, the same inputs can produce different results due to the intrinsic properties of quantum measurements but also due to the high level of noise on near-term hardware; see Sect. 3.2. A typical requirement that needs to be verified is that one obtains a high-quality solution, e.g., a result close to the desired result, with a sufficiently high probability. Here we focus on static verification, while what is sometimes also referred to as dynamical verification is covered in Sect. 3.5.4. The task of verification can be addressed from two sides. First, from a formal point of view, given "working" hardware we need a theoretical proof that the quantum algorithm is correct. Second, from a practical point of view, we need to ensure that the algorithm is implemented correctly in code for the classical and quantum parts of the program. Both parts need verification and the latter finally needs to be correctly translated into the executable circuit; see also Sect. 3.6. The verification of quantum algorithms gives rise to an interesting research question [167, 168, 126]: When quantum computers outperform conventional computers, how can we ensure that the algorithm is correct?

Benchmarking is the quantification of the performance of software and hardware. Because in the current state of QC the question is not yet how fast we can get a result but how good the results are that we get, benchmarking usually refers to assessing the quality of hardware components. So in contrast to conventional computer science, we do not yet compare different software or hardware with metrics like time to solution. In this context, benchmarks are standardized, technology-agnostic methods to evaluate quantum computers. The result of benchmarks are metrics for the performance of a specific device. They should be treated with caution, as they only cover single aspects of the machine, may struggle with the different hardware approaches (see also Sect. 3.2), and only measure the current state of the technology, not its future perspective. Also note that the score is affected by software, in particular the compilation. Any good benchmark should fulfill a number of requirements. It should be accepted by scientists and industry alike. The score of the benchmark is a number or a yes/no answer. The metric allows for a meaningful interpretation, which goes beyond that specific benchmark test. It should not give an advantage to one specific technology by construction, but the values can and will be better for some technologies than others, of course. The benchmarks should be well defined and easy to understand. They should be efficiently implementable, which poses a limitation on the information content in practice and therefore requires them to focus on specific aspects of the performance. They should be reproducible, which is a challenge given the non-deterministic character of quantum computers. Finally, they need to be scalable so they can be applied to small and larger quantum computers to enable tracking of the development progress.

The following quantities and methods are typically considered in the context of benchmarking.

- The fidelity of state preparation, single and two-qubit gates, and measurements. These numbers measure how close the implemented operation and the target operation are.

- Coherence times, which describe how long the coherence of a system, i.e., its ability to interfere, is conserved. In particular, the number of gate operations which can be performed in the coherence time indicates how long quantum computations can be.
- Cross-talk, e.g., how strong idle qubits are affected by gates acting on other qubits. Due to its non-local nature this noise can be difficult to handle.
- Hardware connectivity, i.e., how many qubits can directly interact.
- State and process tomography are methods that allow for a full characterization of a quantum state and a quantum operation, respectively [169, 170, 171].
- Randomized benchmarking [172] is a method to find the average gate fidelity of an important subset of gates, the so-called Clifford gates. It relies on the Gottesman–Knill theorem, which shows that circuits only consisting of such gates can be efficiently simulated on a conventional computer [10]. This then allows for the random insertion of gates into a circuit and efficient inversion of their net effect. Then the deviation from an identity operation is linked to the average fidelity of the gates. One advantage of this method is that the metric is not affected by state preparation and measurement errors.

In order to perform useful reproducible benchmarks, we need to define a suite of standard problems, ideally reflecting interesting target applications (like SPEC benchmarks [173] for different classical hardware) or, e.g., basic operations and algorithms (like LINPACK [174]). Existing benchmark suites for QC include SupermarQ [175] and Arline [130]. There are also benchmark suites tailored toward specific applications, e.g., fermionic quantum simulation [176]. In addition, for the special case of comparing quantum hardware and software, it might be helpful to further specify some constraints on how those problems should be solved as different approaches might not be comparable; e.g., hardcoding the solution is not a fair comparison. This can be tricky to achieve in practice as different assumptions or prior knowledge about the problem is often used in different solution approaches.

For comparison with classical computers, there exists a wide range of possible implementations: we can plug in a classical computer at almost any stage from the level of the original application problem, over a transformed formulation suitable for a quantum algorithm, to the actual operations for a specific hardware (at least for small problems or theoretical runtime considerations). And even on a classical computer, software can be more or less optimized, which influences its runtime by several orders of magnitudes (see, e.g., [177] for an example). So for actual benchmarking results, one needs to provide many additional details on all used implementations as well as on the hardware to actually allow an insightful comparison and interpretation. We further suggest defining separate benchmarking suites to address specific questions in the future:

- **Quantum supremacy**: These benchmarks compare the fastest implementation on a quantum computer with the fastest, elaborated, existing software for classical hardware for different key applications.

- **Near-term practicability**: These benchmarks compare the (estimated) costs of solutions for interesting algorithms (with input data from applications) for different quantum platforms and for classical hardware.
- **Performance and correctness**: These benchmarks assess the accuracy/quality of solutions obtained with different quantum hardware and software stacks for mathematical test problems with known solutions.

4 System Architecture and Implementation

In Sect. 3, we have described the conceptual workflow of quantum computers, from application to actual hardware. The end users are typically ultimately interested in solving their engineering problem, e.g., in simulating the airflow around an aircraft or in finding some optimal resource scheduling. To this end, we aim to construct a platform that allows end users to describe their domain-specific problem and find solutions to it while having to think about the underlying hardware as little as possible. This section describes the technical building blocks we use to construct such a platform. An illustration of the individual components and their connections is provided in Fig. 8.

We aim to construct this platform as domain-independently as possible. To guide our description of the individual components, however, we use an artificial example problem from the automotive domain using this platform. This example problem serves to highlight many of the considerations to be made when constructing a platform for quantum computing. While other use cases will require additional considerations, we believe that this example already suffices to illustrate the most pressing and general concerns platform engineers should consider for a wide swath of use cases.

For our example, consider the goal of developing a new driving function for autonomous vehicles. The engineers implementing this driving function want to evaluate whether it behaves safely in a number of specified driving scenarios. To this end, they specify sets of possible scenarios using traffic sequence charts (TSC) [178]. They then instantiate scenarios that conform to solutions for the given TSC problem and simulate the behavior of the implemented driving function in that scenario [179]. Moreover, they implement a software monitor that observes the simulation and reports unexpected behavior. This is also accompanied by a visualization of the simulation. The full sequence of steps of the simulation shall be automatized. To stay in the frame of a quantum software ecosystem, we further assume that the TSC problem shall be solved using quantum computing hardware. This can, for instance, be done by converting the TSC into a SAT formula and using Grover's algorithm to search for feasible solutions provided by a corresponding quantum oracle gate.

Note that, in an actual application, the TSC is converted into an Satisfiability Modulo Theory (SMT) formula instead of a SAT formula, where the former is a strictly more general model than the latter. There is, however, currently not

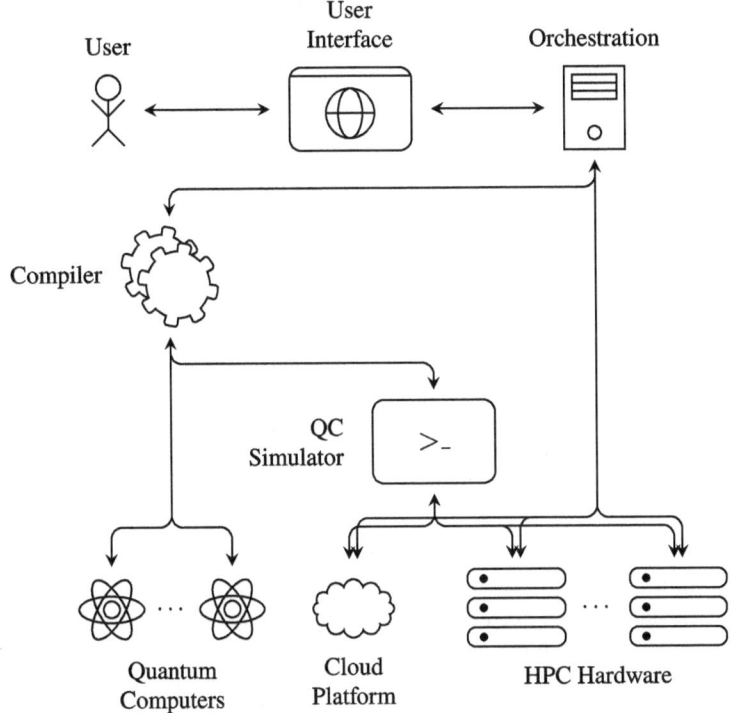

Fig. 8 A technical overview of the platform supporting quantum software developers

a straightforward way to generate solutions for an SMT formula using quantum circuits. Hence, for the sake of example, we assume that the engineers instead generate concrete scenarios via SAT formulas instead of SMT formulas.

In practice, the described simulation steps require heterogeneous hardware: the transformation from TSC to SAT and the extraction of a concrete scenario from a SAT solution can be executed on virtually any hardware without proprietary software. In contrast, finding the solution of the SAT problem and the execution of the simulation requires specialized software, namely SAT solvers, such as Z3 [180], and traffic simulation software, such as CARLA [181], respectively. Moreover, the visualization requires specialized hardware, e.g., graphics processing units (GPUs). As, in this running example, we assume that the engineer wants to find solutions to the SAT formula using some quantum circuit, we also interact with quantum devices.

In order to construct and execute their experiments, the engineers require some interface to the system. This interface provides the engineer with an integrated development environment (IDE) and, once the engineer is satisfied with their specification, passes the problem to some backend for execution. We describe the requirements for that interface in Sect. 4.1. Once the end user has specified the problem, the platform will have to schedule the use of the heterogeneous hardware systems described above. The major novelty of this platform lies in orchestrating the cooperation between classical computing hardware on the one hand, including, e.g., classical workstations, HPC resources, and GPUs, and between QPUs on the other hand. We describe the requirements for this orchestration in Sect. 4.2. The QPUs used during the execution may be implemented in actual hardware or it may be simulated using one of multiple quantum computing simulators. We have described the constraints faced in using existing hardware platforms in Sect. 3.2. The trade-offs to consider when using quantum simulators follow in Sect. 4.3.

4.1 User Interface

Quantum software developers require a straightforward interface for specifying their problems. In our example, the end user must be able to specify the described loop consisting of reading a TSC, calling external software, and performing computations on a well-suited QPU. The end user is not likely to be interested in the specifics of the underlying hardware but instead wants to have the choice of hardware handled by the platform during execution. In contrast, the interface should also cater to experts who are not interested in specifying domain-specific problems but are working on developing novel quantum algorithms. To this end, they require more direct access to the underlying hardware for, e.g., benchmarking.

The interface should allow the user to iterate rapidly on problem formulations e.g., the typical interface of HPC hardware. When using HPC hardware for solving a domain problem, the underlying algorithms and implementations are often mature and well tested. In contrast, when using quantum computing hardware, the underlying algorithms and implementations are constantly evolving and are often adapted to the domain problem at hand. Hence, the platform should allow the end user to rapidly iterate on the formulation of the domain-specific problem.

One approach to satisfy these requirements is allowing users to formulate their problems using a *service-oriented architecture*. In such an architecture, multiple independent software services collaborate to solve the specified problem. In our example above, users could specify one service each for the following tasks:

- Transform a given TSC into an SAT formula
- Construct a quantum circuit that solves this formula.
- Execute the quantum circuit to obtain a solution.
- Transform the solution into a concrete scenario.
- Simulate and monitor the scenario using CARLA [181], obtaining a visualization of the simulation.

The user needs to specify the software and hardware requirements for each service, e.g., that they require a QPU for the third service and CARLA with GPUs for the visualization of the fifth service. They do not necessarily have to implement all services themselves but can rely on other services that users of the platform have implemented and opted to share publicly. Finally, the user must specify the data flow between these services and ask the orchestration component to execute the composed service.

Letting end users define composable services and publishing them to other users has proven successful in the context of data analysis with Apache Nifi [182] and in the context of preliminary design of airplanes, jet fuels, electrical grids, ships, and other complex systems with RCE [183]. Moreover, a graphical user interface that allows users to graphically connect relevant services has been employed successfully for several decades in the field of data acquisition and analysis by LabVIEW [184].

4.2 Orchestration and Data Management

Once the problem has been specified and is given to the orchestration component for execution, that component has to reserve computation time on the initial required computing resource. Our running example requires some computation time on an off-the-shelf workstation which transforms the TSC into an SAT formula and subsequently transforms this formula into a quantum circuit. The orchestration component then has to reserve computation time on some QPU, either real hardware or simulated, to execute the quantum circuit. Once the execution of the quantum circuit has finished and resulted in a solution to the SAT problem, the orchestration component needs to reserve some computation time on an off-the-shelf workstation which transforms this solution into a scenario. Subsequently, the orchestration component needs to reserve computation time on an HPC resource equipped with GPUs to simulate the generated scenario, monitor the simulation, and visualize the simulation if necessary. Finally, the orchestration component needs to repeat the above steps until non-nominal behavior is observed during the simulation.

Our example shows that it is infeasible for the orchestration component to reserve all required computing resources prior to the execution of the initial service. The requirements for the QPU, the available gates, and number of qubits required for the execution of the quantum circuit only become available after the execution of the initial service. Hence, the orchestration component needs to be able to reserve computation time on the fly as results from earlier services become available.

Moreover, the orchestration component needs to take into account external requirements for the chosen computational resources. The visualization of the simulation in the final step of the computation described above may require large maps, textures, or other large data artifacts to visualize the scenario with the required fidelity. If these artifacts are only available to the visualization via a network connection with low bandwidth, the execution time of the complete computation will increase significantly. Hence, the orchestration component needs to be aware of data-intensive parts of the computation and the locality of the required data.

4.3   Use of QC Simulators

In the section Sect. 3.2, we have described the hardware platforms that are currently available for executing quantum circuits. All these platforms are costly, only available in low quantities, do not provide a large number of qubits, and produce noisy results. Although these problems are being addressed in the production of quantum computing hardware research, alternative solutions may tackle these issues.

A promising alternative is the use of quantum computing simulators that adopt classical hardware to simulate the execution of quantum circuits on actual hardware. Simulating such an execution requires significant computing power that is usually only provided by HPC systems. These systems are typically the same ones that execute the classical part of the computation job. Hence, any platform for the execution of quantum computing workloads using simulators must strike a balance between using the HPC resources it has available for the simulation of quantum circuits and using them for classical computation. Moreover, these HPC resources are rarely available for exclusive use by the quantum computing platform. Instead, the resources are also used for "classical" HPC applications. The owner of the resources has to balance their availability between the use by the platform and by the classical applications.

Although the results of the simulations produce data in the same order of magnitude as actual quantum computers (namely a few kilobytes or megabytes), they may offer additional diagnostic data which grows exponentially with the number of simulated qubits. If this data is made available to end users, the platform needs to provide data storage as well as bandwidth for transferring the data to the end user.

5   Conclusion

Quantum computing represents a paradigm shift in computational capabilities, with potential applications in various sectors. A key aspect to unlock its full potential is the establishment of a robust software ecosystem. This ecosystem not only provides the essential infrastructure for operating quantum devices but also serves as a bridge, enabling a broad spectrum of researchers, scientists, and industry experts to explore, use, and enhance the applications of these quantum systems.

Our chapter takes a research-driven approach toward constructing such an ecosystem. We have bifurcated our exploration into two key dimensions. Firstly, we present the conceptual design which encompasses considerations from computational paradigms, applications like quantum simulation, over device-optimized compiling to error handling, verification, and benchmarking. This underscores the theoretical foundation, taking into account the unique challenges and attributes of quantum computing. Secondly, we delve into the system architecture and implementation, focusing on aspects ranging from user interfaces to orchestration, data management, and the critical role of quantum computing simulators. The fusion of these two perspectives ensures a comprehensive understanding and a holistic approach to developing a quantum software ecosystem.

As we step into the future, it is imperative to emphasize that this endeavor is iterative. Practical evaluation and real-world implementation of the proposed ecosystem will undoubtedly reveal areas for improvement. The scientific approach allows the adaptation of the ecosystem, especially given the rapidly evolving quantum hardware landscape. Monitoring these advancements and ensuring flexibility in the response will be critical to remaining aligned with the dynamic nature of quantum computing. By doing so, we pave the way for maximizing the potential of quantum computing, fostering innovation, and moving the field forward.

Acknowledgments This research is part of the projects Algorithms for quantum computer development in hardware-software codesign (ALQU), https://qci.dlr.de/en/alqu, and Classical Integration of Quantum Computers (CLIQUE), https://qci.dlr.de/en/clique, which were made possible by the DLR Quantum Computing Initiative (QCI) and the German Federal Ministry for Economic Affairs and Climate Action (BMWK). Special thanks is due to IQM Quantum Computers and EleQtron for kindly making their respective quantum hardware chip designs available.

References

1. Shor, P.W.: Polynomial-time algorithms for prime factorization and discrete logarithms on a quantum computer. SIAM J. Comput. **26**(5), 1484–1509 (1997). https://doi.org/10.1137/S0097539795293172
2. Lloyd, S.: Universal quantum simulators. Science **273**(5278), 1073 (1996). https://doi.org/10.1126/science.273.5278.1073
3. Harrow, A.W., Hassidim, A., Lloyd, S.: Quantum algorithm for linear systems of equations. Phys. Rev. Lett. **103**, 150502 (2009). https://doi.org/10.1103/PhysRevLett.103.150502
4. Kadowaki, T., Nishimori, H.: Quantum annealing in the transverse Ising model. Phys. Rev. E **58**, 5355 (1998). https://doi.org/10.1103/PhysRevE.58.5355
5. Byrd, G.T., Ding, Y.: Quantum computing: progress and innovation. Computer **56**(01), 20 (2023). https://doi.org/10.1109/MC.2022.3217021
6. Arute, F., Arya, K., Babbush, R., Bacon, D., Bardin, J.C., Barends, R., Biswas, R., Boixo, S., Brandao, F.G.S.L., Buell, D.A., Burkett, B., Chen, Y., Chen, Z., Chiaro, B., Collins, R., Courtney, W., Dunsworth, A., Farhi, E., Foxen, B., Fowler, A., Gidney, C., Giustina, M., Graff, R., Guerin, K., Habegger, S., Harrigan, M.P., Hartmann, M.J., Ho, A., Hoffmann, M., Huang, T., Humble, T.S., Isakov, S.V., Jeffrey, E., Jiang, Z., Kafri, D., Kechedzhi, K., Kelly, J., Klimov, P.V., Knysh, S., Korotkov, A., Kostritsa, F., Landhuis, D., Lindmark, M., Lucero, E., Lyakh, D., Mandrà, S., McClean, J.R., McEwen, M., Megrant, A., Mi, X., Michielsen, K., Mohseni, M., Mutus, J., Naaman, O., Neeley, M., Neill, C., Niu, M.Y., Ostby, E., Petukhov, A., Platt, J.C., Quintana, C., Rieffel, E.G., Roushan, P., Rubin, N.C., Sank, D., Satzinger, K.J., Smelyanskiy, V., Sung, K.J., Trevithick, M.D., Vainsencher, A., Villalonga, B., White, T., Yao, Z.J., Yeh, P., Zalcman, A., Neven, H., Martinis, J.M.: Quantum supremacy using a programmable superconducting processor. Nature **574**(7779), 505 (2019). https://doi.org/10.1038/s41586-019-1666-5

7. Preskill, J.: Quantum computing in the NISQ era and beyond. Quantum **2**, 79 (2018). https://doi.org/10.22331/q-2018-08-06-79

8. Temkin, M.. Investors bet on the technologically unproven field of quantum computing. https://pitchbook.com/news/articles/quantum-computing-venture-capital-funding. Accessed 04 Oct 2023

9. Cohen-Tannoudji, C., Diu, B., Laloe, F.: Quantum Mechanics. Textbook Physics, vol. 1, 1st edn. Wiley, Hoboken (1991)

10. Nielsen, M.A., Chuang, I.L.: Quantum Computation and Quantum Information. Cambridge University Press, Cambridge (2000). https://doi.org/10.1017/CBO9780511976667

11. Schuhmacher, P.K: Decoherence as a resource for quantum information. Ph.D. Thesis, Universität des Saarlandes (2021). https://doi.org/10.22028/D291-35131

12. DiVincenzo, D.P.: The physical implementation of quantum computation. Fortschritte der Physik Progr. Phys. **48**(9–11), 771 (2000). https://doi.org/10.1002/1521-3978(200009)48:9/11<771::AID-PROP771>3.0.CO;2-E

13. Sleator, T., Weinfurter, H.: Realizable universal quantum logic gates. Phys. Rev. Lett. **74**, 4087 (1995). https://doi.org/10.1103/PhysRevLett.74.4087

14. Farhi, E., Goldstone, J., Gutmann, S., Sipser, M.: Quantum computation by adiabatic evolution. Preprint (2000). https://doi.org/10.48550/arXiv.quant-ph/0001106

15. Born, M., Fock, V.: Beweis des Adiabatensatzes. Zeitschrift für Physik **51**(3–4), 165–180 (1928). https://doi.org/10.1007/BF01343193

16. Van Dam, W., Mosca, M., Vazirani, U.: Proceedings 42nd IEEE Symposium on Foundations of Computer Science, pp. 279–287. IEEE, Piscataway (2001). https://doi.org/10.1109/SFCS.2001.959902

17. Aharonov, D., Van Dam, W., Kempe, J., Landau, Z., Lloyd, S., Regev, O.: Adiabatic quantum computation is equivalent to standard quantum computation. SIAM Rev. **50**(4), 755 (2008). https://doi.org/10.1137/080734479

18. Albash, T., Lidar, D.A.: Adiabatic quantum computation. Rev. Modern Phys. **90**(1), 015002 (2018). https://doi.org/10.1103/RevModPhys.90.015002

19. Pfeuty, P.: The one-dimensional Ising model with a transverse field. Ann. Phys. **57**, 79 (1970). https://doi.org/10.1016/0003-4916(70)90270-8

20. Fauseweh, B., Uhrig, G.S.: Multiparticle spectral properties in the transverse field Ising model by continuous unitary transformations. Phys. Rev. B **87**, 184406 (2013). https://doi.org/10.1103/PhysRevB.87.184406

21. Johnson, M.W., Amin, M.H., Gildert, S., Lanting, T., Hamze, F., Dickson, N., Harris, R., Berkley, A.J., Johansson, J., Bunyk, P., et al.: Quantum annealing with manufactured spins. Nature **473**(7346), 194 (2011). https://doi.org/10.1038/nature10012

22. Jünger, M., Lobe, E., Mutzel, P., Reinelt, G., Rendl, F., Rinaldi, G., Stollenwerk, T.: Quantum annealing versus digital computing: an experimental comparison. J. Exper. Algorithmics **26**, 1 (2021). https://doi.org/10.1145/3459606

23. McGeoch, C.C.: Theory versus practice in annealing-based quantum computing. Theoret. Comput. Sci. **816**, 169 (2020). https://doi.org/10.1016/j.tcs.2020.01.024

24. Raussendorf, R., Briegel, H.J.: A one-way quantum computer. Phys. Rev. Lett. **86**, 5188 (2001). https://doi.org/10.1103/PhysRevLett.86.5188

25. Knill, E., Laflamme, R., Milburn, G.J.: A scheme for efficient quantum computation with linear optics. Nature **409**(6816), 46 (2001). https://doi.org/10.1038/35051009

26. Browne, D.E., Rudolph, T.: Resource-efficient linear optical quantum computation. Phys. Rev. Lett. **95**, 010501 (2005). https://doi.org/10.1103/PhysRevLett.95.010501

27. Aharonov, Y., Davidovich, L., Zagury, N.: Quantum random walks. Phys. Rev. A **48**, 1687 (1993). https://doi.org/10.1103/PhysRevA.48.1687

28. Kempe, J.: Quantum random walks: An introductory overview. Contemp. Phys. **44**(4), 307 (2003). https://doi.org/10.1080/00107151031000110776

29. Childs, A.M., Cleve, R., Deotto, E., Farhi, E., Gutmann, S., Spielman, D.A.: Exponential algorithmic speedup by a quantum walk. In: Proceedings of the Thirty-Fifth Annual ACM Symposium on Theory of Computing, STOC '03, pp. 59–68. Association for Computing Machinery, New York (2003). https://doi.org/10.1145/780542.780552
30. Childs, A.M.: Universal computation by quantum walk. Phys. Rev. Lett. **102**, 180501 (2009). https://doi.org/10.1103/PhysRevLett.102.180501
31. Lovett, N.B., Cooper, S., Everitt, M., Trevers, M., Kendon, V.: Universal quantum computation using the discrete-time quantum walk. Phys. Rev. A **81**, 042330 (2010). https://doi.org/10.1103/PhysRevA.81.042330
32. Aharonov, D., Ambainis, A., Kempe, J., Vazirani, U.: Quantum walks on graphs. In: Proceedings of the Thirty-Third Annual ACM Symposium on Theory of Computing, STOC '01, pp. 50–59. Association for Computing Machinery, New York (2001). https://doi.org/10.1145/380752.380758
33. Farhi, E., Gutmann, S.: Quantum computation and decision trees. Phys. Rev. A **58**, 915 (1998). https://doi.org/10.1103/PhysRevA.58.915
34. Schuld, M., Sinayskiy, I., Petruccione, F.: Quantum walks on graphs representing the firing patterns of a quantum neural network. Phys. Rev. A **89**, 032333 (2014). https://doi.org/10.1103/PhysRevA.89.032333
35. Rebentrost, P., Mohseni, M., Lloyd, S.: Quantum support vector machine for big data classification. Phys. Rev. Lett. **113**, 130503 (2014). https://doi.org/10.1103/PhysRevLett.113.130503
36. Mohseni, M., Rebentrost, P., Lloyd, S., Aspuru-Guzik, A.: Environment-assisted quantum walks in photosynthetic energy transfer. J. Chem. Phys. **129**(17), 174106 (2008). https://doi.org/10.1063/1.3002335
37. Whitfield, J.D., Rodríguez-Rosario, C.A., Aspuru-Guzik, A.: Quantum stochastic walks: A generalization of classical random walks and quantum walks. Phys. Rev. A **81**, 022323 (2010). https://doi.org/10.1103/PhysRevA.81.022323
38. Govia, L.C.G., Taketani, B.G., Schuhmacher, P.K., Wilhelm, F.K.: Quantum simulation of a quantum stochastic walk. Quant. Sci. Technol. **2**(1), 015002 (2017). https://doi.org/10.1088/2058-9565/aa540b
39. Schuhmacher, P.K., Govia, L.C.G., Taketani, B.G., Wilhelm, F.K.: Quantum simulation of a discrete-time quantum stochastic walk. Europhys. Lett. **133**(5), 50003 (2021). https://doi.org/10.1209/0295-5075/133/50003
40. Turing, A.M.: On computable numbers, with an application to the entscheidungsproblem. Proc. Lond. Mathemat. Soc. **2**(1), 230 (1937). https://doi.org/10.1112/plms/s2-42.1.230
41. NobelPrize.org. Nobel Prize Outreach AB 2023. The nobel prize in physics 1956. https://www.nobelprize.org/prizes/physics/1956/summary/. Accessed 04 Oct 2023
42. Wilhelm, F.K., Steinwandt, R., Langenberg, B., Liebermann, P.J., Messinger, A., Schuhmacher, P.K., Misra-Spieldenner, A.: BSI Project Number 283 (2018). https://www.bsi.bund.de/SharedDocs/Downloads/DE/BSI/Publikationen/Studien/Quantencomputer/P283_QC_Studie-V_1_2.pdf?__blob=publicationFile&v=1
43. Häffner, H., Roos, C., Blatt, R.: Quantum computing with trapped ions. Phys. Rep. **469**(4), 155 (2008). https://doi.org/10.1016/j.physrep.2008.09.003
44. Monroe, C., Kim, J.: Scaling the ion trap quantum processor. Science **339**(6124), 1164 (2013). https://doi.org/10.1126/science.1231298
45. Brandl, M.F.: A Quantum von Neumann Architecture for Large-Scale Quantum Computing. Preprint (2017). https://doi.org/10.48550/arXiv.1702.02583
46. Clarke, J., Wilhelm, F.K.: Superconducting quantum bits. Nature **453**(7198), 1031 (2008). https://doi.org/10.1038/nature07128
47. Kane, B.E.: A silicon-based nuclear spin quantum computer. Nature **393**(6681), 133 (1998). https://doi.org/10.1038/30156
48. Heinzel, T.: Mesoscopic Electronics in Solid State Nanostructures. Physics Textbook, 2nd edn. Wiley, Hoboken (2007)

49. Hayashi, T., Fujisawa, T., Cheong, H.D., Jeong, Y.H., Hirayama, Y.: Coherent manipulation of electronic states in a double quantum dot. Phys. Rev. Lett. **91**, 226804 (2003). https://doi.org/10.1103/PhysRevLett.91.226804

50. Acín, A., Bloch, I., Buhrman, H., Calarco, T., Eichler, C., Eisert, J., Esteve, D., Gisin, N., Glaser, S.J., Jelezko, F., Kuhr, S., Lewenstein, M., Riedel, M.F., Schmidt, P.O., Thew, R., Wallraff, A., Walmsley, I., Wilhelm, F.K.: The quantum technologies roadmap: a European community view. New J. Phys. **20**(8), 080201 (2018). https://doi.org/10.1088/1367-2630/aad1ea

51. Josephson, B.D.: Possible new effects in superconductive tunnelling. Phys. Lett. **1**(7), 251 (1962). https://doi.org/10.1016/0031-9163(62)91369-0

52. Bladh, K., Duty, T., Gunnarsson, D., Delsing, P.: The single Cooper-pair box as a charge qubit. New J. Phys. **7**(1), 180 (2005). https://doi.org/10.1088/1367-2630/7/1/180

53. Vion, D., Aassime, A., Cottet, A., Joyez, P., Pothier, H., Urbina, C., Esteve, D., Devoret, M.H.: Manipulating the quantum state of an electrical circuit. Science **296**(5569), 886 (2002). https://doi.org/10.1126/science.1069372

54. Koch, J., Yu, T.M., Gambetta, J., Houck, A.A., Schuster, D.I., Majer, J., Blais, A., Devoret, M.H., Girvin, S.M., Schoelkopf, R.J.: Charge-insensitive qubit design derived from the Cooper pair box. Phys. Rev. A **76**, 042319 (2007). https://doi.org/10.1103/PhysRevA.76.042319

55. Mooij, J., Orlando, T., Levitov, L., Tian, L.,Van der Wal, C.H., Lloyd, S.: Josephson persistent-current qubit. Science **285**(5430), 1036 (1999). https://doi.org/10.1126/science.285.5430.1036

56. Van Der Wal, C.H., Ter Haar, A., Wilhelm, F., Schouten, R., Harmans, C., Orlando, T., Lloyd, S., Mooij, J.: Quantum superposition of macroscopic persistent-current states. Science **290**(5492), 773 (2000). https://doi.org/10.1126/science.290.5492.773

57. Pop, I.M., Geerlings, K., Catelani, G., Schoelkopf, R.J., Glazman, L.I., Devoret, M.H.: Coherent suppression of electromagnetic dissipation due to superconducting quasiparticles. Nature **508**(7496), 369 (2014). https://doi.org/10.1038/nature13017

58. Houck, A.A., Koch, J., Devoret, M.H., Girvin, S.M., Schoelkopf, R.J.: Life after charge noise: recent results with transmon qubits. Quant. Inf. Process. **8**(2), 105 (2009). https://doi.org/10.1007/s11128-009-0100-6

59. Clarke, J., Braginski, A.: The SQUID Handbook: Fundamentals and Technology of SQUIDs and SQUID Systems, vol. 1. Wiley, Hoboken (2004). https://doi.org/10.1002/3527603646

60. Lobe, E.: Combinatorial problems in programming quantum annealers. Ph.D. Thesis, Fakultät für Mathematik, Otto-von-Guericke-Universität Magdeburg (2022). https://doi.org/10.25673/89443

61. Motzoi, F., Gambetta, J.M., Rebentrost, P., Wilhelm, F.K.: Simple pulses for elimination of leakage in weakly nonlinear qubits. Phys. Rev. Lett. **103**, 110501 (2009). https://doi.org/10.1103/PhysRevLett.103.110501

62. Paul, W., Steinwedel, H.: Notizen: Ein neues Massenspektrometer ohne Magnetfeld. Zeitschrift für Naturforschung A **8**(7), 448 (1953). https://doi.org/10.1515/zna-1953-0710

63. Paul, W.: Electromagnetic traps for charged and neutral particles. Rev. Mod. Phys. **62**, 531 (1990). https://doi.org/10.1103/RevModPhys.62.531

64. Kielpinski, D., Monroe, C., Wineland, D.J.: Architecture for a large-scale ion-trap quantum computer. Nature **417**(6890), 709 (2002). https://doi.org/10.1038/nature00784

65. Monroe, C., Raussendorf, R., Ruthven, A., Brown, K.R., Maunz, P., Duan, L.M., Kim, J.: Large-scale modular quantum-computer architecture with atomic memory and photonic interconnects. Phys. Rev. A **89**, 022317 (2014). https://doi.org/10.1103/PhysRevA.89.022317

66. Lekitsch, B., Weidt, S., Fowler, A.G., Mølmer, K., Devitt, S.J., Wunderlich, C., Hensinger, W.K.: Blueprint for a microwave trapped ion quantum computer. Sci. Adv. **3**(2), e1601540 (2017). https://doi.org/10.1126/sciadv.1601540

67. Biamonte, J., Wittek, P., Pancotti, N., Rebentrost, P., Wiebe, N., Lloyd, S.: Quantum machine learning. Nature **549**(7671), 195 (2017). https://doi.org/10.1038/nature23474

68. Saggio, V., Asenbeck, B.E., Hamann, A., Strömberg, T., Schiansky, P., Dunjko, V., Friis, N., Harris, N.C., Hochberg, M., Englund, D., Wölk, S., Briegel, H.J., Walther, P.: Experimental quantum speed-up in reinforcement learning agents. Nature **591**(7849), 229 (2021). https://doi.org/10.1038/s41586-021-03242-7
69. Feynman, R.P., et al.: Simulating physics with computers. Int. J. Theor. Phys. **21**(6/7), 467–488 (2018)
70. Fauseweh, B., Schering, P., Hüdepohl, J., Uhrig, G.S.: Efficient algorithms for the dynamics of large and infinite classical central spin models. Phys. Rev. B **96**, 054415 (2017). https://doi.org/10.1103/PhysRevB.96.054415
71. Paeckel, S., Fauseweh, B., Osterkorn, A., Köhler, T., Manske, D., Manmana, S.R.: Detecting superconductivity out of equilibrium. Phys. Rev. B **101**, 180507 (2020). https://doi.org/10.1103/PhysRevB.101.180507
72. Schwarz, L., Fauseweh, B., Tsuji, N., Cheng, N., Bittner, N., Krull, H., Berciu, M., Uhrig, G.S., Schnyder, A.P., Kaiser, S., Manske, D.: Classification and characterization of nonequilibrium Higgs modes in unconventional superconductors. Nat. Commun. **11**(1), 287 (2020). https://doi.org/10.1038/s41467-019-13763-5
73. Fauseweh, B., Zhu, J.X.: Laser pulse driven control of charge and spin order in the two-dimensional Kondo lattice. Phys. Rev. B **102**, 165128 (2020). https://doi.org/10.1103/PhysRevB.102.165128
74. Peruzzo, A., McClean, J., Shadbolt, P., Yung, M.H., Zhou, X.Q., Love, P.J., Aspuru-Guzik, A., O'Brien, J.L.: A variational eigenvalue solver on a photonic quantum processor. Nat. Commun. **5**(1), 4213 (2014). https://doi.org/10.1038/ncomms5213
75. Fauseweh, B., Zhu, J.X.: Quantum computing Floquet energy spectra. Quantum **7**, 1063 (2023). https://doi.org/10.22331/q-2023-07-20-1063
76. Fauseweh, B., Zhu, J.X.: Digital quantum simulation of non-equilibrium quantum many-body systems. Quant. Inf. Process. **20**(4), 138 (2021). https://doi.org/10.1007/s11128-021-03079-z
77. Stollenwerk, T., O'Gorman, B., Venturelli, D., Mandra, S., Rodionova, O., Ng, H., Sridhar, B., Rieffel, E.G., Biswas, R.: Quantum annealing applied to de-conflicting optimal trajectories for air traffic management. IEEE Trans. Intell. Transport. Syst. **21**(1), 285 (2019). https://doi.org/10.1109/TITS.2019.2891235
78. Stollenwerk, T., Lobe, E., Jung, M.: International Workshop on Quantum Technology and Optimization Problems, pp. 99–110. Springer, Berrlin (2019). https://doi.org/10.1007/978-3-030-14082-3_9
79. Stollenwerk, T., Michaud, V., Lobe, E., Picard, M., Basermann, A., Botter, T.: Agile earth observation satellite scheduling with a quantum annealer. IEEE Trans. Aerosp. Electr. Syst. **57**(5), 3520 (2021). https://doi.org/10.1109/TAES.2021.3088490
80. Misra-Spieldenner, A., Bode, T., Schuhmacher, P.K., Stollenwerk, T., Bagrets, D., Wilhelm, F.K.: Mean-field approximate optimization algorithm. PRX Quantum **4**, 030335 (2023). https://doi.org/10.1103/PRXQuantum.4.030335
81. Jordan, S.: Quantum Algorithm Zoo. https://quantumalgorithmzoo.org/. Accessed 04 Oct 2023
82. Montanaro, A.: Quantum algorithms: an overview. npj Quant. Inf. **2**, 15023 (2016). https://doi.org/10.1038/npjqi.2015.23
83. Deutsch, D., Jozsa, R.: Rapid solution of problems by quantum computation. Proc. R. Soc. London. Ser. A Math. Phys. Sci. **439**(1907), 553 (1992). https://doi.org/10.1098/rspa.1992.0167
84. Bernstein, E., Vazirani, U.: Quantum complexity theory. SIAM J. Comput. **26**(5), 1411 (1997). https://doi.org/10.1137/S0097539796300921
85. Simon, D.R.: On the power of quantum computation. SIAM J. Comput. **26**(5), 1474 (1997). https://doi.org/10.1137/S0097539796298637

86. Tilly, J., Chen, H., Cao, S., Picozzi, D., Setia, K., Li, Y., Grant, E., Wossnig, L., Rungger, I., Booth, G.H., Tennyson, J.: The variational quantum eigensolver: A review of methods and best practices. Phys. Rep. **986**, 1 (2022). https://doi.org/10.1016/j.physrep.2022.08.003. The Variational Quantum Eigensolver: a review of methods and best practices

87. Cerezo, M., Arrasmith, A., Babbush, R., Benjamin, S.C., Endo, S., Fujii, K., McClean, J.R., Mitarai, K., Yuan, X., Cincio, L., Coles, P.J.: Variational quantum algorithms. Nat. Rev. Phys. **3**(9), 625 (2021). https://doi.org/10.1038/s42254-021-00348-9

88. McArdle, S., Jones, T., Endo, S., Li, Y., Benjamin, S.C., Yuan, X.: Variational ansatz-based quantum simulation of imaginary time evolution. npj Quant. Inf. **5**, 75 (2019). https://doi.org/10.1038/s41534-019-0187-2

89. Farhi, E., Goldstone, J., Gutmann, S.: A quantum approximate optimization algorithm. Preprint (2014). https://doi.org/10.48550/arXiv.1411.4028

90. Serrano, M.A., Perez-Castillo, R., Piattini, M.: Quantum Software Engineering. Springer Nature, Cham (2022). https://doi.org/10.1007/978-3-031-05324-5

91. Spoletini, P.: Towards quantum requirements engineering. In: 2023 IEEE 31st International Requirements Engineering Conference Workshops (REW), pp. 371–374. IEEE, Piscataway (2023). https://doi.org/10.1109/REW57809.2023.00072

92. Yue, T., Ali, S., Arcaini, P.: Towards quantum software requirements engineering. Preprint (2023). https://doi.org/10.48550/arXiv.2309.13358

93. ELEVATE (Enhanced probLEm solVing with quAntum compuTErs). https://www.dlr.de/sc/en/desktopdefault.aspx/tabid-18455/29433_read-77059/. Accessed 04 Oct 2023

94. DLR Quantum Computing Initiative – We shape the quantum computing ecosystem. https://qci.dlr.de/en/. Accessed 04 Oct 2023

95. Vandersypen, L.M.K., Steffen, M., Breyta, G., Yannoni, C.S., Sherwood, M.H., Chuang, I.L.: Experimental realization of Shor's quantum factoring algorithm using nuclear magnetic resonance. Nature **414**(6866), 883 (2001). https://doi.org/10.1038/414883a

96. Amico, M., Saleem, Z.H., Kumph, M.: Experimental study of Shor's factoring algorithm using the IBM Q experience. Phys. Rev. A **100**, 012305 (2019). https://doi.org/10.1103/PhysRevA.100.012305

97. Skosana, U., Tame, M.: Demonstration of Shor's factoring algorithm for $N = 21$ on IBM quantum processors. Sci. Rep. **11**(1), 16599 (2021). https://doi.org/10.1038/s41598-021-95973-w

98. Zhang, X.M., Li, T., Yuan, X.: Quantum state preparation with optimal circuit depth: Implementations and applications. Phys. Rev. Lett. **129**, 230504 (2022). https://doi.org/10.1103/PhysRevLett.129.230504

99. Cirac, J.I., Blatt, R., Parkins, A.S., Zoller, P.: Preparation of Fock states by observation of quantum jumps in an ion trap. Phys. Rev. Lett. **70**, 762 (1993). https://doi.org/10.1103/PhysRevLett.70.762

100. Wunderlich, H., Wunderlich, C., Singer, K., Schmidt-Kaler, F.: Two-dimensional cluster-state preparation with linear ion traps. Phys. Rev. A **79**, 052324 (2009). https://doi.org/10.1103/PhysRevA.79.052324

101. Berwald, J., Chancellor, N., Dridi, R.: Understanding domain-wall encoding theoretically and experimentally. Philosoph. Trans. Roy. Soc. A: Math. Phys. Eng. Sci. **381**(2241), 20210410 (2023). https://doi.org/10.1098/rsta.2021.0410

102. Chancellor, N.: Domain wall encoding of discrete variables for quantum annealing and QAOA. Quant. Sci. Technol. **4**(4), 045004 (2019). https://doi.org/10.1088/2058-9565/ab33c2

103. Lloyd, S., Schuld, M., Ijaz, A., Izaac, J., Killoran, N.: Quantum embeddings for machine learning. Preprint (2020). https://doi.org/10.48550/arXiv.2001.03622

104. Cross, A.W., Bishop, L.S., Smolin, J.A., Gambetta, J.M.: Open quantum assembly language. Preprint (2017). https://doi.org/10.48550/arXiv.1707.03429

105. Cirq developers. Cirq (2023). https://doi.org/10.5281/zenodo.8161252. Full list of authors: http://github.com/quantumlib/Cirq/graphs/contributors

106. Qiskit contributors. Qiskit: An open-source framework for quantum computing (2023). https://doi.org/10.5281/zenodo.2573505. https://qiskit.org/

107. Svore, K., Geller, A., Troyer, M., Azariah, J., Granade, C., Heim, B., Kliuchnikov, V., Mykhailova, M., Paz, A., Roetteler, M.: Q#: Enabling scalable quantum computing and development with a high-level DSL. In: Proceedings of the Real World Domain Specific Languages Workshop 2018, RWDSL2018. Association for Computing Machinery, New York (2018). https://doi.org/10.1145/3183895.3183901

108. Bichsel, B., Baader, M., Gehr, T., Vechev, M.: Silq: a high-level quantum language with safe uncomputation and intuitive semantics. In: Proceedings of the 41st ACM SIGPLAN Conference on Programming Language Design and Implementation, PLDI 2020, pp. 286–300. Association for Computing Machinery, New York (2020). https://doi.org/10.1145/3385412.3386007

109. Foundation, E.: Qrisp (2023). https://www.qrisp.eu/. Accessed 21 Nov 2023

110. QIR Alliance: QIR Specification (2021). https://github.com/qir-alliance/qir-spec. Accessed 04 Oct 2023

111. Peduri, A., Bhat, S., Grosser, T.: QSSA: an SSA-based IR for quantum computing. In: Proceedings of the 31st ACM SIGPLAN International Conference on Compiler Construction, CC 2022, pp. 2–14. Association for Computing Machinery, New York (2022). https://doi.org/10.1145/3497776.3517772

112. Pérez-Castillo, R., Piattini, M.: Design of classical-quantum systems with UML. Computing 104(11), 2375 (2022). https://doi.org/10.1007/s00607-022-01091-4

113. Usaola, M.P.: In: Short Papers Proceedings of the 1st International Workshop on the QuANtum SoftWare Engineering & Programming, Talavera de la Reina, Spain, February 11–12, 2020, CEUR Workshop Proceedings. Piattini, M., Peterssen, G., Pérez-Castillo, R., Hevia, J.L., Serrano, M.A. (eds.) CEUR-WS.org, vol. 2561, pp. 57–63 (2020). https://ceur-ws.org/Vol-2561/paper6.pdf

114. García de la Barrera, A., García-Rodríguez de Guzmán, I., Polo, M., Piattini, M.: Quantum software testing: State of the art. J. Softw. Evolut. Process 35(4), e2419 (2023). https://doi.org/10.1002/smr.2419

115. Miranskyy, A., Zhang, L., Doliskani, J.: On Testing and Debugging Quantum Software. Preprint (2021). https://doi.org/10.48550/arXiv.2103.09172

116. Wootters, W.K., Zurek, W.H.: A single quantum cannot be cloned. Nature 299(5886), 802 (1982). https://doi.org/10.1038/299802a0

117. Li, G., Zhou, L., Yu, N., Ding, Y., Ying, M., Xie, Y.: Proq: Projection-based Runtime Assertions for Debugging on a Quantum Computer. Preprint (2020). https://doi.org/10.48550/arXiv.1911.12855

118. Liu, J., Byrd, G.T., Zhou, H.: Quantum Circuits for Dynamic Runtime Assertions in Quantum Computation. In: Proceedings of the Twenty-Fifth International Conference on Architectural Support for Programming Languages and Operating Systems, ASPLOS '20, pp. 1017–1030. Association for Computing Machinery, New York (2020). https://doi.org/10.1145/3373376.3378488

119. Campos, J., Souto, A.: QBugs: A Collection of Reproducible Bugs in Quantum Algorithms and a Supporting Infrastructure to Enable Controlled Quantum Software Testing and Debugging Experiments. Preprint (2021). https://doi.org/10.48550/arXiv.2103.16968

120. Zhao, P., Zhao, J., Miao, Z., Lan, S.: Bugs4Q: A Benchmark of Real Bugs for Quantum Programs. Preprint (2021). https://doi.org/10.48550/arXiv.2108.09744

121. Honarvar, S., Mousavi, M.R., Nagarajan, R.: Property-based Testing of Quantum Programs in Q#. In: Proceedings of the IEEE/ACM 42nd International Conference on Software Engineering Workshops, ICSEW'20, pp. 430–435. Association for Computing Machinery, New York (2020). https://doi.org/10.1145/3387940.3391459

122. Gottesman, D.: Theory of fault-tolerant quantum computation. Phys. Rev. A 57, 127 (1998). https://doi.org/10.1103/PhysRevA.57.127

123. Preskill, J.: Lecture Notes for Physics 229: Quantum Information and Computation. California Institution of Technology, Pasadena (1998)

124. Herr, D., Nori, F., Devitt, S.J.: Optimization of lattice surgery is NP-hard. npj Quant. Inf. 3(1), 35 (2017). https://doi.org/10.1038/s41534-017-0035-1

125. Botea, A., Kishimoto, A., Marinescu, R.: In: Proceedings of the Eleventh International Symposium on Combinatorial Search (SoCS2018), vol. 9, pp. 138–142 (2018). https://doi.org/10.1609/socs.v9i1.18463

126. Amy, M., Azimzadeh, P., Mosca, M.: On the controlled-NOT complexity of controlled-NOT-phase circuits. Quant. Sci. Technol. **4**(1), 015002 (2018). https://doi.org/10.1088/2058-9565/aad8ca

127. Amy, M., Maslov, D., Mosca, M., Roetteler, M.: A meet-in-the-middle algorithm for fast synthesis of depth-optimal quantum circuits. IEEE Trans. Comput.-Aided Design Integr. Circ. Syst. **32**(6), 818 (2013). https://doi.org/10.1109/TCAD.2013.2244643

128. Schneider, S., Burgholzer, L., Wille, R.: In: Proceedings of the 28th Asia and South Pacific Design Automation Conference, ASPDAC '23, pp. 190–195 . Association for Computing Machinery, New York (2023). https://doi.org/10.1145/3566097.3567929

129. Nam, Y., Ross, N.J., Su, Y., Childs, A.M., Maslov, D.: Automated optimization of large quantum circuits with continuous parameters. npj Quant. Inf. **4**(1), 23 (2018). https://doi.org/10.1038/s41534-018-0072-4

130. Kharkov, Y., Ivanova, A., Mikhantiev, E., Kotelnikov, A.: Arline Benchmarks: Automated Benchmarking Platform for Quantum Compilers. Preprint (2022). https://doi.org/10.48550/arXiv.2202.14025

131. Khalate, P., Wu, X.C., Premaratne, S., Hogaboam, J., Holmes, A., Schmitz, A., Guerreschi, G.G. , Zou, X., Matsuura, A.Y.: An LLVM-based C++ Compiler Toolchain for Variational Hybrid Quantum-Classical Algorithms and Quantum Accelerators. Preprint (2022). https://doi.org/10.48550/arXiv.2202.11142

132. Epping, M.: Hybrid simplification rules for boundaries of quantum circuits. Preprint (2022). https://doi.org/10.48550/arXiv.2206.03036

133. NVIDIA, Vingelmann, P., Fitzek, F.H.: CUDA (2020). https://developer.nvidia.com/cuda-toolkit

134. Briegel, H.J., Browne, D.E., Dür, W., Raussendorf, R., Van den Nest, M.: Measurement-based quantum computation. Nat. Phys. **5**(1), 19 (2009). https://doi.org/10.1038/nphys1157

135. Lippert, T., Michielsen, K.: In: NIC Symposium 2022: Proceedings, Publication Series of the John von Neumann Institute for Computing (NIC) NIC Series, vol. 51, pp. 3 – 23. NIC Symposium 2022, Jülich, Germany, 29 Sep 2022–30 Sep 2022. Forschungszentrum Jülich GmbH Zentralbibliothek, Verlag, Jülich (2022). https://juser.fz-juelich.de/record/917067

136. HPCQC. Where quantum accelerates the future of supercomputing. https://www.hpcqc.org/. Accessed 04 Oct 2023

137. Janzing, D., Wocjan, P., Beth, T.: Identity check is QMA-complete. Preprint (2003). https://doi.org/10.48550/arXiv.quant-ph/0305050

138. Viamontes, G.F., Markov, I.L., Hayes, J.P.: In: 2007 IEEE/ACM International Conference on Computer-Aided Design, pp. 69–74 (2007). https://doi.org/10.1109/ICCAD.2007.4397246

139. Burgholzer, L., Wille, R.: In: 2020 25th Asia and South Pacific Design Automation Conference (ASP-DAC), IEEE, pp. 127–132. IEEE Press, Piscataway (2020). https://doi.org/10.1109/ASP-DAC47756.2020.9045153

140. Burgholzer, L., Wille, R.: QCEC: A JKQ tool for quantum circuit equivalence checking. Softw. Impacts **7**, 100051 (2021). https://doi.org/10.1016/j.simpa.2020.100051. https://www.sciencedirect.com/science/article/pii/S2665963820300427

141. D-Wave. Ocean. https://github.com/dwavesystems/dwave-ocean-sdk

142. DLR-SC. quark (2023). https://gitlab.com/quantum-computing-software/quark

143. Lobe, E., Lutz, A.: Minor Embedding in Broken Chimera and Derived Graphs is NP-complete. In: Theoretical Computer Science 989 (2024). https://doi.org/10.1016/j.tcs.2023.114369

144. Cai, J., W.G. Macready, Roy, A.: A practical heuristic for finding graph minors. Preprint (2014). https://doi.org/10.48550/arXiv.1406.2741

145. Lobe, E., Schürmann, L., Stollenwerk, T.: Embedding of complete graphs in broken Chimera graphs. Quant. Inf. Process. **20**(7), 1 (2021). https://doi.org/10.1007/s11128-021-03168-z

146. Lobe, E., Kaibel, V.: Optimal sufficient requirements on the embedded Ising problem in polynomial time. Quant. Inf. Process. **22**(305), 1 (2023). https://doi.org/10.1007/s11128-023-04058-2

147. Lidar, D.A.: Review of Decoherence-Free Subspaces, Noiseless Subsystems, and Dynamical Decoupling, pp. 295–354. Wiley, Hoboken (2014). https://doi.org/10.1002/9781118742631. ch11

148. Viola, L., Lloyd, S.: Dynamical suppression of decoherence in two-state quantum systems. Phys. Rev. A **58**, 2733 (1998). https://doi.org/10.1103/PhysRevA.58.2733

149. Lidar, D.A., Birgitta Whaley, K.: Decoherence-Free Subspaces and Subsystems, pp. 83–120. Springer, Berlin (2003). https://doi.org/10.1007/3-540-44874-8_5

150. Mueller, T., Stollenwerk, T., Headley, D., Epping, M., Wilhelm, F.K.: Coherent and non-unitary errors in ZZ-generated gates. Preprint (2023). https://doi.org/10.48550/arXiv.2304. 14212

151. Cai, Z., Babbush, R., Benjamin, S.C., Endo, S., Huggins, W.J., Li, Y., McClean, J.R., O'Brien, T.E.: Quantum Error Mitigation. Preprint (2023). https://doi.org/10.48550/arXiv.2210.00921

152. Endo, S.: Hybrid quantum-classical algorithms and error mitigation. Ph.D. Thesis, University of Oxford (2019). https://ora.ox.ac.uk/objects/uuid:6733c0f6-1b19-4d12-a899-18946aa5df85

153. Temme, K., Bravyi, S., Gambetta, J.M.: Error mitigation for short-depth quantum circuits. Phys. Rev. Lett. **119**, 180509 (2017). https://doi.org/10.1103/PhysRevLett.119.180509

154. Beisel, M., Barzen, J., Leymann, F., Truger, F., Weder, B., Yussupov, V.: Configurable readout error mitigation in quantum workflows. Electronics **11**(19), 2983 (2022). https://doi.org/10. 3390/electronics11192983

155. Gottesman, D.: An Introduction to Quantum Error Correction and Fault-Tolerant Quantum Computation. Preprint (2009). https://doi.org/10.48550/arXiv.0904.2557

156. Bacon, D.: Introduction to Quantum Error Correction, Chap. 2, pp. 46–77. Cambridge University Press, Cambridge (2013). https://doi.org/10.1017/CBO9781139034807.004

157. Roffe, J.: Quantum error correction: an introductory guide. Contemp. Phys. **60**(3), 226 (2019). https://doi.org/10.1080/00107514.2019.1667078

158. Mohseni, M., Rezakhani, A.T., Lidar, D.A.: Quantum-process tomography: Resource analysis of different strategies. Phys. Rev. A **77**, 032322 (2008). https://doi.org/10.1103/PhysRevA.77. 032322

159. Flammia, S.T., Wallman, J.J.: Efficient estimation of pauli channels. ACM Trans. Quant. Comput. **1**(1), 1 (2020). https://doi.org/10.1145/3408039

160. Wimmer, C., Szangolies, J., Epping, M.: Calibration of Syndrome Measurements in a Single Experiment. Preprint (2023). https://doi.org/10.48550/arXiv.2305.03004

161. Shor, P.W.: Scheme for reducing decoherence in quantum computer memory. Phys. Rev. A **52**, R2493 (1995). https://doi.org/10.1103/PhysRevA.52.R2493

162. Steane, A.: Multiple-particle interference and quantum error correction. Proc. R. Soc. Lond. Ser. A Math. Phys. Eng. Sci. **452**(1954), 2551 (1996). https://doi.org/10.1098/rspa.1996.0136

163. Laflamme, R., Miquel, C., J.P. Paz, Zurek, W.H.: Perfect Quantum Error Correction Code. Preprint (1996). https://doi.org/10.48550/arXiv.quant-ph/9602019

164. Bennett, C.H., DiVincenzo, D.P., Smolin, J.A., Wootters, W.K.: Mixed-state entanglement and quantum error correction. Phys. Rev. A **54**, 3824 (1996). https://doi.org/10.1103/ PhysRevA.54.3824

165. Kitaev, A.Y.: Quantum computations: algorithms and error correction. Russ. Math. Surv. **52**(6), 1191 (1997). https://doi.org/10.1070/RM1997v052n06ABEH002155

166. Shor, P.: In: Proceedings of 37th Conference on Foundations of Computer Science, pp. 56–65 (1996). https://doi.org/10.1109/SFCS.1996.548464

167. Gheorghiu, A., Kapourniotis, T., Kashefi, E.: Verification of quantum computation: an overview of existing approaches. Theory Comput. Syst, **63**(4), 715 (2019). https://doi.org/ 10.1007/s00224-018-9872-3

168. Wang, S.A., Lu, C.Y., Tsai, I.M., Kuo, S.Y.: An XQDD-based verification method for quantum circuits. IEICE Trans. Fundam. Electron. Commun. Comput. Sci. **E91-A**(2), 584–594 (2008). https://doi.org/10.1093/ietfec/e91-a.2.584

169. D'Ariano, G.M., Paris, M.G.A., Sacchi, M.F.: Quantum Tomography. Preprint (2003). https:// doi.org/10.48550/arXiv.quant-ph/0302028

170. D'Ariano, G.M., Maccone, L., Presti, P.L.: Quantum calibration of measurement instrumentation. Phys. Rev. Lett. **93**, 250407 (2004). https://doi.org/10.1103/PhysRevLett.93.250407
171. Artiles, L.M., Gill, R.D., Gută, M.I.: An invitation to quantum tomography. J. Roy. Stat. Soc. Ser. B (Statist. Methodol.) **67**(1), 109 (2005). https://doi.org/10.1111/j.1467-9868.2005.00491.x
172. Gaebler, J.P., Meier, A.M., Tan, T.R., Bowler, R., Lin, Y., Hanneke, D., Jost, J.D., Home, J.P., Knill, E., Leibfried, D., Wineland, D.J.: Randomized benchmarking of multiqubit gates. Phys. Rev. Lett. **108**, 260503 (2012). https://doi.org/10.1103/PhysRevLett.108.260503
173. SPEC (Standard Performance Evaluation Corporation). SPEC benchmark and tools. https://spec.org/benchmarks.html. Accessed 04 Oct 2023
174. Dongarra, J.J., Luszczek, P., Petitet, A.: The LINPACK Benchmark: past, present and future. Concurr. Comput. Pract. Exper. **15**(9), 803 (2003). https://doi.org/10.1002/cpe.728
175. Tomesh, T., Gokhale, P., Omole, V., Ravi, G.S., Smith, K.N., Viszlai, J., Wu, X.C., Hardavellas, N., Martonosi, M.R., Chong, F.T.: SupermarQ: A scalable quantum benchmark suite. Preprint (2022). https://doi.org/10.48550/arXiv.2202.11045
176. Dallaire-Demers, P.L., Stechly, M., Gonthier, J.F., Bashige, N.T., Romero, J., Cao, Y.: An application benchmark for fermionic quantum simulations. Preprint (2020). https://doi.org/10.48550/arXiv.2003.01862
177. Röhrig-Zöllner, M., Thies, J., Basermann, A.: Performance of the low-rank TT-SVD for large dense tensors on modern MultiCore CPUs. SIAM J. Sci. Comput. **44**(4), C287 (2022). https://doi.org/10.1137/21m1395545
178. Damm, W., Möhlmann, E., Peikenkamp, T., Rakow, A.: LNCS, pp. 182–205. Springer, Berlin (2018). https://doi.org/10.1007/978-3-319-95246-8_11
179. Kröger, Scheidegger, Becker, Deublein, Fehlberg, Galassi, Hohl, Koester, Zanella: Autonomes fahren. ein treiber zukünftiger mobilität (2022). https://doi.org/10.5281/ZENODO.5907154
180. de Moura, L., Bjørner, N.: TACAS, pp. 337–340. Springer, Berlin (2008). https://doi.org/10.1007/978-3-540-78800-3_24
181. Dosovitskiy, A., Ros, G., Codevilla, F., Lopez, A., Koltun, V.: In: Proceedings of the 1st Annual Conference on Robot Learning, Proceedings of Machine Learning Research. Levine, S., Vanhoucke, V., Goldberg, K. (Eds.) , vol. 78, pp. 1–16. PMLR (2017). https://proceedings.mlr.press/v78/dosovitskiy17a.html
182. Apache Software Foundation, Cloudera, Hortonworks. Apache Nifi. https://nifi.apache.org/. Accessed 04 Oct 2023
183. Boden, B., Flink, J., Först, N., Mischke, R., Schaffert, K., Weinert, A., Wohlan, A., Schreiber, A.: RCE: An integration environment for engineering and science. SoftwareX **15**, 100759 (2021). https://doi.org/10.1016/j.softx.2021.100759
184. Texas Instruments. Laboratory Virtual Instrument Engineering Workbench (LabVIEW). https://www.ni.com/labview. Accessed 04 Oct 2023

Development and Deployment of Quantum Services

Enrique Moguel, Jose Garcia-Alonso, and Juan M. Murillo

Abstract Quantum computing is advancing by leaps and bounds to become a commercial reality. This revolutionary new technology aims to improve essential areas such as cybersecurity, financial services, and medicine. The growth of this technology has encouraged different research centers and big companies such as IBM, Amazon, Microsoft, and Google to dedicate considerable efforts to the development of new technologies that bring quantum computing to the market. However, these technologies are not yet mature and create a major problem of vendor lock-in. Therefore, new techniques and tools are needed to facilitate access to this technology and to allow developers to increase the level of abstraction at which they work. In this chapter, we perform a technical comparison between different quantum computing service providers using a case study by performing empirical tests based on the Traveling Salesman Problem. This study highlights the differences between the major providers. To address these differences and reduce the vendor lock-in effect, we made three proposals: an extension of the Quantum API Gateway to support the different vendors; a code generator making use of a modification of the OpenAPI specification; and a workflow to automate the continuous deployment of these services making use of GitHub Actions. This would allow programmers to deploy quantum code without specific knowledge of the major vendors, which would facilitate access and simplify the development of quantum applications.

Keywords Quantum computing · Quantum software engineering · Quantum services · Techniques and tools

E. Moguel (✉) · J. Garcia-Alonso · J. M. Murillo
Quercus Software Engineering Group, University of Extremadura, Cáceres, Spain
e-mail: enrique@unex.es; jgaralo@unex.es; juan.murillo@cenits.es

189

1   Introduction

Quantum computing has indeed been making significant strides toward becoming a commercial reality [1]. Major technology companies have developed functional quantum computers, and quantum programming languages and simulators have become available. The ability for the general public to access real quantum computers through the cloud has also become a reality [2, 3]. All this is motivating software development companies to take their first steps in the quantum domain by launching their own proposals for the integral development of quantum software [4, 5, 6, 7, 8].

With the advent of the quantum era, computing will take advantage of the robustness and background of classical computing for certain tasks and the computational power of quantum computing to efficiently solve complex problems [9]. These collaborative systems are often referred to as classical-quantum hybrid systems [10, 11]. Leveraging the main principles from service engineering and service computing is a natural approach to managing this coexistence and collaboration.

There are several compelling reasons for adopting a service-oriented approach in this context. First, as quantum hardware technology matures and becomes more cost-effective, companies are likely to adopt quantum infrastructure and quantum software as a service, similar to how they currently use classical computing resources. Large technology companies such as Amazon, Microsoft, IBM, and Google have already started to explore quantum computing [12], and they may offer both classical and quantum computing services in the future.

Second, it's reasonable to assume that quantum systems will initially be used to address specific portions of problems that classical architectures struggle to solve efficiently. For example, in healthcare, quantum computing could accelerate drug discovery and molecular simulations [13]; in finance, it might help analyze complex scenarios and optimize portfolios [14]; or quantum computing could also play a role in cryptography, logistics, climate modeling, and more [15, 16, 17]. The key idea is to leverage quantum capabilities which offer a clear advantage while relying on classical computing for tasks where it remains efficient.

In summary, the coexistence and collaboration between classical and quantum systems are expected to define the quantum computing landscape for the foreseeable future. Leveraging service-oriented principles can help organizations navigate this transition and harness the potential of both classical and quantum computing resources effectively.

Therefore, relying on quantum services is a promising approach to leverage the capabilities of quantum computing in various applications. However, it's important to recognize that invoking a quantum service differs significantly from invoking a classical service due to the unique characteristics of quantum computing.

Conceptually, invoking a quantum program is akin to invoking a classical service in that it involves making a request and receiving a result. However, quantum services introduce complexities related to the inherent nature of quantum computing [18, 19, 20]:

- **Entanglement and Superposition**. Quantum systems can exist in states of entanglement and superposition, which means that they can represent multiple solutions simultaneously. This contrasts with classical systems, where the output is deterministic. Quantum services need to handle these quantum states and provide mechanisms for collapsing them into a single outcome when observed.
- **Quantum Specificity**. Quantum algorithms and their parameters are often highly dependent on the specific quantum hardware on which they run. This makes it challenging to create quantum services that are hardware-agnostic, as classical services typically are. Each quantum architecture may require tailored algorithms and configurations.
- **Error Considerations**. Quantum computations are susceptible to errors due to factors like noise and decoherence. The return of results from a quantum process may be subject to such errors. Additionally, verifying intermediate results during a quantum computation is challenging, as the act of measurement can collapse the quantum state.
- **Diverse Skill sets**. Developing quantum algorithms and services for different quantum architectures demands diverse skill sets. For example, developers working with circuit-based quantum programming need expertise in quantum gates, while those working with quantum annealing require skills in adapting problems to this specific approach.

Given these challenges, creating quantum services that adhere to the principles of service engineering and provide the same level of modularity, reusability, and maintainability as classical services are currently difficult. Quantum service engineering [21], as a specialized field, seeks to address these challenges and develop best practices for designing and deploying quantum services effectively.

In this chapter, we review the background (Sect. 2) in the literature related to quantum service engineering. Subsequently, in Sect. 3 we show an empirical analysis that we have performed for the main quantum computing service providers. Next, in Sect. 4 we show the progress made in standardization in accessing service providers. In Sect. 5 we then advance the work in the area of service generation for quantum computing. Then, in Sect. 6 we define the existing methods and tools for deploying quantum services. Finally, conclusions to this work are presented in Sect. 7.

2 Background

Service-oriented computing (SOC) [22] has played a pivotal role in driving innovation in the computing field over the past few decades [23]. It has significantly impacted both research and industry, leading to transformative changes in the way software is developed and deployed. From service-oriented architectures [24] to cloud computing [25], SOC has had a major impact on both research and industry.

The SOC paradigm revolves around the use of services as fundamental building blocks to enable the development of applications that are fast, cost-effective, interoperable, adaptable, and capable of massive distribution. This paradigm has brought about a fundamental shift in software development, ushering in an era of smart devices and ubiquitous applications that permeate every aspect of our lives.

Some key technological foundations and developments have contributed to the success of SOC:

- **Service-Oriented Architecture (SOA)**: SOA provides a framework for organizing and using services in a flexible and modular manner [26]. It has been instrumental in structuring software systems around services.
- **Semantic Web**: The Semantic Web extends the capabilities of the World Wide Web by adding a semantic layer, enabling more meaningful interactions between machines [27]. It has contributed to the intelligent discovery and composition of services.
- **Standards and Recommendations**: Standards such as OpenAPI [28] and W3C Thing Description [29] have played a crucial role in specifying and describing services in a standardized manner, making it easier for developers to understand and utilize them.
- **Service Composition**: Service composition allows the combination of multiple services or microservices to create higher-level services that can support complex tasks or entire business processes.

The primary goal of these technological advancements has been to enhance flexibility and enable seamless integration in the realm of distributed applications. By adopting SOC principles and technologies, organizations have been able to build more agile and adaptable software systems, driving innovation and transforming various industries.

However, the evolution and benefits seen in classical computing have not yet been fully replicated in the realm of quantum computing. Quantum computers, which are still expensive to build and operate, have followed a model that resembles Quantum Computing as a Service (QCaaS) [30]. This model is somewhat analogous to the classical Infrastructure as a Service (IaaS) [31] model in cloud computing. While QCaaS allows developers to access quantum computers through the cloud, it's important to note that this access is highly dependent on specific quantum hardware, and developers typically require a deep understanding of quantum computing to harness its advantages.

Efforts are underway to increase the level of abstraction and accessibility of QCaaS. Companies like Amazon (Amazon Braket),[1] IBM (IBM Quantum),[2] and Microsoft (Azure Quantum)[3] have introduced platforms that provide a development environment for quantum software engineers. These platforms aim to simplify the

---

[1] https://aws.amazon.com/braket.

[2] https://www.ibm.com/quantum.

[3] https://quantum.microsoft.com.

process of working with quantum computing resources and integrate classical and quantum software.

On the other hand, platforms like QPath[4] offer comprehensive ecosystems that bridge the classical and quantum realms of software development. These platforms provide a quantum development and application life cycle environment, fostering the creation of high-quality quantum software.

In the academic field, research efforts are starting to emerge in the field of quantum software engineering. Some papers focus on translating lessons from classical software engineering to enhance the quality of quantum software [32, 33]. However, there remains a relatively small body of work that specifically addresses the service engineering perspective for quantum and hybrid software [34]. In addition, innovations like Quantum Application as a Service (QaaS) have been proposed to bridge the gap between classical service engineering and quantum software [35, 36]. These initiatives recognize the need for a service-oriented approach to quantum service development.

These developments reflect a growing awareness of the importance of abstracting and simplifying access to quantum computing resources and services [37, 38]. They aim to make quantum computing more accessible to a broader range of developers, including those who may not possess an in-depth understanding of quantum mechanics but can leverage quantum resources for various applications.

Therefore, in the following sections, we will present an empirical study of the main providers of quantum computing services. In addition, we will discuss the main limitations associated with access to this technology. Subsequently, we will delve into the different alternatives proposed in the literature to address these issues.

3   Quantum Providers

The growing interest and investment in quantum computing have positioned it as an emerging commercial reality [32]. Major research centers, large companies, and countries recognize the potential impact of quantum computing on future society. Consequently, quantum computing is on a trajectory to become as popular and well known as classical computing is today [39]. This, combined with the expanding range of applications, makes quantum computing highly attractive to technology companies and researchers alike.

Several prominent computer companies have already developed functional quantum computers. These achievements are the result of substantial efforts and investments in quantum computer construction. Companies are working on processors with increasing numbers of qubits and exploring solutions to address challenges like noise and information loss [40]. For instance, Google presented its Sycamore quantum chip in 2019 with 53 qubits, the Riggetti company at the end of 2022

---

[4] https://www.quantumpath.es.

developed the Aspen-M-3 chip with 80 qubits, and IBM presented Osprey in November 2022, with a 433-qubit quantum processor. In this regard, IBM, one of the leading companies in the development of quantum computers, plans to launch Condor with an 1121-qubit quantum chip by the end of 2023, Flamingo with at least 1386 qubits in 2024, and Kookaburra with no less than 4158 qubits in 2025.

These advancements signal the rapid development of quantum computing and its journey from research laboratories to the broader technology landscape, with potential applications across various industries [1].

The emergence of quantum computing has brought with it a proliferation of quantum programming languages and simulators, making quantum computing resources increasingly accessible. The availability of real quantum computers through cloud platforms has further accelerated this trend, enabling the general public to experiment with quantum computing [4, 6, 5].

This evolution has sparked the interest of software development companies, leading them to explore the development of comprehensive quantum software solutions. In light of these developments, this section undertakes an empirical analysis of quantum computing service providers, examining them from a software engineering perspective. The number of companies offering quantum services has grown significantly, as has the diversity of quantum computers and alternatives for executing quantum algorithms and tasks. With this abundance of choices, the process of selecting the most suitable technology for a given task becomes nontrivial [41].

The primary objective of this analysis is to assess and compare several technological alternatives using consistent criteria. The goal is to provide insights into the strengths and weaknesses of different quantum computing service providers. Additionally, this analysis aims to highlight the challenges and issues faced by quantum software developers who want to use these providers.

To conduct this assessment, a Quantum Phase Estimation (QPE) algorithm has been chosen as a case study. This algorithm will be employed to solve the Travelling Salesman Problem (TSP) and will be developed, deployed, and executed on various quantum machines using different technologies. This case study will provide practical insights into the capabilities and limitations of different quantum computing options for solving real-world problems.

The Traveling Salesman Problem (TSP), as identified by Karp in 1972 [42], falls into the category of NP-hard problems. In this class of problems, if the algorithm is divided into smaller sub-problems, each of these sub-problems is as complex as the original problem. This inherent complexity is one of the reasons for choosing the TSP as a case study. Furthermore, the TSP is notable for lacking an optimal solution found in classical computation. These problems possess a unique characteristic: as the problem size increases, the number of possible solutions typically grows exponentially.

In the analysis that follows, we will examine some of the most popular and innovative solutions available for developing and executing quantum software. Our focus will prioritize integrated tools and options for quantum circuit development provided by these platforms over local alternatives, whenever applicable.

The primary vendors included in this analysis are IBM Quantum,[5] Amazon Braket,[6] Azure Quantum,[7] and Google Quantum AI.[8] While other quantum platforms and service providers were initially considered, they were ultimately excluded for various reasons. Some were excluded because they significantly deviated from the gate-based model architecture used by other quantum computers, rendering a fair comparison difficult (e.g., D-Wave Systems[9]). Others were excluded because they did not function as independent quantum service providers but rather relied entirely on other platforms to provide quantum computing resources for algorithm execution (e.g., QC Ware Forge[10]).

Another platform, Stim [43], which simulates the behavior of stabilizing circuits, was also excluded. It's important to note that Stim does not function as a quantum service provider in the same vein as IBM Quantum or Azure Quantum. Instead, Stim serves as a software tool for simulating the behavior of quantum circuits. While not directly comparable to the gate-based model used by other quantum computers, Stim remains a valuable resource for those interested in quantum computing.

Figure 1 shows a first review of the main vendors included in this study. The figure not only highlights the numerous quantum computers and simulators offered by these vendors but also includes the main languages and libraries they offer for the development of quantum algorithms. Therefore, it can be seen that companies are making great efforts in quantum computing, especially in building quantum computers and processors with a higher number of qubits, as well as offering multiple simulators that allow the study of a quantum system in a programmable way. In addition to quantum hardware, the new paradigm of quantum computing also includes new quantum programming languages and libraries, fundamental in the development of quantum software, with Python being the most common language among the vendors analyzed.

The comparison included in the following sections is performed at different levels, analyzing the vendors themselves along with the services offered, and finally developing a quantum algorithm in each of them and running that algorithm on the quantum hardware provided. Although we have included simulators in the comparison, to analyze the performance and capabilities of these quantum vendors we have exclusively used real quantum computers provided by the vendors analyzed.

To find out what is the best time to perform experiments on the quantum machines of these vendors, we have consulted the specific guidelines and recommendations of each vendor on what is the best time of the day to perform runs on their quantum machines, in addition to having tested over a sufficient period of

---

[5] https://www.ibm.com/quantum.

[6] https://aws.amazon.com/braket.

[7] https://azure.microsoft.com/products/quantum.

[8] https://quantumai.google.

[9] https://www.dwavesys.com.

[10] https://forge.qcware.com.

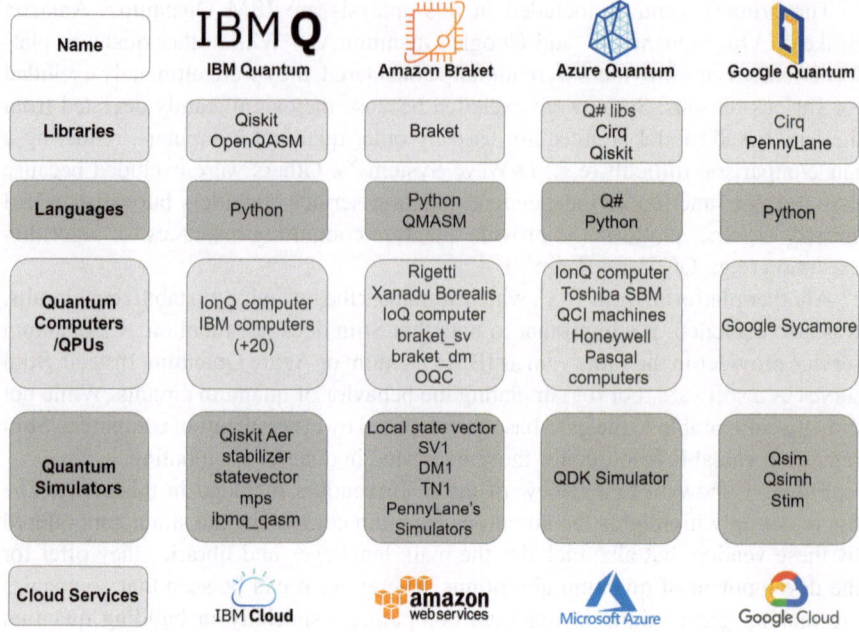

Fig. 1 Overview of quantum providers

time to validate the experiment. In addition, we have also taken into account factors such as the availability of computing resources and the workload of the quantum machine at that time. All this is to achieve more accurate results and to make the vendor comparison effective.

The implementation of the algorithm for each of the vendors analyzed can be found in the Bitbucket repository.[11]

3.1 IBM Quantum

IBM Quantum's decision to provide access to quantum computers via the cloud has been pivotal in democratizing quantum computing. It has allowed researchers, developers, and enthusiasts worldwide to experiment with quantum algorithms without needing specialized hardware.

IBM Quantum offers a comprehensive set of tools and services for quantum computing. Here are some key components of IBM Quantum's quantum computing ecosystem:

---

[11] https://bitbucket.org/spilab/sqj-tsp-code.git.

- **Quantum Computers**. IBM Quantum provides access to a variety of quantum computers through the cloud. These quantum computers have different numbers of qubits and capabilities, allowing users to choose the one that suits their needs.
- **Qiskit**. Qiskit is an open-source quantum computing framework developed by IBM. It provides a rich set of tools and libraries for quantum programming. Users can define quantum circuits, execute them on real or simulated quantum hardware, and work with quantum algorithms. Qiskit supports multiple programming languages, including Python.
- **Qiskit Runtime**. Qiskit Runtime is a cloud-based service offered by IBM Quantum. It allows users to run complex quantum algorithms without having to manage the low-level details of execution. Developers can create quantum programs that leverage Qiskit Runtime to execute on IBM's quantum computers.
- **Quantum Composer**. The Quantum Composer is a graphical user interface provided by IBM Quantum. It simplifies the process of designing quantum circuits using a drag-and-drop interface. Users can visually construct quantum circuits and then export them for execution.
- **OpenQASM**. OpenQASM is an open quantum assembly language developed by IBM. It provides a textual representation of quantum circuits and allows users to define quantum operations at a low level. Quantum circuits written in OpenQASM can be executed on IBM Quantum's hardware.
- **Cloud-Based Access**. IBM Quantum offers cloud-based access to its quantum computers, making it easy for users to run quantum experiments without the need for specialized hardware. Users can access these quantum computers via the IBM Quantum Experience platform.
- **Community and Resources**. IBM Quantum has an active community of researchers, developers, and quantum enthusiasts. They provide extensive documentation, tutorials, and educational resources to help users get started with quantum programming and research.
- **Quantum Software Development Kit (SDK)**. IBM Quantum offers a comprehensive SDK that includes Qiskit, Qiskit Aqua (for quantum applications), Qiskit Aer (for quantum simulation), and other tools for quantum software development.

Overall, IBM Quantum provides a robust ecosystem for quantum computing, making it accessible to a wide range of users, from beginners to experienced researchers and developers.

Table 1 summarizes the analysis of the general aspects of IBM Quantum.

The circuit representing the TSP has been implemented using Qiskit, an open-source SDK for programming quantum circuits based on Python, accessed via Jupyter Notebooks hosted in the IBM Quantum Lab, and by the *Pay-As-You-Go Plan*. In order to be able to use the quantum composition tool, the circuit has also been transformed from a Qiskit format to an OpenQASM 2.0 format. The visual representation of a fragment of the circuit is depicted in Fig. 2.

The process of creating this quantum circuit involves defining six qubits named "unit," eight qubits named "eigen," and six classical bits to store measured results.

Table 1 General aspects analysis of IBM Quantum

Category	Description
Type of quantum technology	Gate-based quantum computing model
Purpose	Develop quantum programs, run them, and analyze the results
QPUs and Simulators	**5 simulators**, of different types, with 5000, 100, 63, 32, and 32 qubits respectively **21 QPUs** grouped by processor type: Eagle (1 QPU of 127 qubits), Hummingbird (1 QPU of 65 qubits), Falcon (19 QPUs from 5 to 27 qubits)
General Characteristics	Medium flexibility, allowing development in Qikist and OpenQASM 2.0
Developer tools	Qiskit Runtime: workloads optimization Quantum Lab: Python Notebooks with Qiskit Quantum Composer: Drag and drop and coding based on OpenQASM 2.0
Plans and pricing	3 different plans (Free Plan, Pay-As-You-Go Plan, and Premium Plan)

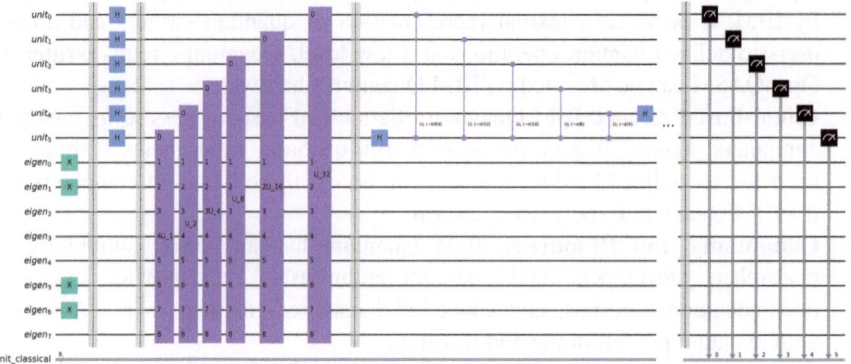

Fig. 2 Partial representation of the TSP implemented with Qiskit in IBM Quantum

The "unit" qubits represent the distances between cities, which are encoded as phases. The "eigen" qubits represent the computational basis states that have eigenvalues associated with them. Quantum gates are then applied to the circuit, including X gates to select input eigenvalues and Hadamard gates to create a superposition state. Also, multiple unitary gates are applied to corresponding qubits before the QFT gate is applied to the "unit" qubits, which are then measured, storing the results in the six classical bits. The complete description of the design of the circuit can be found on Qiskit's official Web site.[12]

Then, we executed the quantum algorithm on IBM Quantum hardware, using a total of 8192 shots. In quantum computing, a "shot" refers to a single execution of

---

[12] https://qiskit.org/textbook/ch-paper-implementations/tsp.html.

a quantum circuit on the quantum computer. The exact number of shots required for a quantum machine to execute an algorithm can vary based on several factors. These factors include the size and complexity of the problem instance being solved, the specific quantum algorithm used, the connectivity of qubits in the quantum hardware, and the level of noise or errors present in the quantum system.

For this particular experiment, a decision was made to use 8192 shots across all providers. This choice aligns with the limits set by quantum service providers to ensure a high quality of service and maintain consistency in the execution of quantum circuits across different platforms [44].

The Traveling Salesman Problem (TSP) algorithm used in this experiment involved executing the same quantum circuit six times, once for each eigenstate. Each eigenstate corresponds to a different route that could potentially solve the TSP. After each circuit execution, the results were collected and analyzed. The analysis aimed to identify which eigenstate had the smallest phase value, indicating the most favorable solution to the TSP. This approach allowed you to determine the associated Hamiltonian cycle, which, in turn, provided the final solution to the TSP for each provider.

IBM Quantum, as a quantum service provider, offers access to a quantum computer with a capacity of up to 127 qubits for circuit execution. We chose to execute your circuit 8192 times, which corresponds to the number of shots, following the terminology of the vendor. This usage resulted in a cost of $8.32 under IBM Quantum's pay-as-you-go pricing model.

In terms of performance, the average running time for executing the algorithm on IBM Quantum hardware was approximately 5.2 seconds. Additionally, there was a queue time of 11.2 seconds, indicating the time it took for your job to be scheduled and executed on the quantum computer.

3.2 Amazon Braket

Amazon Braket is a fully managed quantum computing service provided by Amazon Web Services (AWS). It is designed to accelerate scientific research and software development in the field of quantum computing. Amazon Braket serves as a central access point for a range of quantum computing technologies and supports hybrid approaches that combine classical and quantum computing.

Users can leverage Amazon Braket to experiment with quantum algorithms, develop quantum applications, and explore the potential of quantum computing in various domains. It provides access to quantum hardware, simulators, and a set of development tools to facilitate quantum computing research and application development.

Table 2 summarizes the analysis of the general aspects of Amazon Braket.

Amazon Braket provides a Platform as a Service (PaaS) that enables users to implement and execute quantum algorithms. This platform is designed to seamlessly integrate quantum computing with classical software and supports the development

Table 2 General aspects analysis of Amazon Braket

Category	Description
Type of quantum technology	Gate-based quantum computing, quantum annealing, and hybrid quantum-classical computing
Purpose	Access tools to develop and execute quantum circuits in third-party hardware providers
QPUs and simulators	**Four simulators** (local, sv1, tn1, and dm1), **seven QPUs** from other hardware providers: D-Wave (three QPUs), IonQ (one QPU), Oxford Quantum Circuits (one QPU), and Rigetti (two QPUs)
General Characteristics	Medium flexibility, allowing mainly development through its SDK and the possibility of using Qiskit and OpenQASM 3.0
Developer tools	Amazon Braket SDK with the possibility of using Qiskit or OpenQASM 3.0. Possibility to create hybrid jobs
Plans and pricing	Fixed prices which vary slightly depending on the QPU. Generally: $0.30 for task + $0.00035 for every shot

of hybrid software, which combines classical and quantum elements to address complex problems. Amazon Braket serves as a comprehensive solution for quantum computing in the cloud, offering access to various quantum simulators and quantum computers from different providers.

In Amazon Braket, users can work with a set of quantum simulators, each designed for specific purposes. Additionally, they can access quantum hardware from various providers, allowing for experimentation with different quantum processors. This flexibility and hybrid computing capability makes Amazon Braket a robust platform for building, testing, and deploying quantum-classical applications.

To implement the Traveling Salesman Problem (TSP) algorithm in Amazon Braket, some adaptations were required due to differences in syntax compared to Qiskit, and also because not all gates used in the original TSP circuit were supported by the Rigetti hardware (where the execution was carried out). To address this, a Qiskit provider for Amazon Braket was utilized with Amazon's support. The implementation details can be found in the Bitbucket repository.[13]

Amazon Braket supports circuit execution with up to 80 qubits. In this particular case, the TSP circuit was executed using 8192 shots under a pay-as-you-go plan, resulting in an execution cost of $3.17. The algorithm was run on various machines available through Amazon Braket, with an average total runtime of 9.95 seconds, including a queue time of 30 seconds.

---

[13] https://bitbucket.org/spilab/sqj-tsp-code.git.

Table 3 General aspects analysis of Azure Quantum

Category	Description
Type of quantum technology	Gate-based quantum computing model
Purpose	Access tools to develop and execute quantum circuits in third-party hardware providers
QPUs and Simulators	15+ optimization simulators and QPUs from other hardware providers: IONQ (two QPUs and one simulator), Quantinuum (five QPUs and two simulators)
General Characteristics	High flexibility, allowing development in Q#, Qiskit, and Cirq easily
Developer tools	Quantum Development Kit using Python Notebooks, Q#, Qiskit, and Cirq as language
Plans and pricing	Three different plans (Azure Quantum credits, Pay-as-go, and Subscription)

3.3 Azure Quantum

Azure Quantum is the quantum computing cloud service of Azure developed by Microsoft, with a diverse set of quantum solutions and technologies. It provides access to quantum computers from IonQ and Quantinuum and will soon add Rigetti and Quantum Circuits Inc. In addition, it provides a Quantum Development Kit (QDK) which is a complete SDK that includes a quantum-specific language called Q# and enables anyone to write quantum programs, simulate those programs on a classical computer, and then execute the program on the quantum computer connected to Azure. Thus, Azure Quantum ensures an open, flexible, and future-proofed path to quantum computing that adapts to your way of working and accelerates your progress.

Table 3 summarizes the analysis of the general aspects of Azure Quantum.

The implementation of quantum circuits in Azure Quantum involves the use of Jupyter Notebooks. Azure Quantum offers a higher level of customization, allowing users to choose between Python and Q# as the core of the notebook and select a provider for running quantum jobs, with options including IONQ and Quantinuum.

To perform this validation, we select IONQ. To set up the program for execution on IONQ's quantum hardware within Azure Quantum, several adjustments and modifications are required. Firstly, users need to obtain the *AzureQuantumProvider* by calling the appropriate method and providing the ID of their resources and the region where these resources are located. In Azure Quantum, a resource represents an entity managed by Azure, such as an Azure Quantum workspace, where quantum programs are managed. The specific provider's quantum hardware ID must also be obtained and specified when running the quantum program. Regions in Azure Quantum correspond to geographic locations where resources are hosted, and the chosen region determines the available quantum hardware providers.

The circuit implementation for solving problems like the Traveling Salesman Problem (TSP) in Azure Quantum is conceptually similar to that used in other quantum providers. It involves the definition of various quantum gates as needed for the circuit.

Regarding the execution of the circuit, it is performed on different quantum machines, with the number of qubits in the circuit adjusted to match the maximum number of qubits supported by each machine. In this case, it's possible to run a circuit with a maximum of 29 qubits.

Execution details include the use of 8192 shots in this case with a pay-as-you-go plan, resulting in an execution cost of $0.0143. After running the TSP algorithm on various machines provided by Azure Quantum, the average runtime was approximately 5.15 seconds, with a queue time of 17 seconds included.

3.4   Google Quantum AI

Google has made significant strides in the field of quantum computing, and its Quantum AI division is at the forefront of these efforts. Google Quantum AI is dedicated to advancing quantum computing technologies and making them accessible to researchers and developers for experimentation and problem-solving.

One of Google's notable achievements in quantum computing is the development of the Bristlecone quantum processor. Bristlecone boasts an impressive 72 qubits, which is a significant advancement in quantum hardware. Qubits are the fundamental units of quantum information, and having a large number of them in a quantum processor like Bristlecone opens up new possibilities for quantum computing.

Beyond hardware development, Google is also actively involved in the research and development of quantum algorithms. These algorithms are specifically designed to tackle problems that classical computers struggle with. Quantum machine learning and pattern recognition are among the complex problem domains that Google is exploring with quantum computing.

To facilitate quantum algorithm development and experimentation, Google has introduced an open-source quantum framework called Cirq. This framework is designed for experimenting with noisy intermediate-scale quantum (NISQ) algorithms. NISQ algorithms are quantum algorithms tailored for the limitations and characteristics of current quantum hardware, where the details of the hardware's behavior play a crucial role in algorithm design.

Table 4 summarizes the analysis of the general aspects of Google Quantum AI.

The implementation of the TSP circuit using the Google Quantum AI platform and the Cirq framework shares similarities with the IBM Quantum implementation, but there are some key differences, particularly related to how qubits are defined and manipulated.

In Cirq, qubits can be defined in three different ways: they can be labeled with any name, labeled by a number in a linear array, or labeled by two numbers in

Table 4 General aspects analysis of Google Quantum AI

Category	Description
Type of quantum technology	Gate-based quantum computing model
Purpose	Explore the different solutions for quantum software and hardware, with the possibility of developing circuits and running them in their hardware
QPUs and Simulators	One simulator of 20 qubits and the possibility of creating a QVM. **three QPUs**: Bristlecone (72 qubits), Sycamore (54 qubits), Foxtail (22 qubits)
General Characteristics	Cirq is the only language of development and its hardware has many restrictions, but with the possibility of importing circuits from Quirk or OpenQASM 2.0
Developer tools	Cirq framework and language. Also, other libraries like qsim or Pennylane
Plans and pricing	Free

a rectangular lattice. This flexibility in qubit labeling allows for various ways to represent and organize qubits in a quantum circuit.

Gate application in Cirq is accomplished through a concept called a "Moment," which allows sets of quantum gates to be applied simultaneously to a set of qubits. While Cirq doesn't define gates in the traditional sense as in other quantum frameworks like Qiskit, the Moment concept serves a similar purpose.

The process of measuring qubits in Cirq is similar to other quantum frameworks, with measurements being performed in a regular manner.

However, a notable difference when running a circuit on a real quantum processor with Google Quantum AI is the consideration of the processor's topology. Each quantum processor from Google Quantum AI has a unique topology, which refers to the physical arrangement of qubits and their connectivity. For instance, the Sycamore processor has a square grid layout, while the Bristlecone processor has a linear layout. When designing a quantum circuit for execution on a specific processor, it's essential to account for the topology and connectivity of that particular processor.

In the case of Google Quantum AI, up to 72 qubits are available for circuit execution, and 8192 shots were used in the Free plan with no execution cost. The average total runtime for the TSP algorithm on various Google Quantum AI processors was approximately 8.935 seconds, including a queue time of 8.1 seconds.

3.5 Analysis and Comparison

Upon evaluating these providers and utilizing them to create and run the TSP algorithm, the initial observation is that, while all of them target a common objective, each has been crafted with distinct technology and criteria. Consequently,

Table 5 Overview of the inputs for all experiments

	Max. number of qubits sopported	Cost in $	Number of shots
IBM Quantum	433	8.32	8192
Amazon Braket (Rigetti)	80	3.17	8192
Azure Quantum (IONQ)	29	0.0143	8192
Google Quantum AI	72	Free	8192

each platform is tailored for specific purposes and aligns more effectively with certain projects over others.

Table 5 displays the records encompassing all the conducted experiments on the providers. To sum up, it was determined that the execution utilized 8192 shots for each provider. This choice aligns with the providers' service quality standards, ensuring a robust distribution of results, especially when contending with noise [44]. While executing the algorithm across diverse quantum computers, it became evident that employing a high number of shots, as we have done, proves advantageous [45]. This is due to the presence of noise, which occasionally causes erroneous results, given the ongoing developmental nature of this technology.

Another thing we can easily observe is the maximum number of qubits depending on the machines they offer. Currently, IBM Quantum is the provider supplying the highest number of qubits, followed by Amazon Braket, although this is quite variable depending on the progress of the technologies and the machines they offer respectively.

Another conclusion that can be drawn is the price of running the experiments, which is highly variable from one provider to another, with the least expensive being Azure Quantum and Google Quantum AI, which is free. These prices differ depending on the payment plan chosen and the number of shots.

Another factor to consider when choosing a quantum platform for a project is the specific application or use case. Different quantum platforms offer various functionalities that are tailored to specific applications. For example, IBM Quantum has developed a series of software development kits (SDKs) that provide access to different domains, such as quantum chemistry, optimization, and finance. On the other hand, Google Quantum AI has developed the TensorFlow Quantum library, which allows developers to build and train quantum machine learning models. Similarly, Azure Quantum provides access to the Quantum Development Kit, which includes the Q# programming language and quantum simulators, while Amazon Braket offers integration with different classical computing tools and access to different types of quantum hardware. We know that these factors can influence the decision to choose a quantum platform for specific projects, but they have not been analyzed in depth in the above comparison, as they are more platform-specific, so a fair comparison is not possible. As for the results, as can be seen in Table 6, these are "100100" for all experiments. Despite the inherently probabilistic nature of the

Table 6 Overview of the results for all experiments

	Results	Compiling/ Transpiling time	Queue time	Running time	Total time
IBM Quantum	100100 (consistent)	5.9s	11.2s	5.2s	22.3s
Amazon Braket (Rigetti)	100100 (consistent)	2.2s	30s	9.95s	42.15s
Azure Quantum (IONQ)	100100 (consistent)	4s	17s	5.15s	26.15s
Google Quantum AI	100100 (consistent)	4.801s	8.1s	8.935s	21.836s

TSP algorithm in quantum computing, which arises from the probabilistic nature of quantum mechanics and not just noise or errors, we obtained consistent results in the algorithm runs [46].

The "100100" result in the context of the TSP on quantum machines is the solution that is represented as a state of the quantum machine. The solution is represented as a quantum system's own state, as a binary representation of a solution to the TSP problem, where each digit represents the order of visiting a city in the tour. Concretely, it means that the provider visits cities 1, 2, 3, 3, 4, and 1 in that order. Moreover, these results are consistent because the same result is obtained in all experiments. Consistency is an important property of any computational result, including those obtained using quantum algorithms, because it indicates that the result is reliable and reproducible, as it is in this case. In addition, it can be observed that the elapsed time from launching the run on each platform is different. However, these times are indicative and variable since they depend on the number of users that are sending jobs to the machines at a given time.

After analyzing the implementation of the TSP in each provider, we deduce that it is difficult to work with machines from different providers, without having extensive knowledge about the operation of all of them. We even encounter this problem within the same vendor, where, depending on the machine to be used, the circuit must be implemented differently. In other words, there is a limitation in terms of the programming language or SDK, and the topology of the quantum processor used by the machine to be used for execution [47].

Therefore, it is necessary to work along these research lines in order to solve the problems that still prevail in the access and standardization of the different quantum computing providers. To this end, in the following sections, we will show the research being carried out at different levels: in Sect. 4 we will examine the existing works on the standardization of access to the different providers; in Sect. 5 we will show the existing works on the generation of quantum services; and finally, in Sect. 6 we will consider the existing deployment approaches in this area.

4 Standardization of Access to Quantum Services Use

As can be seen from the previous analysis of different providers, it is necessary to facilitate access so developers can benefit from the advancement of this technology. Along these lines, Ohkura et al. [48] propose a compilation protocol for quantum multiprogramming on NISQ processors. In this work, the researchers pay attention to combining quantum circuits for parallel execution and mapping program qubit variables to physical qubits to reduce unwanted interference among the active set of quantum circuits. They also propose a software-based cross-talk detection protocol that uses a combination of randomized benchmarking methods. The proposed method is characterized by hardware suitability for multiprogramming with relatively low detection costs. In addition, they find a trade-off between success rate and runtime in multiprogramming.

Furthermore, Jonathan Ray's work [49] promotes the connection between quantum simulators from Chinese providers with online platforms for artificial intelligence. In this work, the researcher identifies the main entities investigating the nexus between the two technologies, assesses the pathways, and technological hurdles, and provides pointers for future development.

Also, there are works in the field of security for different quantum providers such as Kaliyanandi et al. [50] in which they propose a holistic approach to load balancing with security in cloud computing. The authors have created the Quantum-Based Security Framework, making use of fuzzy logic. Along these lines, Karacan et al. [51] propose two different quantum attack-resistant structures to ensure secure communication between the subscriber identity module (SIM) and service providers. In these proposed methods, they use the advanced encryption standard (AES-256) for communication with resource-constrained devices, and the N-th degree Truncated polynomial Ring Units (NTRU) encryption system for communication with servers. This proposed method provides authentication, data privacy, and integrity for post-quantum SIM cards.

But in none of these cases is a middleware proposed that allows developers to connect to all quantum machines in an agnostic way. Therefore, Garcia-Alonso et al. [52] have proposed a Quantum API Gateway to solve this problem.

4.1 Quantum API Gateway

An API Gateway is a pattern used for the composition of microservices in applications [53]. It is also a valuable tool for optimizing the deployment strategy of quantum services at runtime. By integrating multiple quantum computing vendors and offering the ability to recommend the best quantum machine based on user-indicated parameters, this gateway can enhance the efficiency and effectiveness of quantum service utilization.

It's important to note that quantum computing is still in its early stages, and the availability of multiple quantum computing platforms from different vendors introduces complexities in terms of selecting the right hardware for a specific task. Solutions like the Quantum API Gateway can help users make more informed decisions by considering various factors when choosing a quantum machine, such as the problem's nature and size, hardware constraints, and performance characteristics.

Additionally, the use of machine learning models to recommend quantum machines based on user inputs is a promising approach. As quantum computing technology continues to evolve, such intelligent decision-making tools may become increasingly essential for users looking to harness the power of quantum computers effectively.

Therefore, Garcia-Alonso et al. [52] proposed a machine learning model implemented to recommend the best quantum machine based on the parameters indicated by the user in the request. In short, it allows for optimizing the deployment strategy of a quantum service at runtime.

The Quantum API Gateway is developed in Python, specifically using the Flask library to define the API with the different endpoints. The project is currently deployed on an AWS server and is presented with a reference implementation for Amazon Braket.

The authors have tested with the Amazon Braket reference implementation, and have extended this tool to cover other vendors, such as IBM Quantum, discussed in Sect. 3.

By integrating multiple vendors with the Quantum API Gateway, and using the TSP algorithm to thoroughly validate this new implementation, the researchers have successfully validated its technological capabilities. The complete system is shown in Fig. 3. The proposed solution significantly improves the deployment and execution of quantum services.

In this work, the researchers use the information presented by the providers about the state of the execution queues on their machines and deploy the quantum service on the best machine of the best platform based on the user's constraints. In this way, the Quantum API Gateway agnostically deploys the quantum services taking into account the constraints and, after receiving the user's requests, returns the response in a standard format for all providers.

The execution process, represented graphically in Fig. 4, starts with a classical machine wishing to invoke a quantum service (step 1). This service call includes input and optimization parameters for the quantum machine, such as the number of qubits, the maximum price to be paid for execution, and the type of machine required for execution: frog or gate. When the Quantum API Gateway receives the service call, it requests information about the state of the machines from the QCaaS provider (step 2) and, through its recommender, chooses the most optimal one to deploy the service (step 3). Once the machine is chosen, it launches the service (step 4) and returns the response in a standard format to the classic machine (step 5). Once the execution is finished, it returns to the quantum machine to recommend the data obtained during the execution (step 6).

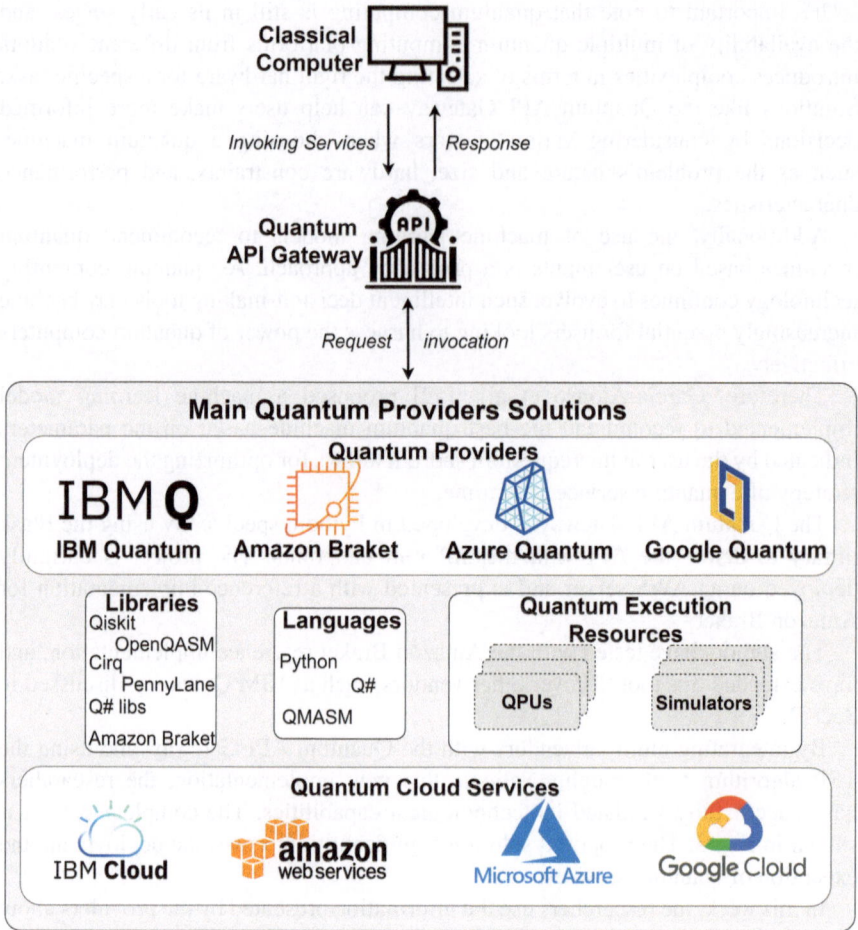

Fig. 3 Quantum providers solutions through Quantum API Gateway

Thus, with this process and by choosing the best computer for each task, the Quantum API Gateway provides advantages over existing methods for using quantum services. For example, it gives developers the flexibility to select at runtime between different providers, depending on the type of code they want to run. This takes into account the number of qubits required for the computation to ensure that only machines with sufficient computational power are used. This information is usually provided by the vendors, being available as static data (e.g., in the case of Amazon Braket) and as back-end information (e.g., in the case of IBM Quantum); this information is specific to each service provider. In addition, the tool allows the flexibility to select between gating-based and annealing-based machines, assuming both quantum service implementations are available. This feature allows for greater efficiency and accuracy in quantum computing.

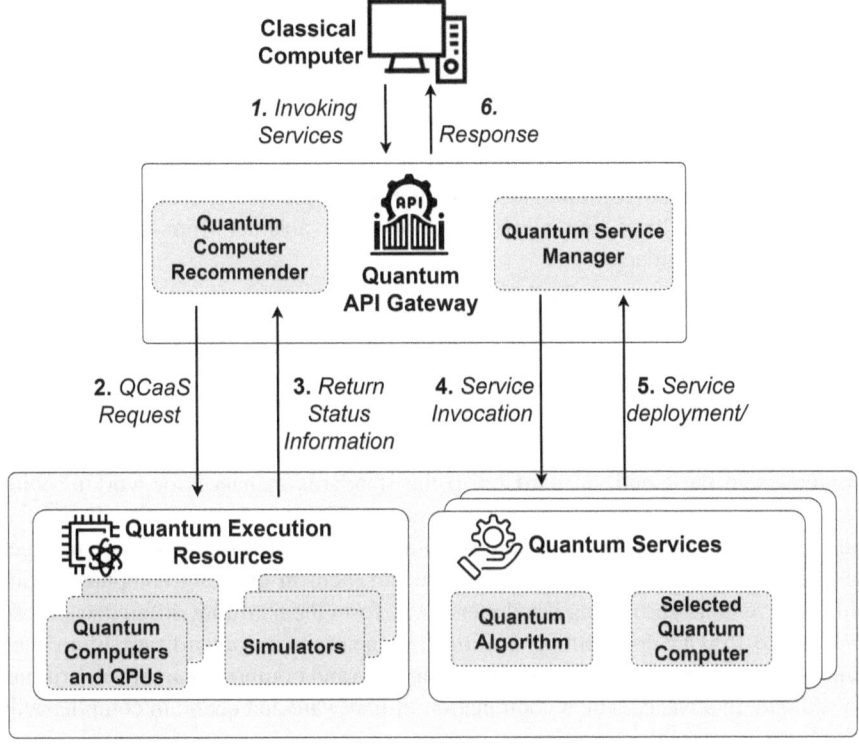

Fig. 4 Quantum API Gateway process

In addition to the number of qubits, the Quantum API Gateway also evaluates the cost of running the chosen computer, taking into account several factors. These include the number of shots the developer needs, the maximum cost he is willing to pay, and the cost per shot. In this context, the triggers refer to the number of iterations needed to find the solution and obtain the results of the service execution.

To calculate the service execution cost, the tool combines the cost per execution with the cost per shot, multiplied by the number of shots. Only machines that meet the cost threshold are selected, and this information is easily accessible from some vendors such as Amazon Braket. However, other providers do not currently offer this type of information at runtime. In these cases, a cost estimate is made from the technical specifications. In the latter case, the choice of vendor is made based on availability, as explained below.

Once the developer selects the machines that meet the cost threshold, Quantum API Gateway checks the availability of quantum computers that meet all these requirements. It then calculates the estimated execution time for each machine, which provides the developer with valuable information to make an informed decision. This is done based on the run context that was also established during the vendor comparison day of the week, the run start time, and the actual time taken by previous runs performed on that computer.

Overall, this process ensures the selection of the most cost-effective and efficient machine to perform the quantum service. Therefore, with these tool enhancements, we ensure that the optimal machine is selected for each service call. By providing a standard format for service responses and incorporating a feedback mechanism for the quantum machine recommender among multiple providers, the entire execution process is streamlined and allows developers to abstract from both quantum machines and providers.

5   Development of Quantum Services

Significant work is already underway with the goal of bringing the way quantum computers in the cloud are used up to the standards managed for working with classical ones. For example, Amazon Braket [54] provides a unified SDK that allows developers to build quantum algorithms in a single programming language, test them on different simulators, and execute them in quantum computers from different vendors abstracting developers away from the hardware differences. Also, works like [55] are contributing to mitigating the problems of hardware differences and availability by providing a method to analyze and optimize quantum algorithms to estimate in advance which combination of hardware and quantum compiler will return the more stable execution.

Nevertheless, the development and operation of quantum service-oriented software is still a complex task very different from the development of classical services which professionals are used to [2]. The lack of advanced operating systems makes it impossible to deploy a quantum service in the same way a classical service is deployed. Alternatively, a classical service can be deployed that executes a quantum task when called, adding an additional layer of indirection and complexity to the system [56, 57]. The queuing system used to run tasks in most quantum computers makes it very difficult to know or estimate the response time of a given quantum task, making it impossible to work with service-level agreements that guarantee any kind of service quality. The low abstraction level of most quantum programming languages and algorithms makes the quantum source code very dependent on the specific hardware where it is designed to be run, preventing developers from taking advantage of the availability of different quantum computers through the cloud. The availability of advanced tools and methodologies for the development of quantum services is very limited, making developers use low abstraction level techniques that are error-prone and offer few of the benefits and amenities of modern software development tools. To address some of these problems, different research initiatives are emerging.

That said, there is a clear need to provide developers with tools to assist them in the generation of quantum services. In this line of work, Weder et al. [58] focus on some of the problems related to the orchestration of quantum and classical services in hybrid systems. To address them, they propose the use of an orchestration mechanism based on TOSCA to coordinate the different services. The same authors propose in [59] a provenance mechanism to simplify the selection of a suitable quantum computer to execute a certain quantum service.

On the other hand, there are emerging works to provide APIs for hybrid quantum-classical computing, such as Qiskit Runtime [60] and Quantum Intermediate Representation (QIR) [61]. These works are intended to allow users to efficiently execute workloads and serve as a common interface between languages and quantum computing platforms.

All these proposals, even though they raise the abstraction level of quantum service development and simplify the creation of complex hybrid solutions in which classical and quantum services coexist, are still far away from the classical development of service-oriented software. Additional support is needed for the creation of quantum services so current services developers can more easily transition to the quantum domain, mitigating the lack of a skilled quantum workforce [62] and facilitating the creation of a new generation of hybrid systems.

In this section, we propose an adaptation of the OpenAPI tools to support quantum services. OpenAPI is one of the most widely used standards for API description and, for this purpose, defines a vendor-independent description format for REST-compliant services [63]. The acceptance of the REST architectural style as a method and protocol for manipulating and exchanging data between different systems has greatly changed the development of Web services. Nowadays, RESTful Web services have become a standard for the development of Web APIs [64]. However, as APIs proliferated, the need for both humans and computers to discover and understand the capabilities of services without accessing the source code or documentation became clear [65]. The OpenAPI Specification[14] is one of the most widely used alternatives among developers for defining, documenting, and implementing APIs in a standardized way. This standard facilitates the design of APIs using different supporting tools (Swagger Editor, OpenAPI Explorer, etc.), providing a well-defined structure that complies with the standard and considerably reduces API implementation time [66].

By allowing the creation of quantum services through the use of OpenAPI, we not only simplify the process of creating these services but also facilitate the transition from classical services developers by providing them with the same set of tools and support mechanisms they are used to.

5.1 OpenAPI Specification for Quantum Services

To implement a classic service using OpenAPI, a developer needs to combine two main aspects: the business logic of the service, which is specific to each service, and

---

the endpoint of the service. Using the OpenAPI specification the service endpoint is defined, using a standard interface that is language-independent for RESTful APIs. This makes it possible to discover and understand the features of the service without having to access the source code or documentation and to define the service and its input and output parameters. From this specification, using a source code generator, the code structure is generated, in a programming language chosen by the developer, where the business logic of the service is then added to have a fully operative Web service.

Therefore, to address the current state of the art in quantum services, in this work, we will use OpenAPI in a similar way as it is being used for the implementation of classical services. Specifically, the code generator called OpenAPI Generator[15] will be modified to support the process of defining and creating quantum Web services. To achieve this, an extension of the OpenAPI specification, including custom properties, and an extension of the OpenAPI Generator, to allow for defining and generating code for quantum applications, have been developed.

For the integration of the business logic of quantum services, we will use a graphical quantum programming tool that allows drag-and-drop operations to build quantum circuits. Specifically, the open-source quantum circuit composer Quirk[16] will be used to develop the business logic of quantum services. Quirk is an open-source solution implemented with JavaScript and can be run in the Web browser and helps in rapid creation of quantum circuit prototypes. So, it offers programmatic access to the quantum circuit composed through a graphical editor. Nevertheless, it can be easily replaced by any other tool for quantum circuit creation that offers programmatic access to the code so it can be integrated with the OpenAPI Specification.

In this way, starting from an OpenAPI specification, enriched with custom quantum properties, and a quantum circuit it is possible to automatically generate the source code of the quantum service. For this work, we will use the Python programming language for the generated services, as it is one of the most widely used languages in quantum software development [67]. Note that the programming language for the generation of quantum services can be changed to any other language supported by the OpenAPI Generator with the appropriate modifications to support quantum services.

In order to carry out the generation of hybrid classical-quantum services, the following process is proposed, which is depicted in Fig. 5, and is summarized by the following steps:

1. **Define Business Logic as a Quantum Circuit**. This step involves designing the quantum algorithm or logic that you want to expose as a service. You use the Open Quirk Composer or a similar tool to create the quantum circuit that

---

[15] https://openapi-generator.tech.

[16] https://algassert.com/quirk.

Fig. 5 Quantum services
definition process with
OpenAPI

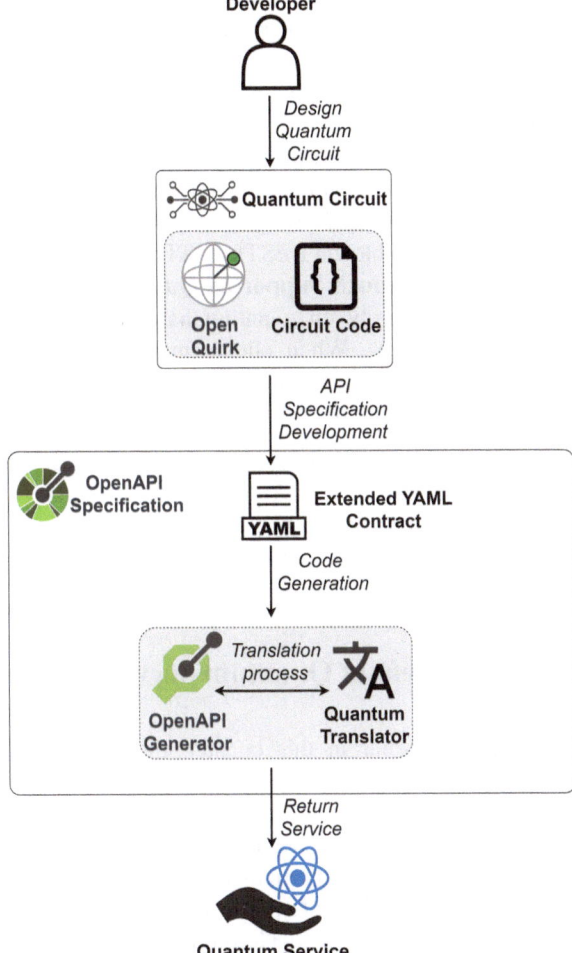

represents this logic. This quantum circuit encapsulates the core functionality of
the quantum service.

2. **Define Service Endpoints with OpenAPI**. In parallel with defining the quantum
   circuit, you also specify the service endpoints that will expose this quantum
   logic using the OpenAPI Specification. This YAML-based specification outlines
   the available endpoints, their input and output formats, and any other relevant
   information about the API.
3. **Link Quantum Circuit to Service Endpoint**. To connect the quantum logic to
   a specific service endpoint, you include the Open Quirk URL of the quantum
   circuit within the YAML specification of the API. This linkage is crucial as
   it associates the quantum algorithm with the API endpoint that will trigger its
   execution.

4. **Generate Quantum Service Source Code**. This is where the proposed extension of the OpenAPI code generator comes into play. It generates the source code for the quantum services based on the quantum circuit and the API specification. This source code is generated in Python, using the Flask[17] Web application framework.
5. **Deployment of Quantum Services**. Once you have the source code for the quantum services, you can deploy them. Deploying these services typically involves hosting them on a server or a cloud platform. The quantum services are now accessible via RESTful API calls to the specified endpoints.
6. **Execution Through Supported Quantum Providers**. To execute the quantum services, they rely on quantum hardware providers (e.g., IBM Quantum or Amazon Braket). When clients make requests to the API endpoints, these services trigger the execution of the associated quantum algorithm on the chosen quantum hardware provider.

This process enables developers to create quantum services that are exposed through a RESTful API, making them accessible to other services or applications. It combines the principles of service-oriented architecture with quantum computing to create a flexible and accessible quantum computing infrastructure.

6 Deployment of Quantum Services

As discussed earlier in this chapter, the integration of quantum services with classical services presents unique challenges due to the inherent constraints of quantum systems.

However, there remains a gap in the literature when it comes to the development of quantum services. In particular, there is a need for tools and methodologies to support the development of quantum services that are on par with those available for classical cloud services [68]. Currently, there is some work focusing on bringing the advantages of service-oriented computing (SOC) to quantum computing. One example is Kumara et al.'s [69] theoretical presentation of a SOC-based methodology that allows quantum and classical developers and programmers to collaboratively create hybrid applications. All this translates into a lack of resources that limits the ability of developers to create and deploy quantum services in an efficient and scalable way [70].

In this section, we focus on bringing the development of quantum services closer to that of classical cloud services by adapting existing tools and methodologies to support quantum services.

To this end, we propose a pipeline for the generation and deployment of quantum services by adapting techniques from the DevOps methodology for continuous

---

[17] https://flask.palletsprojects.com.

software integration [71]. Specifically, we propose a modification of the OpenAPI specification and its code generator to generate quantum services, as well as the automation of the continuous deployment (CD) process for their deployment in ready-to-consume containers. This is done through a DevOps-based workflow for continuous software integration and deployment, using the GitHub Actions tool. To validate this workflow, a complete process has been developed through the following steps: an API has been specified for the services, the code for these services has been automatically generated with the OpenAPI extension, the services have been automatically deployed on an AWS server using the GitHub Actions tool and Docker, and their correct operation has been manually verified by analyzing the generated code and making the necessary calls to the services.

6.1 Continuous Deployment of Quantum Services

To realize a continuous deployment similar to those that already exist in classical computing, we have designed and implemented a pipeline that integrates the automatic generation of code and its deployment in containers ready to be consumed by developers. For this implementation, we have used a tool offered by the repositories hosted on GitHub, a well-known code management platform. Specifically, the tool used is GitHub Actions, which allows the developer to define what he wants to do with the code every time a change occurs in the repository. This tool allows for defining a workflow composed of the desired steps to be executed after a change is made to the repository.

The proposed pipeline can be seen in Fig. 6.

The first step is to define the business logic of the service as a quantum circuit using Open Quirk, indicating the Open Quirk URL of the created circuit or directly indicating a URL where the source code in Qiskit language (obtained from IBM Quantum Composer) is located.

Therefore, for the integration of the business logic of quantum services, we use a graphical quantum programming that allows drag-and-drop operations to build quantum circuits. Specifically, the aforementioned quantum circuit composer called Open Quirk is used to develop the business logic of quantum services.

Then, in the second step, the quantum API is defined, for which an API contract must be established with OpenAPI, as explained in Sect. 5.1.

At this point it should be noted that for the execution of services that have been automatically generated, a prior configuration of the environment with the credentials of the providers is necessary. Without this prior configuration, services may not be accessible or the available functionality may be limited. The credentials are typically given by the providers, such as Amazon Web Services (AWS) or IBM, and may include a password, secret key, and region.

Returning to the process defined in our pipeline, the process continues by automating with GitHub Actions the generation of the code for quantum services. The manual process of the developers ends with a commit to the repository, and

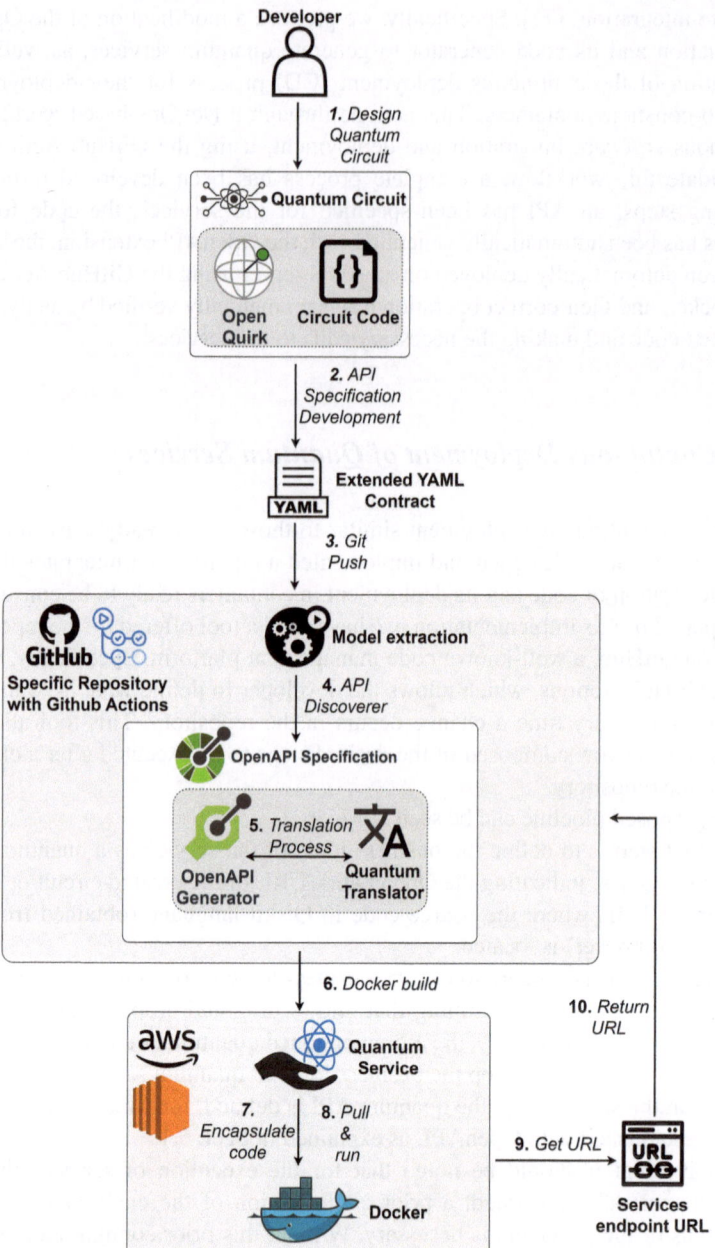

Fig. 6 Automatic quantum services deployment pipeline

the process of automatic generation and deployment of the services begins (step 3). Next, the repository specification is checked for correct formatting. To do this, the code of the services is generated with the modified version of the OpenAPI code generator (steps 4 and 5). If the code is generated correctly, the next task is to automatically deploy the services in a container (step 6). To do this, a request is made to the deployment API deployed on the AWS server. This request contains the URL to the YAML file containing the specification, and the credentials to configure execution on the providers.

The server receives the GitHub Shares call, generates and encapsulates the code in a container (step 7), and deploys it by exposing it on the first free port (step 8). Once ready, it returns the URL where the generated services are hosted. This URL will be visible to the developer at the end of the workflow execution (steps 9 and 10).

7 Conclusion

In this chapter we have presented an introduction to the emerging field of service-oriented computing for quantum computing; also, we have presented some of the current limitations in the construction and use of quantum services through a practical study of the most important service providers in the market such as IBM Quantum, Amazon Braket, Azure Quantum, and Google Quantum. In addition, we have indicated the need and the different alternatives existing in the literature on the possibility of adapting techniques and methods of classical service engineering to the quantum world.

This study will serve to enable service developers familiar with high-level abstraction tools that simplify the process of developing and deploying classical services to have an easier transition to quantum service development.

For all these reasons, in this chapter, we have proposed the Quantum API Gateway tool, which is a middleware that will allow access to any service provider in a developer-agnostic way, and that will facilitate standardization in accessing different quantum service providers (Sect. 4.1). Furthermore, we propose a method to standardize the process of defining quantum services using the OpenAPI specification, providing an extension of the OpenAPI Code Generator specification capable of generating the source code of quantum services from an API specification and a quantum circuit (Sect. 5.1). Additionally, and to facilitate the automatic deployment of these quantum services, we have developed a workflow for the continuous deployment of the generated code in Docker containers using the GitHub Actions tool, encapsulating the code in a container, returning to the developer the URL where the services are deployed (Sect. 6.1).

With the proposals presented in this chapter, we aim to make quantum computing more accessible by offering tools and techniques for the automatic generation and deployment of quantum services. By automating the deployment process, our tools bring quantum computing closer to developers by making it more similar to what they already know in classical computing.

Acknowledgments This work has been partially funded by MCIN/AEI/10.13039/5011000110 33 and by the European Union 'Next GenerationEU/PRTR, by the Ministry of Science, Innovation and Universities (projects PID2021-1240454OB-C31, TED2021-130913B-I00, PDC2022-133465-I00). It is also supported by the QSALUD project (EXP 00135977/MIG-20201059) in the lines of action of the Center for the Development of Industrial Technology (CDTI); by the Ministry of Economic Affairs and Digital Transformation of the Spanish Government through the Quantum ENIA project call—Quantum Spain project; by the European Union through the Recovery, Transformation, and Resilience Plan—NextGenerationEU within the framework of the Digital Spain 2025 Agenda; by the European Union under the Agreement—101083667 of the Project TECH4E-Tech4effiencyEDIH regarding the Call: DIGITAL-2021-EDIH-01 supported by the European Commission through the Digital Europe Program; and by the Regional Ministry of Economy, Science and Digital Agenda of the Regional Government of Extremadura (GR21133).

References

1. MacQuarrie, E.R., Simon, C., Simmons, S., Maine, E.: The emerging commercial landscape of quantum computing. Nature Rev. Phys. 2(11), 596–598 (2020). https://doi.org/10.1038/s42254-020-00247-5
2. Rojo, J., Valencia, D., Berrocal, J., Moguel, E., Garcia-Alonso, J., Rodriguez, J.M.M.: Trials and tribulations of developing hybrid quantum-classical microservices systems (2021). https://doi.org/10.48550/arXiv.2105.04421
3. Romero-Álvarez, J., Alvarado-Valiente, J., Garcia-Alonso, J., Moguel, E., Murillo, J.M.: A graph-based healthcare system for quantum simulation of medication administration in the aging people. In: Gerontechnology IV, pp. 34–41. Springer, Évora, Portugal (2022). https://doi.org/10.1007/978-3-030-97524-1_4
4. Pérez-Castillo, R., Piattini, M.: The quantum software engineering path. In: International Workshop on Software Engineering & Technology (Q-SET'20) Co-located with IEEE International Conference on Quantum Computing and Engineering (IEEE Quantum Week 2020) Broomfield, Colorado, USA, October, 2020. CEUR Workshop Proceedings, vol. 2705, pp. 1–4. CEUR-WS.org. http://ceur-ws.org/Vol-2705/invited1.pdf
5. Wille, R., Van Meter, R., Naveh, Y.: Ibm's qiskit tool chain: Working with and developing for real quantum computers. In: Design, Automation & Test in Europe Conference & Exhibition (DATE), Florence, Italy, pp. 1234–1240 (2019). https://doi.org/10.23919/DATE.2019.8715261
6. Bergholm, V., Izaac, J., Schuld, M., Gogolin, C., Alam, M.S., Ahmed, S., Arrazola, J.M., Blank, C., Delgado, A., Jahangiri, S., others: Pennylane: Automatic differentiation of hybrid quantum-classical computations. arXiv preprint (2018). https://doi.org/10.48550/arXiv.1811.04968
7. Piattini, M., Serrano, M., Perez-Castillo, R., Petersen, G., Hevia, J.L.: Toward a quantum software engineering. IT Prof. **23**(1), 62–66 (2021). https://doi.org/10.1109/MITP.2020.3019522
8. Pérez-Castillo, R., Serrano, M.A., Piattini, M.: Software modernization to embrace quantum technology. Adv. Eng. Software **151**, 102933 (2021). https://doi.org/10.1016/j.advengsoft.2020.102933
9. Sodhi, B.: Quality attributes on quantum computing platforms. arXiv preprint (2018). https://doi.org/10.48550/arXiv.1803.07407
10. McCaskey, A., Dumitrescu, E., Liakh, D., Humble, T.: Hybrid programming for near-term quantum computing systems. In: IEEE International Conference on Rebooting Computing (ICRC), pp. 1–12 (2018). https://doi.org/10.1109/ICRC.2018.8638598

11. McCaskey, A.J., Lyakh, D.I., Dumitrescu, E.F., Powers, S.S., Humble, T.S.: Xacc: a system-level software infrastructure for heterogeneous quantum–classical computing. Quantum Sci. Technol. **5**(2), 1–17 (2020). https://doi.org/10.48550/arXiv.1911.02452

12. Digital Journal: Topological Quantum Computing Market Is Likely to Experience a Tremendous Growth in Near Future (2022). https://www.digitaljournal.com/pr/topological-quantum-computing-market-is-likely-to-experience-a-tremendous-growth-in-near-future-microsoft-ibm-google-d-wave-systems

13. Zinner, M., Dahlhausen, F., Boehme, P., Ehlers, J., Bieske, L., Fehring, L.: Toward the institutionalization of quantum computing in pharmaceutical research. Drug Discovery Today **27**(2), 378–383 (2022). https://doi.org/10.1016/J.DRUDIS.2021.10.006

14. Pistoia, M., Ahmad, S.F., Ajagekar, A., Buts, A., Chakrabarti, S., Herman, D., Hu, S., Jena, A., Minssen, P., Niroula, P., Rattew, A., Sun, Y., Yalovetzky, R.: Quantum Machine Learning for Finance (2021). https://doi.org/10.1109/ICCAD51958.2021.9643469 2109.04298

15. Cheng, J.K., Lim, E.M., Krikorian, Y.Y., Sklar, D.J., Kong, V.J.: A Survey of Encryption Standard and Potential Impact Due to Quantum Computing. In: IEEE Aerospace Conference Proceedings (2021). https://doi.org/10.1109/AERO50100.2021.9438392

16. Alvarado-Valiente, J., Romero-Álvarez, J., Moguel, E., Garcia-Alonso, J., Murillo, J.M.: Quantum-classical software for drug prescription simulation in aging people. Gerontechnology **21**, 1–1 (2022). https://doi.org/10.4017/GT.2022.21.S.557.OPP7

17. Alvarado-Valiente, J., Romero-Álvarez, J., Moguel, E., García-Alonso, J., Murillo, J.M.: Towards a classical-quantum platform for pharmacogenetic simulations. In: Gerontechnology V, pp. 187–192. Springer, Évora, Portugal and Cáceres, Spain (2023). https://doi.org/10.1007/978-3-031-29067-1_20

18. Sanchez-Rivero, J., Talaván, D., Garcia-Alonso, J., Ruiz-Cortés, A., Murillo, J.M.: Operating with Quantum Integers: An Efficient 'Multiples of' Oracle (2023). https://doi.org/10.48550/arXiv.2304.04440

19. Sanchez-Rivero, J., Talaván, D., Garcia-Alonso, J., Ruiz-Cortés, A., Murillo, J.M.: Some Initial Guidelines for Building Reusable Quantum Oracles (2023). https://doi.org/10.48550/arXiv.2303.14959

20. Sanchez-Rivero, J., Talavan, D., Garcia-Alonso, J., Ruiz-Cortes, A., Murillo, J.: Automatic generation of an efficient less-than oracle for quantum amplitude amplification. In: International Workshop on Quantum Software Engineering (Q-SE), pp. 26–33. IEEE Computer Society, Los Alamitos, CA, USA (2023). https://doi.org/10.1109/Q-SE59154.2023.00011

21. Ravichandran, T., Rai, A.: Quality management in systems development: An organizational system perspective. MIS Q. Manag. Inf. Syst. **24**(3), 381–410 (2000). https://doi.org/10.2307/3250967

22. Papazoglou, M.P., Georgakopoulos, D.: Introduction: service-oriented computing. Commun. ACM **46**(10), 24–28 (2003). https://doi.org/10.1145/944217.944233

23. Papazoglou, M.P.: Service-oriented computing: concepts, characteristics and directions. In: Proceedings of the Fourth International Conference on Web Information Systems Engineering, 2003. WISE 2003, pp. 3–12 (2003). https://doi.org/10.1109/WISE.2003.1254461

24. Papazoglou, M.P., van den Heuvel, W.-J.: Service oriented architectures: approaches, technologies and research issues. VLDB J. **16**(3), 389–415 (2007). https://doi.org/10.1007/s00778-007-0044-3

25. Papazoglou, M.P., Traverso, P., Dustdar, S., Leymann, F.: Service-oriented computing: State of the art and research challenges. Computer **40**, (2007). https://doi.org/10.1109/MC.2007.400

26. World Wide Web Consortium: Web Services Architecture (2004). https://www.w3.org/TR/2004/NOTE-ws-arch-20040211/

27. Berrocal, J., Garcia-Alonso, J., Murillo, J.M., Canal, C.: Rich contextual information for monitoring the elderly in an early stage of cognitive impairment. Pervasive Mobile Comput. **34**, 106–125 (2017). https://doi.org/10.1016/j.pmcj.2016.05.001

28. OpenAPI Initiative: The OpenAPI Specification Repository (2021). https://github.com/OAI/OpenAPI-Specification

29. Kaebisch, S., McCool, M., Korkan, E.: Web of Things (WoT) Thing Description (2017). https://www.w3.org/TR/wot-thing-description11/
30. Rahaman, M., Masudul Islam, Md.: A review on progress and problems of quantum computing as a service (qcaas) in the perspective of cloud computing. Global J. Comput. Sci. Technol. (2015). https://computerresearch.org/index.php/computer/article/view/1279
31. Marston, S., Li, Z., Bandyopadhyay, S., Zhang, J., Ghalsasi, A.: Cloud computing - the business perspective. Decis. Support Syst. 51(1), 176–189 (2011). https://doi.org/10.1016/j.dss.2010.12.006
32. Zhao, J.: Quantum software engineering: Landscapes and horizons. CoRR abs/2007.07047 (2020). https://doi.org/10.48550/arXiv.2007.07047
33. Piattini, M., Peterssen, G., Pérez-Castillo, R.: Quantum computing: A new software engineering golden age. ACM SIGSOFT Softw. Eng. Notes 45(3), 12–14 (2020). https://doi.org/10.1145/3402127.3402131
34. Valencia, D., Garcia-Alonso, J., Rojo, J., Moguel, E., Berrocal, J., Murillo, J.M.: Hybrid classical-quantum software services systems: Exploration of the rough edges. In: Quality of Information and Communications Technology, pp. 225–238. Springer, Algarve, Portugal (2021). https://doi.org/10.1007/978-3-030-85347-1_17
35. Barzen, J., Leymann, F., Falkenthal, M., Vietz, D., Weder, B., Wild, K.: Relevance of near-term quantum computing in the cloud: A humanities perspective. In: Cloud Computing and Services Science - 10th International Conference (CLOSER) 2020, Prague, Czech Republic, May 7-9, 2020, Revised Selected Papers. Communications in Computer and Information Science, vol. 1399, pp. 25–58. Springer, Prague, Czech Republic (2020). https://doi.org/10.1007/978-3-030-72369-9_2
36. Moguel, E., Rojo, J., Valencia, D., Berrocal, J., Garcia-Alonso, J., Murillo, J.M.: Quantum service-oriented computing: current landscape and challenges. Software Q. J. 30(4), 983–1002 (2022). https://doi.org/10.1007/s11219-022-09589-y
37. Piattini, M., Peterssen, G., Pérez-Castillo, R., Hevia, J.L., Serrano, M.A., Hernández, G., García Rodríguez de Guzmán, I., Paradela, C.A., Polo, M., Murina, E., Jiménez, L., Marqueño, J.C., Gallego, R., Tura, J., Phillipson, F., Murillo, J.M., Niño, A., Rodríguez, M.: The talavera manifesto for quantum software engineering and programming. In: Short Papers Proceedings of the 1st International Workshop on the QuANtum SoftWare Engineering & pRogramming, Talavera de la Reina, Spain, February 11–12, 2020. CEUR Workshop Proceedings, vol. 2561, pp. 1–5 (2020). https://www.aquantum.es/wp-content/uploads/2020/03/Talavera_Manifesto.pdf
38. Moguel, E., Berrocal, J., García-Alonso, J., Murillo, J.M.: A roadmap for quantum software engineering: applying the lessons learned from the classics. In: International Workshop on Software Engineering & Technology (Q-SET 2020) (2020). https://ceur-ws.org/Vol-2705/short1.pdf
39. Gyongyosi, L., Imre, S.: A Survey on quantum computing technology. Comput. Sci. Rev. 31, 51–71 (2019). https://doi.org/10.1016/J.COSREV.2018.11.002
40. Grumbling, E., Horowitz, M.: Quantum computing: progress and prospects. National Academies of Sciences, Engineering and Medicine (2019). https://nap.nationalacademies.org/catalog/25196/quantum-computing-progress-and-prospects
41. Alvarado-Valiente, J., Romero-Álvarez, J., Moguel, E., García-Alonso, J., Murillo, J.M.: Technological diversity of quantum computing providers: a comparative study and a proposal for api gateway integration. Software Q. J. (2023). https://doi.org/10.1007/s11219-023-09633-5
42. Karp, R.M.: Reducibility among combinatorial problems. Complex. Comput. Comput., 85–103 (1972). https://doi.org/10.1007/978-1-4684-2001-2_9
43. Gidney, C.: Stim: a fast stabilizer circuit simulator. Quantum 5 (2021). https://doi.org/10.22331/q-2021-07-06-497
44. Mandviwalla, A., Ohshiro, K., Ji, B.: Implementing grover's algorithm on the ibm quantum computers. In: 2018 IEEE International Conference on Big Data (Big Data), pp. 2531–2537 (2018). https://doi.org/10.1109/BigData.2018.8622457

45. Bisicchia, G., García-Alonso, J., Murillo, J.M., Brogi, A.: Dispatching shots among multiple quantum computers: an architectural proposal. In: International Workshop on Quantum Software Engineering and Technology (QCE23). IEEE Quantum Week 2023 (2023)
46. Srinivasan, K., Satyajit, S., Behera, B.K., Panigrahi, P.K.: Efficient quantum algorithm for solving travelling salesman problem: An ibm quantum experience (2018). https://doi.org/10.48550/arXiv.1805.10928
47. Aparicio-Morales, Á.M., Herrera, J.L., Moguel, E., Berrocal, J., Garcia-Alonso, J., Murillo, J.M.: Minimizing deployment cost of hybrid applications. In: International Workshop on Quantum Software Engineering and Technology (QCE23). IEEE Quantum Week 2023 (2023)
48. Ohkura, Y., Satoh, T., Van Meter, R.: Simultaneous execution of quantum circuits on current and near-future nisq systems. IEEE Trans. Quantum Eng. **3**, (2022). https://doi.org/10.1109/TQE.2022.3164716
49. Ray, J.: China at the nexus of ai and quantum computing. Chinese Power and Artificial Intelligence: Perspectives and Challenges, 155–172 (2022). https://doi.org/10.4324/9781003212980-12
50. Kaliyanandi, M., Murugan, J., Subburaj, S.K., Ganesan, S., Gandhimathinathan, V.: Design and development of novel security approach designed for cloud computing with load balancing. Adv. Intell. Appl. Innov. Approach **2760**, 050005 (2023). https://doi.org/10.1063/5.0126814
51. Karacan, E., Karakaya, A., Akleylek, S.: Quantum secure communication between service provider and sim. IEEE Access **10**, 69135–69146 (2022). https://doi.org/10.1109/ACCESS.2022.3186306
52. Garcia-Alonso, J., Rojo, J., Valencia, D., Moguel, E., Berrocal, J., Murillo, J.M.: Quantum software as a service through a quantum api gateway. IEEE Internet Comput. **26**, 34–41 (2022). https://doi.org/10.1109/MIC.2021.3132688
53. Romero-Álvarez, J., Alvarado-Valiente, J., Moguel, E., Canal, C., García-Alonso, J., Murillo, J.M.: Leveraging api specifications for scaffolding quantum applications. In: International Workshop on Quantum Software Engineering and Technology (QCE23). IEEE Quantum Week 2023 (2023)
54. Amazon: Amazon Braket. Accelerate Quantum Computing Research. https://aws.amazon.com/braket/
55. Salm, M., Barzen, J., Leymann, F., Weder, B.: Prioritization of compiled quantum circuits for different quantum computers. In: 2022 IEEE International Conference on Software Analysis, Evolution and Reengineering (SANER), pp. 1258–1265 (2022). https://doi.org/10.1109/SANER53432.2022.00150. IEEE
56. Alvarado-Valiente, J., Romero-Álvarez, J., Arias, D., Terres, E.B., Garcia-Alonso, J., Moguel, E., Bringas, P.G., Murillo, J.M.: Improving the quality of quantum services generation process: Controlling errors and noise. In: Hybrid Artificial Intelligent Systems, pp. 180–191. Springer, Salamanca, Spain (2023). https://doi.org/10.1007/978-3-031-40725-3_16
57. Alvarado-Valiente, J., Romero-Álvarez, J., Díaz, A., Rodríguez, M., García-Rodríguez, I., Moguel, E., Garcia-Alonso, J., Murillo, J.M.: Quantum services generation and deployment process: A quality-oriented approach. In: Quality of Information and Communications Technology, pp. 200–214. Springer, Aveiro, Portugal (2023). https://doi.org/10.1007/978-3-031-43703-8_15
58. Weder, B., Barzen, J., Leymann, F., Zimmermann, M.: Hybrid quantum applications need two orchestrations in superposition: A software architecture perspective. In: 2021 IEEE International Conference on Web Services (ICWS), pp. 1–13 (2021). https://doi.org/10.48550/arXiv.2103.04320 . IEEE
59. Weder, B., Barzen, J., Leymann, F., Salm, M., Wild, K.: Qprov: A provenance system for quantum computing. IET Quantum Commun. **2**(4), 171–181 (2021). https://doi.org/10.1049/qtc2.12012
60. Johnson, B.: Qiskit runtime, a quantum-classical execution platform for cloud-accessible quantum computers. Bull. Am. Phys. Soc. (2022). https://research.ibm.com/publications/qiskit-runtime-a-quantum-classical-execution-platform-for-cloud-accessible-quantum-computers

61. Heim, B.: Universal quantum intermediate representation. In: APS March Meeting Abstracts, vol. 2021, pp. 34–009 (2021). https://ui.adsabs.harvard.edu/abs/2021APS..MARM34009H/abstract
62. Hilton, J.: Building the quantum workforce of the future. Forbes Technology Council (2019). https://www.forbes.com/sites/forbestechcouncil/2019/06/19/building-the-quantum-workforce-of-the-future/
63. Schwichtenberg, S., Gerth, C., Engels, G.: From open api to semantic specifications and code adapters. In: 2017 IEEE International Conference on Web Services (ICWS), pp. 484–491 (2017). https://doi.org/10.1109/ICWS.2017.56. IEEE
64. Soni, A., Ranga, V.: Api features individualizing of web services: Rest and soap. Int. J. Innov. Technol. Explor. Eng. **8**(9), 664–671 (2019). https://api.semanticscholar.org/CorpusID:241888945
65. Karavisileiou, A., Mainas, N., Petrakis, E.G.M.: Ontology for openapi rest services descriptions. In: 2020 IEEE 32nd International Conference on Tools with Artificial Intelligence (ICTAI), pp. 35–40 (2020). https://doi.org/10.1109/ICTAI50040.2020.00016
66. Romero-Álvarez, J., Alvarado-Valiente, J., Casco-Seco, J., Moguel, E., Garcia-Alonso, J., Canal, C., Murillo, J.M.: Developing high-level abstractions for creating quantum services: Openapi and asyncapi. In: Symposium and Summer School On Service-Oriented Computing (SummerSOC 2023), Crete, Greece (2023)
67. Silva, V.: Practical Quantum Computing for Developers: Programming Quantum Rigs in the Cloud Using Python, Quantum Assembly Language and IBM QExperience. Apress, USA (2018). https://doi.org/10.1007/978-1-4842-4218-6
68. Romero-Álvarez, J., Alvarado-Valiente, J., Moguel, E., Garcia-Alonso, J.: Quantum web services: Development and deployment. In: Web Engineering, pp. 421–423. Springer, Alicante, Spain (2023). https://doi.org/10.1007/978-3-031-34444-2_39
69. Kumara, I., Van Den Heuvel, W.-J., Tamburri, D.A.: Qsoc: Quantum service-oriented computing. In: Symposium and Summer School on Service-Oriented Computing, pp. 52–63 (2021). https://doi.org/10.1007/978-3-030-87568-8_3. Springer
70. Alvarado-Valiente, J., Romero-Álvarez, J., Moguel, E., García-Alonso, J.: Quantum web services orchestration and management using devops techniques. In: Garrigós, I., Murillo Rodríguez, J.M., Wimmer, M. (eds.) Web Engineering, pp. 389–394. Springer, Alicante, Spain (2023). https://doi.org/10.1007/978-3-031-34444-2_33
71. Romero-Alvarez, J., Alvarado-Valiente, J., Moguel, E., Garcia-Alonso, J., Murillo, J.M.: A workflow for the continuous deployment of quantum services. In: IEEE International Conference on Software Services Engineering (SSE), pp. 1–8 (2023). https://doi.org/10.1109/SSE60056.2023.00015

Engineering Hybrid Software Systems

Luis Jiménez-Navajas, Ricardo Pérez-Castillo, and Mario Piattini

Abstract Quantum computing is getting closer and closer to bringing all its potential applications to our lives. This means that in a few years the current IT will evolve into hybrid software systems where quantum and classical computing paradigms should be designed, developed, and operated together. This is a big challenge that will require software modernization processes for transforming and migrating legacy software systems (which may include adding new existing quantum software) toward such hybrid software systems. This chapter discusses the challenges of hybrid software and how software modernization (based on architecture-driven modernization) can be used as a reengineering solution for an effective evolution of classical and quantum software.

Keywords Quantum software · Software modernization · Hybrid software systems · Architecture-driven modernization · KDM · UML

1 Introduction

When its associated technology is sufficiently mature, quantum computing is expected to make a great impact on information systems and, in general, on business and society [1, 2]. Technology giants such as Amazon, IBM, Google, and Microsoft are investing a lot of resources in developing this new paradigm, whether by creating new languages [3–5], researching the creation of better quantum computers, or enabling quantum services [6]. This growing interest in quantum computing and its potential impact on various fields [7] has led to the emergence of a vibrant quantum ecosystem comprising startups, research labs, and consortia. In 2021,

L. Jiménez-Navajas · R. Pérez-Castillo (✉)
University of Castilla-La Mancha, Talavera de la Reina, Spain
e-mail: ricardo.pdelcastillo@uclm.es

M. Piattini
University of Castilla-La Mancha, Ciudad Real, Spain

© The Author(s) 2024
I. Exman et al. (eds.), *Quantum Software*,
https://doi.org/10.1007/978-3-031-64136-7_9

Zapata Computing conducted a survey of 300 leaders at large global enterprises (information and technology officers and other executive levels) with estimated 2021 revenues of over $250 million. In this survey, 74% of enterprise leaders agreed that "those who fail to adopt quantum computing solutions will fall behind" [8].

Companies that are eager to benefit from quantum software may want to adapt their classical software systems to the quantum computing paradigm. For example, companies researching the creation of certain materials or pharmaceuticals will be forced to adopt quantum software, since its performance is better than classical software with these types of problems [9].

The effective adoption of quantum software does not imply a total discarding of the classical software systems but rather a progressive evolution in which quantum software could be integrated in some parts. There are several reasons for which a partial adoption is expected instead of a whole revolution. The first reason is that quantum computing can solve very specific problems [10], which implies that (1) not everything can be better solved with a quantum algorithm, and even doing so, (2) those quantum programs could not represent a performance gain compared to classical software [10]. Additionally, while current classical software systems were in place, those systems probably have embedded a large amount of mission-critical knowledge (specifically in the source code) that is still extremely valuable for the organizations. That embedded knowledge is probably not present anywhere else, so it is extremely difficult and risky to preserve and migrate such knowledge in new software systems developed from scratch [11].

Consequently, in the near future, it is expected to find organizations with hybrid software systems, which combine both quantum and classical software. Quantum software components will perform those complex operations that classical software cannot perform in a reasonable time. Typically, these operations will be executed through the services provided by quantum computing providers [12], usually in the cloud. On the other hand, the classical software will manage those request/response interactions with quantum software, e.g., sending the input with which the quantum software will work, and then receiving and processing the output of the quantum software execution.

The evolution of classical software systems, in isolation, has been previously addressed by software reengineering [13–15]. With the advent of quantum computing, some adaptations have been suggested to meet the underlying challenges of the evolution from/toward hybrid software systems [16]. First, quantum algorithms must be capable of being integrated into the existing software systems. Also, the replacement of its classical counterparts must take place in an integrated way. Second, once the classical software system has evolved, new functionalities inspired in and based on the quantum computing paradigm must be introduced in the target hybrid software system [17].

In order to carry out the evolution of classical software systems toward hybrid software systems, a quantum software modernization process has been proposed [18]. This process is a solution based on reengineering and, more specifically, on *architecture-driven modernization* (ADM) [19]. ADM is the evolution of traditional reengineering following the *model-driven engineering* (MDE) principles, in order to address the standardization and automation challenges [20]. This modernization process facilitates the analysis, refactoring, and transformation of an existing software system to support new requirements, the migration of systems, or even their interoperability. Thanks to the MDE principles, this process is agnostic to the quantum software technology and programming languages, following the quantum software engineering principles set out in the Talavera Manifesto [21].

The remainder of this chapter is structured as follows. First, it discusses the challenges that quantum software brings to the existing software systems and the transformation that it entails. Then, it discusses the process of quantum software modernization for evolving from/toward hybrid software systems. After this, a running example illustrates how the modernization process works. The last section draws some conclusions.

2 Classical-Quantum Software Systems

Once companies have access to quantum service providers, those companies that would take advantage of this technology will start to consider adapting some of their business processes. However, as mentioned above, the classical part is expected not to be fully replaced. There are several reasons for this. Firstly, quantum algorithms help us solve specific tasks, and the business model of some companies probably does not allow them to employ these algorithms. Another reason might be that the implementation of their software systems with quantum software would not make a significant difference in performance since the functions that these systems accomplish are simplistic regarding quantum computing, while the cost of its implementation would skyrocket.

Hybrid software systems are expected to be composed of two main parts, classical and quantum software. Classical software implements all those functions that do not make sense to "quantumfy," and which will perform a transformation of the output of the quantum functions into legible information. Quantum software implements such functions, either in the cloud or through simulations. Figure 1 shows the usual execution process of a hybrid program. The two parts are not isolated from each other. The input the quantum algorithm needs to process is provided by the classical part, previously stored in the memory. Then, the quantum part prepares the algorithm (either adiabatic or gate based) and manipulates the qubits to process the input. Finally, the qubits are measured, and the output of the algorithm (now classical data) can be processed by the classical part and thus by the users.

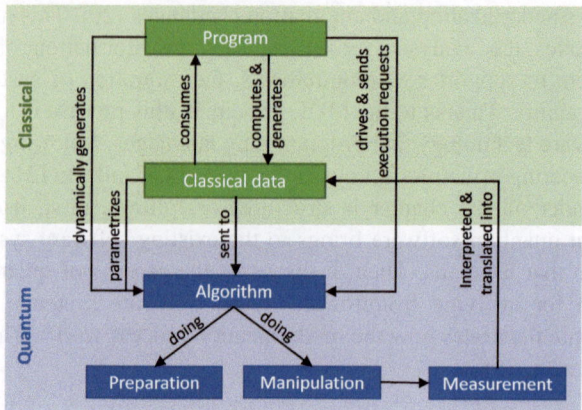

Fig. 1 Execution process of a hybrid program

2.1 Challenges of Hybrid Software

Once it is understood that companies will not completely replace their current software systems to start from scratch with quantum systems, it is time to discuss what kinds of companies or organizations could benefit from the evolution of their current software systems.

Companies that will be able to take advantage of quantum computing and will consider evolving their software systems will have to face several challenges and will have to study which components or functions to evolve. In the vast majority of cases, this evolution would consist of carrying out the most demanding operations in a quantum provider's cloud [22]. This would be one of the scenarios to be faced, figuring out which functions to evolve and which algorithms that are isolated in third-party systems should be used, while communications with cloud providers would be done through classical computing, i.e., the classical software system would evolve into a software system with quantum software components.

Another scenario could occur if organizations want to take advantage of the quantum computing hype and start to move their business models toward the new paradigm. This would imply a direct evolution of their software systems toward hybrid ones, as they will still have certain business processes that remain implemented by classical computing.

Since today's computational power for noisy intermediate-scale quantum (NISQ) devices is still limited to a degree, several NISQ devices could be used in a distributed quantum computing architecture [23]. This will entail another important challenge for the mentioned evolution toward hybrid software systems.

According to [24], hybrid software systems will also face obstacles in code portability, tool integration, program validation, and in the orchestration of workflow development. These problems together with the low maturity of the quantum solutions market will lead to another important challenge. Today, there exists a huge volatility in quantum technology (quantum computers, programming languages, development tools, etc.). Thus, today's companies that bet on a specific technology could find tomorrow that such technology has become obsolete.

3 Quantum Software Modernization

In this section, the overall quantum software modernization is explained. For a better understanding, as the process presented is based on ADM, first the traditional software reengineering and its evolution to architecture-driven modernization is explained. Then, how the evolution toward hybrid software systems may be achieved is described.

3.1 Traditional Reengineering

All technologies evolve over time, and so the software should evolve consequently. This evolution can have negative effects on software systems developed in the past, like degradation or aging. This implies that information systems can be turned into *legacy* information systems, which means that the source code that was developed could be technologically obsolete [25]. Reengineering allows "the preservation of the business knowledge, making possible to carry out evolutionary maintenance of the legacy information systems assuming low risks and low costs" [26]. The overall reengineering process is typically presented as a "horseshoe" model [27]; see Fig. 2, where reengineering consists of three main phases:

- *Reverse engineering:* the information system is analyzed to identify its components and interrelationships and create abstract representations of the system in another form or at a higher level of abstraction.
- *Restructuring:* the transformation from one representation form to another at the same relative abstraction level. This phase can consist of refactoring, i.e., the internal structure is improved while preserving the subject system's external behavior (functionality and semantics). Or additionally, it can add new functionality at this abstraction level.
- *Forward engineering:* the final phase consists of the renovation by generating the new source code and other software artifacts at a lower abstraction level.

Software reengineering projects have traditionally failed when dealing with specific challenges like the standardization and automation of the reengineering process [28]. First, standardization constitutes a challenge since the reengineering processes have typically been conducted in many different ad hoc ways. Reengineering projects must, therefore, focus their efforts on a better definition of the process. Furthermore, the code cannot be the only software asset that the standardization covers, since "the code does not contain all the information that is needed" [29].

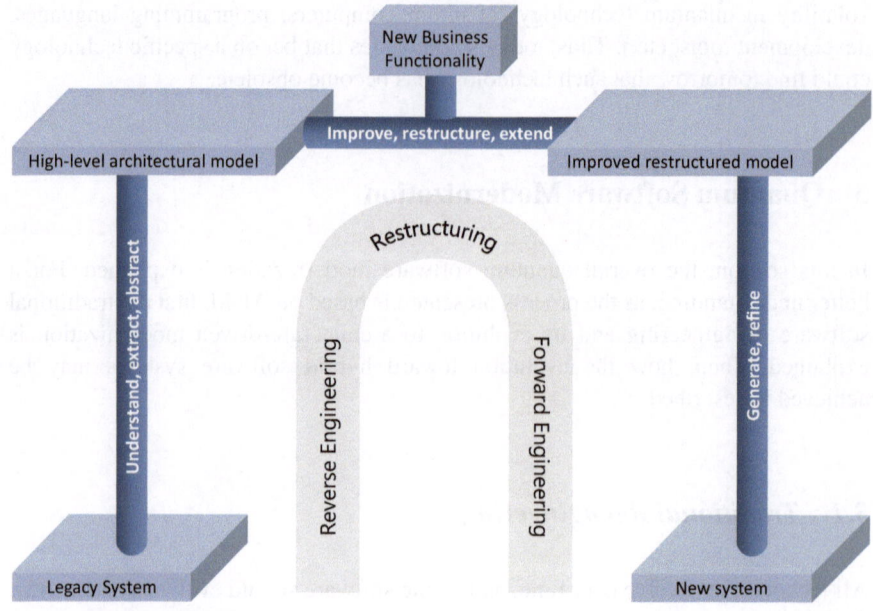

Fig. 2 Horseshoe software reengineering model

The reengineering process must be formalized to ensure an integrated management of all the knowledge involved in the process, such as source code, data, business rules, and so on.

Second, automation is also a particularly important problem. In order to prevent failure in large complex legacy information systems, the reengineering process must be mature and repeatable [30]. In addition, the reengineering process needs to be aided by automated tools in order to enable companies to handle the maintenance costs [28].

3.2 *Architecture-Driven Modernization*

In order to address the mentioned challenges, traditional reengineering evolved toward architecture-driven modernization (ADM) [31]. ADM consists of the use of tools that facilitate the analysis, refactoring, and transformation of existing systems toward a modernization for supporting new requirements, their migration, or even their interoperability. To accomplish this, ADM makes use of reengineering and model-driven engineering (MDE) principles [32], i.e., software artifacts are represented and managed as models, and automatic model transformation is defined between them. Thus, ADM attempts to address the mentioned flaws of the traditional reengineering.

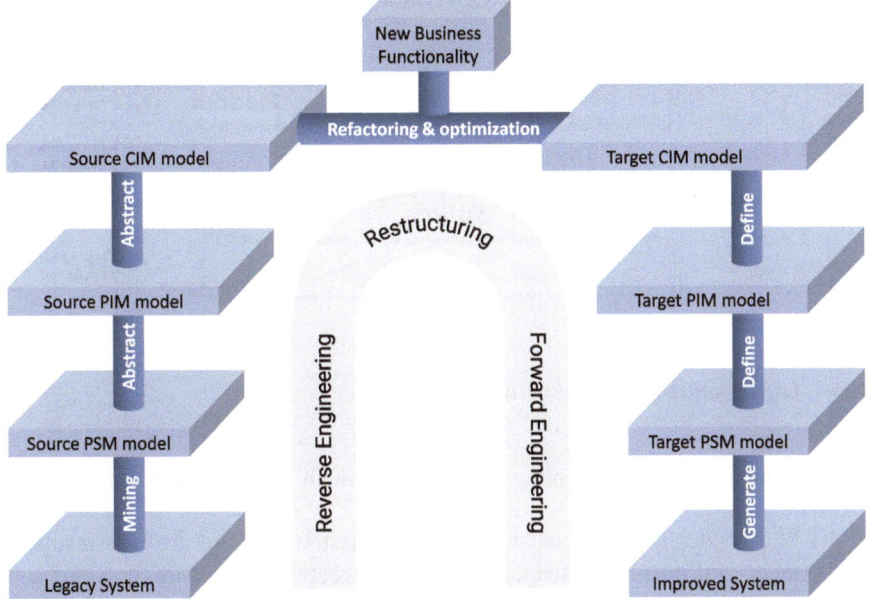

Fig. 3 Horseshoe modernization model

The horseshoe reengineering model has been adapted to ADM, and it is known as the horseshoe modernization model (see Fig. 3). There are three kinds of models in the horseshoe model [33]:

- *Computation-independent model (CIM)* is a view of the system from the computation-independent perspective at a high abstraction level. A CIM does not show details of the system's structure. CIMs are sometimes called domain models and play the role of bridging the gap between the domain experts and experts in the system design and construction.
- *Platform-independent model (PIM)* is a view of a system from the platform-independent perspective at an intermediate abstraction level. A PIM has a specific degree of technological independence to be suitable for use with several different platforms of a similar type.
- *Platform-specific model (PSM)* is a view of a system from the platform-specific perspective at a low abstraction level. A PSM combines the specifications in the PIM with the details that specify how that system uses a particular type of platform or technology.

As a part of the ADM initiative, the Object Management Group (OMG) released the Knowledge Discovery Metamodel (KDM) within a broad set of proposed standards [34]. KDM addresses the main challenges that appear in the modernization of legacy information systems, and it is the cornerstone of the set of proposed standards, since the other standards are defined around KDM [35]. KDM uses the

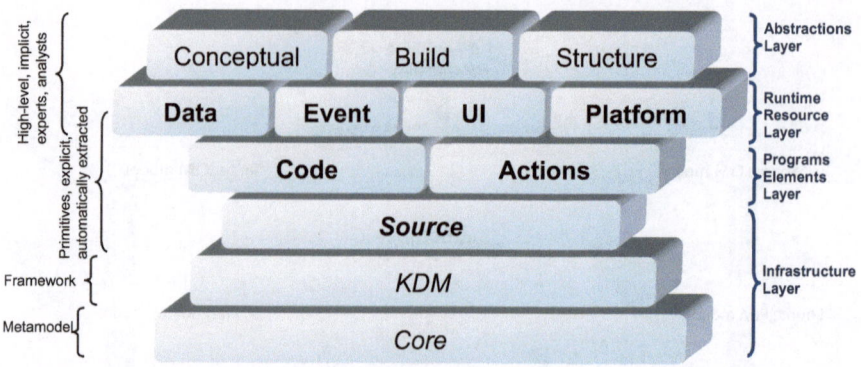

Fig. 4 Layers, packages, and concerns in KDM

OMG's standards for representing the models through XML Metadata Interchange (XMI).

KDM provides a metamodel which represents the software artifacts involved in the legacy information system, providing an accurate view of its functions and structures. Reverse engineering techniques use KDM to build high abstraction level models in a bottom-up manner starting from software legacy artifacts.

The KDM specification has different perspectives [35], and, in order to simplify the management of its structure, four layers were designed. Each layer is, therefore, based on the previous one, and each of them contains several packages representing different concerns related to legacy information systems. Different KDM packages and layers could be used depending on the artifacts analyzed (cf. Fig. 4).

According to the horseshoe modernization model, the ADM-based process can be categorized into three kinds of modernization processes [36]. These depend on the abstraction level reached in the reverse engineering phase. The reverse engineering phase is probably the most important phase in the horseshoe modernization model. This is because this activity conditions the abstraction level achieved in each kind of modernization process and, therefore, the resources provided and possibilities to restructure legacy information systems. A higher abstraction level usually implies a greater amount of knowledge and rich information which provide the modernization process with more restructuring possibilities.

Figure 5 shows the three kinds of modernization processes depending on the maximum abstraction level reached during the reverse engineering phase:

- *Technical Modernization.* This kind of modernization considers the lowest abstraction level and is historically that which is most applied to legacy systems. A company conducts a technical modernization project when it wishes to deal with platform or language obsolescence, new technical opportunities, conformance to standards, system efficiency, system usability, or other similar modernization factors. This is sometimes not strictly considered to be a modernization process since it focuses solely on corrective and preventive modifications,

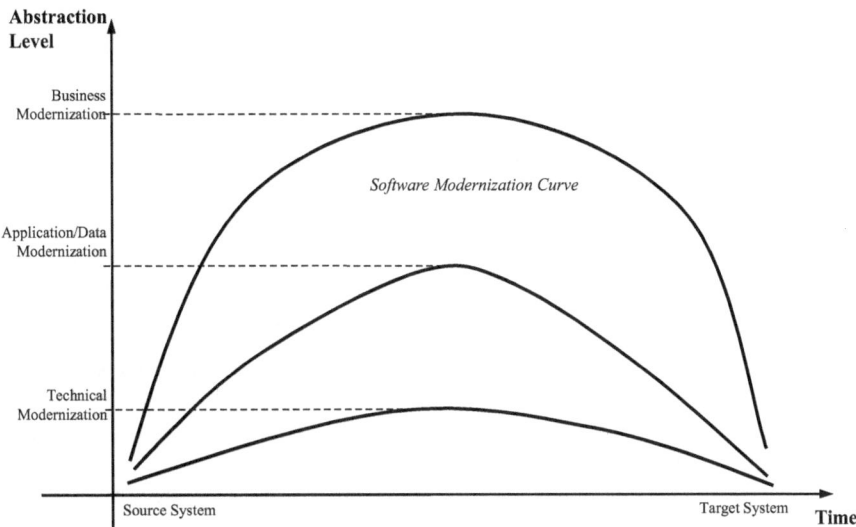

Fig. 5 Three kinds of horseshoe modernization models

but in any case, it addresses adaptive or perfective modifications according to the modernization definition.

- *Application/Data Modernization.* This kind of modernization considers an intermediate abstraction level since it focuses on restructuring a legacy system at the level of application and data design to obtain the target system. This kind of modernization is driven by several modernization factors such as improving the system reusability, reducing the delocalized system logic or system complexity, and applying design patterns. There is a fine line between this kind of modernization and the previous one, but that line is crossed when there is some impact on the system design level.

- *Business Modernization.* This kind of modernization increases the abstraction level to the maximum. The restructuring phase therefore takes place at the level of business architecture, i.e., the business rules and processes that govern a legacy system in the company. Apart from technical models and application/data models, this kind of modernization also incorporates business semantic models which are a key asset in (1) preserving the business knowledge embedded in legacy systems and (2) aligning the company's business requirements with the future target systems.

3.3   Software Modernization of Hybrid Software Systems

Software engineering has evolved as new (or adapted) technologies and methodologies are emerging to deal with the mentioned challenges of hybrid software
systems. Now, because of the new quantum paradigm, new difficulties have emerged
as explained previously.

A solution based on reengineering and, more specifically on ADM [19], was
already proposed in [18] to achieve the evolution of classical software systems
toward hybrid ones. That solution introduced "quantum software modernization"
and ensured that it could be used in three different use cases:

- *Use case 1.* To integrate existing quantum algorithms into new hybrid software
  systems
- *Use case 2.* To evolve actual/classical legacy software systems toward hybrid
  software systems
- *Use case 3.* To implement new business operations supported by quantum
  software into the target hybrid software system

Figure 6 shows the overall process of quantum software modernization. In this
process, it is proposed to employ already existing standards such as KDM (already
presented) or unified modeling language (UML). The first phase, which can be
seen on the left-hand side of Fig. 6, consists of reverse engineering, where a model

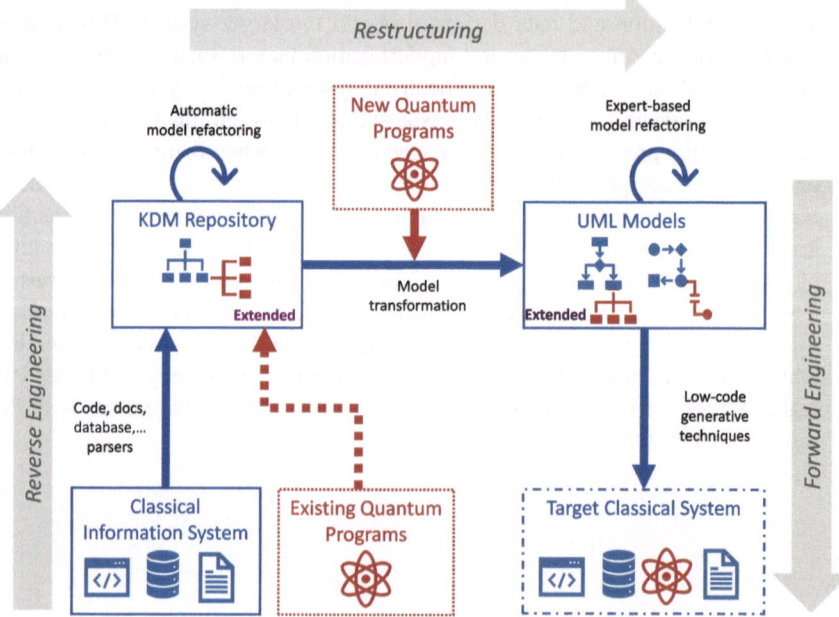

Fig. 6 Quantum software modernization approach [37]

represents the different components of a system in a technology-agnostic way. This model is built through the analysis of the artifacts of the classical system (use case 1) and quantum elements—if they exist (use case 2). The second phase, at the top center of Fig. 6, is restructuring. The extended KDM that were previously generated are transformed into high abstraction level models. Also, new quantum programs or business process could be added to the design of the target software system (use case 3). The metamodel chosen was UML since it is a widely known modeling language that has been widely embraced in the industry and which follows the technology-agnostic philosophy of the reverse engineering phase. Finally, on the right-hand side of Fig. 6, the forward engineering phase is depicted. In this final step of the quantum software modernization process, various tools can be used to automatically generate code fragments of the hybrid system designed employing the extended UML models.

The quantum software modernization process can be used for any case that aims at the evolution of a classical software system toward a hybrid one. To illustrate the overall software modernization process, let us imagine a legacy shipping routing system belonging to a logistics company. In this case, the company is intended to implement a quantum algorithm that, taking advantage of quantum parallelism, calculates the optimal route. Firstly, the company could explore the development of a quantum algorithm that calculates optimal routes (programs for similar problems already exist, at least for the quantum annealing device [38]). Secondly, once the quantum algorithm is developed, the company could have a quantum program, which needs to be operated almost manually. Finally, the company will need to integrate with other parts of the existing classical software systems. This is crucial since the input parameters for the quantum algorithms come from those classical systems. The output of the quantum algorithms is essential for the classical counterparts, so that users can make decisions based on them. In this scenario, the proposed software modernization process might consist of:

- Reverse engineering to get the KDM representing both the classical software system and the quantum program. This quantum program could be an implementation of a quantum circuit in a quantum programming language, but not the graphical quantum circuit. This is where the change of the abstraction level lies, since to model a quantum program in KDM, one necessarily must change the abstraction level.
- Based on a model transformation, the target hybrid software system is restructured. In this phase, the UML representations of the quantum program are integrated with the classical system representations, resulting in the design of the target hybrid software system. To cover all aspects of the model transformation, expert-based model refactoring would be employed. In this example, the integration of classical software parameters and quantum response integration could be modeled.
- Finally, in the forward engineering phase, the source code backbone for the target hybrid software system is generated, at least the backbone that can then be completed by engineers.

4 Example of Application for the Software Modernization Process

This section shows an example of the application of the quantum software modernization process to illustrate all the involved artifacts and the tasks performed within this process. This section has been divided into three subsections, one for each phase of the software modernization process (i.e., reverse engineering, restructuring, and forward engineering). However, since there is already literature on the generation of KDM from the source code of classical software systems, the reverse engineering phase focuses on the generation a KDM from quantum software and, in particular, from OpenQASM3 [39]. Then, the restructuring phase performs the transformation of KDM to UML, and the forward engineering phase introduces the automatic quantum code generation.

4.1 Reverse Engineering of Quantum Code

Despite all the efforts of OMG and the Architecture-Driven Modernization Task Force (ADMTF) to build a robust standard with the potential to represent all the components of an information system that are needed for modernization, they never considered the quantum paradigm since quantum computing was not relevant in 2003 when the ADMTF was formed. Therefore, it is necessary to "extend the KDM metamodel through its built-in extension mechanism to support the representation of the different quantum entities" [40]. The KDM's default extension mechanism is the extension family; Fig. 7 depicts the different components within this mechanism that can be found in a quantum programming language. The KDM extension is referred to hereinafter as "Q-KDM."

Whenever quantum programs are analyzed by reverse engineering, the Q-KDM must appear in the KDM generated from the respective quantum program. In addition, each quantum component (i.e., a quantum gate or a qubit) is also defined in the KDM according to its operation. Table 1 shows the definition of the quantum elements that may appear in a quantum program along with its Q-

```
<extensionFamily>
    <stereotype name="quantum programming language" />
    <stereotype name="quantum program" />
    <stereotype name="quantum operation" />
    <stereotype name="quantum gate" />
    <stereotype name="qubit" />
    <stereotype name="qubit measure" />
    <stereotype name="control qubit" />
    <stereotype name="qubit array" />
</extensionFamily>
```

Fig. 7 Q-KDM extension (extracted from [40])

Table 1 Mapping of quantum elements to KDM along with the extension family

Quantum element	KDM element	Extension family element
Quantum program	CodeModel	Quantum program
Quantum operation	CallableUnit	Quantum operation
Quantum gate	ActionElement	Quantum gate
Qubit	Storable and ParameterUnit	Qubit or qubit array
Quantum control	ActionRelation	Control qubit

```
1 OPENQASM 3.0;
2 include "stdgates.inc";
3
4 qubit[2] q;
5
6 h q[0];
7 cx q[0], q[1];
8 m q[0];
9 m q[1];
```

Fig. 8 Example of an OpenQASM3 program and its analogous quantum circuit

KDM extension. For example, if a qubit appears in a quantum algorithm, this qubit will be represented in KDM as a *StorableUnit* or *ParameterUnit* and will also point to the extension family stereotype "qubit" or, if it is a qubit array, "qubit array." Associating quantum elements with their corresponding extension family stereotypes allows us to extend the semantics of KDM, since stereotypes may be used to indicate a difference in meaning or usage between two elements with identical structures [41]. This is necessary since the elements of quantum software are radically different from the elements that appear in classical software, which forces us to extend the metamodel to preserve as much information as possible. In addition, it is preferred to use standards already embraced by the industry as these have greater tool support and dominance by industry experts.

This extension, as presented in [40], makes it possible to generate KDM by analyzing programs developed in any quantum programming language. The left side of Fig. 8 shows an example of a short program implementing the Bell state developed in OpenQASM3 [39]. In this program, in line 4, an array of two qubits is defined; in line 6, a Hadamard's gate is applied to the first qubit. Then, a controlled not is applied to qubits 0 and 1 in line 7. Finally, the qubits are measured in lines 8 and 9. The right side of Fig. 8 shows the same implementation of the Bell state but using the quantum circuit composer of IBM quantum experience [42].

Figure 9 depicts a shortened version of the generated KDM from the Open-QASM3 program shown in Fig. 8. The extension family defined on Fig. 7 can be seen from lines 8 to 17 of Fig. 9. In lines 21 and 22, a qubit is declared as a

```xml
1  <xml version="1.0" encoding="UTF-8"?>
2  <kdm:Segment xmlns:kdm="http://www.omg.org/spec/KDM/20160201/kdm"
3  xmlns:xmi=http://www.omg.org/XMI xmi:version="2.0"name="bell.qasm">
4   <extensionFamily xmi:id="id.0" name="quantum extension">
5    <stereotype name="quantum programming language" xmi:id="id.1" />
6    <stereotype name="quantum circuit" xmi:id="id.2" />
7    <stereotype name="quantum operation" xmi:id="id.3" />
8    <stereotype name="quantum gate" xmi:id="id.4" />
9    <stereotype name="qubit" xmi:id="id.5" />
10   <stereotype name="qubit measure" xmi:id="id.6" />
11   <stereotype name="control qubit" xmi:id="id.7" />
12   <stereotype name="qubit array" xmi:id="id.8" />
13  </extensionFamily>
14  <model xmi:type="code:CodeModel" name="bell.qasm" xmi:id="id.13">
15  <codeElement xmi:type="code:CompilationUnit" name="bell.qasm"
16  xmi:id="id.14" />
17   <codeElement xmi:id="id.21" xmi:type="code:StorableUnit"
18   name="q[2]" stereotype="id.8" />
19   <codeElement xmi:id="id.22" xmi:type="action:ActionElement"
20   kind="operator" name="Hadamard" stereotype="id.4">
21    <source language="OpenQASM3" snippet="h q[0]" />
22    <actionRelation xmi:id="id.23" xmi:type="action:Addresses"
23    from="id.22" to="id.21" />
24    <codeElement xmi:id="id.24" name="0" xmi:type="code:Value"
25    stereotype="id.5" />
26    <actionRelation xmi:id="id.25" xmi:type="action:Reads"
27    from="id.22" to="id.21" />
28    <actionRelation xmi:id="id.27" xmi:type="action:Flow"
29    from="id.22" to="id.28" />
30   </codeElement>
31   <codeElement xmi:id="id.28" xmi:type="action:ActionElement"
32   kind="operator" name="Controlled Not" stereotype="id.4">
33    <source language="OpenQASM3" snippet="cx q[0],q[1]" />
34    <actionRelation xmi:id="id.29" xmi:type="action:Addresses"
35    from="id.28" to="id.21" />
36    <codeElement xmi:id="id.30" name="0" xmi:type="code:Value"
37    stereotype="id.5" />
38    <codeElement xmi:id="id.32" name="1" xmi:type="code:Value"
39    stereotype="id.5" />
40    <actionRelation xmi:id="id.31" xmi:type="action:Reads"
41    from="id.28" to="id.21" stereotype="id.7" />
42    <actionRelation xmi:id="id.33" xmi:type="action:Reads"
43    from="id.28" to="id.21" />
44    <actionRelation xmi:id="id.35" xmi:type="action:Flow"
45    from="id.28" to="id.36" />
46   </codeElement>
47  <codeElement xmi:id="id.36" xmi:type="action:ActionElement"
48   kind="operator" name="Measure" stereotype="id.4">
49   <source language="OpenQASM3" snippet="m q[0]" />
50   <actionRelation xmi:id="id.37" xmi:type="action:Addresses"
51   from="id.36" to="id.21" />
52   <!--Reduced for code simplification--!>
53  </codeElement>
54  <codeElement xmi:id="id.42" xmi:type="action:ActionElement"
55  kind="operator" name="Measure" stereotype="id.4">
56   <source language="OpenQASM3" snippet="m q[1]" />
57   <actionRelation xmi:id="id.43" xmi:type="action:Addresses"
58   from="id.42" to="id.21" />
59   <!--Reduced for code simplification--!>
60  </codeElement>
61 </model>
62 </kdm:Segment>
```

Fig. 9 Resulting KDM file of the previous OpenQASM3 program

StorableUnit, as a qubit, on reflection, is just a variable which stores a result (the qubit's state). This element points to id of "qubit array" in the extension family with the attribute "stereotype." Finally, from line 23 to 81 are described the action and the data flow of the different quantum gates that appear in the algorithm. For example, lines 23 to 36 represent the abstraction of the Hadamard's gate. In that part, line 25 specifically holds the textual representation (i.e., "h q[0]"), in lines 26 and 27 the qubit in which is applied (by means of the ids), and, in lines 34 and 35, the next quantum gate which acts (with the "actionRelation" of type "Flow"). From lines 37 to 54, the controlled not gate is described in KDM, pointing to the two different registers of the qubit array, and from lines 55 to 80, the two final measure gates are described.

4.2 Restructuring

For the restructuring phase of the quantum software reengineering process, the well-known UML standard has been selected. The restructuring phase consists of the generation of high-level models where the relevant redesigns for the subsequent generation of the target hybrid software system are conducted. To perform this task, UML [43] has been chosen as the modeling language given that it is such a popular metamodel in the industry (it is an OMG and ISO/IEC standard), with a wide variety of tools available and a large community of software engineers who are proficient in this metamodel. It is worth highlighting the good results obtained when using UML for the analysis and design of software systems [43].

During the design of hybrid software systems, problems may occur concerning the representation of the new semantics and building blocks that quantum software can bring. However, like KDM, UML is not designed to represent the particular elements that may appear in a quantum algorithm, such as quantum gates or qubits. This is the reason it is necessary to create an extension of the metamodel. UML offers three extension mechanisms [44]:

- *A new instance of the Meta-Object Facility (MOF) model.* This approach consists of creating a completely new metamodel based on MOF. The result of this heavyweight approach is a new domain-specific modeling language (DSML).
- *Derivation of a new UML metamodel.* This approach adds new metamodel elements to the existing one. As occurs with the first approach, it creates a different metamodel, but it at least considers the original UML metamodel as it is.
- *UML profile.* This is a lightweight extension approach that is based on the UML built-in extension mechanism, UML profiling. UML profiles are created as a set of stereotypes, tagged values, and constraints defined for some of the existing UML elements.

Of these three options, the last one has been chosen, i.e., to extend UML through the creation of a UML profile. There were two reasons for implementing it in this way: all models generated using such a profile will be fully compliant with the UML standard; and, in addition, it is easier to maintain extensions that have been defined as UML profiles, since the associated modeling tools do not need to be adjusted after each change. Furthermore, there is already a UML quantum profile that represents quantum elements through class and sequence diagrams [45].

The quantum UML profile, previously proposed in [46], allows the representation of quantum programs through activity diagrams (see Fig. 10). On the right-hand side of Fig. 10 can be seen the different stereotypes added to the metamodel to represent the quantum components that might appear in a quantum program: quantum circuit, qubit, quantum gate, controlled qubit, measure, and reset. Then, on the left-hand side of Fig. 10, an excerpt of the UML metamodel for representing activity diagrams is shown. Finally, the arrows which point from the stereotypes to the different metaclass elements indicate that the stereotype extends the properties of the metaclass elements. The UML extension is referred to hereinafter as "Q-UML."

The root element of a model which represents a quantum circuit will be a metaclass of type activity with the <<QuantumCircuit>> stereotype. Inside this activity, the qubits are typified as *ActivityPartition* with the <<Qubit>> stereotype because it is intended that the qubits are seen as horizontal lines where the quantum gates can be placed (as is done by IBM Quantum Experience [42] or any circuit composer). The quantum gates are represented by the metaclass action but with the <<QuantumGate>> stereotype—but depending on what action they perform on the qubits, different metaclasses and stereotypes can be assigned. Further details of Q-UML can be seen in [46].

The designed KDM-to-UML model transformation can be formally defined in Atlas Transformation Language (ATL) [47]. An ATL transformation program is composed of rules that define what elements of the input metamodel are transformed in other elements regarding the output metamodel. A key part for designing the model transformation is to define the input and output metamodels. The input metamodel is an extension of KDM which allows the identification of quantum elements proposed in [18]. The output metamodel is the ECORE metamodel for UML version 2.5.1, which defines the abstract syntax of UML. This ECORE metamodel can be seen in [48] and contains the UML model description compliant with the EMOF metamodel [49]. EMOF stands for Essential MOF and "it provides a straightforward framework for mapping MOF models to implementations such as JMI and XMI for simple metamodels" [50]. The UML metamodel is used as is, although a quantum UML profile as depicted in [51] is used for modeling quantum circuits as the UML activity diagram.

Having defined the metamodels, the design of the ATL transformation attempts to identify which quantum entities could match with elements of the UML metamodel. The transformation accomplished follows a top-down order. Thus, the first KDM elements transformed to UML are those that group the remaining nested elements, i.e., the *Segment* element as the KDM's root element (which may contain, from different perspectives, the description of a whole system, including its components and interrelationships [52]. The last, and more atomic, KDM element is the

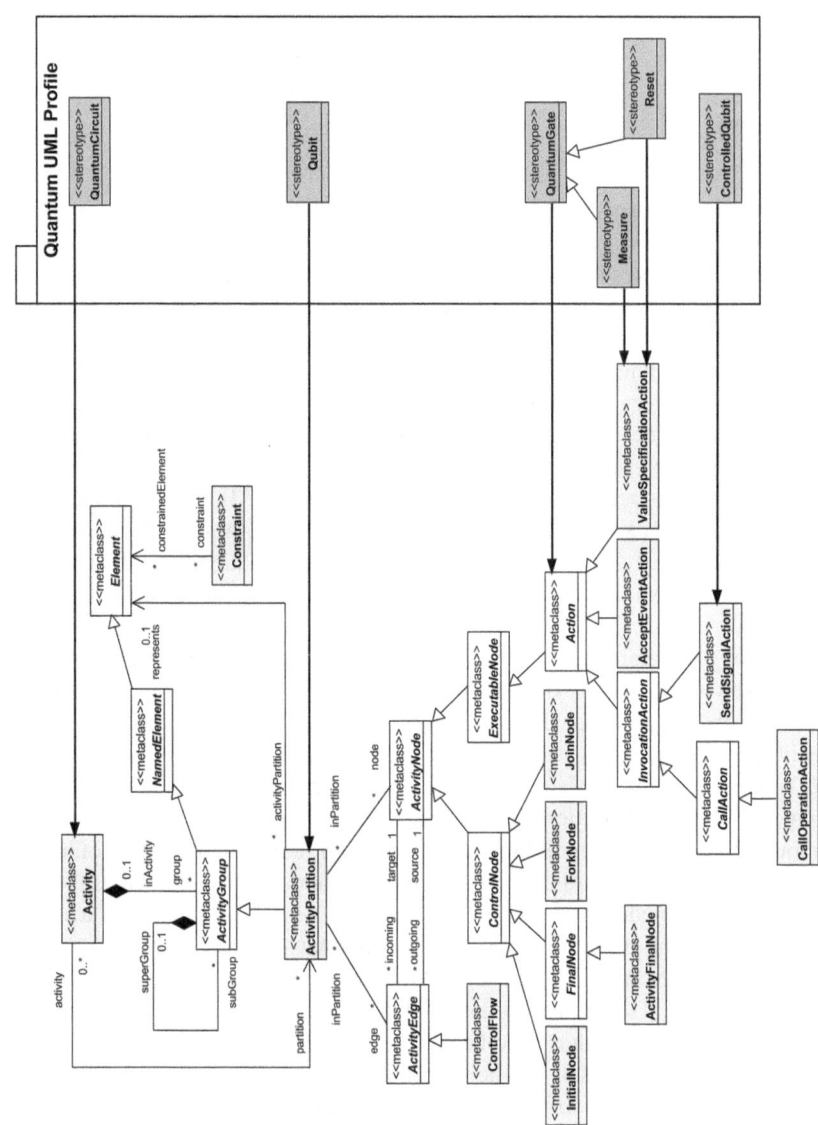

Fig. 10 Quantum UML profile extracted from [46]

Table 2 Summary of the transformations accomplished

Quantum element	Input KDM	Output UML
Quantum program	CompilationUnit	Interaction
Quantum operation	CallableUnit	Activity
Qubit declaration	StorableUnit	ActivityPartition
Quantum gate	ActionElement	CallOperationAction/ AcceptEventAction/ SendSignalAction
Data flow between gates	Flow	ControlFlow

actionRelation, which specifies on which qubit a quantum gate acted and its flow control.

Table 2 shows a short summary of the transformations carried out. On the left side the quantum element is analyzed, the middle of the table shows the KDM definition, and the right side shows its UML transformation.

As previously explained, the UML standard is defined as a metamodel compliant with MOF. Every metamodel has two separate but related syntaxes: "i) an abstract syntax that describes the concepts in the language, their characteristics and interrelationships; and ii) a concrete syntax that defines the specific textual or graphical notations required for the abstract elements" [52]. Although the ATL model transformation can generate UML models from KDM, these UML models are the abstract syntax representation, while a second transformation from the abstract to the concrete syntax representation allows us to visualize the UML diagrams in a graphical way.

To carry out the graphical representation, several tools that perform the same process of drawing an activity diagram based on a model were studied, for example visual paradigm [53] and jsUML2 [54]. jsUML2 was chosen because it is an open-source library and supports designing use cases, classes, and activity diagrams, among others, as well as JavaScript-based web applications. This entails the advantage of a better integration into a REST API solution.

Although the quantum algorithms modeled with the quantum UML profile are valid according to the standard, in order to represent them graphically with jsUML2, it is necessary to modify the models so that the library will generate activity diagrams. Among the different types of diagrams that jsUML2 allows to design, activity diagrams have been chosen for modeling quantum programs according to the UML extension. This is due to the UML models built with the UML profile belonging to the abstract syntax specification of UML activity diagrams.

Figure 11 shows the result of the graphical UML activity diagram after the KDM-to-UML model transformation and the definition of its concrete syntax using jsUML2 of the OpenQASM3 program depicted in Fig. 8. The activity diagram contains an activity with the name of the quantum program, two qubits (one for each register), and four gates: a Hadamard's gate, a controlled not split into two elements for a better comprehension of the diagram, and two measurement gates. All those elements, that are represented from quantum programs, are depicted with

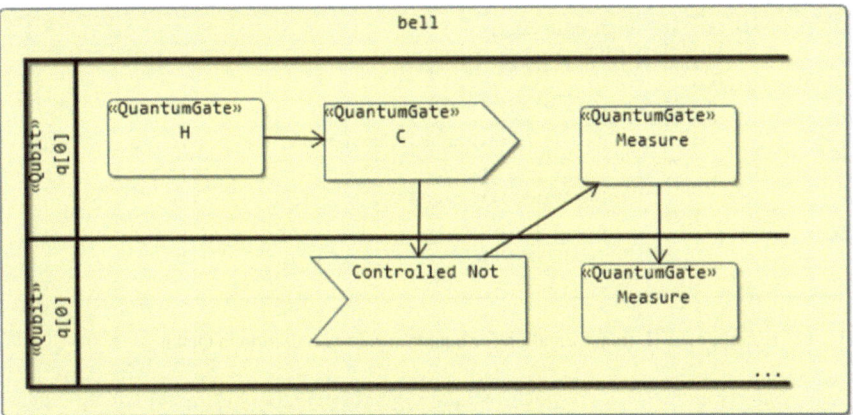

Fig. 11 UML activity diagram using jsUML2

its correspondent stereotype, which enables an extension in the syntax of UML to represent properly such quantum elements.

4.3   Forward Engineering

The proposed model-to-text transformation considers two types of UML diagrams according to the quantum UML profile: (1) the class diagram which provides the comprehensive static view of the system, representing how classes and packages are organized, and (2) the activity diagram which serves to model the dynamics (algorithms or quantum circuits) of certain quantum software components. The output for the target hybrid software is Python and its quantum software extension, Qiskit [55]. Today, both languages are widely used, both in classical and quantum software development. In addition, Qiskit supports the generation of OpenQASM quantum assembly code, which is the basis of other quantum programming languages. Despite this, the transformation could be adapted to other models and programming languages according to the MDE approach.

The transformation process is made in two steps, which can be considered as two independent model-to-text transformation steps executed in a row (the transformation code is available in [56]). In the first step, the quantum software is generated from the extended UML activity diagrams that represent quantum circuits. In the second step, the Python code (classical software) is generated from the UML class diagrams, which also uses quantum stereotypes defined in the UML profile. Such information is extremely relevant to define dependencies and relationships between classical and quantum code. Because of this, the quantum code generation is done first.

```
1   [*QUANTUM GATES*]
2      [% var initial = getInitialNode();
3         if(initial == null){
4            "There is no InitialNode".println();
5         } else{
6            var actual = initial.outgoings.target.get(0);
7            var type = actual.toString().split(' ').get(0).split('@').get(0);
8            while(not(type == "org.eclipse.uml2.uml.internal.impl.ActivityFinalNodeImpl")){
9               var gate = checkGateType(actual);
10              if (not (gate == "pass")){%]
11                 [%=circuitName%].[%=gate%]
12              [%}
13              actual = nextNode(actual);
14              type = actual.toString().split(' ').get(0).split('@').get(0);
15           }
16        }%]
```

Fig. 12 Excerpt of EGL transformation for quantum gates generation in Qiskit

4.3.1 UML Activity Diagrams to Qiskit Code

The first Epsilon Generation Language (EGL) transformation generates a Python (*.py*) file for each activity diagram (that represents a quantum circuit). The Python file first adds all the Qiskit imports, and then it will generate a *QuantumCircuit* object representing the quantum circuit. All the quantum elements (registers, gates, measures, etc.) will be added to that object. First, a quantum register (by using *QuantumRegister* class) is generated, which groups the number of qubits that are used by the circuit. According to the quantum UML profile, every *Lane* element represents a qubit in the circuit. Similarly, *a ClassicalRegister* object is generated (and added to the circuit) for every qubit affected by a measure operation (i.e., a UML *Action* element stereotyped with <<Measure>>). Second, the *QuantumCircuit* object is instantiated by using as parameters both registers (quantum and classical). After that, quantum gates are added to the circuit, as well as the measure operations. Quantum gates are modeled in the UML activity diagrams as "Action" elements stereotyped with <<QuantumGate>> (see Fig. 12). It is crucial to preserve the order of quantum gates, since quantum circuit does not define an explicit execution flow. Another important question is the controlled gates, which are modeled as a pair of two elements and one constraint between them: a *SendSignalAction* (on the qubit used for the control) and an *AcceptEventAction* (on the qubit in which the gate is applied). In this case, the EGL transformation should consider the relationship between those two elements applied in different *Lane* elements; at the same time, the order of the remaining gates is kept. Finally, the circuit is generated, and made persisted in the target Python file, through the EGL template.

4.3.2 UML Class Diagrams to Python Code

The second EGL transformation generates the Python code for the classical software, from the UML class diagrams. Of course, there already exist tools for classical code generation from UML class diagrams. The difference is that the classical code is generated with some relationships with the previous Qiskit code.

```
1  [%function getAttributeType(attribute) : String{
2      if(attribute.type.name == null)
3          return getDataType(attribute.type.eProxyURI.toString().split('#').get(1));
4      else if(attribute.type.name == "qiskit.circuit.QuantumCircuit")
5          for(activity in activities.replace(' ', '').split(','))
6              if(not(attribute.name == null))
7                  if((activity.replace(' ', '_').replace('-', '_')) ==
8                  (attribute.name.replace(' ', '_').replace('-', '_').toLowerCase()))
9                      return attribute.name;
10     return getDataType(attribute.type.name);
11 }
```

Fig. 13 Excerpt for the EGL function for classical-quantum code integration

In this sense, the first mapping considers *Packages* and generates the respective directory structure to store the Python files for each *Class*. For each *Class*, all the *attributes* are generated in code. It is necessary to establish a mapping between the predefined UML data types and the available Python data types (of course this is parameterizable). Along with the *attributes*, the respective functions for the public interface, i.e., *getters* and *setters*, are defined. Finally, the *operations* defined in the UML *classes* are defined as functions in the Python code. The function signature is created in the target class with the parameters and the return type. Obviously, these operations are empty and must be completed by developers.

Apart from those transformation rules, the quantum code is integrated along with the classical code. The following conditions are checked to do such integration: (1) there is a UML *class* stereotyped as <<Quantum Driver>>; (2) there is a dependency from the previous *class* to a different UML *class* stereotyped as <<Quantum>> (which represents the quantum circuit); and (3) the <<Quantum>> class name matches with the name of the *.py* file previously generated from a UML activity diagram. As a result, the generated source code for the <<Quantum Driver>> class contains a Qiskit *QuantumCircuit* attribute with the name of the target <<Quantum>> class (see Fig. 13).

As a result, the generated code defines the skeleton of the classic classes, while the existing code presents fully functional code. The generated code of the quantum circuit varies in the order of application of some gates, but only in cases where it does not affect the result, so those can be considered as functionally equivalent circuits.

Although there are several generative techniques for both classical and quantum software, these were provided in isolation. However, this model-to-text transformation generates both classical (Python) and quantum (Qiskit) code in combination from the high-level design in UML of hybrid software systems. This transformation completes the software modernization process from/to hybrid software systems.

Figure 14 shows the output of the model-to-text transformation, from the UML activity diagram (depicted in Fig. 11) to a hybrid program (Python file importing the IBM quantum's Software Development Kit (SDK) Qiskit). In lines 3 and 4, the Qiskit's libraries are imported. Then, the qubits are declared in lines 7 and 8, and in line 11 the quantum circuit (*Bell*) is initialized with the qubits previously declared. Finally, from lines 13 to 16, the quantum gates act on the quantum circuit.

```
1  # -*- coding: utf-8 -*-
2
3  from qiskit import QuantumCircuit, QuantumRegister,
4  ClassicalRegister
5  from numpy import pi
6
7  q1 = QuantumRegister(1, 'q1')
8  q0 = QuantumRegister(1, 'q0')
9
11 Bell = QuantumCircuit(q1, q0)
12
13 Bell.h(q0)
14 Bell.cz(q0, q1)
15 Bell.measure(q0)
16 Bell.measure(q1)
```

Fig. 14 Output Qiskit program

5 Conclusions

Every day we are coming closer to a world where organizations can have access to quantum computers or be able to run quantum software that improves or benefits their business models. Moreover, the estimated predictions point to a large increase in the value of quantum software services developed regarding the new quantum computing paradigm.

However, the organizations which could benefit from quantum computing are not yet ready for this paradigm leap. It has always been said that it is not the strongest that survives but the one that adapts the best. This phrase can be applied to our context since, in a not-too-distant future, the organizations that best adapt their business models (hence, their software systems) or create new strategies considering the new paradigm, with which organizations will be able to survive to competence.

In this context, quantum software modernization has been introduced in this chapter as a solution to conduct the evolution of classical software systems toward hybrid software systems. This process makes the combination of both computing paradigms, quantum and classical, easier. This process consists of three phases, reverse engineering, restructuring, and forward engineering. These phases have been illustrated in this chapter, although the overall modernization process follows the MDE principles, and, therefore, it could be instantiated with different (meta)models.

The main implication of the quantum software modernization process for practitioners is a set of challenges that may appear during the evolution of classical software systems toward hybrid software systems. Thus, software modernization helps the companies to identify which components from their business models could be evolved, and how, or even start new businesses following this new paradigm using techniques and standards which have been proved to be effective in solving such problems.

References

1. Zhao, J., Quantum Software Engineering: Landscapes and Horizons. 2020.
2. Gupta, S., Sharma, V.: Effects of quantum computing on businesses. In: 2023 4th International Conference on Intelligent Engineering and Management (ICIEM). IEEE (2023)
3. Cross, A.: The IBM Q experience and QISKit open-source quantum computing software. In: APS March Meeting Abstracts (2018)
4. Svore, K., et al.: Q#: Enabling scalable quantum computing and development with a high-level DSL. In: Proceedings of the Real World Domain Specific Languages Workshop 2018. Association for Computing Machinery, Vienna (2018) Article 7
5. Hancock, A., et al. Cirq: A Python Framework for Creating, Editing, and Invoking Quantum Circuits. 2019.
6. Kessler, E.J.A.O.T.T., Introduction to Quantum Computing on AWS. 2020.
7. Alsalman, A.I.S.: Accelerating quantum readiness for sectors: risk management and strategies for sectors. J Quant Inf Sci. 13(2), 33–44 (2023)
8. Zapata Computing, The First Annual Report on Enterprise Quantum Computing Adoption. 2022.
9. McArdle, S., et al.: Quantum computational chemistry. Rev Modern Phys. 92(1), 015003 (2020)
10. Aaronson, S.J.S.A.: The limits of quantum computers. Sci Am. 298(3), 62–69 (2008)
11. Pérez-Castillo, R., Mas, B., Pizka, M.: Understanding legacy architecture patterns. In: 2015 International Conference on Evaluation of Novel Approaches to Software Engineering (ENASE) (2015)
12. Garcia-Alonso, J., et al.: Quantum software as a service through a quantum API gateway. IEEE Internet Computing. 26(1), 34–41 (2021)
13. Colanzi, T., et al.: Are we speaking the industry language? The practice and literature of modernizing legacy systems with microservices. In: 15th Brazilian Symposium on Software Components, Architectures, and Reuse (2021)
14. Khadka, R., et al.: How do professionals perceive legacy systems and software modernization? In: Proceedings of the 36th International Conference on Software Engineering (2014)
15. Comella-Dorda, S., et al.: A Survey of Legacy System Modernization Approaches. Carnegie-Mellon Univ Pittsburgh, PA, Software Engineering Inst (2000)
16. Pérez-Castillo, R., Serrano, M.A., Piattini, M.: Software modernization to embrace quantum technology. Adv Eng Softw. 151, 102933 (2021)
17. Heim, B., et al.: Quantum programming languages. Nat Rev Phys. 2(12), 709–722 (2020)
18. Jiménez-Navajas, L., Pérez-Castillo, R., Piattini, M.: Reverse engineering of quantum programs toward KDM models. In: 13th International Conference on the Quality of Information and Communications Technology (QUATIC), pp. 249–262. Springer International Publishing, Faro, Portugal. (Online Conference) (2020)
19. Pérez-Castillo, R., de Guzmán, I.G.R., Piattini, M.: Architecture-driven modernization. In: Modern Software Engineering Concepts and Practices: Advanced Approaches, pp. 75–103. IGI Global (2011)
20. Favre, J.-M., Towards a Basic Theory to Model Model Driven Engineering. 2011.
21. Piattini, M., et al.: The Talavera Manifesto for Quantum Software Engineering and Programming. In: QANSWER (2020)
22. MacQuarrie, E.R., et al.: The emerging commercial landscape of quantum computing. Nat Rev Phys. 2(11), 596–598 (2020)

23. Ferrari, D., et al.: Compiler design for distributed quantum computing. IEEE Trans Quantum Eng. **2**, 1–20 (2021)
24. McCaskey, A., et al.: Hybrid programming for near-term quantum computing systems. In: 2018 IEEE International Conference on Rebooting Computing (ICRC) (2018)
25. Ulrich, W.M., Legacy Systems: Transformation Strategies. 2002.
26. De Lucia, A., et al.: Emerging Methods, Technologies, and Process Management in Software Engineering, pp. 1–276 (2007)
27. Kazman, R., Woods, S.G., Carriere, S.J.: Requirements for integrating software architecture and reengineering models: CORUM II. In: Reverse Engineering – Working Conference Proceedings, pp. 154–163 (1998)
28. Sneed, H.M.: Estimating the costs of a reengineering project. In: Proceedings of the 12th Working Conference on Reverse Engineering, pp. 111–119. IEEE Computer Society (2005)
29. Müller, H.A., et al.: Reverse engineering: a roadmap. In: Proceedings of the Conference on The Future of Software Engineering. ACM, Limerick, Ireland (2000)
30. Canfora, G., Penta, M.D.: New Frontiers of Reverse Engineering. In: 2007 Future of Software Engineering. IEEE Computer Society (2007)
31. Ulrich, W.M. and P.H. Newcomb, Information Systems Transformation, 2010.
32. Schmidt, D.C.: Developing applications using model-driven design environments. IEEE Comp Society. **39**(2), 25–32 (2006)
33. Miller, J., Mukerji, J.: MDA Guide Version 1.0.1. www.omg.org/docs/omg/03-06-01.pdf, p. 62. OMG (2003)
34. OMG: Architecture-Driven Modernization Standards Roadmap. https://www.omg.org/adm/ADMTF%20Roadmap.pdf (2009)
35. Pérez-Castillo, R., De Guzmán, I.G.R., Piattini, M.: Knowledge discovery metamodel-ISO/IEC 19506: a standard to modernize legacy systems. Comp Standards Interf. **33**, 519–532 (2011)
36. Khusidman, V., Ulrich, W.: Architecture-Driven Modernization: Transforming the Enterprise. DRAFT V.5. http://www.omg.org/docs/admtf/07-12-01.pdf, p. 7. OMG (2007)
37. Jiménez-Navajas, L., Pérez-Castillo, R., Piattini, M.: KDM to UML model transformation for quantum software modernization. In: International Conference on the Quality of Information and Communications Technology, pp. 211–224. Springer (2021)
38. Weinberg, S.J., et al.: Supply chain logistics with quantum and classical annealing algorithms. Sci Rep. **13**(1), 4770 (2023)
39. Cross, A.W., et al., OpenQASM 3: A Broader and Deeper Quantum Assembly Language. 2021.
40. Jiménez-Navajas, L., Pérez-Castillo, R., Piattini, M.: Reverse engineering of quantum programs toward KDM models. In: International Conference on the Quality of Information and Communications Technology, pp. 249–262. Springer (2020)
41. ISO/IEC: Knowledge Discovery Meta-model (KDM). https://www.iso.org/standard/32625.html (2009)
42. IBM: IBM Quantum Experience Webpage. https://quantum-computing.ibm.com/
43. OMG: UML 2.5.1. https://www.omg.org/spec/UML/2.5.1/PDF (2017)
44. Ribo, J.M. J. Franch Gutiérrez A Two-Tiered Methodology to Extend the UML Metamodel. 2002.
45. Pérez-Delgado, C.A., Perez-Gonzalez, H.G.: Towards a quantum software modeling language. In: Proceedings of the IEEE/ACM 42nd International Conference on Software Engineering Workshops (2020)
46. Pérez-Castillo, R., Jiménez-Navajas, L., Piattini, M.: Modelling quantum circuits with UML. In: Second International Workshop on Quantum Software Engineering (Q-SE 2021). IEEE Computer Society, Madrid (2021) (Online). p. In Press
47. Foundation, E.: ATL – A Model Transformation Technology. https://www.eclipse.org/atl/
48. UML ECORE. https://github.com/ricpdc/qrev-api/blob/main/qrev-api/resources/metamodels/uml.ecore
49. Eclipse: EMF, ECore & Meta Model. 27/03/2021. https://www.eclipse.org/modeling/emft/search/concepts/subtopic.html

50. OMG: The Essential MOF (EMOF) Model. https://it-dev.mpiwg-berlin.mpg.de/svn/JET/trunk/doc/latex/Diplomarbeit/websources/OMG/06-01-01.pdf (2006)
51. Pérez-Castillo, R., Jiménez-Navajas, L., Piattini, M.: Modelling quantum circuits with UML. In: 43rd ACM/IEEE International Conference on Software Engineering Workshops. 2021 IEEE/ACM 2nd International Workshop on Quantum Software Engineering (Q-SE), pp. 7–12. IEEE Computer Society, Virtual (2021) (originally in Madrid, Spain)
52. OMG. Architecture-Driven Modernization: Knowledge Discovery Meta-Model (KDM). https://www.omg.org/spec/KDM/1.4/PDF (2016)
53. Visual Paradigm's Homepage. https://www.visual-paradigm.com/
54. Romero, D.J.R.: jsUML2 – A lightweight HTML5/javascript library for UML 2 diagramming. http://www.jrromero.net/tools/jsUML2
55. Qiskit, I.: Getting Started with Qiskit. https://qiskit.org/documentation/tutorials/circuits/1_getting_started_with_qiskit.html (2022)
56. Cantalejo, I.: EGL Scripts for Transforming Quantum UML Models into Python Code. https://github.com/ivyncm/PythonGenerator/tree/main/EGLtemplates (2023)

Part III
Quantum Software Laboratory

Trapped-Ion Quantum Computing

Albert Frisch, Alexander Erhard, Thomas Feldker, Florian Girtler,
Max Hettrich, Wilfried Huss, Georg Jacob, Christine Maier,
Gregor Mayramhof, Daniel Nigg, Christian Sommer, Juris Ulmanis,
Etienne Wodey, Mederika Zangerl, and Thomas Monz

Abstract The future of quantum information processing requires a stable hardware platform to execute quantum circuits reliably and with low error rates, such that solutions for industrial applications can be built on top of it. Trapped-ion quantum computing, among other platforms, currently proves to be very suitable for the transition from tabletop, lab-based experiments to rack-mounted, on-premise systems which allow operation in data center environments. Several technical challenges need to be solved and controlling many degrees of freedom needs to be optimized and automated, before industrial applications can be successfully implemented on quantum computers situated within data centers. These necessary developments range from the architecture of an ion trap that fundamentally defines the supported instruction sets, over the control electronics and laser systems, which limit the quality of qubit operations, to the optimized compilation of quantum circuits based on qubit properties and gate fidelities. In this chapter, we give an introduction to the ion-trap quantum computing platform, present the current technical state of the art of Alpine Quantum Technologies' ion-trapping hardware and rack-based quantum computing systems, and highlight parts of the execution stack.

Keywords Quantum computing · Trapped ions · Gate model · Quantum performance · Alpine Quantum Technologies (AQT)

The original version of the chapter has been revised. A correction to this chapter can be found at https://doi.org/10.1007/978-3-031-64136-7_14

A. Frisch (✉) · A. Erhard · T. Feldker · F. Girtler · M. Hettrich · W. Huss · G. Jacob · C. Maier · G. Mayramhof · D. Nigg · C. Sommer · J. Ulmanis · E. Wodey · M. Zangerl
Alpine Quantum Technologies GmbH, Innsbruck, Austria
e-mail: albert.frisch@aqt.eu

T. Monz
Alpine Quantum Technologies GmbH, Innsbruck, Austria

Institut für Experimentalphysik, Universität Innsbruck, Innsbruck, Austria

1 Overview

In recent years, quantum computing (QC) has taken shape as a multidisciplinary research and development field extending in many dimensions, i.e., spanning from theoretical to experimental disciplines as well as from research and development to engineering. Quantum algorithms and their applications touch a plethora of scientific and industrial fields while user communities start to become aware of their possible implications in the near future. Ultimately, the goal is to make distinct QC resources, i.e., superposition, entanglement, and randomness, available for real-world application workloads, which will be able to benefit from quantum advantage [1]. Trapped-ion QC is a very promising architecture that continuously proves to be a stable platform to execute quantum algorithms reliably. This platform has recently started to push toward integration in data centers and high-performance computing (HPC) environments [2].

Substantial efforts are taken to provide low-threshold programmatic access to execute quantum algorithms on existing QC hardware provided by various vendors. Mostly, access is implemented via so-called quantum software development kits (SDKs) in combination with application programming interfaces (APIs). While SDKs and APIs enable the execution of quantum circuits, they also clearly separate the quantum computing infrastructure from the classical computing infrastructure. For a tighter integration of classical compute nodes and quantum processing units (QPUs), significant software and hardware development will be necessary in the near future [3].

The following section starts with an overview of different QC platforms in Sect. 1.1, followed by a short introduction to ion-trap technology (Sect. 1.2). In Sect. 2 we focus on aspects of the Alpine Quantum Technologies (AQT) hardware, from the ion trap (Sect. 2.1), mounted in a vacuum chamber setup (Sect. 2.2), to the full-scale rack-mounted system (Sect. 2.3). Subsequently, we outline some of the most important aspects of the quantum performance in Sect. 3, which includes 20-qubit control (Sect. 3.1), gate fidelities (Sect. 3.2), and coherence times (Sect. 3.3), as well as the quantum volume (QV) of the whole system (Sect. 3.4). In Sect. 4 we describe important parts of our software stack, i.e., the AQT cloud platform (Sect. 4.1), circuit transpilation (Sect. 4.2), and the radio frequency (RF) pulse scheduler (Sect. 4.3). We conclude with an outlook for future steps to facilitate the realization of a heterogeneous, hybrid HPC-QC infrastructure (Sect. 4.4).

1.1 Quantum Computing Platforms

For several quantum computing system approaches more or less detailed roadmaps have been proposed on how to construct large-scale QC systems. The promising platforms include trapped ions, superconducting systems, neutral atoms, photons, quantum dots, and semiconductors. For reasons of completeness, note that more

Table 1 Characteristic features of different QC platforms for selected properties split into the two categories of universal and analog QC, based on [5, 6, 7, 8]. Note that no clear preference can be given due to dependencies and trade-offs between several parameters. Some QC platforms might belong to both categories

Universal QC	Number of qubits	Qubit lifetimes	Gate times	Single-qubit gate fidelities	Quantum volume
Superconducting qubits	LARGE (100+)	~ 0.5 ms	~ 10–50 ns	$\sim 99.9\%$	MEDIUM
Trapped ions	MEDIUM (<100)	$\sim 50 +$ s	~ 1–$50\,\mu$s	$\sim 99.99\%$	HIGHEST
Neutral atoms	LARGE	~ 1 s	~ 100 ns	$\sim 99\%$	
Photons	SMALL (<10)	N/A	~ 1 ns	$\sim 99.9\%$	
Quantum dots	SMALL	~ 1–10 s	~ 1–10 ns	$\sim 99\%$	
Semiconductors	SMALL	$\sim 100\,\mu$s	~ 10–$20\,\mu$s	$\sim 99\%$	
Analog QC	**Number of qubits**	**Problem sizes**			
Quantum annealer	LARGE	MEDIUM			
Trapped ions	LARGE	MEDIUM			
Neutral atoms	LARGE	MEDIUM			

avenues to building a quantum computer exist, but most other systems are still in a very early stage of development. Each of these technologies has its advantages, but also challenges that need to be overcome. To put trapped-ion quantum computers into perspective, we compare selected metrics of those QC platforms which are currently in the focus of start-ups and larger commercial entities in Table 1. The comparison should serve as a rough overview to indicate that each platform has its strengths and weaknesses, and why there is no clear "winning approach" at the moment. We note that for a detailed evaluation which also considers fundamental dependencies between different parameters, other comparisons can be found in the literature [4, 5, 6].

1.2 Ion Traps Background

Devices for trapping charged particles have been developed in the context of studying atomic, molecular, and optical physics in the mid-twentieth century, long before the field of quantum information science emerged. Hence, there is a vast body of literature covering the various aspects of this field [9, 10, 11, and references therein]. The following subsection therefore certainly doesn't attempt to broadly cover ion-trap physics as a whole, but is only meant to provide a minimum of necessary context to a technically inclined, but not necessarily physics-trained, audience.

Generally speaking, ion traps, especially Paul traps [11], are devices which capture and keep charged atomic or molecular particles at a fixed position in space, well isolated from the environment. This is achieved by creating a confining electrical potential, which is generated by a set of electrodes that are connected to RF and DC voltages. Such a setup provides a physical system with the following key features which make it an excellent platform for QC:

- Ions of one species are *identical*, allowing for keeping the control mechanisms the same for all of them.
- The physics of the ions and thus their behavior in the ion trap is described by *quantum mechanics*.
- *Undesired external influences* can be effectively suppressed, if the system is set up in a suitable ultra-high vacuum (UHV) environment with proper electromagnetic shielding.
- *Desired external control* of the system can be effectively exercised, typically mediated by electromagnetic fields in the RF, micro-wave (MW), and optical regime.

These very properties are the reason that such systems can fulfill all the *DiVincenzo's criteria* for realizing quantum computation [12]. Moreover, it has been shown that all the required basis operations for QC can be performed in a fault-tolerant way [13, 14, 15]. While quantum error correction comes at the price of a considerable resource overhead, it is expected to be key for large-scale QC in the future [1, 16, 17, 18, 19]. The quality of control on trapped-ion systems is also documented by the fact that a *quantum volume* of 2^{19} has been reported on such a system [20], the highest number across all quantum computing platforms so far.

1.2.1 Paul Traps

Currently the most widely used variant of an ion trap for quantum computing is the *Paul trap*, named after Wolfgang Paul, who was awarded the Nobel Prize in Physics in 1989 for his contributions to the field of trapped ions. It emerged as a modification of apparatuses used to create atomic and molecular beams for spectroscopy research [11].

Paul traps work by applying suitable voltages to a set of electrodes that result in trapping charged particles. No additional magnetic fields are used, as, e.g., in the case of Penning traps [21]. Since it is not possible to create an electric potential with a minimum in all three spatial dimensions using only static voltages, according to *Earnshaw's theorem*, a combination of DC and AC voltages is used to create a harmonic pseudo-potential, i.e., an effective quasi-static potential for particles with a specific mass [22, 23, 24].

Physical realizations of Paul traps have been evolving over time, starting from larger setups with parabolic-shaped electrodes, to smaller devices, providing higher trap frequencies and increased optical access for interaction with laser fields and photon detection purposes. Another concept in trap design is mapping all electrodes to a two-dimensional structure, which then yields planar *chip traps*, which can be produced using established micro-fabrication techniques. There is no single design

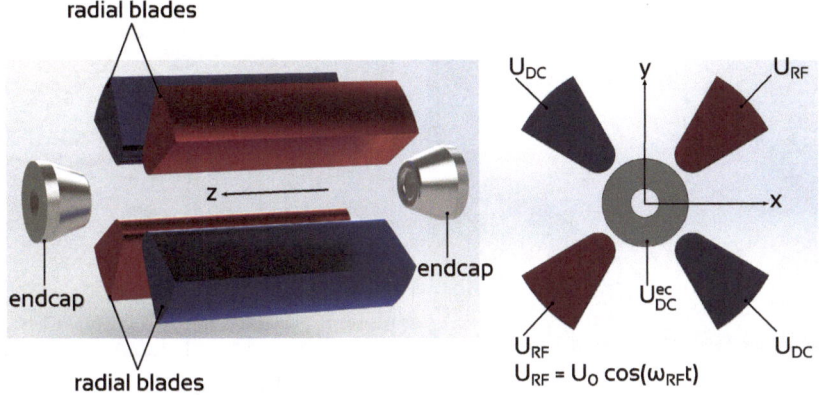

Fig. 1 X-shaped Paul trap designed by AQT. Holes in the endcap electrodes allow for optical access along the axial direction

that fits all the purposes ranging from quantum computation and communication to quantum sensing. Different architectures and their main features are described in more detail in Sect. 1.2.2.

1.2.2 Ion-Trap Architectures

The design details of the employed trap, i.e., the choice of materials, the geometry of its electrodes, its dimensions, the fabrication process, etc., play a major role when it comes to the performance of a trapped-ion QC system.

A currently widely used design can be seen in Fig. 1. The X-shaped electrode structure ensures extensive optical access while providing high trap frequencies using still manageable electrode voltages. High-quality quantum operations of 50 ions have been demonstrated in this kind of trap [25]. For more detailed information on such a trap, see Sect. 2.1.

Another approach to trap design is segmentation and miniaturization [26, 27, 28, 29, 30, 31, 32]. A few such traps are shown in Fig. 2. Segmented traps feature multiple dynamic and possibly independent trapping potentials, which allow for dynamic transport and reconfiguration of ion crystals during operation to achieve scalability for trapped-ion QC systems. Production of those devices usually requires various micro-fabrication techniques due to their design complexity. This increased complexity also limits the performance of those devices in many cases; e.g., maintaining low heating rates during operation remains a persisting challenge, transport and reconfiguration of the ion crystals takes up additional computational time, and the complexity of circuit compilation increases. Moreover, controlling the individual segments of those traps requires suitable low-noise control of a large number of individual DC voltages. Mitigation strategies include cooling such traps

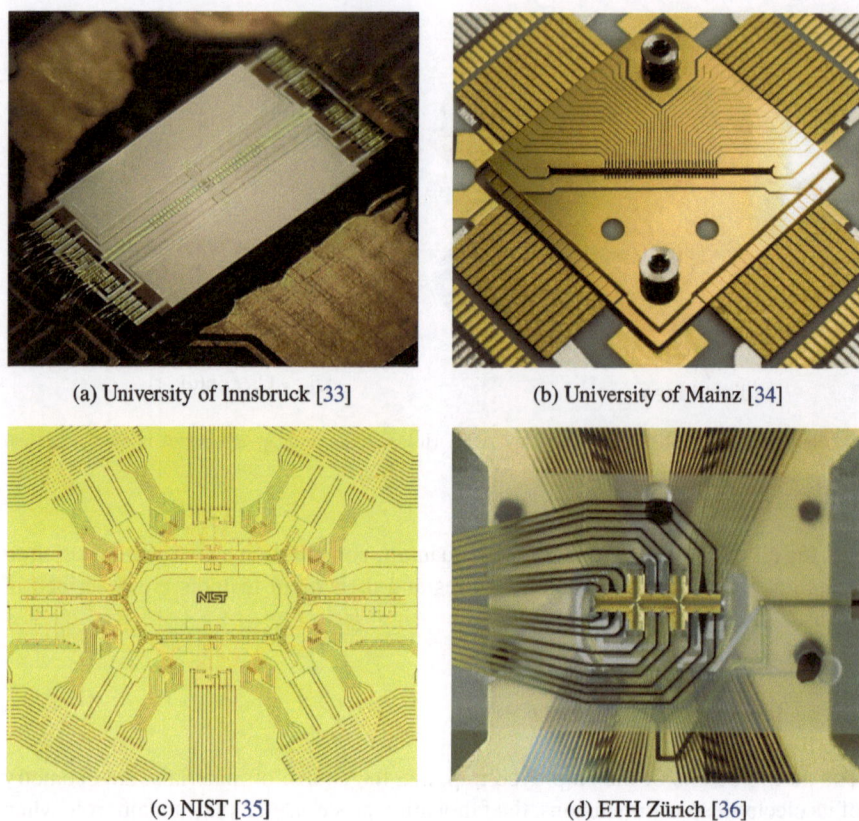

(a) University of Innsbruck [33] (b) University of Mainz [34]

(c) NIST [35] (d) ETH Zürich [36]

Fig. 2 Examples of microstructured ion traps. (**a**) shows a planar trap, where multiple electrodes are connected to the same DC voltage, enabling parallel ion transport operations, (**b**) shows a multilayered segmented 3D ion trap (wire-bond connections missing in the image), (**c**) shows a planar trap with a closed *racetrack*-shaped electrode structure, and (**d**) shows a 3D trap featuring cross-shaped intersections

to cryogenic temperatures and/or operating the system with more than one ionic species, which enables cooling of the quantum register during operation.

While impressive results could be achieved going down that route [20, 29], the accompanying complexity still largely ties such systems to laboratory environments, while systems employing traps as shown in Fig. 1 can be engineered in such a fashion that a deployment as part of a QC system in standard data centers is possible (see Sect. 2).

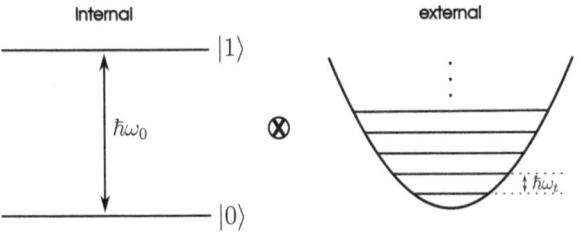

Fig. 3 Simplified internal and external degrees of freedom of one ion in a trap. The internal degree of freedom is an electronic two-level system with the qubit-states $|0\rangle$ and $|1\rangle$ and an energy difference of $\hbar\omega_0$. The external degree of freedom is the ion confined in a harmonic potential with an energy difference $\hbar\omega_t$, with ω_t denoting the trap frequency

1.2.3 Ion Crystals as Qubit Registers

Ions in a Paul trap have an *external degree of freedom*, describing the motional state of the particles in the trapping potential, and an *internal degree of freedom*, describing the electronic state of the ions (see Fig. 3). The most important aspect of external degrees of freedom can be described as a standard quantum mechanical harmonic oscillator in three dimensions [23]. The confining trapping potential of a Paul trap is chosen, such that ω_z is relatively small compared to ω_x and ω_y. Consequently, the ions will line up along the z-axis of the trap. The resulting *linear ion crystal* can then be used as a *qubit* register, where a qubit is the most fundamental unit of quantum information, just as the regular bit is for classical information processing. The quantum mechanical *state* of a qubit in general is described by $|\psi\rangle = \alpha|0\rangle + \beta|1\rangle$ with $\alpha, \beta \in \mathbb{C}$ and $|\alpha|^2 + |\beta|^2 = 1$. Upon measurement, the *superposition state* of the qubit collapses, and is projected onto either $|0\rangle$ or $|1\rangle$. For further details about the concept and physics of qubits, we refer the reader to the literature [4, 37].

Describing the internal degree of freedom is in general a more complex atomic physics problem, depending on the ionic species. For more details on that topic, we again refer the reader to the literature [38, 39]. In the present context, it is sufficient to be aware that ions employed for QC purposes offer two suitable electronic energy levels. A transition between these two levels can be driven to implement gate operations. The respective states are then referred to as $|0\rangle$ and $|1\rangle$, and can be distinguished by a measurement.

In the absence of any external interaction, this system is described by the Hamiltonian

$$H = \frac{1}{2}\hbar\omega_0\sigma_z + \hbar\omega_t\left(a^\dagger a + \frac{1}{2}\right),$$ (1)

with $\hbar$ being the reduced Planck's constant, $a^\dagger$ and a the creation and annihilation operator of the harmonic oscillator describing the motion of the ion respectively, ω_0 the transition frequency between the internal states $|0\rangle$ and $|1\rangle$, ω_t the trap frequency, given by the electrode configuration and the operational parameters of the ion trap, and σ_z the respective Pauli matrix.

A suitable driving field, usually an external laser field with the frequency ω_L, is applied to couple the internal and/or external states of the ions. We focus on the following three cases:

- *Resonant Laser Field*

  If $\omega_L = \omega_0$, the external field only drives the transition between the ion's internal states $|0\rangle$ and $|1\rangle$. We refer to that transition as the carrier (car) transition. ϕ_L denotes the phase of the driving field. The resulting Hamiltonian [23] reads:

$$H_{\text{car}} = \hbar\frac{\Omega}{2}\left(e^{i\phi_L}\sigma^+ + e^{-i\phi_L}\sigma^-\right) \tag{2}$$

- *Red Motional Sideband*

  If $\omega_L = \omega_0 - \omega_T$, the interaction affects the internal and the motional states of the ion crystal. An excitation of the internal state goes along with a de-excitation of the motional state and vice versa. We call that transition the red sideband (rsb) transition.

$$H_{\text{rsb}} = i\hbar\eta\frac{\Omega_{n,n-1}}{2}\left(e^{i\phi_L}a\sigma^+ + e^{-i\phi_L}a^\dagger\sigma^-\right) \tag{3}$$

- *Blue Motional Sideband*

  If $\omega_L = \omega_0 + \omega_T$, the interaction also affects the internal and the motional states of the ion crystal. Now, an excitation of the internal state goes along with an excitation of the motional state and vice versa. We call that transition the blue sideband (bsb) transition.

$$H_{\text{bsb}} = i\hbar\eta\frac{\Omega_{n,n+1}}{2}\left(e^{i\phi_L}a^\dagger\sigma^+ + e^{-i\phi_L}a\sigma^-\right) \tag{4}$$

Here, Ω is the *Rabi frequency*, describing the timescale of the dynamics of the system induced by the external driving field, $\sigma^\pm = \sigma_x \pm i\sigma_y$ a combination of Pauli matrices, and η the Lamb-Dicke Parameter, and the indices n designate the number states of the motional harmonic oscillator. For more details on the underlying physics, please refer to the standard textbook literature on quantum mechanics, e.g., [40].

Single-Qubit Gates

An initial state $|\Psi(t_0)\rangle$ is converted to a final state at the end of the interaction of duration t_1 by means of the time evolution operator $U(t)$, $|\Psi(t_1)\rangle = U(t)|\Psi(t_0)\rangle$. For time-independent Hamiltonians, as H_{car}, which needs to be employed in this case, it reads explicitly

$$U_{SQ}(t) = \exp\left(-\frac{i}{\hbar}H_{cart}\right) = \begin{pmatrix} \cos(\frac{\Omega}{2}t) & -ie^{-i\phi_L}\sin(\frac{\Omega}{2}t) \\ -ie^{i\phi_L}\sin(\frac{\Omega}{2}t) & \cos(\frac{\Omega}{2}t) \end{pmatrix} = R(\theta, \phi) \tag{5}$$

which is identical to the canonical definition of an $R(\theta, \phi)$ gate operation [37, 4], with $\phi = \phi_L$ and $\theta = \Omega t$.

$R_z(\theta)$ gate operations

$$R_z(\phi) = \begin{pmatrix} \cos(\frac{\phi}{2}) - i\sin(\frac{\phi}{2}) & 0 \\ 0 & \cos(\frac{\phi}{2}) + i\sin(\frac{\phi}{2})) \end{pmatrix} \tag{6}$$

can be implemented in a virtual fashion, i.e., without employing actual pulses, but by changing the phases of all subsequent pulses [41].

Two-Qubit Gates
Engineering a suitable interaction with a bichromatic light field employing a red and blue sideband interaction simultaneously allows for the implementation of a two-qubit gate operation of the Mølmer-Sørensen type [42, 43]. The time evolution operator reads

$$U_{MS} \propto \exp\left(i\frac{\theta}{2}S_x^2\right)$$
$$= \begin{pmatrix} \cos(\frac{\theta}{2}) & 0 & 0 & -i\sin(\frac{\theta}{2}) \\ 0 & \cos(\frac{\theta}{2}) & -i\sin(\frac{\theta}{2}) & 0 \\ 0 & -i\sin(\frac{\theta}{2}) & \cos(\frac{\theta}{2}) & 0 \\ -i\sin(\frac{\theta}{2}) & 0 & 0 & \cos(\frac{\theta}{2}) \end{pmatrix} = R_{xx}(\theta), \tag{7}$$

which is identical to the canonical definition of a $R_{xx}(\theta)$ gate operation [37]. Here, $S_x = \sigma_x^{(i)} + \sigma_x^{(j)}$ is the global spin operator of the target ions i and j. This generates the maximally entangled state for the case $\theta = \pi/2$

$$U_{MS}|00\rangle = \frac{1}{\sqrt{2}}(|00\rangle - i|11\rangle). \tag{8}$$

2 Trapped-Ion Hardware

In general, many hardware components and devices are required to build a QC system with high-quality qubits and high-fidelity quantum gate operations. Several trade-offs need to be considered and optimized during the design process that are conductive for the targeted, out-of-laboratory or industrial, operational conditions.

Thus, the hardware and system design needs to ensure that the device operates to the required physical, environmental and quantum, as well as interface specifications. In the case of trapped ions, these requirements include keeping qubits in an adequate electromagnetic environment, shielded from the surroundings, and at the same time enabling well-controlled qubit operations during execution of quantum algorithms, qubit state detection, and communication to the user.

An efficient approach to implement such complex system designs is based on a modular architecture. In this case, the hardware components are hierarchically structured into exchangeable subassemblies, with interfaces in between, ideally allowing them to be modeled by a hardware description in software. Tight integration of quantum physics subsystems, i.e., the trapped ions coupled to electromagnetic fields, with various other subsystems, such as high-precision laser light sources, real-time electronic control, electro-optical distribution networks, as well as classical compute and network systems, is required. In the following sections, we describe the main elements of a device that we have assembled and are operating at AQT, starting with the ion trap *PINE trap* in Sect. 2.1 and vacuum and control setup for operating the trap *PINE set-up* in Sect. 2.2. In Sect. 2.3 we elaborate on how the complete system is installed within a standardized 19″ rack that is compatible with operation in data center environments.

2.1 Ion-Trap Device

The *PINE trap* as shown in Fig. 4 is a high-precision ion trap built upon the well-tested design of the University of Innsbruck and the Institute of Quantum Optics and Quantum Information of the Austrian Academy of Sciences. The initial design was further optimized for high thermal and electrical conductivity to minimize parasitic heating effects, as well as for precision manufacturing to allow a reproducible production process.

The trap features heating rates of < 10 phonons/s, as demonstrated in Fig. 5, especially an axial heating rate of < 1 phonon/s for a trap frequency of about 500 kHz. That low number is key for performing high-fidelity two-qubit gate operations as described in 1.2, where the ion–ion interaction is mediated by the ion crystal's motional mode. The performance of the PINE trap on that front fulfills the requirements for fault-tolerant gate operation. Furthermore, the high optical access with a numerical aperture (NA) > 0.5 allows for tightly focusing laser fields on the ion string, minimizing cross-talk to neighboring ions during addressing operations. Those key performance indicators make the PINE trap an excellent device for the storage and coherent manipulation of trapped particles in general.

The trap can be integrated in a custom-built vacuum system that contains standard vacuum components. Electrical contacts to the trapping electrodes, up to four compensation electrodes, and temperature sensors can be accessed by standardized electrical vacuum feedthroughs. The choice of materials and fabrication process leads to a reduced trap-temperature over RF-power dependency of < 5 K/W,

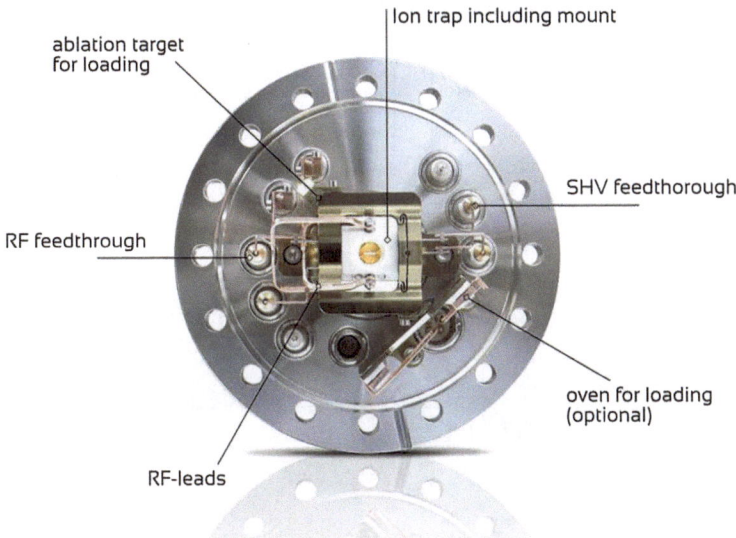

Fig. 4 The *PINE trap* is mounted on an ultra-high-vacuum flange and connected RF and safe high-voltage (SHV) feedthroughs for electrical supply. This trap has been already utilized by research groups to demonstrate outstanding results in the field of QC and high precision metrology [13, 44], and trap various atomic- and molecular ion species

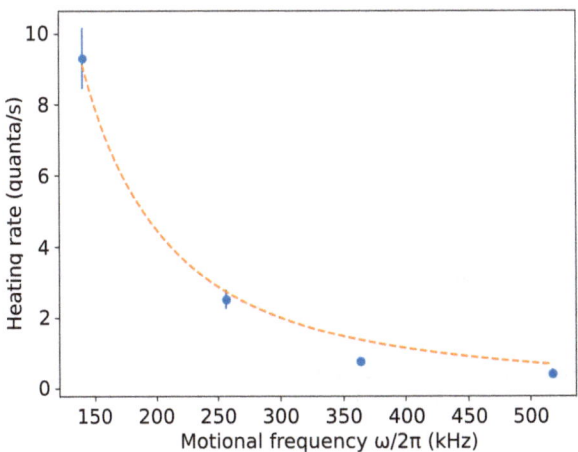

Fig. 5 The *PINE trap* features heating rates of below 10 phonons/s within its typical operating range and of below 1 phonon/s for an axial trap frequency of 500 kHz specifically, which allows the trap to be used for fault-tolerant quantum operations

PINE SET-UP

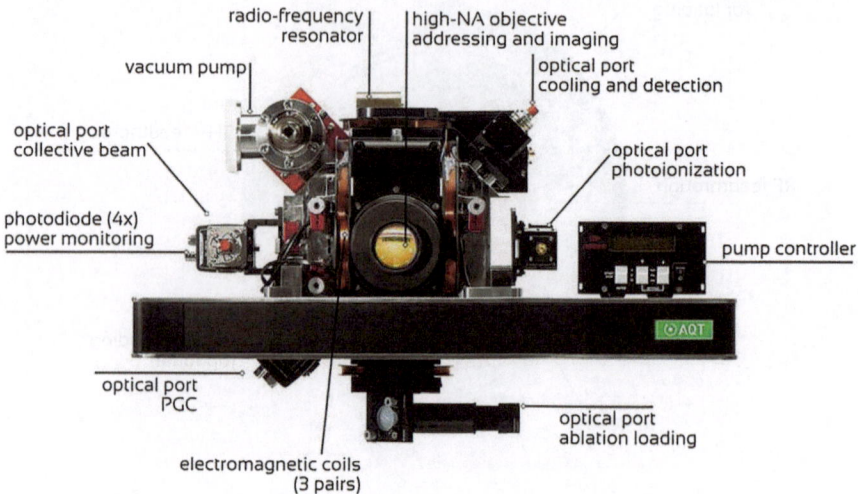

Fig. 6 The *PINE setup* includes the *PINE trap* mounted in an ultra-high-vacuum chamber with required pump and controller, optical access for all laser beams for ablation loading, cooling, detection, and polarization gradient cooling (PGC) as well as imaging and addressing of trapped ions via a high numerical aperture (NA) objective, electromagnetic coils, and an RF resonator

minimizing mechanical drifts due to changing temperature during operation with non-constant RF-power.

2.2 Ion-Trap Setup

The *PINE setup* is an ion-trapping assembly based on the modular hardware approach (see Fig. 6). The heart of the setup is the *PINE trap*, which is located inside an ultra-high-vacuum chamber facilitating a low background-gas collision rate of $< 0.02\,\mathrm{s}^{-1}$. Such a collision rate translates to less than one collision per ion with a background gas particle per minute, which is important when considering the maximal width of a quantum circuit as the overall collision rate grows linearly with the number of ions. Optical interfaces for qubit manipulation are provided via dedicated fiber ports. The objective with a high numerical aperture (NA) of up to 0.6 fulfills two purposes. Firstly, it allows for focusing down a laser beam to a spot size of $< 1\mu\mathrm{m}$ to address single ions with low cross-talk to next neighbors. Secondly, it can efficiently collect fluorescence photons for reliable state detection using the electron shelving technique [38] within a detection time of less than $200\,\mu\mathrm{s}$. The ion species can be selected by choosing respective targets for ablation loading, and up to two ablation targets can be configured for multi-ion species applications. This

PINE SET-UP
suitable for a 19-inch rack installation

Fig. 7 This configuration of the *PINE setup* is ready to be mounted into a standard 19″ rack with easy access by mounting it on sliding rails which act as a drawer that can be pulled out of the rack. Additionally, it features a vibration isolation stage, a scientific camera for imaging purposes, and an electromagnetic shielding structure

configuration allowed the setup to achieve the world's largest maximally entangled quantum state with 24 calcium-ion qubits [44], superseded recently by the creation of a 32-qubit maximally entangled state [45].

2.3 Quantum Computer in a Rack

The *MARMOT system* is a complete trapped-ion quantum computer that fits inside two standardized 19″ racks by mounting the *PINE setup* on sliding rails as shown in Fig. 7. In that system, tens of individually addressable qubits can be prepared and worked with, depending on the scientific application and performance requirements (see more details in Sect. 3).

The *MARMOT system* has been designed to target standard HPC facilities, data centers, industrial environments, or even office spaces (see Fig. 8). Operated remotely and supplied from just a single phase power wall outlet, the device does not require special access, cooling, vibration insulation, or further requirements typically associated with other quantum devices. To date, this system has been used as a testbed to investigate quantum benefits in the fields of chemistry, risk

Fig. 8 A photograph of the *MARMOT system* which is a 19″-rack-mounted room-temperature quantum computer, having a less than $2\,m^2$ footprint and a power consumption of less than $2\,kW$. Designed for the installation at HPC infrastructures and data centers, the *PINE setup* is located behind a front plate on the bottom of the left rack, while the full laser system and stabilization is placed in the right rack

analysis, portfolio optimization [46], probabilistic networks [47], random numbers for cryptographic applications [48], and more.

3 Quantum Performance

Characterizing and qualifying manufactured hardware components is a fundamental task before using any device. The goal of our specific QC device is to use it for quantum information processing and execution of quantum circuits. Therefore, a well-characterized and well-specified QC system requires measuring its properties, including the quality of qubits in various aspects. Typical examples are the quality of isolation from the environment and from each other, how well their quantum state can be controlled, and what their collective quantum performance is, which eventually defines the quality of the whole QC system.

In the following, we describe several QC hardware performance metrics that we have applied to characterize our *MARMOT system*. We start with the parasitic coupling of the laser light field to neighboring ions within the qubit register, so-called qubit cross-talk, in Sect. 3.1, the single-qubit error rate within the range for enabling fault-tolerant quantum gate operations in Sect. 3.2, the qubit coherence times in Sect. 3.3, and the quantum volume for simplified QC performance benchmarking in Sect. 3.4.

3.1 20-Qubit Control

In our trapped-ion quantum computer, we move a single or several laser beams onto the position of a single or multiple ions, respectively. Applying discrete laser pulses onto the ions effectively changes the encoded quantum information. Ideally, the laser light would hit only the targeted ion(s) and nothing else, which is a requirement that can rarely be fulfilled in ion crystals with more than two ions. Thus, it is important to characterize the undesired coupling of the laser light field via the coupling strength of non-targeted ions relative to the addressed ion. Typical numbers are within the range of 1–3%, but in Fig. 9 we present the full cross-talk matrix, which gives an average coupling to next-neighbor qubits of only 0.58% in a 20-qubit register.

Such low levels of cross-talk convert into error rates in the 10^{-5} range, which is compatible with fault-tolerant requirements and enables the execution of quantum algorithms on the *MARMOT system* without considering complicated error mitigation routines. Supporting fault-tolerant universal quantum gate operations provides a pathway to go beyond so-called noisy intermediate-scale quantum (NISQ) devices [1], which, as a proof of concept, has been recently demonstrated with trapped-ion qubits using a *PINE trap* [13].

Furthermore, increasing the number of high-quality qubits should result in benefits for the end user and gradually increase the QC system performance levels. It provides a solid basis for implementing use cases on NISQ devices ranging from finance to chemistry [49, 50] and several more [1].

3.2 Single-Qubit Error Rates

Errors in quantum processors are one of the largest roadblocks toward the implementation of quantum applications resulting in a computational benefit. While controlling larger numbers of qubits for creating larger quantum states for computing is demanding, an even more challenging aspect is to at least maintain, but ideally significantly improve, the performance of the quantum gate operations at the same time. In terms of quantum processor description, this entails details such as

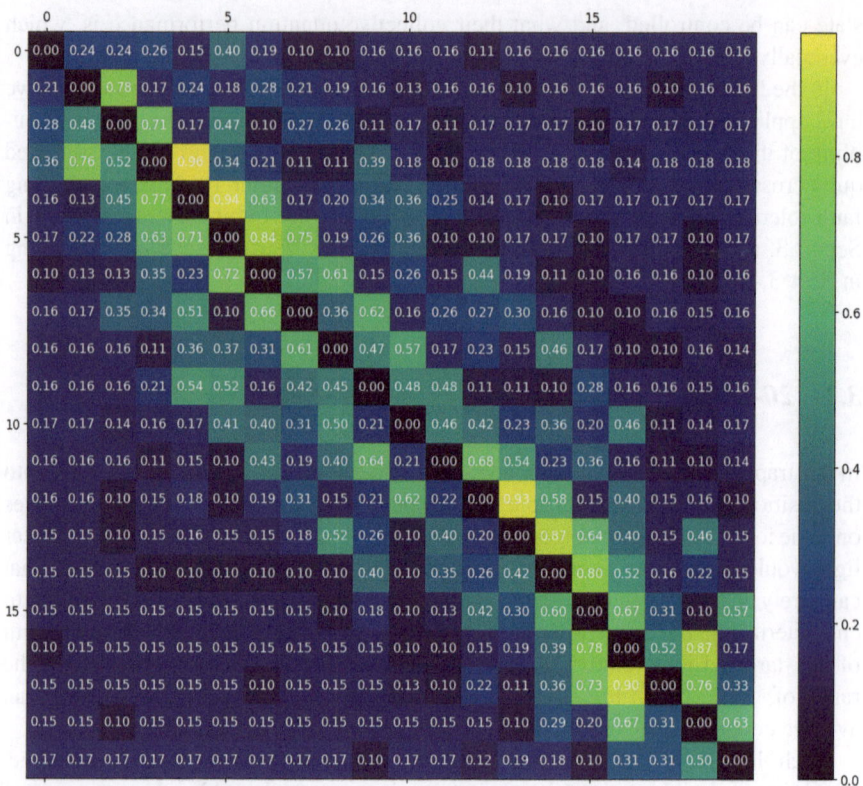

Fig. 9 Cross-talk matrix for a qubit register consisting of 20 individual ions. We characterize the couplings between individual qubits by driving Rabi oscillations on a single ion and measuring the excitation on other qubits. The mean value of the ratio of the coupling to the next-neighbor qubits is 0.58%. In terms of error rates, this corresponds to the 10^{-5} range and is consistent with the requirements for fault-tolerant quantum computers

realizing *Markovian dynamics*, e.g., the order of gate operations has no effect on the achieved performance, stability of the system, negligible cross-talk between qubits, as well as a sufficient connectivity.

One possible source of errors is the single-qubit error rate, for which we present individual measurements on 10 qubits in Fig. 10. We determined the fidelity for single-qubit gates using local randomized gates [51, 52], which are randomly and uniformly sourced from the Clifford group. In addition, the inverse element is calculated and placed at the end of the sequence to reverse the previous operations and ideally return the qubit to its initial state. In doing so, the average success probability (SP) of returning the qubit to its initial state decreases with N according to

$$SP(N) = Ap^N + B, \tag{9}$$

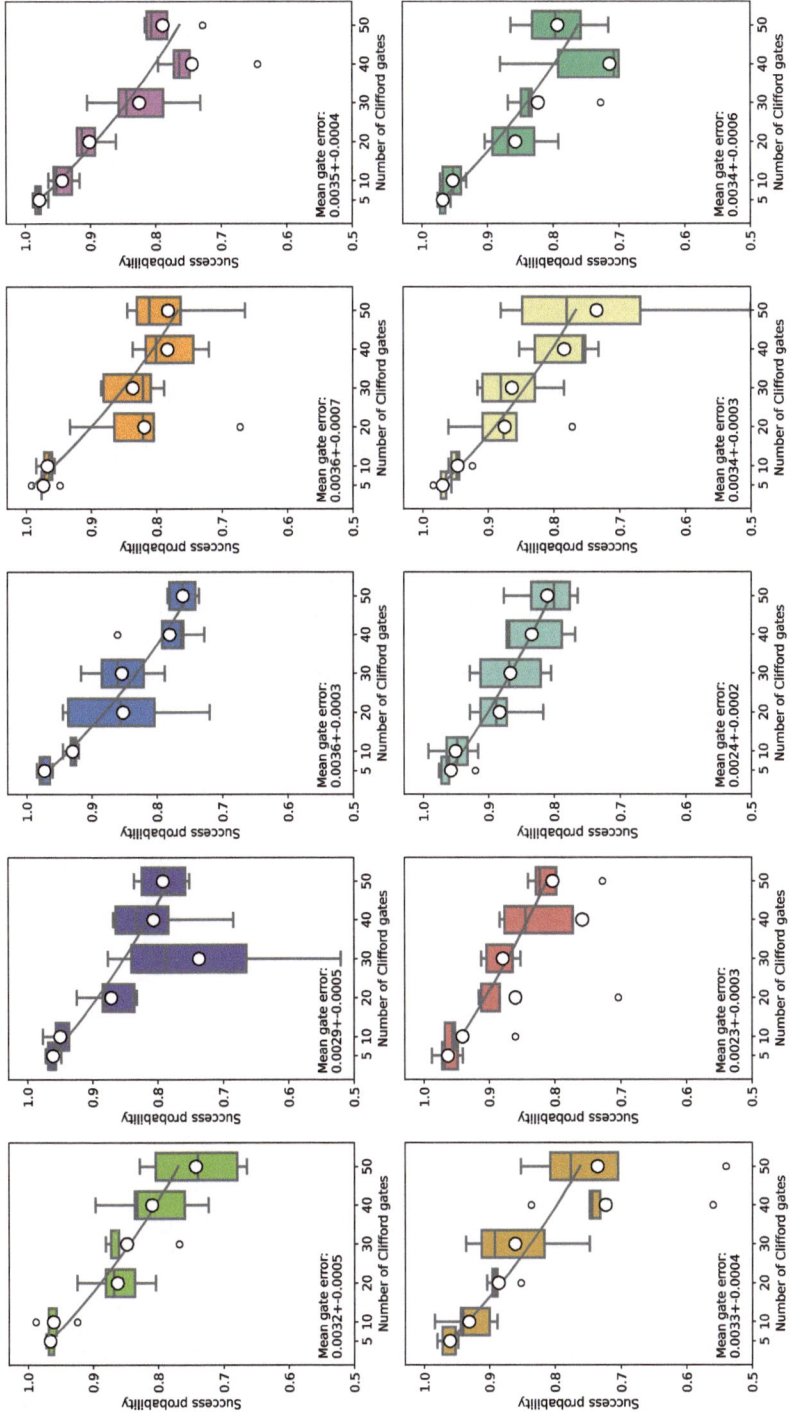

Fig. 10 Randomized benchmarking of single-qubit gates in a ten-qubit register. Each qubit achieves an error rate of less than 1 in 1000

with p the mean gate error and A and B free fitting constants with expected values of $1 - 1/2^n$ and $1/2^n$, respectively, where n is the number of qubits per gate operation and thus $n = 1$ for single-qubit gate operations. For the presented measurements, we implemented random sequences with $N = 5, 10, 20, 30, 40,$ and 50 Clifford elements, where each element consists of several X and Y gate operations, on average about 1.7 gate operations per Clifford element. For each sequence length N we realize 50 random repetitions. A fit to the experimental data yields mean gate errors that are given for each ion in Fig. 10. On average, the qubit register features an error rate that is less than 1 in 1000.

3.3 Quantum Memory Lifetime

In contrast to a classical computer, where information is stored in binary states, a QPU stores information in superpositions of binary quantum states specified by relative phases and amplitudes. Storage and manipulation of such quantum information can be fragile and susceptible to disturbances from the environment, leading to information loss and thus reduction in quantum performance. The effect of this disturbance can be quantified by the lifetime of the quantum information, referred to as quantum memory lifetime, which is depicted in Fig. 11.

The quantum memory lifetime is dominated by two effects that can be witnessed on qubits. The first effect describes the decay of qubit excitation resulting from energy exchange between an ion and its environment. The respective rate is described by the so-called T_1 time which is limited by the natural lifetime of the energy levels constituting the qubit system. Individual measurements of T_1 for 20 qubits are shown in Fig. 12. The second effect stems from information loss due to scrambling of the phase relation in the superposition state predominantly induced

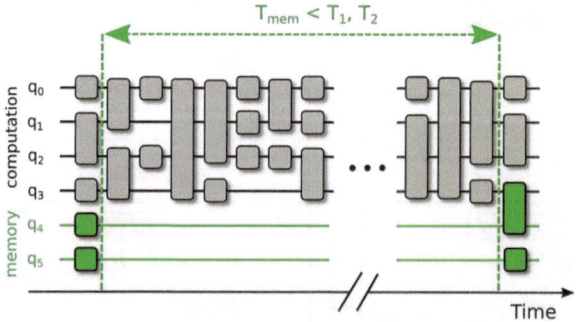

Fig. 11 Lifetime of memory qubits T_{mem} in comparison to coherence times of computational qubits T_1 and T_2. Considering typical gate times on the order of 10 to 100 μs, the quantum memory persists for the equivalent of up to 10,000 quantum gate operations. Such circuit depths can be challenging for some platforms (see Sec. 1.1 and Table 1)

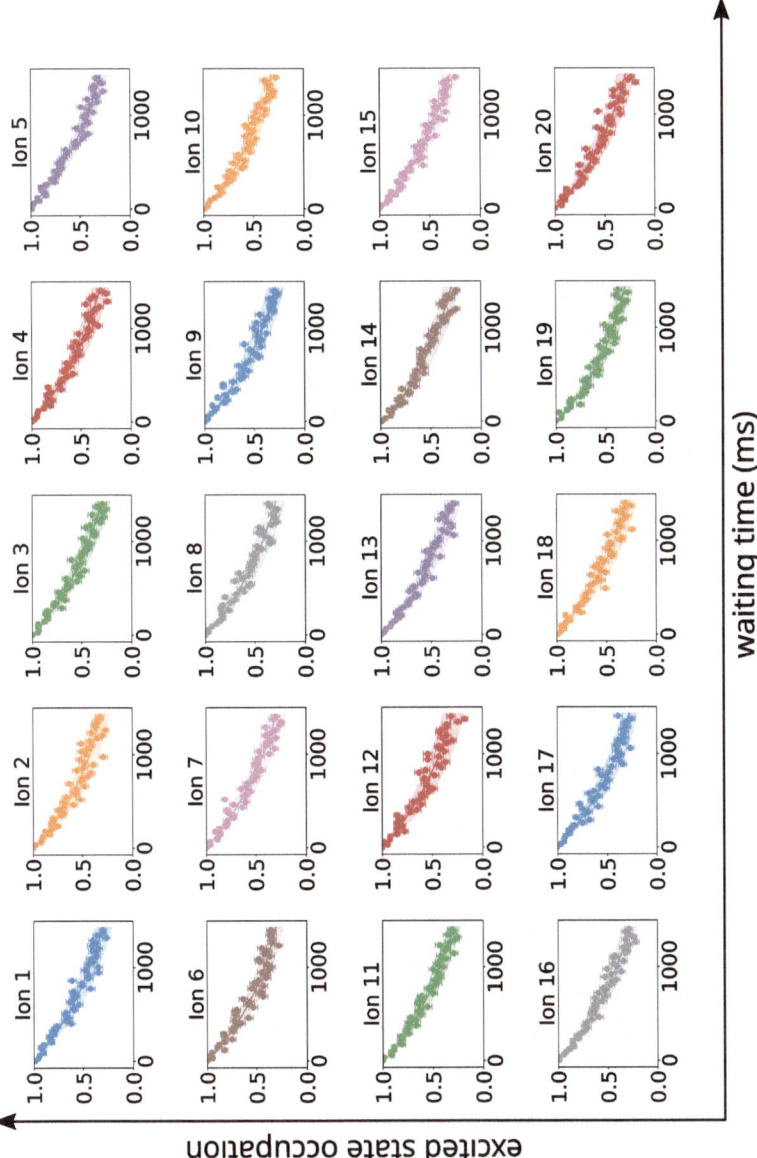

Fig. 12 T_1 times for individual qubits in a register of 20 ions. All qubit lifetimes match within one standard deviation to an average of $T_1 = 1.14\,\text{s} \pm 0.06\,\text{s}$ and agree with the natural lifetime of the qubit transition $T_{1,\text{nat}} = 1.165\,\text{s} \pm 0.011\,\text{s}$ [53]

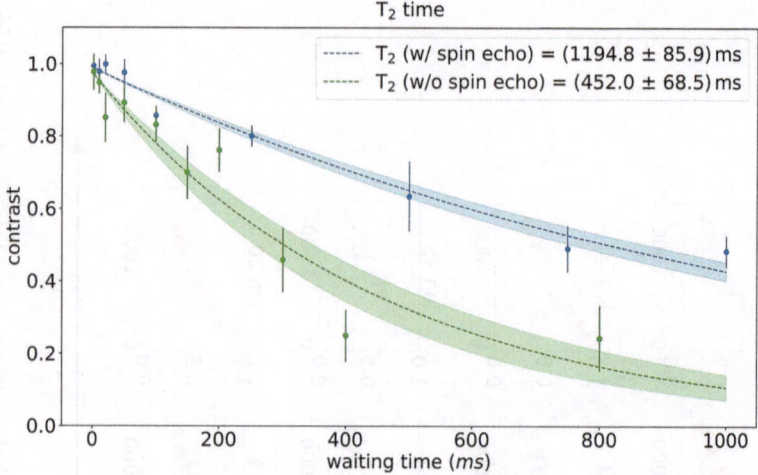

Fig. 13 T_2 time of the qubit transition. The blue and green dots represent the measurement results derived from a standard Ramsey experiment and a Ramsey measurement with spin echo refocusing, respectively. We determine the T_2 time by fitting exponential decays to the two experiments with results given in the legend

by laser light field and magnetic field fluctuations. It is described by the T_2 time, with its measurement presented in Fig. 13. Ideally, both the T_1 and T_2 times should be significantly longer than the time it takes to manipulate the qubits. Physically, the ultimate limit for the T_2 time of the quantum system is given by the lifetime T_1 by $T_2 < 2T_1$, i.e., a well-isolated quantum system should demonstrate T_2 times on the order of T_1.

Here, we present the T_1 and T_2 times measured in the *MARMOT system*. We first highlight the identical behavior of all ions in the qubit register, exemplified by the time $T_1 = 1.14\,\text{s} \pm 0.06\,\text{s}$, measured for each ion in a register of 20 ions. A laser linewidth of less than 1 Hz and highly stable magnetic fields provide us with an excellent T_2 time between 0.5 and 1.2 s. Accordingly, the quantum memory persists for the equivalent of up to 10,000 quantum gate operations based on gate times on the order of 10 to 100 μs, visualized in Fig. 11.

The identical nature of all qubits, in combination with low error rates and all-to-all connectivity, allows us to reduce circuit compilation and calibration overhead. This simplifies the implementation of quantum applications, making the trapped-ion QPU a preferable platform for QC.

3.4 Quantum Volume

The quantum volume (QV) test is a benchmark that tries to assess and describe the computational performance of a QC system with a single number [54]. The higher the number, the more powerful the computer, where the QV is either limited by the number of available qubits or by the circuit size that can be implemented with reasonable success probability. Although there are many more possible benchmarks available [55], the QV test is one of the simplest and most commonly used benchmarks at the moment and allows us to compare different universal QC systems, independent of their platform or architecture.

The QV on the AQT QC system was determined by running 870 random QV test circuits in total. We show an example in Fig. 14. The test resulted in a mean heavy output probability (HOP) of 0.714 ± 0.015 with twice the standard deviation of $2\sigma = 0.031$. Thus, the measured HOP is above the required threshold of 2/3 with 99.89% confidence. The implemented circuits were generated using Qiskit [37]. The random circuits were further optimized using methods which include Block combination, Block approximation, mirroring, and arbitrary angles for entangling gate operations [56]. This procedure yields a QV of 128 with the corresponding measurement shown in Fig. 15. While higher QV values have been recently achieved by Quantinuum in the US [45], to our knowledge, so far 128 is the largest QV measured on a universal quantum computer which has been designed, built, and located in Europe. It's also worth noting that QV scales exponentially with the number of qubits.

Using the programming language Python and various supported QC interfaces, the implementation of the presented QV test requires only a few lines of code in Qiskit, which makes it an easy-to-use, synthetic benchmark to characterize the holistic performance of a QC system. As an extension to synthetic benchmarks in general, efforts have recently been made to define application-specific benchmarks for easier comparison of real operational performances of QC systems [57, 58, 59].

4 Software

Executing quantum algorithms with sufficiently high quality is the primary goal for every QC system, and to provide those capabilities for a given application, a suitable software stack is required. From top to bottom, the stack includes an interface for user input, remote connectivity, queue and job management, compilation and transpilation of quantum circuits, scheduling and generation of RF and laser pulse objects, processing quantum instructions, controlling electronics and components, and result processing, to name the most important parts.

The secondary goal of the software stack is operating and maintaining a QC system in an unattended fashion for a long period of time, which requires automatic calibrations of QC components and parameters, monitoring and reporting of important system properties, ensuring data integrity and security, and supporting classical administrative and operational tasks.

In the next subsections we will present details about the cloud QC platform (Sect. 4.1), circuit transpilation (Sect. 4.2), and the RF pulse scheduler (Sect. 4.3) developed and used by AQT.

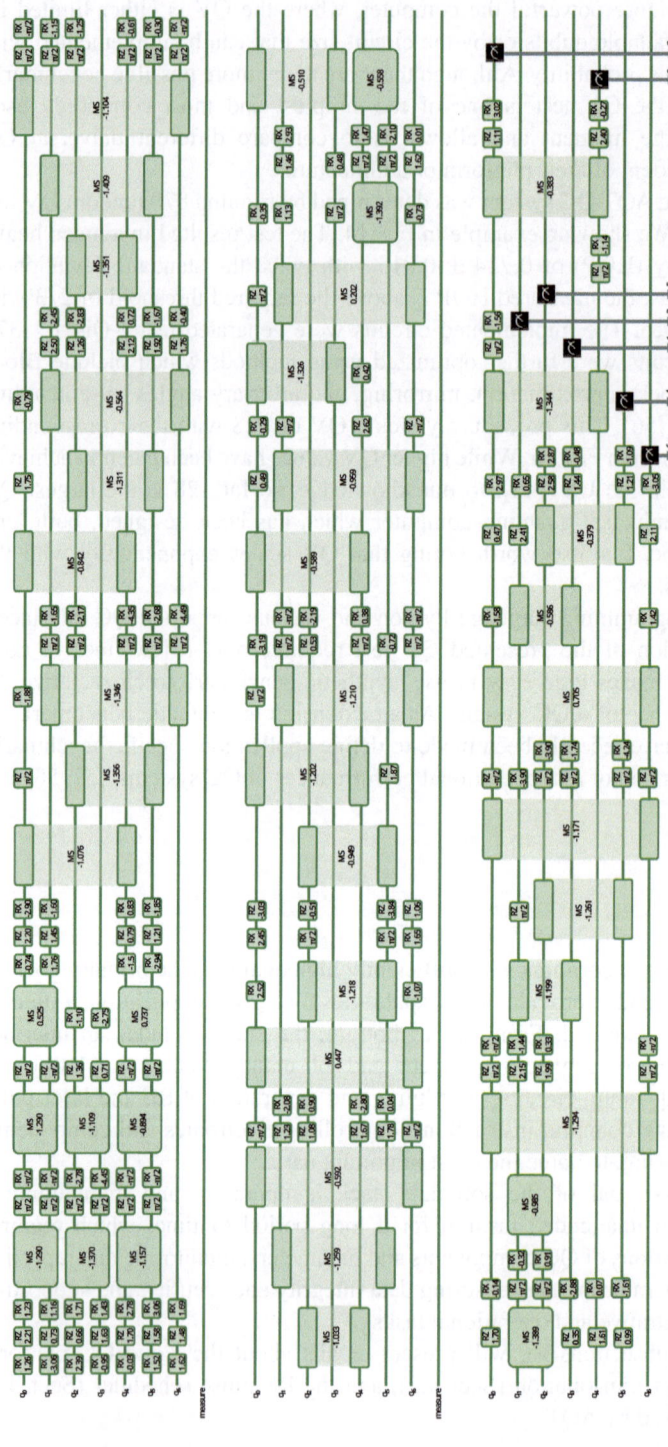

Fig. 14 The quantum volume test consists of a series of random quantum circuits. A random circuit starts with the preparation of the qubits, followed by the implementation of several local single-qubit gates and interleaving two-qubit gates. Finally, the state of the qubits is measured and the result is obtained in the form of a classical bit string. The number of qubits (vertical extent) corresponds to the circuit width and the number of gate realizations (horizontal extent) describes the circuit depth

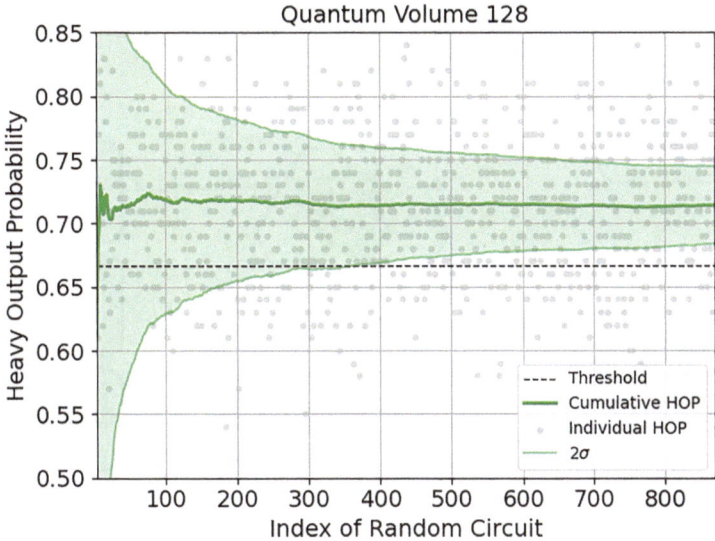

Fig. 15 For the quantum volume test to be successful, the heavy output probability (HOP) must be above the specified threshold of 2/3. The data shows that the mean HOP is above this threshold and the associated uncertainty decreases as the number of random circuits increases. Eventually, the HOP exceeds the threshold by more than two standard deviations (2σ), which certifies that the AQT *MARMOT system* has a quantum volume of 128

4.1 Cloud Platform

Access to the AQT QC systems is provided through a dedicated cloud platform. A client can submit circuits to the quantum computer for processing with a so-called representational state transfer (REST) call to the cloud platform API. The circuit is defined in a service-specific JSON format and transmitted in the HTTP request body. Once completed, the circuit results can be requested from the same API. The REST API is protected through token authentication.

The service provided by the cloud platform is of an asynchronous nature. This means that when a circuit is transmitted for processing, the connection is not kept alive until the result is available. A submission results in an immediate response instead, containing a job ID. This job ID is then used to request the state of the processing task and to retrieve the result once it is ready.

Internally, a submitted circuit is stored in the database, which acts like a queue. The quantum computer queries the cloud portal for circuits to process. Similar to the submission of circuits, this is also done through a REST API call. If an unprocessed circuit is available in the database, it will be processed by the quantum computer followed by yet another REST call to submit the result to the cloud platform. The result is stored in the database and will be returned to the client upon request. The

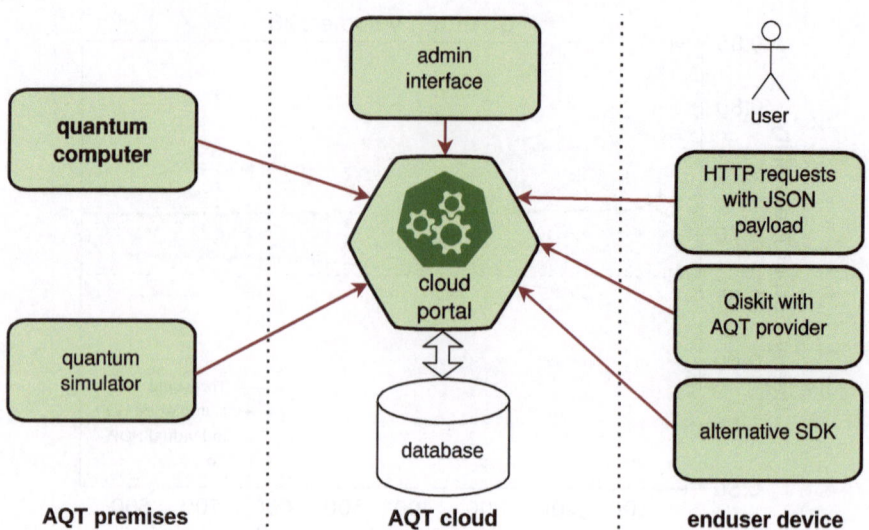

Fig. 16 Overview of the AQT cloud QC architecture. The cloud portal is the central component that allows users to submit workloads which are retrieved and processed by the quantum computers

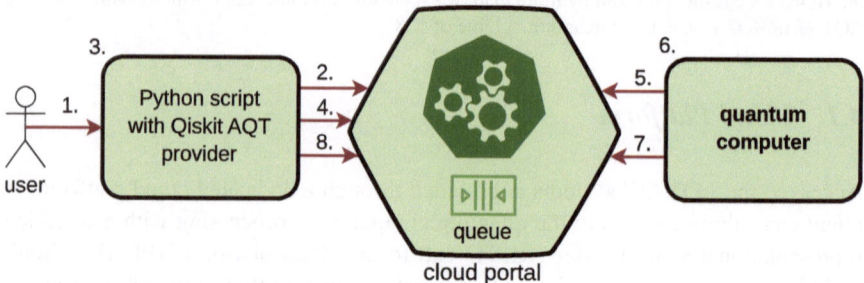

Fig. 17 A step by step illustration of the cloud portal workflow: The user executes a Qiskit script (1) which retrieves the QC capabilities (2) and transpiles into circuits compatible with the AQT QC systems (3). The transpiled circuits are transmitted to the cloud portal (4) and they are retrieved (5) and processed by the quantum computer (6). The results are returned to the cloud portal (7), and are then retrieved by Qiskit and the user (8)

high-level architecture of the cloud portal is illustrated in Fig. 16, a typical workflow is shown in Fig. 17, and a Qiskit code example in Listing 1.

It is possible to directly use the REST API, but a usage via a suitable quantum SDK is much more convenient and user friendly: the SDK takes care of creating the JSON payload as well as communication with the cloud platform. After submitting a circuit it will regularly request its processing state in the background and retrieve the result once it is ready. This allows existing code based on any of these libraries to be readily used on the *MARMOT system*.

Listing 1 Basic example of using the Qiskit AQT provider, which creates and executes a 4-qubit Greenberger–Horne–Zeilinger (GHZ) state on the *MARMOT system*

```
 1  import qiskit
 2  from qiskit import QuantumCircuit
 3
 4  from qiskit_aqt_provider.aqt_provider import AQTProvider
 5
 6  # Ways to specify an access token (in precedence order):
 7  # - as argument to the AQTProvider initializer
 8  # - in the AQT_TOKEN environment variable
 9  # - if none of the above exists, default to an empty string
10  #   to the default workspace only.
11  provider = AQTProvider("token")
12
13  # The backends() method lists all available computing backends.
14  # Printing it renders it as a table that shows each backend's
15  # containing workspace.
16  print(provider.backends())
17
18  # Retrieve a backend by providing search criteria.
19  # The search must have a single match. For example:
20  backend = provider.get_backend("marmot", workspace="default")
21
22  # Create a 4-qubit GHZ state
23  qc = QuantumCircuit(4)
24  qc.h(0)
25  qc.cx(0, 1)
26  qc.cx(0, 2)
27  qc.cx(0, 3)
28  qc.measure_all()
29
30  result = qiskit.execute(qc, backend, shots=200).result()
31
32  if result.success:
33      print(result.get_counts())
34  else:
35      print(result.to_dict()["error"])
```

4.2 Circuit Transpilation

The existence of universal gate sets allows QC manufacturers to focus on implementing a limited set of gate operations and rely on algebraic manipulations to rewrite any valid quantum gate combination in terms of the gate set implemented by the targeted hardware. The cloud platform described in Sect. 4.1 exposes the native gates operation, which are implemented by the AQT quantum computers. These gate operations are exactly those that trapped-ion platforms can implement with minimal overhead (see Sect. 1.2).

The gate-level transpilation of quantum circuits, which maps arbitrary quantum gates to those implemented by the target hardware, is performed ahead of the AQT cloud platform API. This offers maximum transparency for the API consumers and allows fine-tuning of the quantum circuit, e.g., for optimizing execution speed.

The AQT provider for the Qiskit SDK exposes transpilation targets and custom transformation passes that strive to optimally rewrite an arbitrary quantum circuit to be ready for execution on AQT hardware. The general architecture is that of the built-in Qiskit transpiler [60], with the following notes:

1. *Optimization Stage*
   Sequences of single-qubit rotations on the same qubit are factored into the ZXZ form, taking advantage of the virtual nature of the R_z operations.
2. *Scheduling Stage*
   $R_x(\theta)$ operations are rewritten as $R(\theta, \phi = 0)$ and rotation angles are wrapped, exploiting the periodicity of R and R_{xx} operations in θ. For $R(\theta, \phi = 0)$ operations, due to hardware limitations, rotation angles $\theta < \theta_s$ are split into two laser pulses as $R(\theta < \theta_s, \phi) = R(\pi, \phi + \pi)R(\theta + \pi, \phi)$. The threshold θ_s is an implementation detail, typically set around $\pi/5$. For $R_{xx}(\theta)$ operations, the following rules are applied recursively for wrapping θ in the entangling operations until $\theta \in [0, \pi/2]$:

$$R_{xx}(\theta) \rightarrow \begin{cases} R_{xx}(\theta) & 0 \le \theta \le \pi/2 \\ R_z^{(1)}(\pi)R_{xx}(|\theta|)R_z^{(1)}(\pi) & -\pi/2 \le \theta < 0 \\ R^{(1)}(\pi, 0)R^{(2)}(\pi, 0)R_{xx}(\theta - \text{sign}(\theta)\pi) & |\theta| < 3\pi/2 \\ R_{xx}(\theta - 2\pi) & \text{otherwise.} \end{cases}$$

$$(10)$$

Remarkably, the angle-wrapping rules require the knowledge of the numeric value of the rotation angles. This is incompatible with the caching strategy adopted by the standard implementation of the Qiskit `Sampler` and `Estimator` primitives to minimize the transpilation overhead, e.g., when sampling different parametrizations of the same circuit. The specialized implementations of these primitives, `AQTSampler` and `AQTEstimator`, use a two-stage transpilation pass, where the first one performs most of the work and is cached, while the second one is restricted to wrapping the rotation angles and is not cached.

4.3 Radio Frequency Pulse Scheduler

In a classical computer, a program written in a high-level programming language needs to be compiled into the language that is native to the respective hardware. The same applies to quantum computers, but their quantum algorithms are meant to be processed on different components of the QC systems, e.g., first on classical

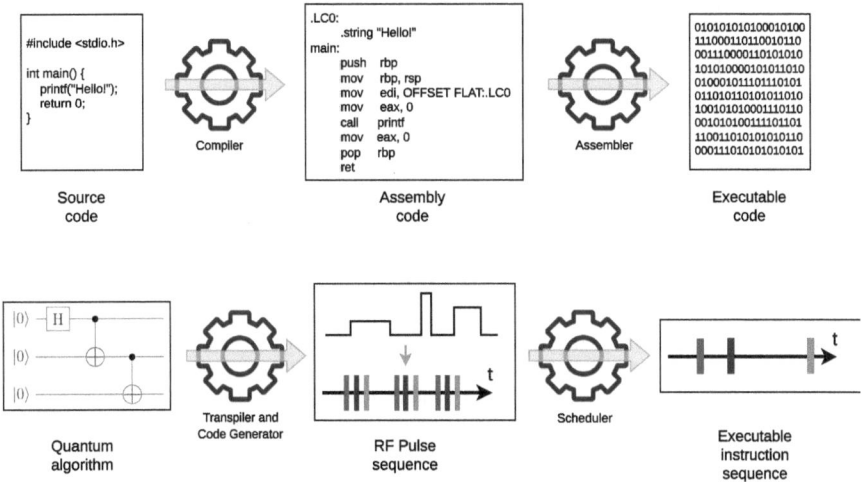

Fig. 18 Schematic illustration of the compilation process of a classical computer (top) compared to the transpilation, code generation, and scheduling of instructions for a quantum device (bottom). After translating gate operations into RF pulses and the respective instructions to generate them, the instructions are scheduled along a timeline to create an instruction sequence that is executable on the target hardware

compute hardware and later on real-time control electronics. Such algorithms are typically designed on the level of quantum gate operations and then translated first into pulses needed to realize the gate operations. In a further step, the pulses are translated into instructions specific to the electronic devices of the target system. These instructions are directed at RF pulse generators to create RF pulses and, subsequently, pulsed laser signals. For the laser pulses to perform the desired operations on the qubits, the instructions need to be scheduled for execution on the real-time hardware with very high precision in timing, frequency, and amplitude. A schematic illustration of the transpilation and scheduling pipeline is shown in Fig. 18.

While the translation into the pulse- and instruction-level representation is done by the control software itself, the scheduling of instructions is done by the RF pulse scheduler software. Figure 19 shows the relation between the control software and the RF pulse scheduler package that is called from a driver component within the control software. The scheduler software is aware of the hardware constraints and applies a series of transformations to the instruction sequence in order to make it executable. The constraints from the RF pulse electronics include that there is a limited number of channels for instructions to run in parallel, as well as the need for a sufficiently large distance along the timeline between two instructions on the same channel.

In its current setup, the RF pulse electronics uses 15 different instructions, identified by a unique opcode, shown in Listing 2. Each instruction corresponds

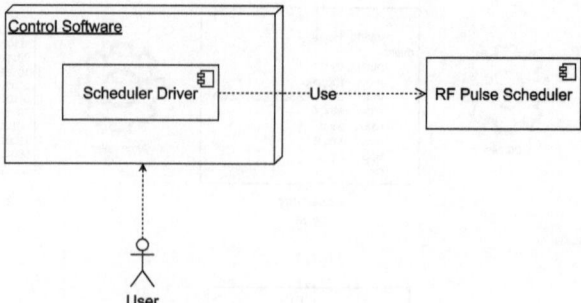

Fig. 19 Context diagram showing the relation of the control software and the RF pulse scheduler software package. The RF pulse scheduler is called from a scheduler driver component within the control software to retrieve an executable instruction sequence. Image (modified) from [61]

Listing 2 A list of the instruction set available to the scheduler. EVENT does not correspond to a physical operation. It serves as a marker for visualization purposes

```
 1 DDS_OUTPUT_DISABLE
 2 DDS_OUTPUT_ENABLE
 3 DDS_SINGLE_TONE_SETUP
 4 PHASER_OUTPUT_DISABLE
 5 PHASER_OUTPUT_ENABLE
 6 PHASER_SINGLE_TONE_BOX_DOWN
 7 PHASER_SINGLE_TONE_BOX_UP
 8 PHASER_SINGLE_TONE_SETUP
 9 PHASER_SINGLE_TONE_SHAPE_DOWN
10 PHASER_SINGLE_TONE_SHAPE_UP
11 TTLCOUNTER_START
12 TTLCOUNTER_STOP
13 TTL_OUTPUT_DISABLE
14 TTL_OUTPUT_ENABLE
15 EVENT
```

to a physical channel of the control electronics. The EVENT instruction serves as a marker and is removed before forwarding the instruction schedule to the hardware.

An executable instruction sequence is then sent to the RF pulse electronics via remote procedure calls (RPCs). The electronics is based on field-programmable gate arrays (FPGAs) that schedule real-time input/output (RTIO) events for frequency synthesizers based on the instruction schedule that was received. Eventually, the frequency synthesizers create RF pulses with the respective frequency, amplitude, and length to drive acousto-optical modulators (AOMs). The AOMs are used to mix the RF pulses with the laser light and thus create the pulsed laser signals for manipulating the qubit states.

4.4 High-Performance Computing Integration

It has been proposed that QC would serve as a natural accelerator to HPC in the form of a QPU [62]. QC systems in general may provide performance boosts for classically hard algorithms leading to an accelerated time-to-solution or to reduced costs of generating the solution. Recent activities and initiatives aim to bring QC and HPC technologies closer together in a step-wise process. In a first step, different QC platforms and technologies will be installed on premise at HPC facilities and evaluated for their readiness to operate in data center environments. The next step will focus on integrating the QC systems into HPC nodes, until ultimately the QPU can be used as an accelerator within the classical compute cluster. Some of the challenges of such an accelerator hardware have been outlined for the system-level integration part in [3, 62] and for the software development part in [2, 63].

As the HPC integration activities do not select between or prefer a specific QC platform or hardware vendor, it is very important to establish definitions of common standards and interfaces. First discussions have started in the context of several initiatives, but the work is ongoing, and will require a significant amount of communication effort between all participating entities. For example, the development of a domain-specific language that covers both HPC and QC user communities seems to be a simple but nonetheless important task. We give an example for three different definitions of a QPU in case of a trapped-ion quantum computer in Fig. 20 to further illustrate the challenge of a common interface. The dashed boxes indicate definitions of a QPU according to different sources or vendors. Only the largest

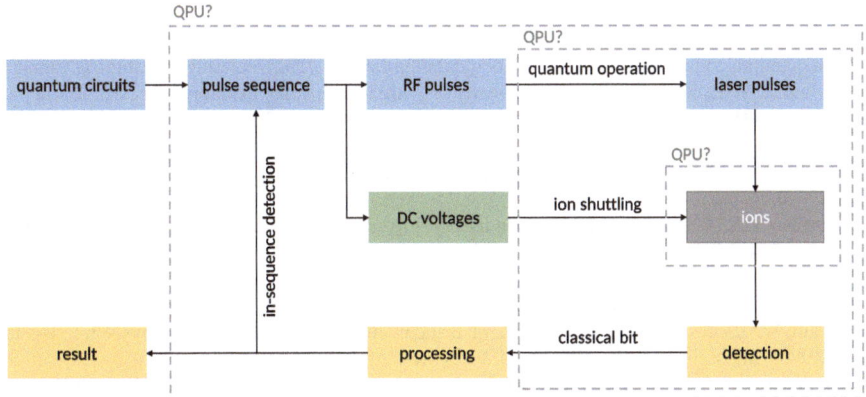

Fig. 20 Schematic diagram of a system-level model with the direction of the flow of information shown by black arrows, the forward direction highlighted by blue and green boxes, and the feedback direction by orange boxes. Note that boxes are representing different types of objects, from abstract software objects, e.g., quantum circuits and pulse sequence, to physical objects, e.g., RF or light pulses, respectively. The dashed boxes indicate that there does not yet exist an agreement between different hardware vendors of where the boundary of a quantum processing unit (QPU) is located

box corresponds to the proposal presented in [62], in which the scope of the QPU covers a quantum control unit ("pulse sequence" and "processing"), a quantum execution unit ("RF pulses," "laser pulses," "DC voltages," and "detection"), as well as the qubit register ("ions"), with labels corresponding to components as shown in Fig. 20. These considerations demonstrate that the integration landscape is still fractured, without clear common standards and definitions, which is understandable for currently early stages of software development in this area.

The explanations above have outlined the similarities and differences between a quantum computer and classical compute infrastructure. The next step is to bring QC systems into an HPC environment to accelerate the classical compute capabilities using quantum algorithms, but also push QC capabilities to a next level by the standardized integration into a non-lab environment.

References

1. Preskill, J.: Quantum Computing in the NISQ era and beyond. Quantum **2**, 79 (2018). https://doi.org/10.22331/q-2018-08-06-79
2. Schulz, M., Ruefenacht, M., Kranzlmüller, D., Schulz, L.B.: Accelerating hpc with quantum computing: It is a software challenge too. Comput. Sci. Eng. **24**, 60–64 (2022). https://doi.org/10.1109/MCSE.2022.3221845
3. Humble, T.S., et al.: Quantum computers for high-performance computing. IEEE Micro. **41**, 15–23 (2021). https://doi.org/10.1109/MM.2021.3099140
4. Nielsen, M.A., Chuang, I.L.: Quantum Computation and Quantum Information. Cambridge University Press, Cambridge (2000)
5. Popkin, G.: Quest for qubits. Science **354**, 1090–1093 (2016). https://www.science.org/doi/abs/10.1126/science.354.6316.1090
6. Bobier, J.-F., Langione, M., Tao, E., Gourévitch, A.: What happens when 'if' turns to 'when' in quantum computing? https://www.bcg.com/publications/2021/building-quantum-advantage
7. Mądzik, M.T., et al.: Precision tomography of a three-qubit donor quantum processor in silicon. Nature **601**, 348–353 (2022). https://doi.org/10.1038/s41586-021-04292-7
8. Wang, C., et al.: Towards practical quantum computers: transmon qubit with a lifetime approaching 0.5 milliseconds. npj Quantum Inf. **8**, 3 (2022). https://doi.org/10.1038/s41534-021-00510-2
9. Brown, L.S., Gabrielse, G.: Geonium theory: Physics of a single electron or ion in a penning trap. Rev. Mod. Phys. **58**, 233–311 (1986). https://link.aps.org/doi/10.1103/RevModPhys.58.233
10. Ghosh, P.K.: Ion Traps. Oxford University Press, Oxford (1995)
11. Paul, W.: Electromagnetic traps for charged and neutral particles. Rev. Mod. Phys. **62**, 531–540 (1990). https://link.aps.org/doi/10.1103/RevModPhys.62.531
12. DiVincenzo, D.P.: The physical implementation of quantum computation. Fortschritte der Physik **48**, 771–783 (2000). https://doi.org/10.1002/1521-3978(200009)48:9/11<771::AID-PROP771>3.0.CO;2-E
13. Postler, L., et al.: Demonstration of fault-tolerant universal quantum gate operations. Nature **605**, 675–680 (2022). https://doi.org/10.1038/s41586-022-04721-1
14. Ryan-Anderson, C., et al.: Realization of real-time fault-tolerant quantum error correction. Phys. Rev. X **11**, 041058 (2021). https://link.aps.org/doi/10.1103/PhysRevX.11.041058

15. Hilder, J., et al.: Fault-tolerant parity readout on a shuttling-based trapped-ion quantum computer. Phys. Rev. X **12**, 011032 (2022). https://link.aps.org/doi/10.1103/PhysRevX.12.011032

16. Shor, P.: Fault-tolerant quantum computation. In: Proceedings of 37th Conference on Foundations of Computer Science, pp. 56–65 (1996). https://doi.org/10.1109/SFCS.1996.548464

17. Preskill, J.: Reliable quantum computers. Proc. Roy. Soc. Lond. A Math. Phys. Eng. Sci. **454**, 385–410 (1998). https://royalsocietypublishing.org/doi/abs/10.1098/rspa.1998.0167

18. Aliferis, P., Gottesman, D., Preskill, J.: Quantum accuracy threshold for concatenated distance-3 codes. arXiv quant–ph/0504218 (2005). https://doi.org/10.48550/arXiv.quant-ph/0504218

19. Terhal, B.M.: Quantum error correction for quantum memories. Rev. Mod. Phys. **87**, 307–346 (2015). https://link.aps.org/doi/10.1103/RevModPhys.87.307

20. cbaldwin1, mlk621, khmayer01, ZackMassa.: Quantinuum hardware quantum volume data (2023). https://github.com/CQCL/quantinuum-hardware-quantum-volume

21. Dehmelt, H.: Experiments with an isolated subatomic particle at rest. Rev. Mod. Phys. **62**, 525–530 (1990). https://link.aps.org/doi/10.1103/RevModPhys.62.525

22. Wineland, D., et al.: Experimental Primer on the Trapped Ion Quantum Computer, chap. 3, pp. 57–84. Wiley (1999). https://onlinelibrary.wiley.com/doi/abs/10.1002/3527603093.ch3

23. Leibfried, D., Blatt, R., Monroe, C., Wineland, D.: Quantum dynamics of single trapped ions. Rev. Mod. Phys. **75**, 281–324 (2003). https://link.aps.org/doi/10.1103/RevModPhys.75.281

24. Steane, A.: The ion trap quantum information processor. Appl. Phys. B **64**, 623–643 (1997). https://doi.org/10.1007/s003400050225

25. Kranzl, F., et al.: Controlling long ion strings for quantum simulation and precision measurements. Phys. Rev. A **105**, 052426 (2022). https://link.aps.org/doi/10.1103/PhysRevA.105.052426

26. Kielpinski, D., Monroe, C., Wineland, D.J.: Architecture for a large-scale ion-trap quantum computer. Nature **417**, 709–711 (2002). https://doi.org/10.1038/nature00784

27. Kaushal, V., et al.: Shuttling-based trapped-ion quantum information processing. AVS Quantum Sci. **2**, 014101 (2020). https://doi.org/10.1116/1.5126186

28. Ragg, S., Decaroli, C., Lutz, T., Home, J.P.: Segmented ion-trap fabrication using high precision stacked wafers. Rev. Sci. Instrum. **90**, 103203 (2019). https://doi.org/10.1063/1.5119785

29. Pino, J.M., et al.: Demonstration of the trapped-ion quantum CCD computer architecture. Nature **592**, 209–213 (2021). https://doi.org/10.1038/s41586-021-03318-4

30. Holz, P.C., et al.: 2D linear trap array for quantum information processing. Adv. Quantum Technol. **3**, 2000031 (2020). https://onlinelibrary.wiley.com/doi/abs/10.1002/qute.202000031

31. Bowler, R., et al.: Coherent diabatic ion transport and separation in a multizone trap array. Phys. Rev. Lett. **109**, 080502 (2012). https://link.aps.org/doi/10.1103/PhysRevLett.109.080502

32. Walther, A., et al.: Controlling fast transport of cold trapped ions. Phys. Rev. Lett. **109**, 080501 (2012). https://link.aps.org/doi/10.1103/PhysRevLett.109.080501

33. © University of Innsbruck.: https://quantumoptics.at/en/research/cryotrap.html

34. Kaufmann, H.: A Scalable Quantum Processor. Ph.D. thesis, University of Mainz (2017)

35. © National Institute of Standards and Technology.: https://www.nist.gov/image/racetrackiontrapjpg

36. © ETH Zürich.: https://tiqi.ethz.ch/research/equal-experiment.html

37. Qiskit.: https://qiskit.org

38. Schindler, P., et al.: A quantum information processor with trapped ions. New J. Phys. **15**, 123012 (2013). https://dx.doi.org/10.1088/1367-2630/15/12/123012

39. Blinov, B.B., Leibfried, D., Monroe, C., Wineland, D.J.: Quantum computing with trapped ion hyperfine qubits. Quantum Inf. Process. **3**, 45–59 (2004). https://doi.org/10.1007/s11128-004-9417-3

40. Cohen-Tannoudji, C., Diu, B., Laloë, F.: Quantum Mechanics; 1st edn. Wiley, New York, NY (1977). https://cds.cern.ch/record/101367. Trans. of : Mécanique quantique. Paris : Hermann, 1973

41. McKay, D., Wood, C.J., Sheldon, S., Chow, J.M., Gambetta, J.M.: Efficient Z gates for quantum computing. Phys. Rev. A **96**, 022330 (2017). https://doi.org/10.1103/PhysRevA.96.022330

42. Sørensen, A., Mølmer, K.: Quantum computation with ions in thermal motion. Phys. Rev. Lett. **82**, 1971–1974 (1999). https://link.aps.org/doi/10.1103/PhysRevLett.82.1971

43. Sørensen, A., Mølmer, K.: Entanglement and quantum computation with ions in thermal motion. Phys. Rev. A **62**, 022311 (2000). https://link.aps.org/doi/10.1103/PhysRevA.62.022311

44. Pogorelov, I., et al.: Compact ion-trap quantum computing demonstrator. PRX Quantum **2**, 020343 (2021). https://link.aps.org/doi/10.1103/PRXQuantum.2.020343

45. Moses, S.A., et al.: A race track trapped-ion quantum processor. arXiv 2305.03828 (2023). https://doi.org/10.48550/arXiv.2305.03828

46. Sanz-Fernandez, C., et al.: Quantum portfolio value forecasting. arXiv 2111.14970 (2021). https://doi.org/10.48550/arXiv.2111.14970

47. Braun, M.C., et al.: Quantum amplitude estimation with error mitigation for time-evolving probabilistic networks. arXiv 2303.16588 (2023). https://doi.org/10.48550/arXiv.2303.16588

48. Foreman, C., Wright, S., Edgington, A., Berta, M., Curchod, F.J.: Practical randomness amplification and privatisation with implementations on quantum computers. Quantum **7**, 969 (2023). https://doi.org/10.22331/q-2023-03-30-969

49. Woerner, S., Egger, D.J.: Quantum risk analysis. npj Quantum Inf. **5**, 15 (2019). https://doi.org/10.1038/s41534-019-0130-6

50. Cerezo, M., et al.: Variational quantum algorithms. Nature Rev. Phys. **3**, 625–644 (2021). https://doi.org/10.1038/s42254-021-00348-9

51. Emerson, J., Alicki, R., Życzkowski, K.: Scalable noise estimation with random unitary operators. J. Opt. B Quantum Semiclassical Opt. **7**, S347 (2005). https://dx.doi.org/10.1088/1464-4266/7/10/021

52. Dankert, C., Cleve, R., Emerson, J., Livine, E.: Exact and approximate unitary 2-designs and their application to fidelity estimation. Phys. Rev. A **80**, 012304 (2009). https://link.aps.org/doi/10.1103/PhysRevA.80.012304

53. Kreuter, A., et al.: Experimental and theoretical study of the $3d\,^2D$–level lifetimes of $^{40}\mathrm{Ca}^+$. Phys. Rev. A **71**, 032504 (2005). https://link.aps.org/doi/10.1103/PhysRevA.71.032504

54. Cross, A.W., Bishop, L.S., Sheldon, S., Nation, P.D., Gambetta, J.M.: Validating quantum computers using randomized model circuits. Phys. Rev. A **100**, 032328 (2019). https://link.aps.org/doi/10.1103/PhysRevA.100.032328

55. Eisert, J. *et al.* Quantum certification and benchmarking. Nature Rev. Phys. **2**, 382–390 (2020). https://doi.org/10.1038/s42254-020-0186-4

56. Baldwin, C.H., Mayer, K., Brown, N.C., Ryan-Anderson, C., Hayes, D.: Re-examining the quantum volume test: Ideal distributions, compiler optimizations, confidence intervals, and scalable resource estimations. Quantum **6**, 707 (2022). https://doi.org/10.22331/q-2022-05-09-707

57. Martiel, S., Ayral, T., Allouche, C.: Benchmarking quantum coprocessors in an application-centric, hardware-agnostic, and scalable way. IEEE Trans. Quantum Eng. **2**, 1–11 (2021). https://doi.org/10.1109/TQE.2021.3090207

58. Lubinski, T., et al.: Application-oriented performance benchmarks for quantum computing. IEEE Trans. Quantum Eng. **4**, 1–32 (2023). https://doi.org/10.1109/TQE.2023.3253761

59. Chen, J.-S., et al.: Benchmarking a trapped-ion quantum computer with 29 algorithmic qubits. arXiv 2308.05071 (2023). https://doi.org/10.48550/arXiv.2308.05071

60. Qiskit.: Qiskit transpiler documentation. https://qiskit.org/documentation/apidoc/transpiler.html

61. Zangerl, M.: Porting and Optimization of RF Pulse Scheduling for Trapped-Ion Quantum Computing. Bachelor's thesis, University of Innsbruck (2023)

62. Britt, K.A., Mohiyaddin, F.A., Humble, T.S.: Quantum accelerators for high-performance computing systems. In: 2017 IEEE International Conference on Rebooting Computing (ICRC), pp. 1–7 (2017). https://doi.org/10.1109/ICRC.2017.8123664
63. McCaskey, A.J., Lyakh, D.I., Dumitrescu, E.F., Powers, S.S., Humble, T.S.: XACC: a system-level software infrastructure for heterogeneous quantum–classical computing. Quantum Sci. Technol. **5**, 024002 (2020). https://dx.doi.org/10.1088/2058-9565/ab6bf6

Quantum Software Engineering and Programming Applied to Personalized Pharmacogenomics

José Luis Hevia, Ezequiel Murina, Aurelio Martínez, and Guido Peterssen

Abstract Providing personalized drug therapy to polymedicated patients is a very complex situation, as not even the most powerful supercomputer in the world could, in a reasonable amount of time, process the enormous number of variables required. Fortunately, quantum computing opens up new possibilities in this field, especially thanks to its ability to efficiently combine a large number of variables. We present the basic idea of an extensible algorithm to deal with genetic polymorphisms, pharmacological polytherapy, and clinical condition, and the implementation of a prototype that allows for the calculation of the ideal dose for each patient considering their genomics and drug interaction. To this end, we have applied best practices of quantum software engineering to the development of quantum/classical software systems.

Keywords QuantumPath · Quantum software engineering · qSOA

1 Introduction

During the last century, a process of transition has been taking place in the health field, so that the prevalence of infectious diseases has been progressively displaced by chronic diseases. This makes the elderly population (over 65) the largest consumer of pharmaceuticals. The prescription of multiple drugs exposes the polymedicated elderly to treatment failures and a higher risk of adverse reactions, since physiological changes related to aging can alter pharmacokinetic and pharmacodynamic properties [1].

The elderly often receive drugs for the treatment of minor symptoms (including adverse effects of other drugs), but the use of these drugs is often inappropriate, since their benefit is low, their cost is high, and the new drug may cause additional

J. L. Hevia (✉) · E. Murina · A. Martínez · G. Peterssen
Quantum Software Technology, Madrid, Spain
e-mail: jluis.hevia@aquantum.es; ezequiel.murina@aquantum.es;
aurelio.martinez@aquantum.es; guido.peterssen@aquantum.es

© The Author(s) 2024
I. Exman et al. (eds.), *Quantum Software*,
https://doi.org/10.1007/978-3-031-64136-7_11

toxicity. In these patients, the risk of adverse effects increases and, consequently, the risk of hospitalization and death. In studies on hospitalized patients, between 12% and 58.5% receive an inappropriate drug [2]. This is not only a health problem but also a problem of great economic importance since the cost of medicines is constantly increasing and is already a serious problem for the national health authorities.

However, providing safe and effective drug therapy to the elderly is a complex situation due to numerous reasons, especially the management of numerous variables. In addition, the amount of information to be considered is of such magnitude (note that some 32,000 pharmaceutical products are allowed on the market) that with current tools, it is unmanageable.

The problem is that currently not even the most powerful supercomputer in the world could, in a reasonable time, process the huge number of variables needed to give an adequate answer. Hence, we consider it necessary to explore quantum computing as a possible solution to this problem through the application of the most appropriate methods, practices, techniques, technologies, and tools of quantum computing to create a reliable quantum/classical system that overcomes the information processing limits existing in the classical IT domain and, in this way, contribute to a sustainable response to the diseases and needs arising from aging.

2 Quantum Health

Today, we can already use quantum computers, which not only allow us to simulate nature much better but also to run algorithms that require massive parallel computations, which are impractical for "classical" computers. In fact, the 2020s is the "quantum decade," in which "quantum computing is poised to expand the scope and complexity of the business problems we can solve" [3], thus offering a true "quantum advantage."

Quantum computing is based on the counterintuitive principles of quantum mechanics, such as superposition and entanglement. There are different types of quantum technologies that have made it possible to build various quantum computers [4, 5]. It is currently possible to distinguish two main quantum computing paradigms: quantum gate-based computing and quantum annealing. Currently, there are already dozens of programming languages [6] and several development environments for building quantum software systems [7]. Although today quantum gate machines still have challenges to overcome to become fully operational, quantum annealing computers are beginning to offer services very close to production, which at least brings quantum experimentation closer to new information systems.

Three key potential quantum computing use cases are central to the healthcare industry's ongoing transformation: diagnostic assistance, insurance premiums and pricing, and precision medicine [3]. There are several applications of quantum computing in medicine and health [8–12].

We have worked for the last 3 years in the QHealth project "Quantum Phar-macogenomics applied to aging" whose goal is to increase the longevity and quality of life of the elderly, thanks to the investigation of the relationships between genetic determining factors and other variables of the health trajectory of the elderly throughout their lives, including the reaction that medications can trigger in this group, in such a manner that the possible adverse effects that a certain medication may have on the health of an elderly person can be predicted based on their history of taking medications, their effects, and their physiological and genetic conditions. The members of the project are the University Institute for Biosanitary Research of Extremadura (INUBE), the University of Castilla-La Mancha (UCLM), the University of Extremadura (UNEX), and the companies aQuantum (Alhambra IT), Gloin, and Madrija. It is the first major research project on quantum computing applied to life sciences to receive funding from the Spanish Center for the Technological and Industrial Development (CDTI), in the call of the Health Mission Program.

To achieve this objective, we designed the scientific, methodological, and technological models necessary for the conception of the scientific and technical foundations of a hybrid classical/quantum system, capable of carrying out opti-mizations and simulations that are impossible to carry out in reasonable execution times in classic computers, which, thanks to the integration with classic health applications, provides the results of the system to the health professionals in charge of prescribing medicines for the elderly.

QuantumPath® [13] was chosen as the general-purpose quantum platform of the project, because of its 100% agnosticism, no limit on the scaling required for the execution of the experiments, support of the two quantum technological approaches (gates and annealing), and its qSOA® architecture, ensuring the viability of real-time integration of quantum services with classic health systems (see Fig. 1). In the QHealth project, quantum annealing computing technology has been the focus, but thanks to the QuantumPath platform, when the time comes, quantum gates can also be exploited, thanks to their general purpose.

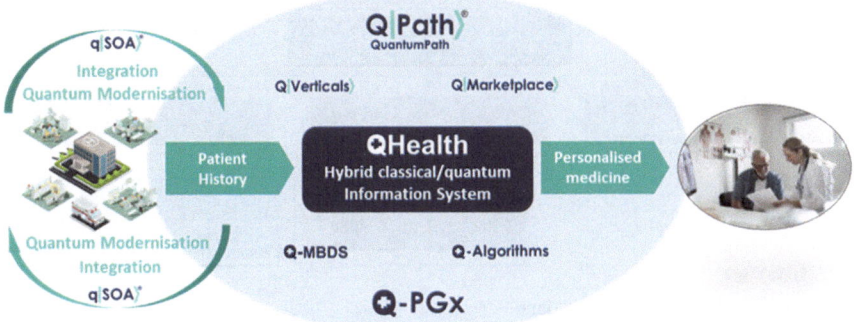

Fig. 1 Overview of the QHealth project

3   Qualitative Description of the Computational Problem

To address this complex situation, the Q-PGx model (from Quantum Pharmacogenomics) (Fig. 2) was proposed by INUBE, led by Dr. Adrian Llerena, Director of
INUBE and President of the Spanish Society of Pharmacogenetics and Pharmacogenomics (SEFF), which will make it possible to determine the factors related
to pharmacogenetic variability and the interindividual difference in drug response,
for which several sets of variables have also been defined: genetic polymorphisms,
pharmacological polytherapy, and clinical conditions.

The joint management of all the variables will allow the generation of prediction
scenarios of interindividual and intraindividual variability according to temporal
variables, something unimaginable without the quantum solutions proposed by the
QHealth project.

The interrelation of all these data of the variables of the Q-PGx model (Fig. 3)
will make it possible to achieve the fundamental objective of the project: *to define
the optimal dosage of each drug for each patient*, at each time it is prescribed, totally
personalized and with high precision.

It is a matter of addressing the interindividual and intraindividual (transtemporal)
variability of each patient, scenarios that are unimaginable and unfathomable in
current pharmacotherapy with classical IT. This will make it possible to create
personalized medicine services that are only feasible with quantum computing.

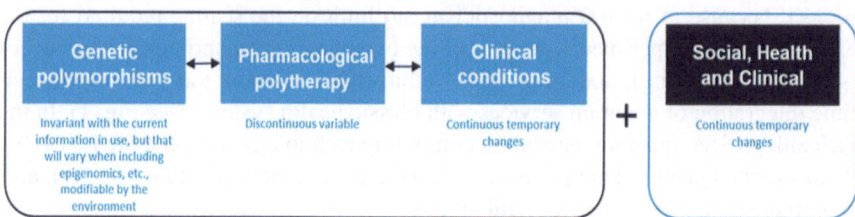

Fig. 2 Q-PGx model: QHealth's variables

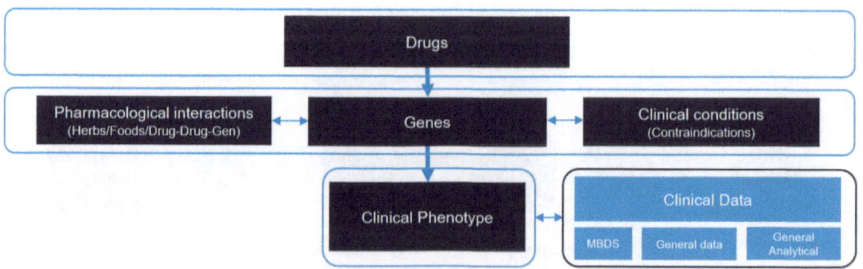

Fig. 3 Q-PGx Model: QHealth's data

Table 1 Metabolizing activity—drug response

Metabolizing activity (phenotype)	Response to drug administration (standard dose)
Null	Poisoning
Diminished	Poisoning
Normal	Expected effect
Increased	Null effect

In a first approximation of the domain of the problem, we will work with a limited set of variables that are closely related to the speed of the drug metabolization process:

- Pharmacogenetics (depending on the individual genetic endowment)
- Drug interactions (depending on the treatment package)

The speed at which the body metabolizes a medication is linked to its effectiveness and the possible side effects that it may entail. The body is expected to eliminate a drug within a certain period. One of the factors influencing the previous response to a drug is genetics, the variability of which determines the individual's metabolizing activity (phenotype), which can be classified into various groups as shown in Table 1.

As can be seen in Table 1, the effect that a drug causes in a patient will be the desired one only if the individual's metabolizing activity is qualified as "normal." This happens for most individuals, who share the most common genotypes, and based on which the standard dose of the drug is established. However, there is a part of the population for which, potentially, the drug in question will not have the desired effect, causing intoxication if the metabolic activity is null or decreased, or an absence of any beneficial effect, in the case of increased metabolic activity. Therefore, knowing the metabolic response of the patient under ideal conditions based on their genotype, although it is obviously not the only factor to consider, will be the starting point of the predictive model that will be carried out.

Within the information search process carried out in the framework of the QHealth project, work has been done on the collection of information on a broad range of drugs and the associated genetic biomarkers, and subsequently, the variables have been defined that allow the variants to be related to the genetics associated with each biomarker and with the different metabolizing responses (phenotype). This process is schematized in Fig. 4.

Fig. 4 Relationship between a drug and the metabolizing capacity of a patient through their genotype

Table 2 Genetic information

Genetic information				
Active principle	Biomarker gene (en)	Haplotype	Variant identification (rsID)	Phenotype associated with genotype
Clopidogrel	CYP2C19	*1	wt	Normal
		*2	rs12769205 rs4244285 rs3758581	Null
		*3	rs4986893 rs3758581	Null
		*4	rs12248560 rs28399504 rs3758581	Null
		*5	rs3758581 rs56337013	Null
		*6	rs72552267 rs3758581	Null
		*7	rs72558186	Null
		*8	rs41291556	Null
		*9	rs17884712 rs3758581	Diminished
		*10	rs6413438 rs3758581	Diminished
		*11	rs58973490 rs3758581	Normal
		*12	rs3758581 rs55640102	Unknown

The result, which has been incorporated into the QHealth knowledge base, is a set of data tables that make it possible to quickly relate the genotype of a patient to the expected metabolic response (phenotype) to a certain drug. An example of this data can be seen in Table 2, where the biomarker CYP2C19, a metabolizer of the drug clopidogrel, is related to the known genetic variants and their associated activity.

One of the challenges in drug prescription is the need to identify and avoid, as far as possible, interactions between drugs. When different drugs are administered to a patient, there is the possibility of adverse reactions because one of the drugs may increase or decrease the effect of another drug. This type of interaction, known as gene–drug–drug interaction, hereinafter DDI (drug–drug interaction), involves the process by which drugs are metabolized in the body.

The metabolization of drugs is carried out by enzymes, and after taking a drug it is expected that it will be eliminated from the body in a certain period. However, what if the drug removal process takes longer than expected? In this case, the drug could accumulate in the body, which could lead to a case of intoxication, or an excess of the pharmacological effect of the drug could be generated. Induction or inhibition of enzymes can affect drugs directly or indirectly through a transcription factor.

If the enzymes responsible for the metabolization of drug A are inhibited or induced by other drugs, then the bioavailability of drug A will be higher or lower than expected, making it toxic or less effective:

- Inhibition implies a slower metabolism of the drug → toxicity.
- Induction implies a faster metabolism of the drug → ineffectiveness.

Apart from metabolism-based interactions, drug–drug interactions can also occur due to induction or inhibition of transporters. Transporters are primarily responsible for the cellular uptake or efflux of drugs. Transporters play an important role in drug clearance since drugs can only be metabolized after they are transported to liver cells. However, transporter-based drug interactions have not been as well studied as metabolism-based interactions.

4   Analytical Description of the Computational Problem

The general computational problem must consider the variability in dosages over time (Fig. 5). There will be a continuous type of variability, such as renal or hepatic function, as well as discrete, discontinuous, or pulsed variability, such as the pharmacological prescription. An example of the latter, that is, of drug administration within the framework of a medical treatment, is the following:

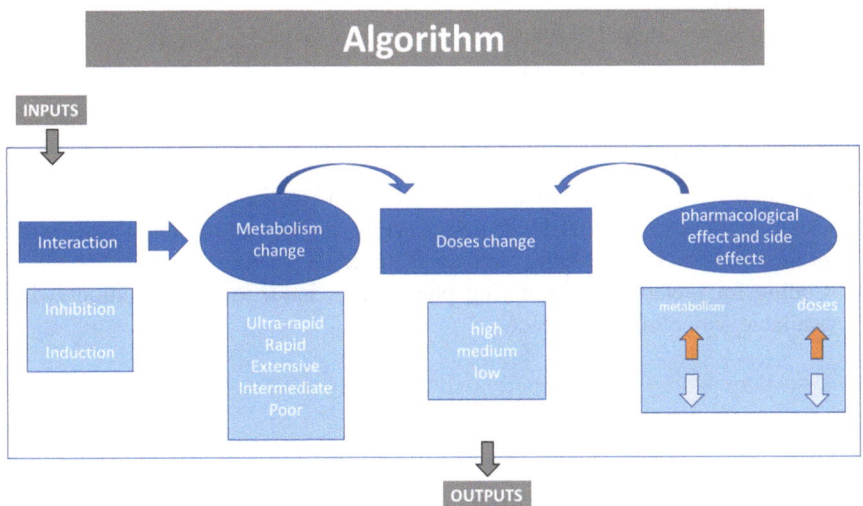

Fig. 5 QHealth's pharmacogenomic problem

The recommended total daily dose of **topiramate** for migraine prophylaxis in adults is **100 mg/day, divided into two doses.** Dose adjustment should start with 25 mg daily, administered in the evening, for 1 week. Subsequently, the dose will be increased, at 1-week intervals, by 25 mg/day. If the patient cannot tolerate the titration regimen, the dose escalation intervals may be extended.

In more analytical terms, what is desired is to study the correlations between genetic and clinical variables, drug interactions, and temporal variability. The latter increases the dimensionality of the problem at a magnitude that justifies the use of quantum technologies for its approach.

One of the main objectives of the algorithm will be predictability in terms of the selection of the drug to be administered and the administration schedule. The modification of the regimen (dose of a drug and administration over time) is considered, as well as the selection and modification of the number of drugs administered. Regarding the initial prediction framework, it would be determined by the following:

- All drugs are administered for the first time.
- For the most diseases, there are pre existing drugs, and the question is to add or remove.

The interest of staying on a clinical description plane is emphasized, that is, one wants to study whether a given drug should be chosen or not (dose and co-medication) and what will happen to the patient. However, when interactions are considered, the evidence corresponds to a biochemical level (laboratory or animal model). Work will then be done on the development of a "coarse-grained" model that incorporates interactions with clinical and regulatory evidence. To stay on the clinical plane, the mathematical model will include the following points:

- Genes: present/absent in degrees for enzymes
- Clinical factor: altered, yes/no
- Interaction: exists/nonexistent

Regarding the correlations, initially those of type will be considered:

- Gene-mediated drug–drug
- Quantitative, which block by quantity and depend on the dose
- Qualitative ones that block by degree of activity in the enzyme and whose source of information comes from experimental studies
- Coding for metabolism-modifying phenomena: induction or inhibition (when available with clinical evidence)

5   QHealth Information System

This section provides an overview of the QHealth information system, starting with its functionality, describing its technical features, and ending with the details of its implementation.

5.1   Functional Overview

Software systems developed for healthcare, given their intended use, need to be high quality, extensible, scalable, high performance, and highly secure. Therefore, building reliable software systems for healthcare requires the application of software engineering best practices and the team's experience in the development of critical software solutions. Carrying out projects of this type, incorporating quantum computing, has the added complexity that quantum software engineering is just taking its first steps and that the experience accumulated in the design, development, and implementation of this type of project is accumulating its first cases.

Therefore, conceiving, designing, and testing the feasibility of the QHealth information system has involved the challenge of researching and defining the best options for the development of a hybrid quantum/classical health software system capable of integrating efficiently with existing classical health systems. In addition, it has been necessary to ensure the delivery of quality, professionally tested quantum software solutions; to devise a security model specifically designed for quantum projects as well as to define a management framework for quantum computing services; and to design a valid model for the governance and management of quantum architectures and quantum platforms.

The technical validity of the research results of the QHealth project is directly related to the demonstration, through a wide variety of proof of concepts (PoCs), of the feasibility of applying quantum software engineering and programming research results to hybrid quantum/classical software systems that can be used by healthcare specialists as just another tool in their work environment. The work for the demonstration of this technical feasibility has represented challenges of high complexity but, thanks to the research and technologies selected for the PoCs of the project, we can show the basis of a hybrid quantum/classical system for health specialists to work with personalized pharmacogenomics solutions.

Each query that can be made to the system will be based on several contexts determined by the interaction with the specialist. In this interaction, the specialist will determine what data is to be collected for what type of query. From a base Hamiltonian expression, each context will introduce new elements to the expression in the form of constraints. The data collected from the medical system (via the QHealth dashboard, Fig. 6) will then compose a graph structure established in the project design, which will allow for correlation of patient information according to the context.

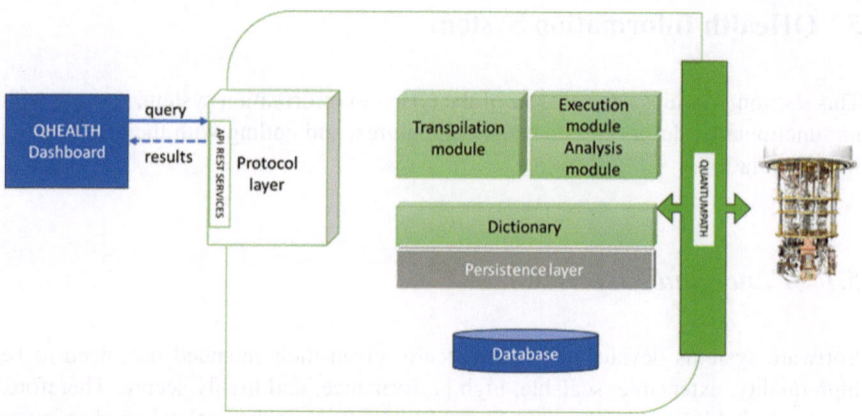

Fig. 6 System overview

Implementing this information as input to the system, and post-processing the request through the dictionary elements of the system, the assets—agnostics, in intermediate language—necessary to be able to execute the request to the quantum machine(s) managed in the system will be generated. At this point, the QuantumPath® platform makes this execution possible, as well as collecting the response that will be encoded according to the problem. The system will therefore decode the answer and provide, according to the context of the query, an answer with the required information in the form of a suggestion to the specialist, so that he/she can continue with his/her work.

As a proof of concept of the integration of the quantum software with the classical one in the QHealth software system, it has been possible to generate Windows applications based on Microsoft .NET technology that have exploited annealing circuits to validate client layer designs. Thanks to QuantumPath's qSOA® technology, fully transparent connectivity to the QHealth system use cases was possible, so that they can be exploited from a classic client application (Fig. 7).

5.2 *Technical Features*

In the design of the technical solution, all the key elements of an information system based on n-layers have been taken into account, having as requirements by design all the key elements of a mature system that also incorporates a new disruptive quantum technology that will evolve very fast in the coming years. These key elements include:

- Scalability of services. By design, automation services are structured to exploit queues. By means of centralized queues receiving actions, services compete to provide the best performance and optimization of actions. The system supports

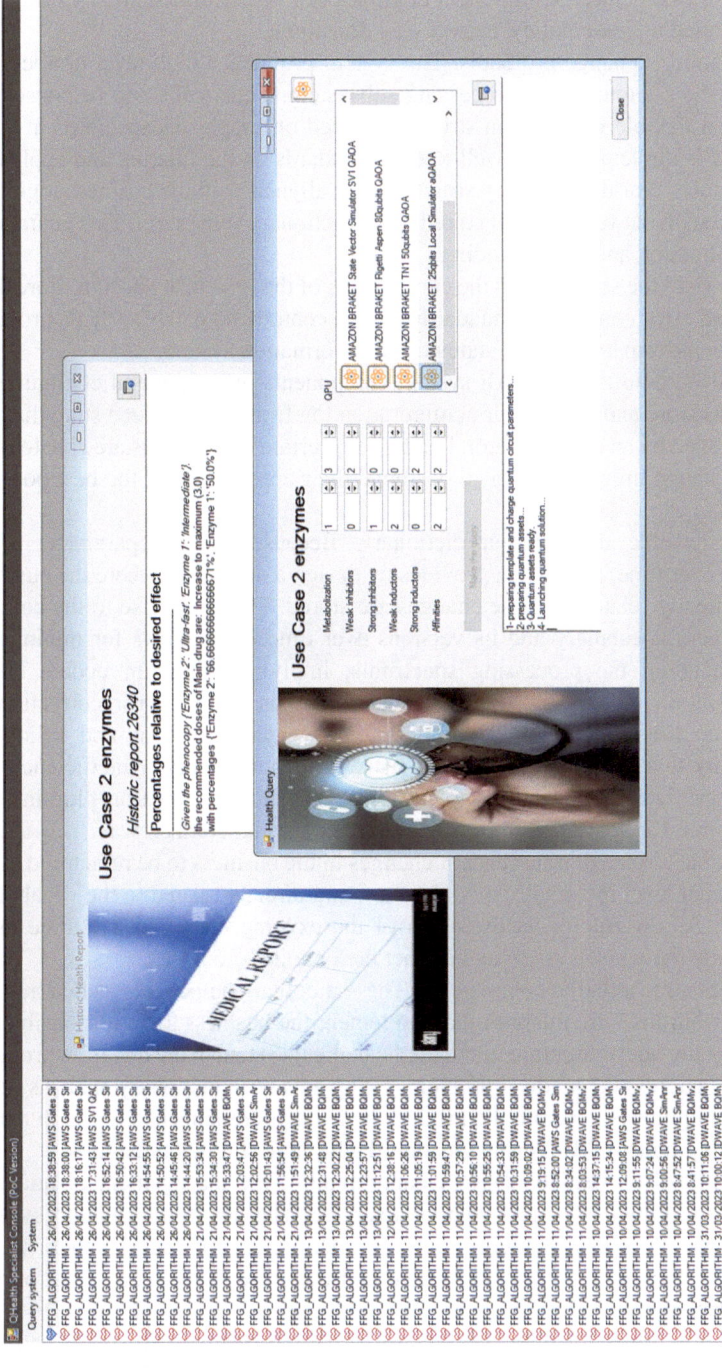

Fig. 7 QHealth application

prioritization, categorization, failover protection, and dynamic scalability in elastic infrastructures. Component upgrades can be performed hot, by designing a controlled upgrade policy, minimizing downtime.

- Information exchange protocols. The system provides a high-level protocol for calling the computational processing subsystem. Thus, calls and responses are based on flexible information structures based on graphs encapsulated in high-level APIs implemented on well-known standards on the Internet and applied to the business world. The query structures are aligned with the business logic and mapped with the vocabularies stored in the dictionary subsystem. This guarantees their validation and understanding.
- Telemetry of the services. All the components of the system, by design, store their trace and error control in a standardized and centralized database. This provides real-time information on the status of the information system.
- Centralized configuration. All system components in the general configuration elements store and query their configuration log from a centralized store that can be managed by an administrator. In addition, certain components are able to react to the change immediately or to postpone their applications at the best possible time.
- Time-extensible transpilation dictionary. Because medical parameters may change over time, the system provides by design a dictionary where the business rules directly related to these changes are stored. This gives rise to the concept of business vocabulary and its versions over time. This allows for minimizing and extending the processing spectrums, implying minimum update times, incorporation of specializations depending on the client, error correction in minimum times, etc. and, very importantly, a query analysis and validation capability that is able to assist the query and identify errors or inefficiencies in the query. This dictionary is directly related to the transpilation plug-ins and responsible for applying the business logic in a parameterized way. This allows new business rules or transcendent changes in the business to be refactored at the component level in a totally modular way, and directly related to the vocabulary version. A new rule or an extension of the existing ones will not force us to recompile the whole system and impact the ongoing processes.
- Extensible transpilation components. These modular components, called transpilation "plug-ins," are the ones that implement the business logic responsible for adapting the query structure of the medical client system to the quantum products that will address the medical problem. Using advanced dictionary analysis rules, these components generate the product logics that are launched to the quantum processing units (QPUs) using QuantumPath® agnostic functionalities.
- Scalability of QPUs. Thanks to QuantumPath®, the management of quantum technology providers is provided as a service. The health information system, by design, takes into account all these functionalities by adding them to the telemetry and configuration subsystem and therefore to the administration and management system.
- Information protection. Given the nature of the information to be processed, it is necessary to contemplate—by design—the protection of data and its life cycle in

the system. Encryption procedures in transit, storage, and anonymization of the source medical data are elements defined by design in the conception of all the modules that will make up the vertical information system.

- Governance. IT governance is an element of corporate governance, aimed at improving the overall management of IT and deriving improved value from investment in information and technology. IT governance frameworks enable organizations to manage their IT risks effectively and ensure that the activities associated with information and technology are aligned with their overall business objectives, in this case, a Health IT system—which will have an extra level of protection of sensitive data. IT governance enables an organization to:

  - Demonstrate measurable results against broader business strategies and goals
  - Meet relevant legal and regulatory obligations, such as those set out in the GDPR (General Data Protection Regulation)
  - Assure stakeholders they can have confidence in your organization's IT services
  - Facilitate an increase in the return on IT investment
  - Comply with certain corporate governance or public listing rules or requirements

Thanks to this "backend" system design, the "client" medical information system responsible for the treatment of each patient's medical data will have as a viable method a high-level query channel to process elements not available with classical computers for the specialist. Thanks to the system's vocabularies, a specialist will be able to generate a type of query with medical information elements related to the areas of knowledge discussed in the previous points. This query will flow through the business channels provided by the quantum information system and will return an answer in acceptable (minute) times. The system also offers the possibility to set up simulations based on additional variables and parameters that could not be handled with the limitations of the "classical" systems.

5.3   Implementation Details

As discussed in the functional overview in Sect. 5.1, the QHealth information system has involved the challenge of investigating and defining the best options for the development of a hybrid quantum/classical health software system capable of integrating efficiently with existing classical health systems.

It should be noted that quantum computing technologies establish a new paradigm in the overall architecture of an information system, and it is necessary to establish as a premise that this new technology must be added to a "traditional" information system as a new type of modular component to be interconnected in some way. This already means that in our way of thinking we are introducing the terms "classical systems," "quantum systems," and "hybrid systems."

As in the design of a classic information system, the new hybrid information system will be adapted to the design rules of an architecture based on layers—and their best practices—distributed and modular. One of these layers will be formed by the new services supported by quantum computing. As with classical systems, these layers will be coupled to the overall system following patterns of loosely coupled elements, and therefore it will be necessary to define interconnection, adaptation, and execution elements, as well as telemetry for the control of each and every one of the integrated components.

5.3.1 Interconnection Layer and Information Protocol

In order that in our solution the classic system used by the health specialist can access the services capable of accessing the algorithm that uses the quantum advantage, it is necessary to provide an interconnection layer under a distributed call model that will consist of an interface based on REST API services (Fig. 8) standardized on the Internet and highly flexible information structures, parameterizable and extensible in time and context. These information structures will be the tree and the network where its computer representation will be based on the JSON standard, both for the input and the response.

Since the information system starts from a query, the query will act as input and will be composed of the syntactic elements necessary to be able to provide the need, the known input data, and the elements that need to be calculated, as well as a structure of response to the query. For this purpose, the structure will have a format:

- **Queries**. An object that groups one or several query type objects.
  A query object is a network that represents the data associated with an analysis query and will have the properties that will make it possible to identify the medical objects that are provided as input rules.

  - *Edges* → Array of edge type objects, each of which represents an edge of the network. These elements will allow for establishing the relationship rules between the different nodes and the values that affect this relationship.
  - *Questions* → Array of objects of type question, each of which represents a question to be solved by the algorithm. These questions will be information needs established by the medical specialist and that the system will take with the elements to be ascertained through the quantum advantage algorithm.

From the query, the QHealth vertical will activate the processing and translation modules to generate the classic-quantum products needed to compose the required response. This required response will also have its established format:

- **queries_response**. Object array of query response's type.
  A query response object represents the answers to the questions of a given query and will consist of the metadata necessary to provide the required data. Since there can be multiple query terms—batch query mode—there can be multiple

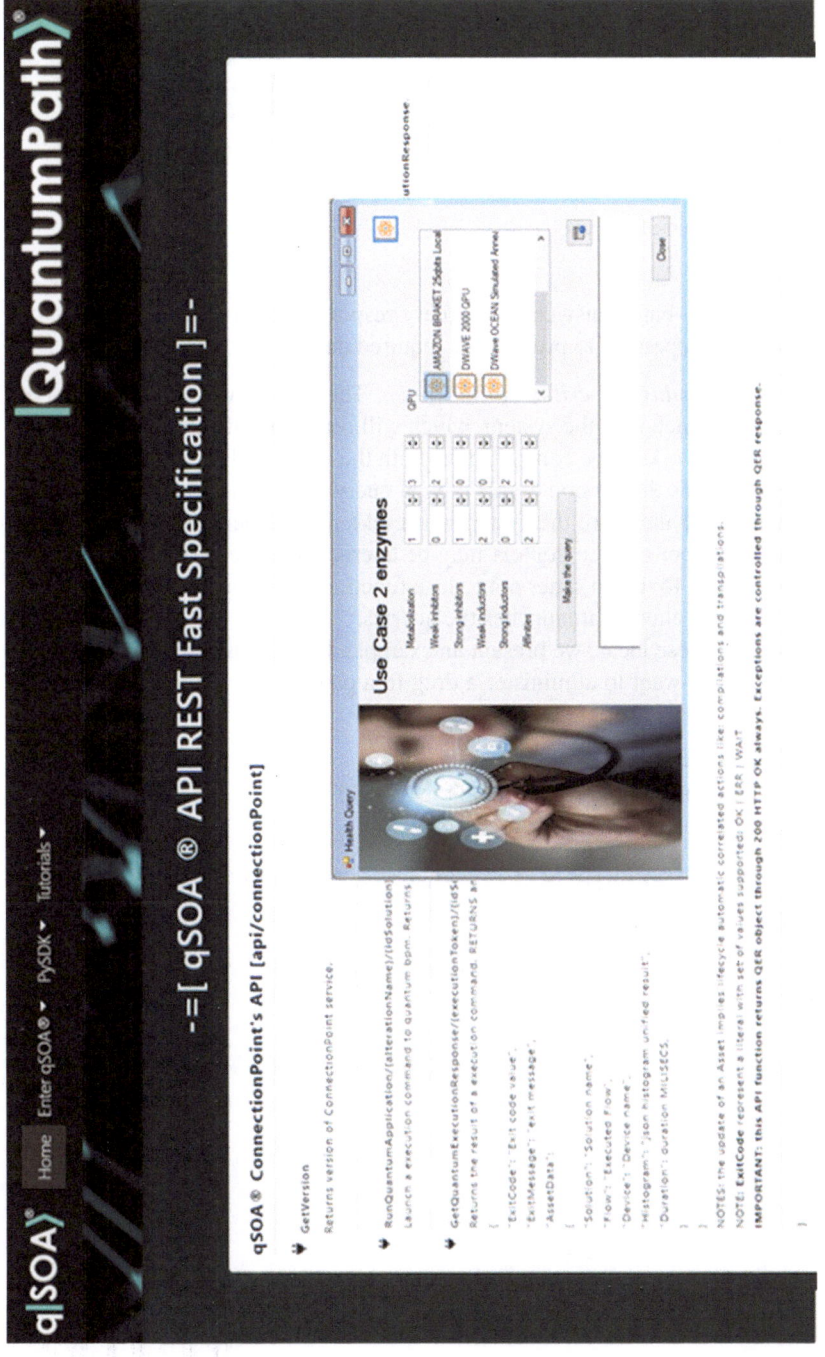

Fig. 8 Distributed layers using protocols and communication for quantum solutions isolation

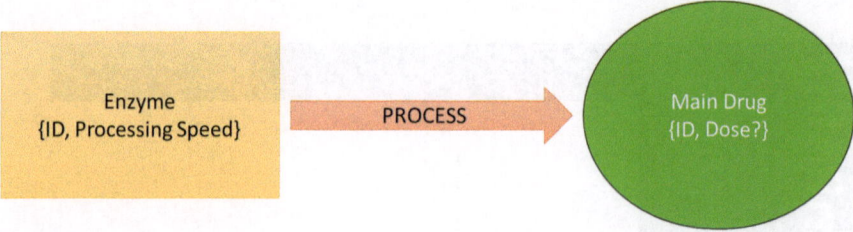

Fig. 9 Example of a medical query

answer terms—batch answers. The query response object will be composed of the metadata necessary to provide the required data.

Context and timing are critical at this point. The context will establish the type of query to be launched to the system, which will determine the number of nodes of the trees and networks to be composed for both the query and the response, and the time will determine the version of this type of query. Over time a given context may be refactored, and therefore the system must take into account that the definitions and requirements of a given context may be altered. And the system must be able to react and adapt to this in order not to lose functionality at any time depending on the version of the client that launches the queries.

To illustrate these ideas, we present an example, from a basic context (Fig. 9).

Question: We want to administer a drug to a patient, and we need to know the optimal dose for this patient.

Entry data:

- Drug to be administered to the patient: N05AX07
- Enzyme that metabolizes the drug: CYP2A6

    – Enzyme processing speed as a function of genotype: slow (0)

Output data:

- Most appropriate dose of the drug to be administered

Query JSON:
```
{
  "graphs": [
    {
      "id": "newQuery",
      "nodes": [
        {
          "id": "enzyme1",
          "type": "Processor",
          "label": "a processor",
```

(continued)

```
            "metadata": {
                       "P": 1
                 }
        },
        {
           "id": "drug1",
           "type": "Signal",
           "label": "a drug",
           "metadata": {
                    "Value": "undefined"
           }
        },
      ],
      "edges": [
            {
           "id": "edge1",
           "type": "Process",
           "source": "enzyme1",
           "target": "drug1"
        }
      ],
   "questions": [
            {
           "id": "question1",
           "type": "0",
           "node_id": "drug1"
        }
    ]
}
```

Response JSON:

```
{
   "queries_response": [
     {
        "id": "newQuery",
        "questions": [
           {
             "id": "question1",
             "response":  "1
           }
        ]
      }
   ]
}
```

5.3.2 Execution Layer: Transpilation, Execution, and Post-processing

This layer is responsible for processing the query, preparing an execution engine that will be responsible for "understanding" what is desired, and performing all the necessary steps and processes to provide an answer. Among these steps, the most critical is the one that generates the necessary elements to take the quantum advantage of the pharmacogenomics algorithm that responds to the contexts studied with the specialists. The execution module will rely on the transpilation, dictionary, and telemetry subsystems to prepare the products to be executed on a quantum computer and post-process their response to return to the classical system the data it needs. For this purpose:

- The transpilation module (Fig. 10) will be responsible for analyzing and validating the query received, in such a way that it can identify the context and generate a mathematical product that is compatible with the quantum computing principle selected as a technological alternative: quantum computing by annealing.
- By using a platform-agnostic product, such as the one provided by QuantumPath®—the first viable technological alternative selected for this information system—this process is simplified since high-level metalanguages are used that are perfectly adapted to the definition of the mathematical product mentioned above, providing multiple advantages to the system under investigation: adaptation to the technology, minimization of risks in time, and optimal selection of the required quantum technology, among others.
- The dictionary module (Fig. 11) is responsible for providing the necessary tools to the transpilation module to generate the necessary quantum products to enable the launch of a quantum circuit compatible with the selected technology. QuantumPath® generates the metalanguage elements necessary to compose a platform-agnostic quantum circuit. The dictionary module is critical to the system, since it makes it possible to define the contexts, the terms that are associated with rules, and the rules that make it possible to associate the input metadata with the variables of the quantum circuit to be generated. This module is parameterized in database and plug-ins under extensible design.

The dictionary module contains different types of instances of "vocabularies" adapted to the context. Let's say, for example, that you want to validate an input query based on the simplest context (context 1). The grammar that can validate the rules of the query can be defined with a regular expression rule:

{"name": "Context1", "def": "id-ty-so-ta-MePr-"}
{{"name": "Context2", "def": "–a regular expression–",{ . . . more rules . . . }}

If a query like the one proposed in Code 1 arrives, the regular expression will validate the validity of the sentence, while identifying the context and making it possible to load the dictionary objects associated with context 1, to generate the mathematical expressions, and by extension, from these, the quantum product would be generated (Fig. 12).

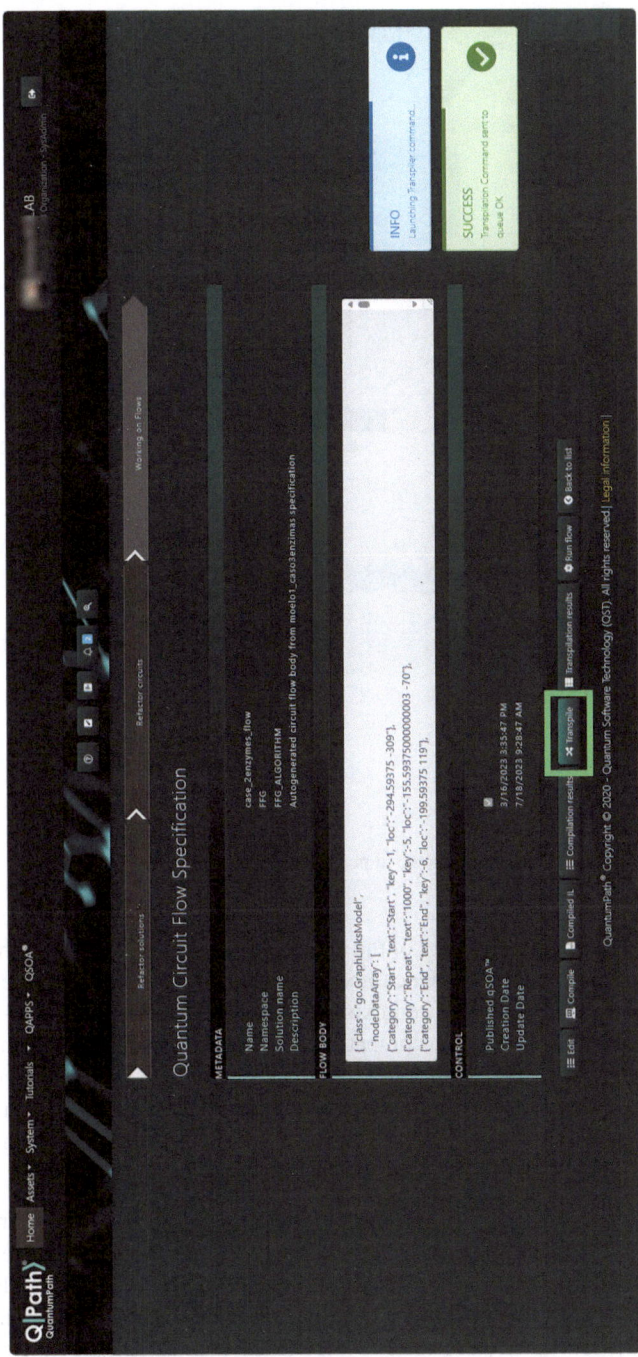

Fig. 10 Transpilation features of the QuantumPath®

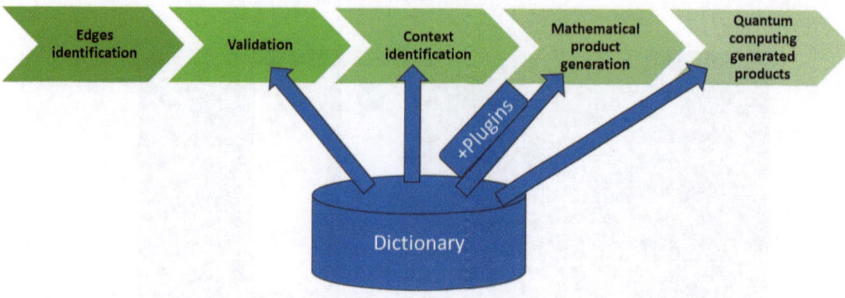

Fig. 11 Dictionary module role

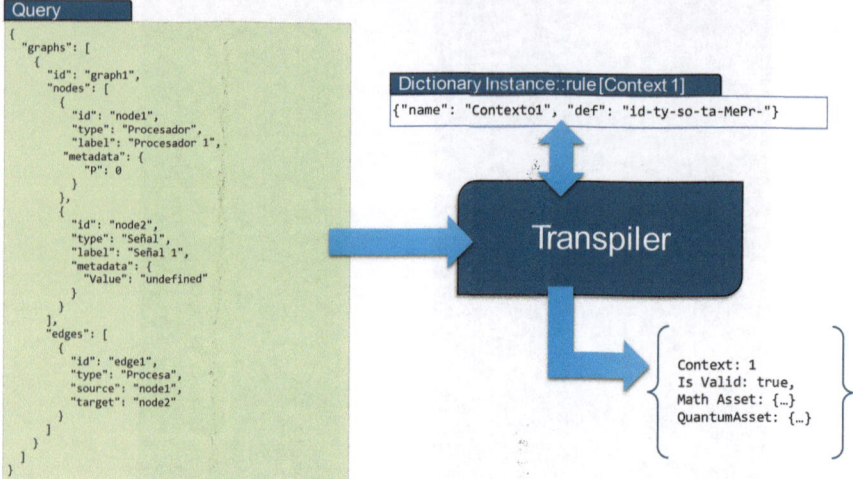

Fig. 12 Transpiler plus dictionary instance to process the query

Thanks to this dynamic capacity of the system, it is possible to make it grow over time with new contexts as experience and knowledge in the health area expands, as well as to refactor existing contexts—in response to improvements and/or corrections—maintaining context compatibility with the systems that demand the use case in a specific context. This is done in such a way that the platform's evolutions do not interrupt its execution at any time due to these dynamic and adaptable elements of the information system. This is a 24×7 execution with loosely coupled systems that adapt to change and favor continuous deployment.

- The execution module. It is the module directly responsible for the interconnection with the quantum computers established by configuration in the system governance. Starting with the products generated by the transpiler, calls to the quantum computing system are generated, and the processed responses are collected and formatted according to the standard established in the protocol (Fig. 13). Thanks to agnostic products such as the one selected in the QHealth project, the quantum system can be modified in a flexible and tool-guided way.

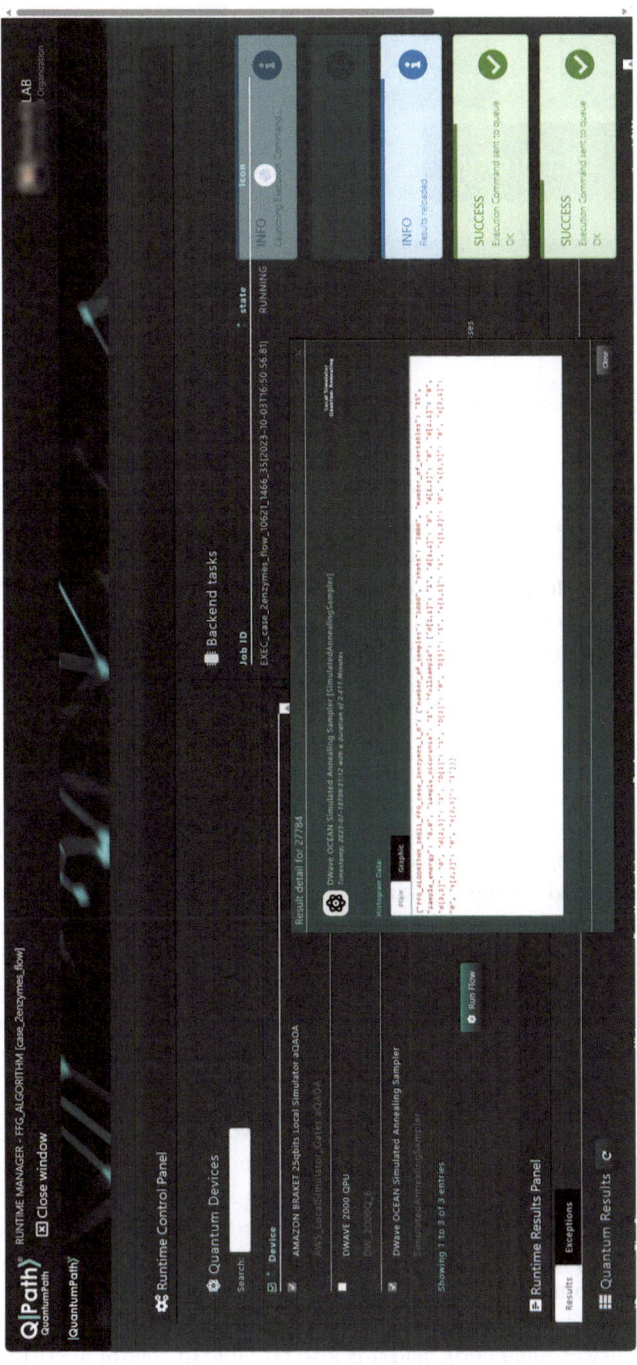

Fig. 13 Running an agnostic quantum use case

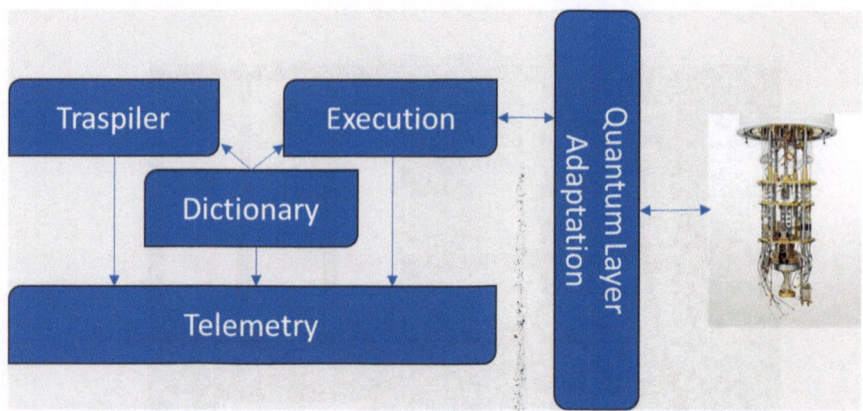

Fig. 14 Dependencies between modules

Likewise, the quantum computer technology can be adapted to the best conditions of a manufacturer and the one that offers the best fidelity for the type of call made. Moreover, other aspects associated with the quantum devices provided by a given vendor should be considered, as for example, cost controlling, reliability, availability, queue contention, etc. In the case of not working with an agnostic product such as QuantumPath®, the dictionary could always be adapted to a particular specialized hardware to generate the quantum products from the mathematical expression, which would negatively affect the adaptation of the system to future changes in these technologies. Figure 14 shows the dependencies between the different modules.

- The telemetry module, as a transversal module, provides a store of trace, control, and timing records of each and every one of the events generated in the aforementioned modules, in such a way that, from all its stored information, business data can be extracted to feed the different governance tools mentioned above. For the purposes of the project, the telemetry log provides a calling standard in the form of an API, and each of the executable elements of the previous modules is coded with an event code and a trace type, in such a way that everything is categorized and prepared to generate data extraction processes to feed the system's analysis systems.

Finally, after the whole process, the response would be returned to the classic client system for further post-processing and treatment until it reaches the specialist.

Thanks to all the telemetry collected (Fig. 15) and the high parameterization of the system, the governance module will enable the management, control, and monitoring of the processes carried out in the system. For example, if we focus on managing quantum resources, it provides a high value in the governance of the system in the access to complete statistics of use of quantum devices by supplier, fidelity in the answers, and costs, and it is also possible to control the risk in case a

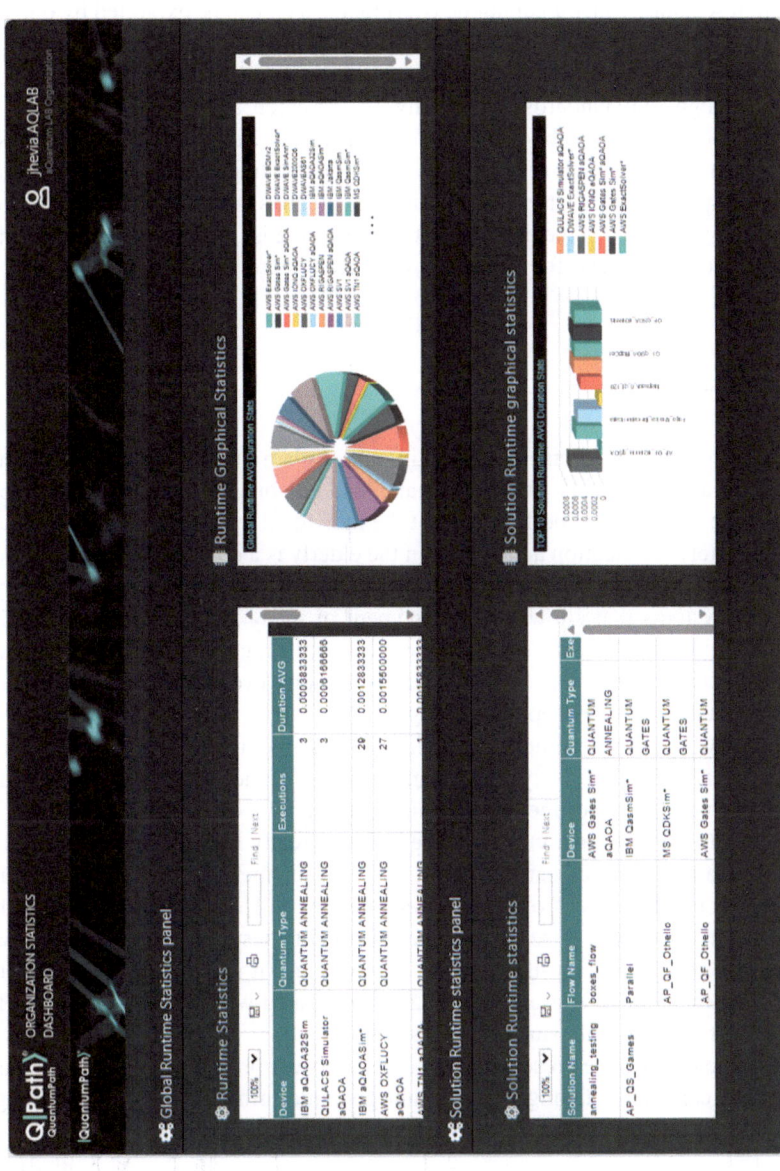

Fig. 15 Analytical information for decision-making

supplier stops being online and it is necessary to look for a technological alternative, and all directly on the environment already in production and with very low reaction times.

In the general architecture of the system, the service-oriented role of these layers and its high scalability factor cannot be overlooked, as it can be exploited by one or many classic clients identified by an information system that does not necessarily have to be part of this project but can integrate with this technology by means of highly recognized standards. Potentially, the research and development of the QHealth project can itself be a service platform that will serve health centers, hospitals, or any other health-related entity that is able to transmit the query data and collect the response to offer it in its functionalities, thanks to the quantum advantage in times that will make viable the analysis of the specialist almost in real time both for a specific operation and for a batch set of operations.

6 Conclusion

The goal of precision medicine is to identify and explain the relationships between interventions and treatments, on the one hand, and outcomes, on the other, in order to provide the best medical performance at the individual level.

Unfortunately, medication adjustment in the elderly is a complex and unresolved challenge and is currently carried out by trial and error. Therefore, the availability of software systems that allow the management of many variables could make it possible to optimize the choice of the most optimal drug combination, the most suitable prescribing regimen, and modeling situations over time, thus making it possible to establish the appropriate strategy.

Fortunately, quantum computing makes it possible to deal with enormous numbers of variables and analyze them in a timely manner to help the physician give the appropriate dose of medicine to his patients.

However, to achieve quantum software that can really be used in health information systems, it is necessary to build it in an engineering way and without forgetting the good practices of software engineering [14]. In fact, in the QHealth project, we have had to propose tools for design, quality, testing, estimation, process management, etc. to develop the project. Furthermore, it should not be forgotten that the quantification software must be easily integrated with existing classical IT systems, where most of the patient data resides.

In this chapter, we have presented a quantum software prototype that implements an algorithm capable of taking into account genomic information and drug–drug interactions.

Acknowledgments This work is part of the QHealth: Quantum Pharmacogenomics Applied to Aging (2020 CDTI Missions Program) project funded by the Spanish Ministry of Science and Innovation and European Regional Development Fund (ERDF). We would like to thank all the members of the project for their help and collaboration.

References

1. Merle, L., Laroche, M.L., Dantoine, T., Charmes, J.P.: Predicting and preventing adverse drug reactions in the very old. Drugs Aging. **22**, 375–392 (2005). https://doi.org/10.2165/00002512-200522050-00003
2. Fahrni, M.L., Azmy, M.T., Usir, E., Aziz, N.A., Hassan, Y.: Inappropriate prescribing defined by STOPP and START criteria and its association with adverse drug events among hospitalized older patients: a multicentre, prospective study. PLoS One. **14**, 1–20 (2019). https://doi.org/10.1371/journal.pone.0219898
3. IBM: The Quantum Decade. A Playbook for Achieving Awareness, Readiness, and Advantage. IBM Institute for Business Value (2023) https://www.ibm.com/thought-leadership/institute-business-value/report/quantum-decade
4. Ezratty, O.: Understanding Quantum Technologies, 5th edn. https://www.oezratty.net/wordpress/2022/understanding-quantum-technologies-2022/ (2023)
5. Piattini, M., Serrano, M.A., Pérez-Castillo, R., Peterssen, G., Hevia, J.L.: Toward a quantum software engineering. IT Prof. **23**(1), 62–66 (2021)
6. Serrano, M.A., Cruz-Lemus, J.A., Pérez-Castillo, R., y Piattini, M.: Quantum software components and platforms: overview and quality assessment. ACM Comput Surv. **55**(8), 164:1–164:31 (2023)
7. Hevia, J.L., Peterssen, G., Ebert, C., Piattini, M.: Quantum computing. IEEE Softw. **38**(5), 7–15 (2021)
8. Cordier, B.A., Sawaya, N.P.D., Guerreschi, G.G., McWeeney, S.K.: Biology and Medicine in the Landscape of Quantum Advantages. https://arxiv.org/pdf/2112.00760.pdf
9. Exploring Quantum Computing Use Cases for Life Sciences. Decoding Secrets of Genomes, Drugs, and Proteins. IBM Institute for Business Value. https://www.ibm.com/downloads/cas/EVBKAZGJ
10. Silva, G.S.M., Droguett, E.L.: Quantum Machine Learning for Health State Diagnosis and Prognostics. https://arxiv.org/ftp/arxiv/papers/2108/2108.12265.pdf
11. The Disruptive Power of Quantum Computing in Precision Medicine. https://coruzant.com/op-ed-p/quantum-solace/the-disruptive-power-of-quantum-computing-in-precision-medicine/
12. Rasool, R.U. et al. (2022). Quantum Computing for Healthcare: A Review.. https://www.techrxiv.org/articles/preprint/Quantum_Computing_for_Healthcare_A_Review/17198702/1
13. Hevia, J.L., Peterssen, G., Piattini, M.: QuantumPath: a quantum software development platform. Softw Pract Experience. **52**(6), 1517–1530 (2022)
14. M. Piattini, G. Peterssen, R. Pérez-Castillo, J. L. Hevia et al. 2020. The Talavera Manifesto for Quantum Software Engineering and Programming.. http://ceur-ws.org/Vol-2561/paper0.pdf.

References

Text illegible.

Challenges for Quantum Software Engineering: An Industrial Application Scenario Perspective

Cecilia Carbonelli, Michael Felderer, Matthias Jung, Elisabeth Lobe, Malte Lochau, Sebastian Luber, Wolfgang Mauerer, Rudolf Ramler, Ina Schaefer, and Christoph Schroth

Abstract Quantum software is becoming a key enabler for applying quantum computing to industrial use cases. This poses challenges to quantum software

C. Carbonelli · S. Luber
Infineon Technologies AG, Neubiberg, Germany
e-mail: cecilia.carbonelli@infineon.com; sebastian.luber@infineon.com

M. Felderer
Institute of Software Technology, German Aerospace Center (DLR), Cologne, Germany

University of Innsbruck, Innsbruck, Austria

University of Cologne, Cologne, Germany
e-mail: michael.felderer@dlr.de

M. Jung
University of Würzburg, Würzburg, Germany
e-mail: m.jung@uni-wuerzburg.de

E. Lobe
Institute of Software Technology, German Aerospace Center (DLR), Brunswick, Germany
e-mail: elisabeth.lobe@dlr.de

M. Lochau (✉)
University of Siegen, Siegen, Germany
e-mail: malte.lochau@uni-siegen.de

W. Mauerer
Technical University of Applied Sciences/Siemens AG, Regensburg, Germany
e-mail: wolfgang.mauerer@othr.de

R. Ramler
Software Competence Center Hagenberg, Hagenberg, Austria
e-mail: rudolf.ramler@scch.at

I. Schaefer
Karlsruhe Institute of Technology, Karlsruhe, Germany
e-mail: ina.schaefer@kit.edu

C. Schroth
Fraunhofer IESE, Kaiserslautern, Germany
e-mail: christof.schroth@iese.fraunhofer.de

© The Author(s) 2024
I. Exman et al. (eds.), *Quantum Software*,
https://doi.org/10.1007/978-3-031-64136-7_12

311

engineering in providing efficient and effective means to develop such software. Eventually, this must be reliably achieved in time, on budget, and in quality, using sound and well-principled engineering approaches. Given that quantum computers are based on fundamentally different principles than classical machines, this raises the question if, how, and to what extent established techniques for systematically engineering software need to be adapted. In this chapter, we analyze three paradigmatic application scenarios for quantum software engineering from an industrial perspective. The respective use cases center around (1) optimization and quantum cloud services, (2) quantum simulation, and (3) embedded quantum computing. Our aim is to provide a concise overview of the current and future applications of quantum computing in diverse industrial settings. We derive presumed challenges for quantum software engineering and thus provide research directions for this emerging field.

Keywords Quantum computing · Software engineering · Quantum software engineering · Industrial use cases · Software development

1 Introduction

Quantum computers (QCs) are a reality today, but quantum software development is in its very infancy. Although many small-/medium-sized quantum programs have been written over the years to demonstrate the potentials of quantum computing, barely any of these examples can be seriously called *quantum software*. In other words, there is no such thing as quantum software to date [28].

In this regard, *software engineering* (SE) is concerned with supporting and improving the development, application, and maintenance of software-intensive systems [92]. SE employs scientific methods, business principles, structured process models, and predefined quality goals to cope with the complexity of software as a whole. Current mainstream SE research for classical (i.e., non-quantum) software comprises design principles (e.g., high-level modeling languages fostering abstraction and modularity), development practices (e.g., tasks, roles, and responsibilities), and tool support (e.g., Integrated Development Environment (IDEs), code generation, static analysis, version control, issue tracking, unit testing, debugging, etc.). This perspective of SE research on software development is, however, mismatching the current status of quantum software. Zhao et al. were some of the first to coin the term *quantum software engineering* (QSE) to summarize any effort to adopt established SE principles and practices to make them also work for quantum software [111]. However, in this chapter, we take on a contrary perspective: research on QSE should, as a first step, identify, understand, and tackle short-term engineering challenges for better support of, usually fully manually crafted, small-/medium-scale quantum programs today (i.e., focusing on the programming and deployment phases). More sophisticated and mature concepts including high-level software abstraction as propagated, for instance, in the context of requirements elicitation, object-oriented design patterns, software maintenance and evolution, and re-engineering are out of scope for now due to the lack of any accessible examples and use cases. To meet the short-term goals, quantum SE should first of all focus on the following challenges.

- Make quantum computing accessible to developers and users through appropriate processes, methods, and tools.
- Facilitate hybrid quantum computing through a combination of classical SE and QSE concepts based on a generic description of a computational problem and (quantum) platform constraints.
- Provide benchmarks and benchmarking processes, methods, and tools for assessing quantum advantage as well as constraints that arise from the integration of quantum software components in an overall (hybrid) software system.

Our goal is to assess the short-term requirements and challenges of SE in the upcoming era of quantum computing. These requirements and challenges are already relevant to the noisy intermediate-scale quantum (NISQ) era. In contrast to other recent works on this subject [111, 6, 101, 110], we do not follow a top-down approach, but instead, illustrate the status quo of QSE by considering a selection of industrial application scenarios. For each application scenario, we first provide a short general description and then describe selected recent use cases to characterize the common aspects of the respective scenarios. Based on these descriptions, we derive in a bottom-up manner the key challenges for QSE with respect to these application scenarios. Our goal is to gain a better understanding of the principles and practices that will most likely support the development of software systems that solve problems that, at least partly, involve quantum computations. Our claim is that, from an SE point of view, quantum computation is not a new programming paradigm in the first place, but, first of all, a new *computational architecture*. The novel conceptual thinking required for effectively exploiting the frequently promised *quantum advantage* is crosscutting all classical development phases and hierarchies of software systems. Quantum computing will thus potentially influence SE as a whole as we know it today [89]. Nevertheless, we argue that established solutions developed in SE research over the past decades will not all suddenly become inappropriate and obsolete due to the advent of quantum computing, but instead require careful rethinking and adjustments to also cope with the key characteristics of quantum software. Many of these characteristics and possible side effects apparent in quantum computations have been considered before in other contexts, whereas the inherent pervasiveness of these characteristics in a quantum setting is indeed a novel aspect. These characteristics include, for instance, the probabilistic nature of computational outcomes and the lack of reference architectures (although Qiskit may be seen as a de facto standard today for the majority of computational approaches).

   "While many of quantum computing's promised capabilities could be revolutionary, the realization of this promise requires breakthroughs in several areas, including improvements in the quality of qubits, error correction, and a demonstrable set of practical applications" [28]. The inflated expectations may result in a *quantum winter* similar to what we experienced with AI, where it took a long time to turn promising theoretical concepts into reality. Thus, the immediately necessary contributions of the SE community to advancing quantum computing lie in moving from first demonstrable examples to real-world applications with practical impact.

2 Paradigmatic Application Scenarios

We next describe potential application domains of QSE by means of paradigmatic application scenarios as illustrated in Fig. 1:

- **Application Scenario 1.** Provide quantum computing capabilities as a cloud service to solve optimization problems or machine learning tasks (quantum-computing-as-a-service).
- **Application Scenario 2.** Perform physical simulations with quantum programs developed by domain experts in a machine-oriented low-level manner.
- **Application Scenario 3.** Embed quantum processing units (QPUs) as integrated components into hybrid safety- or mission-critical software systems with a special focus on nonfunctional properties.

The selection of these application scenarios is driven by industrial and academic experiences of the authors and is aligned with the core use cases of the QUTAC Consortium [11]. Our aim is to illustrate the diversity of application domains and different perspectives on quantum computing, ranging from recent black-box and white-box views to embedded quantum computing.

Fig. 1 Application scenarios for quantum computing

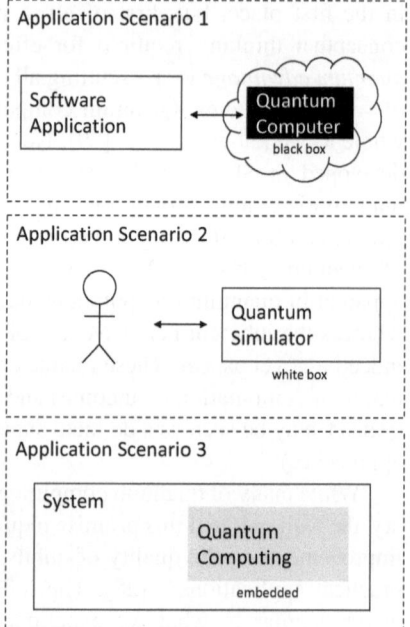

2.1   Application Scenario 1: Quantum Cloud Services

2.1.1   Use Cases and Examples

Quantum computing brings new opportunities for **solving optimization problems**, which are among the first industrial applications of the technology [11]. One example is the *flight-gate assignment (FGA)* problem in airport and air traffic planning, where the assignment of incoming flights to gates shall be optimized to minimize transfer times [94, 81]. This scheduling problem belongs to a class of NP-hard combinatorial optimization problems. Further examples include *Electronic Design Automation* (EDA) such as placement and routing on design chips and fault detection in electrical power networks [68], trajectory optimization in air traffic management [95], paint-shop scheduling [108], and planning problems in highly individualized mass production [9].

NP-hardness implies that, in practice, real-world instances can only be solved by approximation algorithms or heuristics. Here, quantum computers, taking advantage of entanglement, superposition, and interference, could potentially speed up and improve the optimization. One key property of the mentioned problems is that they can be solved **offline**: one problem instance is solved once, usually without critical time constraints, and the result is used to do something substantial, either conducting further research or going in an operational state, for instance, by applying the optimized flight schedule in an airport scenario.

2.1.2   Approaches and Challenges

A possible solution to bypass insufficient local computational power for effectively solving hard optimization problems is to **pass the work to a quantum cloud system**. For instance, D-Wave's Leap service [23] provides connections to quantum annealers or IBM's Qiskit interfacing to their quantum machines [71].

It has been argued that handling the offloading of such computations does not pose any new challenges to SE [50] as quantum computing essentially appears as a black box with well-defined interfaces. However, an open issue is to properly design such interfaces and to **formulate optimization problems** being tractable by quantum processing units (QPUs). First, an emerging optimization problem may be identified as computational bottlenecks within larger application contexts. These problems are either spotted by mathematical analysis during the design phase or during an optimization stage using a profiler; ideally, they match one of the known quantum primitives [39]. To this end, developers have to **refactor the overall software system** to isolate and replace the computational component by calls to quantum cloud services. Yet, there may be many such components that are closely tied to specific requirements of the overall system and which are the result of decades' worth of research and optimization [24]. This makes replacing them a nontrivial endeavor. Examples include subtasks of database management systems like join ordering [84, 85], multi-query optimization [98] or transaction scheduling [15].

Using quantum computing to speed up tasks previously solved by components designed and optimized for classical computers thus requires careful analysis. This includes understanding the underlying problem as well as exploring possible quantum speedups under varying workloads, input data characteristics, etc., while simultaneously retaining crucial, yet unrelated functional and nonfunctional properties of the overall system. Established SE techniques and tools (e.g., for performance analysis and refactoring) may help.

However, it is fair to say that the understanding of **what benefits quantum computers can provide** for what specific problems **is far from being well understood** in comparison to the state of the art in classical algorithms, and *also* in terms of system architecture.

While the potential speedups of seminal approaches [64] like Shor's algorithm (and, more generally, quantum phase estimation) or Grover search are rigorously established, the impact of imperfections on these algorithms makes any practical application considerations quickly prohibitive [43]. Likewise, even the actual requirements on the hardware of future machines for comparatively simple co-variables like the number of qubits is subject to discussion, and depends not only on many low-level details of the underlying hardware, but also on the actual payload algorithms [78]. A substantial body of the existing literature is dedicated to establishing a comprehensive understanding of the theoretical advantages of quantum sampling approaches [44]. Yet, concrete applications of these techniques are thinly spread, and their practical gain especially in comparison to existing heuristics and approximations is still under initial exploration [27].

The situation becomes even less straightforward for the more recent class of variational quantum algorithms and quantum approximate optimization algorithm (QAOA)-style approaches [17, 13]. While it is known that an efficient simulation of specific variants of QAOA would have strikingly unattractive and unexpected consequences for some of the pillars of computational complexity theory, entirely classical replacements for other variants are also known [61]. Likewise, the understanding of how to construct efficient classical surrogates for variational algorithms has considerably increased recently [87, 86], and restricts potential quantum advantage to increasingly narrower domains. When—unavoidable—practical constraints are taken into account [105, 79], determining a fair basis for comparison is a not yet satisfactorily resolved problem [12, 46], even ignoring the substantial limitations of currently available hardware.

A major challenge is to identify, factor out, and transform optimization subtasks suitable for quantum computers or annealers and their specific computing architectures [25, 48]. Several transformation steps usually reformat the optimization problem. In addition, "glue" code to connect classic and quantum parts is required. Tools like Quark [55][1] enable users to easily formulate and transform optimization

---

[1] See also the list of contributors (link in PDF).

problems, and to handle experiment dispatch and analysis. Likewise, approaches for recommending solution strategies for optimization problems using quantum approaches have been suggested [70]. However, such tools to support interacting and experimenting with quantum computers are still subject to research [103].

2.1.3 Conclusions

We are in the phase of evaluating the potentials of quantum computing in solving optimization problems. Providing such capabilities as reliable (black-box) services, however, requires an improved understanding of machine properties obtained from experiments and benchmarking. This necessitates many iterations of interactions with the quantum hardware for parameter tuning. Software development efforts, therefore, increase significantly when dealing with quantum hardware in contrast to well-established classical approaches as this fine-tuning requires not only software skills but also deeper knowledge in fundamental quantum physics. We assume this up-front investment will eventually pay off: if a fast heuristic solution is available and easy to access, a user will simply call quantum optimizers as a black-box cloud service over a well-defined interface, hiding transformation complexity and specific hardware requirements.

Summary Quantum cloud services will allow for accelerating mathematical optimization problems. Automatic means of transforming existing formulations into quantum descriptions have become available; yet, it remains a software architecture and engineering challenge to identify appropriate problems. Integrating quantum solvers into applications from a black-box perspective, including interface design, remains a minor SE challenge. However, the underlying quantum computing software stack, including the compilation and hybrid computing process, requires new quantum software engineering approaches.

2.2 Application Scenario 2: Quantum Simulation

2.2.1 Use Cases and Examples

Quantum simulation is one of the most promising application scenarios for quantum computing. It can help in understanding real-world chemistry and physics phenomena, improving design methodologies and making experiments much more effective. Simulating quantum mechanics on classical computers is a hard computational problem,[2] and determining relevant properties of quantum systems, e.g., finding their minimal energy, is even harder. To efficiently simulate a quantum system, the simulator might rely on quantum-mechanical dynamics. The basic idea of a quantum simulator is to use a controllable quantum platform to replicate dynamic or static properties of another, usually less controllable, quantum system [51]. This is similar to using wind tunnels for testing aerodynamic properties of reduced-scale models in a controlled environment, and then to transfer gained information to full-scale objects in the (uncontrolled) real world. With the rapid growth of quantum computing capabilities, the interest in **(quantum) material science** has also risen significantly. This field targets a large variety of applications ranging from the *design of more efficient batteries and catalysts* to the study of *innovative sensing materials for consumer and automotive applications* [66].

For the latter task, many candidate compounds have to be efficiently screened and evaluated to select or design the best materials with respect to the desired properties. This implies large effort and costs in terms of material procurement, measurement equipment, and setup. Direct simulations of the material properties could drastically reduce the required resources and significantly accelerate the discovery process reducing time-to-market. Here, quantum systems promise a fast and more precise simulation tool of real-world mechanisms than their conventional counterparts.

Likewise, the study of new storage materials and the development of innovative battery technology is being pushed by several emerging and established applications, ranging from electric and light electric vehicles to solar energy storage systems and robotics. Researchers aim at understanding the mechanisms impacting efficiency, stability, and faster charging of battery operations to predict real-world performance. Yet the first fundamental step, again, remains the selection of apt chemical compounds. New families of disruptive active materials such as Lithium-Ion (Li-ion) and Lithium-Sulfur (Li-S) offer four times higher energy density than Li-ion batteries. From a modeling perspective, it is crucial to describe the solid electrolyte interphase forming on the battery anode and to define its durability and long-term performance. Classic DFT, multi-physics simulations, and measurements have not provided satisfactory answers particularly in terms of accuracy . Quantum computing can offer a closer characterization of the key chemical properties of battery cells such as equilibrium cell voltages, ionic mobility, and thermal stability.

---

[2] Problems efficiently solvable by QC belong to complexity class bounded-error quantum polynomial (BQP), the quantum analog of BPP. The relation between BQP and classical classes like NP poses many open questions. The **dynamics** of a quantum system (compute output of a quantum circuit given an initial state) is BQP-hard [36], which makes it likely intractable for classical computers, but doable for quantum machines for a class of natural Hamiltonians in BPQ. Inferring *global* properties of a quantum system (given a quantum circuit, is there a state that produces a desired output? What is the minimum energy eigenstate for a given Hamiltonian?) belong into QMA, a probabilistic quantum analog of NP [1], and is intractable even for quantum computers . It is even possible to give physical problems that are undecidable, at least within the limit of infinite size [22]. Quantum SE needs to be aware of such peculiarities to properly ascertain the feasibility of architectures and designs by avoiding illusory, inflated expectations of potential gains.

The quantum simulation often boils down to obtaining the ground state energies of various molecules of increasing complexity [26]; likewise, physical characteristics like dipole moments have also been calculated [77].

2.2.2 Approaches and Challenges

Programmable universal quantum computers can simulate quantum mechanical processes [18, 40, 7, 54, 16]. Such simulations are specified using software (e.g., using **domain-specific languages**), which takes this topic into the focus of SE. However, different approaches to quantum simulation (analog simulation, digital simulation, combinations thereof, and hybrid quantum-classical algorithms) differ in their implications. In each case, and in contrast to other forms of quantum computation, quantum simulation requires **awareness of the Hamiltonian** underlying the task (the Hamilton operator (or *Hamiltonian*) of a system is, roughly speaking, a mathematical object[3] that provides information about a physical system. It is closely related to the energy spectrum,[4] and governs time-evolution of a quantum system. The Schrödinger equation combines Hamiltonian and quantum states, which are mathematically described by the wave function, into a differential equation).

Analog quantum simulators [18, 20] are physical systems that mimic other quantum systems (or a class of models) by closely reproducing the system's characteristics. Hence, their Hamiltonian should be as similar as possible to the simulated system. *Digital quantum simulation* is based on decomposing the Hamiltonian into operations implementable in the simulator by single- and two-qubit gate operations. This is more flexible than analog quantum simulators and enables us to overcome the limitations of the simulator system itself. Furthermore, it allows for quantum error correction and universality in a *"fully universal"* quantum

---

[3] We have been deliberately careful to avoid confusing the physical concept of a dynamical observable that can be measured with the mathematical operator/object to which it corresponds in the formal description.

[4] Many textbooks on quantum mechanics simply state that the Hamiltonian represents the total energy of a system, sometimes requiring this as a fundamental postulate. There are reasons to avoid such strong statements, both from a fundamental perspective (in the canonical approach of replacing physical quantities in the Hamilton function H of classical mechanics with operator-valued quantities, H is always conserved, but does, as Legendre transform of the Langrangian, not automatically equate to the sum of potential and kinetic energy; the approach to deriving a quantum Hamiltonian from energy-momentum relations delivers different results for the non-relativistic and relativistic case; and approaches based on space-time symmetries need to introduce empirical factors that relate the quantum Hamiltonian to classical energies), and from a practical point of view that concerns the software engineering aspects of quantum simulations. It is fairly common in this field to work with *effective Hamiltonians* that describe only degrees of freedom relevant for a particular task (for instance, Spin Hamiltonians in spectroscopy, the Ligand Field Hamiltonian of coordination chemistry, or the Hückel Hamiltonian for aromatic systems, which all carry a certain relevance for quantum chemistry), and therefore do not deliver a complete energy spectrum. Correctness checks, invariants, and the interpretation of results must adapt to such circumstances, and require awareness from the software side.

computer. If the simulator offers a universal set of perfect quantum gates, then the model can simulate a wide class of Hamiltonians [54], albeit the computing effort may vary depending on the types of gates. Some implementation technologies for QCs in use today are particularly well suited for quantum simulators. An example is Rydberg atom arrays [63, 102] that provide identical and long-lived qubits with strong coherent interactions. To represent the physical properties of the simulated system, the properties of the simulator correspond well to these, especially when analog simulation steps are involved. At least for this aspect, this challenges the idea that abstraction layers [10], despite proven useful classically, can satisfactorily eliminate differences between implementation platforms.

Industrial experience with quantum simulation problems gained by some of the authors shows that the exact boundary between digital simulation and optimization is not always clear. Especially quantum-classical hybrid algorithms—most importantly, the variational quantum eigensolver (VQE) [97]—rely on optimization methods to determine observables like the ground state energy of molecules based on a physical model. It is hypothesized that VQE, which at its core is independent of the simulated problem, will provide improved modeling accuracy over classical approaches like DFT. However, engineering challenges remain such as hardware-dependent **noise compensation**, an understanding of the differences between the many available variants of VQE [34] (requiring **problem-dependent benchmarking** [76]), and **determining optimal quantum-classical splits**. Especially the latter topics fall within the responsibilities of SE, but it might also be possible to improve noise handling based on software-centric methods. Also, the **depth reduction of circuits** generated from Hamiltonian descriptions is an important goal, in which compilers may play a crucial role (see, e.g., [30, 49, 82]). As with other use cases, resource usage and scalability in general need to be addressed by QSE.

Despite initial steps taken on problems of industrial scale, explorations are still in an early phase with already important collaborations emerging between large chemical and computing technology corporations [19]. Currently, the effort of finding appropriate Hamiltonian models by far exceeds the software implementation effort; knowledge of physical principles and details by far outranks the challenges of transcribing these into the quantum framework. While the modeling task in the classical domain is routinely reduced to a well-informed parametrization of canned DFT software, quantum tools—even given existing frameworks support [71]—require high manual programming effort.

2.2.3 Conclusions

SE tasks in quantum simulation include algorithm selection, determining the influence of mathematical/physical details on nonfunctional and functional properties, and comparing quantum and hybrid architectures to classical approaches and heuristics. Many revolve, in a broader sense, around the topic of **testing**. As the goal of quantum simulation is to exceed the computational capabilities of classical approaches, this opens up new research challenges. Testing quantum simulations comprises ensuring (a) model correctness and (b) correctness of circuits generated from the model. After establishing a Hamiltonian description of the system, empirical measurements on the actual physical system can be performed and compared to the simulation results. The resulting circuit generator is then trusted, and quantum simulation based on the generators can be used to explore the properties of novel, previously unexplored materials.

From an SE point of view, recent attempts lift established techniques for end-to-end testing of classical computations to components with probabilistic behavior [62, 41, 35, 38]. This includes novel notions of testing oracles based on distance measures for execution trace distributions and statistical criteria for approximating error probability by the number of repetitions of test runs. More involved quantum phenomena like superposition and entanglement of computational states are not yet properly addressed by these approaches. This, first of all, requires new abstractions concerning the notion of *observations* in testing reflecting the destructive nature of quantum measurements which obstructs established testing practices like interactive debugging [62].

Further properties of quantum states and circuits are also not suited to established testing methods: as there are usually no classical control branches in quantum circuits, structural code coverage criteria are not applicable, which renders well-established, elementary software testing concepts [92] useless. Likewise, localization of faults is unlike harder for quantum circuits than for classical programs, given that entangled states can intertwine arbitrary parts of a circuit and mutually influence each other . Not just the stochastic nature of quantum measurements but also the impact of imperfection and noise in quantum circuits obstruct the definition of proper test oracles. Here, we need to distinguish unavoidable variations caused by quantum measurements from variations due to (classically) probabilistic algorithmic elements from variations induced by noise and imperfection. Distinguishing between such different probability distributions is no new challenge, but there are quantum specifics: for instance, the amount of information to be recorded for a meaningful statement (e.g., by estimating the required number of samples for a desired precision and bounded error probability via Hoeffding's inequality [65], or randomized measurement procedures [31] that estimate quantum properties from classical observations) requires future research in QSE. Well-principled guidelines can eliminate the need for individual software engineers to be aware of such statistical peculiarities.

Other verification approaches for quantum simulation include up-front correctness validation of models (e.g., finding physical invariants that can be probed with accessible measurements), equipping a model's software representation (or the representation of the simulation approach) with a formal semantics honors quantum aspects (e.g., [58, 14, 21, 32]) that allows us to verify specific properties and correctness of generated modeling circuits by decomposition techniques (see, e.g., [67, 99]).

Summary Quantum simulation can benefit from established means of SE to formulate and describe models of physical systems whose properties can be simulated on quantum computers. Efforts evolve more around a physical understanding of the employed models rather than programming. Validation and verification techniques, as well as architectural decomposition into quantum and classical aspects, will rely on established, yet to be adapted SE approaches.

2.3   Application Scenario 3: Embedded Quantum Computing

2.3.1   Use Cases and Examples

Embedded software systems are purpose-built for specific tasks. In contrast to general purpose and high-performance computing systems (Application Scenario 1), embedded systems operate under restricted resources, on specific hardware platforms, and have to meet distinct quality requirements like **real-time constraints or safety guarantees**. Safety measures prevent material damage and harm to individuals and deeply influence hardware and software co-design of classical embedded software [57].

2.3.2   Approaches and Challenges

We recently observed a convergence between embedded systems and high-performance computing [42], for instance, in autonomous driving, avionics, and control systems. We expect embedded systems to require even more computational resources in future applications. Hence, quantum computing may also play an important role in **hybrid embedded scenarios** by utilizing **quantum accelerators** for solving particular computational tasks [105]. To the best of our knowledge, no approaches have been investigated so far to facilitate quality assurance techniques and tools for embedded quantum computing. Meeting these requirements in QPU accelerated hybrid systems is complicated by the dominance of iterative, probabilistic algorithms; yet, since almost all known quantum algorithms that operate on perfect error-corrected quantum systems are also inherently *probabilistic* [56], the problem will also extend after the NISQ area. Open research questions include how to improve understanding of termination properties and convergence toward sufficiently accurate results in iterative algorithms [33, 3], as well as the role of classical optimization components [114, 96] and result degradation. But, perhaps counter-intuitively, also possible improvements [53] by imperfections and noise [4, 100] are important research questions.

In many application domains, embedded co-design development processes must achieve (safety) certifications. It is an open question how established approaches can be adapted to quantum computing including entirely novel qualification approaches aligned with QPU peculiarities. Therefore, we may expect that system engineering will play a larger role in hybrid embedded quantum computing than for classical applications.

Prior work in safety-critical embedded systems deals with probabilistic algorithms and machine learning (e.g., neural networks) in the context of unreliable hardware. Measures include redundant computation, error correction [93], as well as more high-level concepts like safety cages [45] and static partitioning [73], *Digital Dependability Identities* (DDI) [74], and *Dynamic Risk Management* (DRM) [75]. It is not obvious if and how these approaches can be adopted for quantum computing. It is also crucial to consider how to integrate QPUs into existing embedded development processes and infrastructures. This includes interface design (at the physical and protocol level) to ensure proper timing and co-scheduling of computational tasks offloaded to a quantum component. The integration of QPUs further impacts the software operating systems level and middleware layers. Given the strong influence of imperfection of QPUs in the near and midterm [13], QPU integration will also impact co-design of hardware and algorithms to ensure computational advantages for a given set of problems. The established approaches to hardware–software co-design are currently adapted to interactions between QPUs and classical system components [52, 5], with efforts ranging from traditional embedded systems design to integration with high-performance computing [105, 88], all of which also pose software engineering challenges. The feasibility of co-design decisions strongly depends on the underlying physical implementation technology, which influences the quality properties of any software executed on top.

Since embedded systems are employed in industrial and cost-sensitive domains, economic considerations are also important in a quantum setting, especially given that even in the upcoming era of fully error-corrected quantum computers (but even more so in the NISQ era), different physical implementations of the computational concepts will offer different characteristics depending on their physical implementation [104]. A quantum approach with marginal improvement over existing solutions at the expense of inflating the bill of materials (or other development costs) is neither intellectually satisfying nor economically desirable. Embedded quantum SE must consider these issues.

2.3.3   Conclusions

The main challenges to enable hybrid embedded quantum computing include novel co-design principles and practices to adopt quality assurance techniques (e.g., embedded systems testing) and corresponding certification processes to a quantum setting. This is particularly crucial in safety-critical application domains. In the near term, we may expect quantum computing to find its way into large-scale embedded systems only (e.g., in CT scanners). In contrast, the physical size of recent quantum computers is the main limiting factor for small-scale, mobile use cases such as automotive *Electronic Compute Units* (ECU). These limitations of first-generation QPU are not quantum inherent, and future quantum technology may provide quantum accelerators fitting into small, well-integrated embedded systems.

Summary We expect that QPUs, given increasing miniaturization, will be deployed as accelerators in embedded use cases. This requires applications (and extensions) of established co-design methods from embedded SE that also lean substantially toward systems engineering. Quality assurance, certification requirements, and economic and physical constraints will play pronounced roles.

3 Promises and Perils of Quantum Software Engineering

3.1 Promises and Opportunities

Application scenario 1 is aligned with classical SE for developing complete software solutions by making use of quantum cloud services, whereas application scenario 2 crosscuts classical SE and instead seeks support of craftsmanship by individual experts. Application scenario 3 demands principles and practices similar to systems engineering for quality-aware integration of heterogeneous software/hardware components on a computational platform. From these observations, we conclude that the work with quantum computing is, and will be, similar to the development process using embedded accelerators, such as GPUs or special-purpose hardware (see Fig. 2). Similar to hardware–software co-design approaches, we expect that hardware–software–QC co-design processes will be required to split classical from quantum software parts [29, 69]. Likewise, a number of proposals have been made regarding more general questions of software architecture for quantum-classical hybrid systems, for instance [90, 80, 37].

After the diverse software parts are completed and tested as separate units (taking into account that quantum aspects bring additional challenges to reproducibility aspects [60]), an integration test step is required. Ideally, those steps will be embedded into continuous engineering processes [8], e.g., by making use of virtual hardware platforms or simulators for faster feedback cycles. We next discuss challenges of QSE by considering the respective SE phases. While many of these challenges have already been mentioned in recent surveys on QSE [111], our attempt is to relate these aspects to the insights gained from all three application scenarios described above.

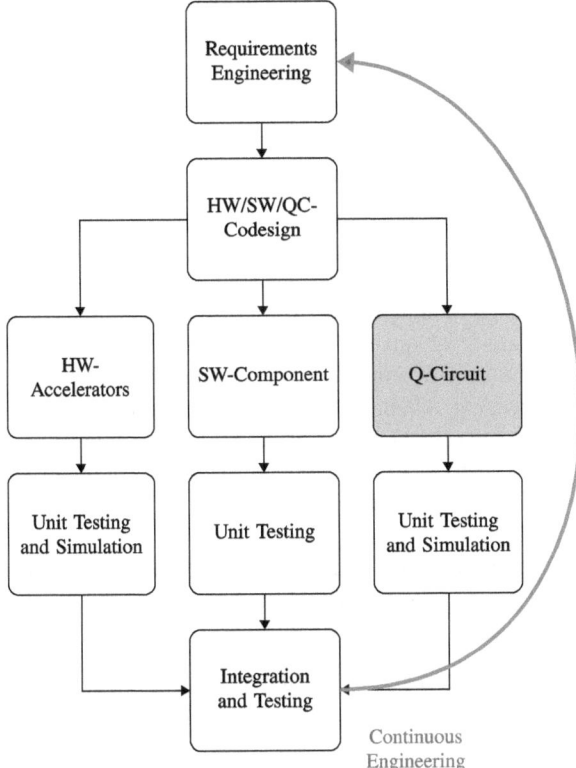

Fig. 2 Quantum software development process

Requirements Engineering The requirements engineering phase will not fundamentally change as requirements, by definition, deal with the *What?* and not the *How?* in software projects. Hence, system-level requirements for QC do not substantially differ from classical requirements. However, new types of nonfunctional requirements specific to quantum software in combination with quantum hardware might become relevant.

Systems Design/Architecture (Hardware–Software–QC Co-Design) In this phase, the problem splitting between classical and quantum tasks takes place: the engineer decides which parts of the overall problem are solved by classical computations and which ones by quantum solutions. This requires architectural guidelines and patterns, as well as interface descriptions for interactions between classical and quantum data.

Programming Languages and Implementation (Q-Circuit) In this phase, algorithms need to be realized for the classical as well as for the quantum parts of a given problem. For the classical part, programming languages and compilation is well known. However, for implementing quantum algorithms, we currently rely on gate-level languages (even in case of seemingly higher-level quantum programming languages like Q#). While gate-level languages are essentially the quantum equivalent to classical assembly languages, for more efficient implementation, we need appropriate high-level quantum programming abstractions. Furthermore, we need programming guidelines and idioms, as well as design patterns for quantum programming languages. [107] Design by contract for quantum software.

Compilation and Deployment (Q-Circuit) Today, each quantum hardware comes with its own hardware specifics, e.g., gates that can be implemented easily or at all and to which qubits these gates can apply. This requires machine-specific compilation and transpilation techniques. OpenQASM is only becoming a de facto standard for hardware-level quantum programming. In order to allow for more efficient development and execution of quantum programs, we need a common intermediate language, e.g., OpenQASM, and generic compilation techniques. This includes instruction set selection and back-end optimization that can be easily adapted and configured for specific hardware. Here, ideas for classical compiler-compilers may become useful again to automatically generate hardware-specific compilers.

This aspect naturally includes devising new methods to (statically) check desirable properties and guarantees of quantum programs at compile time; the first steps in this direction have already been taken [112, 47, 106, 72].

Testing and Verification In the spirit of the V-model and similar development models, the approaches in this phase complement the approaches of the respective development phases. Recent techniques for testing and verification of (partly) probabilistic hybrid software systems may provide a conceptual foundation for ensuring that the observed output behavior of quantum components conforms to a given specification [41, 62, 109, 35, 2]. Corresponding black-box techniques are applicable at the functional unit level as well as the system integration level of the hybrid system, by abstracting from any internal details of quantum components (application scenarios 1 and 3). In contrast, in the case of a white-box setting (application scenario 2), it is not obvious how to adopt established techniques for software testing (e.g., interactive debugging [62]) and verification of quantum computations. The first step in this direction may be to find sound abstractions that properly reflect quantum-specific phenomena like superposition and entanglement of computational states and the destructive nature of quantum measurements. As always, testing and verification aim at improving software quality and minimizing the number of bugs; the first steps in the direction of understanding the quantum-specific aspects of these goals have been taken [113].

3.2 Perils

Quantum computing will benefit from established software engineering techniques. The synthesis of both fields will likely put a few new topics on the joint research agenda. However, there is also good reason to predict that quantum software engineering will (a) likely not radically change most established means of software engineering and (b) not benefit from inapt, straightforward adaptations of existing insights. In particular, we argue that this concerns the use of modeling languages and adaptations of development processes.

Albeit special-purpose quantum languages are available, most development activities in the NISQ either comprise using quantum functionalities on the API level or constructing gate sequences that are applied on qubits. Dispatching and orchestration aspects are embedded into a classical host scripting language, typically Python [71, 91]. The translation between different APIs is currently near-trivial [83]. Special-purpose quantum programming languages (or extensions to classical languages) promise to lift the specification or verification of quantum *algorithms* to more appropriate levels of abstraction that require less manual handling of details. We are not aware of an argument as to why abstraction levels that transcend algorithmic implementation details, and thus avoid quantum specifics, would necessarily need to be crafted differently than in the classical case. Of course, it is possible to use mechanisms like UML that were intended to model software designs for describing low-level details of qubits, quantum registers, and gates. Yet it would also be possible to model classical bits, registers and electronic gates using UML in the same way; since we are not aware of any beneficial application of such a technique to the best of our knowledge, this underlines the importance of not mixing modeling techniques targeted at high levels of abstraction with low-level details. While the *design* of algorithms for quantum systems is entirely different from classical algorithms (and systematic methods range among the most challenging unsolved problems in the field), implementation details in general almost never concern modeling at a higher level [10], and should therefore continue not to do so in quantum software development.

Again to the best of our knowledge, using entirely nonstandard development processes in specific domains is not commonly reported in the literature. Likewise, we are unaware of specially crafted software development processes—unlike architectures—that are beneficial when components like GPU accelerators or target domains like cloud deployments are considered. As we have argued in the use case discussion above, GPUs can be seen as computational accelerators (in local appliances) or cloud resources (in distributed systems), which by analogy suggests that any such specially crafted processes will not lead to pronounced advantages. Additionally, software engineering research often finds little to no difference [59] when the implications of various forms of (social) process interactions between developers are studied for software in different domains. This insight further strengthens the hypothesis that quantum software development can be based on existing processes, and inherit the advantages and disadvantages of each approach.

Consequently, we find it unlikely that quantum software engineering in any of the scenarios described in this chapter will require entirely new development processes, or nontrivial modifications of existing approaches. Since no substantial body of quantum software exists yet, mining quantitative empirical evidence toward one side or another will likely not be conclusive at this stage. While it cannot be ruled out that, for instance, UML will be an appropriate tool to design algorithms at gate and qubit level, or that entirely new development processes will need to be devised to implement quantum software, we call for caution before making overly ambitious statements without conclusive evidence, which could either be derived from sound ab initio considerations or empirically observed from mounting industrial and academic experience with creating concrete quantum software.

4   Summary and Outlook

Quantum computing is still in a very early stage with major challenges ahead. Many of these challenges have to be addressed by advancing quantum computing at the hardware level. Nevertheless, quantum computing will not only be pushed by innovations in physics, leading to advancements in quantum hardware, but progress can also be expected by a pull effect caused by innovative future applications. Or, according to the aforementioned quote by Deshpande [28], realizing practical applications is indeed in the domain of SE.

Nevertheless, quantum software development will not cause a revolution in SE, neither today nor in the foreseeable future. The overall aim of many SE principles (e.g., separation of concerns, encapsulation, and information hiding, just to name a few) is exactly to be agnostic to diverse (existing and future) computational platforms. Hence, we should be more interested in those characteristics of quantum computations which have been exotic corner cases in SE until now but will soon become omnipresent in quantum software development.

Moreover, quantum software development today mostly happens at source code level and reaching downwards to assembly level. Quantum programming today mostly means to custom-tailor a quantum solution to a very specific instruction set of a specifically developed special-purpose quantum computer. The tendency in mainstream SE today is, however, to abstract exactly from those low-level details and instead focus on requirements and design issues. Hence, recently outdated, former core disciplines of mainstream SE research like compiler construction and instruction set architecture design will become highly relevant again.

Acknowledgments This work is supported by the German Federal Ministry of Education and Research within the funding program Quantum technologies—from basic research to market, contract numbers 13N16303 (IS) and 13N15647/13NI6092 (WM). WM also acknowledges support from the High-Tech Agenda of the Free State of Bavaria. The work is further partly supported by the Austrian ministries BMK, BMAW, and the State of Upper Austria in the frame of the FFG COMET competence center INTEGRATE at SCCH as well as by BMBWF via the project QuantumReady (RR). We also acknowledge the use of IBM Quantum services and the Fraunhofer quantum computer in Ehningen for this work (MJ).

References

1. Aaronson, S.: Quantum Computing Since Democritus. Cambridge University Press, USA (2013). ISBN:0521199565

2. Abreu, R., et al.: Metamorphic Testing of Oracle Quantum Programs. In: 2022 IEEE/ACM 3rd International Workshop on Quantum Software Engineering (Q-SE), pp. 16–23 (2022). https://doi.org/10.1145/3528230.3529189

3. Akshay, V., et al.: Reachability deficits in quantum approximate optimization. Phys. Rev. Lett. **124**(9), 090504 (Mar. 2020). https://doi.org/10.1103/PhysRevLett.124.090504. https://link.aps.org/doi/10.1103/PhysRevLett.124.090504

4. Alam, M., Ash-Saki, A., Ghosh, S.: Design-Space Exploration of Quantum Approximate Optimization Algorithm under Noise. In: 2020 IEEE Custom Integrated Circuits Conference (CICC), pp. 1–4 (2020). https://doi.org/10.1109/CICC48029.2020.9075903

5. Algaba, M.G., et al.: Co-design quantum simulation of nanoscale NMR. Phys. Rev. Res. **4**(4), 043089 (Nov. 2022). https://doi.org/10.1103/PhysRevResearch.4.043089. https://link.aps.org/doi/10.1103/PhysRevResearch.4.043089

6. Ali, S., Yue, T., Abreu, R.: When software engineering meets quantum computing. Commun. ACM **65**(4), 84–88 (Mar. 2022). ISSN:0001-0782. https://doi.org/10.1145/3512340

7. Altman, E., et al.: Quantum simulators: Architectures and opportunities. PRX Quantum **2**(1), 017003 (2021)

8. Antonino, P.O., et al.: Enabling Continuous Software Engineering for Embedded Systems Architectures with Virtual Prototypes. In: Cuesta, C.E., Garlan, D., Pérez, J. (eds.) Software Architecture, pp. 115–130. Springer International Publishing, Cham (2018). ISBN:978-3-030-00761-4

9. Awasthi, A., et al.: Quantum Computing Techniques for Multi-Knapsack Problems (2023). https://doi.org/10.48550/ARXIV.2301.05750. https://arxiv.org/abs/2301.05750

10. Bass, L., Clements, P., Kazman, R.: Software Architecture in Practice. SEI Series in Software Engineering. Addison-Wesley (2003). ISBN:9780321154958

11. Bayerstadler, A., et al.: Industry quantum computing applications. EPJ Quantum Technol. **8**(1), (Nov. 2021). https://doi.org/10.1140/epjqt/s40507-021-00114-x. https://epjquantumtechnology.springeropen.com/track/pdf/10.1140/epjqt/s40507-021-00114-x.pdf

12. Becker, C.K.-U., Gheorghe-Pop, I.-D., Tcholtchev, N.: A Testing Pipeline for Quantum Computing Applications. In: Proceedings of the IEEE International Conference on Quantum Software. IEEE (2023)

13. Bharti, K., et al.: Noisy intermediate-scale quantum algorithms. Rev. Mod. Phys. **94**(1), 015004 (Feb. 2022). https://doi.org/10.1103/RevModPhys.94.015004. https://link.aps.org/doi/10.1103/RevModPhys.94.015004

14. Bichsel, B., et al.: Silq: A High-Level Quantum Language with Safe Uncomputation and Intuitive Semantics. In: Proceedings of the 41st ACM SIGPLAN Conference on Programming Language Design and Implementation, PLDI 2020, pp. 286–300. Association for Computing Machinery, London, UK (2020). ISBN:9781450376136. https://doi.org/10.1145/3385412.3386007

15. Bittner, T., Groppe, S.: Avoiding Blocking by Scheduling Transactions Using Quantum Annealing. In: Proceedings of the 24th Symposium on International Database Engineering & Applications, IDEAS '20. Association for Computing Machinery, Seoul, Republic of Korea (2020). ISBN:9781450375030. https://doi.org/10.1145/3410566.3410593

16. Blatt, R., Roos, C.F.: Quantum simulations with trapped ions. Nature Phys. **8**(4), 277–284 (2012)

17. Blekos, K., et al.: A Review on Quantum Approximate Optimization Algorithm and Its Variants (2023). arXiv:2306.09198 [quant-ph]

18. Buluta, I., Nori, F.: Quantum simulators. Science **326**(5949), 108–111 (2009). https://doi.org/10.1126/science.1177838. eprint: https://www.science.org/doi/pdf/10.1126/science.1177838. https://www.science.org/doi/abs/10.1126/science.1177838

19. Business Value II for: The Quantum Decade: A Playbook for Achieving Awareness, Readiness, and Advantage. IBM Institute for Business Value (2021). ISBN:9781737401100. https://books.google.de/books?id=MeN%5C_zgEACAAJ
20. Cirac, J.I., Zoller, P.: Goals and opportunities in quantum simulation. Nature Phys. **8**(4), 264–266 (2012). https://doi.org/10.1038/nphys2275
21. Cross, A., et al.: OpenQASM 3: A broader and deeper quantum assembly language. ACM Trans. Quantum Comput. **3**(3), (Sept. 2022). ISSN:2643-6809. https://doi.org/10.1145/3505636
22. Cubitt, T.S., Perez-Garcia, D., Wolf, M.M.: Undecidability of the spectral gap. Nature **528**(7581), 207–211 (2015). https://doi.org/10.1038/nature16059
23. D-Wave Systems Inc.: D-Wave Systems Leap Cloud Service (2023). https://cloud.dwavesys.com/leap/ visited 2023-03-03
24. De Andoin, M.G., et al.: Comparative Benchmark of a Quantum Algorithm for the Bin Packing Problem. In: 2022 IEEE Symposium Series on Computational Intelligence (SSCI), pp. 930–937. IEEE (2022)
25. Deb, A., Dueck, G.W., Wille, R.: Exploring the potential benefits of alternative quantum computing architectures. IEEE Trans. Comput. Aided Des. Integr. Circuits Syst. **40**(9), 1825–1835 (2020)
26. Delgado, A., et al.: Simulating key properties of lithium-ion batteries with a fault-tolerant quantum computer. Phys. Rev. A **106**(3), 032428 (Sept. 2022). https://doi.org/10.1103/PhysRevA.106.032428. https://link.aps.org/doi/10.1103/PhysRevA.106.032428
27. Deng, Y.-H., et al.: Solving graph problems using Gaussian Boson sampling. Phys. Rev. Lett. **130**(19), 190601 (May 2023). https://doi.org/10.1103/PhysRevLett.130.190601. https://link.aps.org/doi/10.1103/PhysRevLett.130.190601
28. Deshpande, A.: Assessing the quantum-computing landscape. Commun. ACM **65**(10), 57–65 (2022)
29. Dey, N., et al.: QDLC – The Quantum Development Life Cycle (2020). arXiv:2010.08053 [cs.ET]
30. Ding, Y., et al.: Systematic Crosstalk Mitigation for Superconducting Qubits via Frequency-Aware Compilation. In: 2020 53rd Annual IEEE/ACM International Symposium on Microarchitecture (MICRO), pp. 201–214 (2020). https://doi.org/10.1109/MICRO50266.2020.00028
31. Elben, A., et al.: The randomized measurement toolbox. Nature Rev. Phys. **5**(1), 9–24 (2023). https://doi.org/10.1038/s42254-022-00535-2
32. Evans, A., et al.: MCBeth: A Measurement Based Quantum Programming Language (2022). arXiv:2204.10784 [cs.PL]
33. Farhi, E., Goldstone, J., Gutmann, S.: A Quantum Approximate Optimization Algorithm (2014). https://doi.org/10.48550/ARXIV.1411.4028. https://arxiv.org/abs/1411.4028
34. Fedorov, D.A., et al.: VQE method: a short survey and recent developments. Mater. Theory **6**(1), 2 (2022). https://doi.org/10.1186/s41313-021-00032-6
35. Feng, Y., Duan, R., Ying, M.: Bisimulation for quantum processes. ACM Trans. Program. Lang. Syst. **34**(4), (2012). https://doi.org/10.1145/2400676.2400680
36. Fortnow, L.: One Complexity Theorist's View of Quantum Computing. In: Electronic Notes in Theoretical Computer Science. 31 CATS 2000 Computing: the Australasian Theory Symposium, pp. 58–72 (2000). ISSN:1571-0661. https://doi.org/10.1016/S1571-0661(05)80330-5. https://www.sciencedirect.com/science/article/pii/S1571066105803305
37. Furutanpey, A., et al.: Architectural Vision for Quantum Computing in the Edge-Cloud Continuum. In: Proceedings of the IEEE International Conference on Quantum Software. IEEE (2023)
38. Garcìa de la Barrera, A., et al.: Quantum software testing: State of the art. J. Software Evol. Process **35**(4), e2419 (2023). https://doi.org/10.1002/smr.2419. https://onlinelibrary.wiley.com/doi/abs/10.1002/smr.2419
39. Gemeinhardt, F.G., Wille, R., Wimmer, M.: Quantum k-community detection: algorithm proposals and cross-architectural evaluation. Quantum Inf. Process. **20**(9), 302 (2021)

40. Georgescu, I.M., Ashhab, S., Nori, F.: Quantum simulation. Rev. Modern Phys. **86**(1), 153 (2014)
41. Gerhold, M., Stoelinga, M.: Model-based testing of probabilistic systems. Formal Aspects Comput. **30**(1), 77–106 (Jan. 2018). ISSN:0934-5043. https://doi.org/10.1007/s00165-017-0440-4
42. Girbal, S., et al.: On the convergence of mainstream and mission-critical markets. In: 2013 50th ACM/EDAC/IEEE Design Automation Conference (DAC), pp. 1–10 (May 2013). https://doi.org/10.1145/2463209.2488962
43. Greiwe, F., Krüger, T., Mauerer, W.: Effects of Imperfections on Quantum Algorithms: A Software Engineering Perspective. In: Proceedings of the IEEE International Conference on Quantum Software. IEEE (2023)
44. Hangleiter, D., Eisert, J.: Computational advantage of quantum random sampling. Rev. Modern Phys. **95**(3), (July 2023). https://doi.org/10.1103/revmodphys.95.035001
45. Heckemann, K., et al.: Safe Automotive Software. In: König, A., et al. (eds.) Knowledge-Based and Intelligent Information and Engineering Systems, pp. 167–176. Springer, Berlin, Heidelberg (2011). ISBN:978-3-642-23866-6
46. Herrmann, N., et al.: Quantum Utility—Definition and Assessment of a Practical Quantum Advantage. In: Proceedings of the IEEE International Conference on Quantum Software. IEEE (2023)
47. Klamroth, J., et al.: QIn: Enabling Formal Methods to Deal with Quantum Circuits. In: Proceedings of the IEEE International Conference on Quantum Software. IEEE (2023)
48. Kole, A., et al.: Improved mapping of quantum circuits to IBM QX architectures. IEEE Trans. Comput. Aided Des. Integr. Circuits Syst. **39**(10), 2375–2383 (2019)
49. Kreppel, F., et al.: Quantum Circuit Compiler for a Shuttling-Based Trapped-Ion Quantum Computer (2022). https://doi.org/10.48550/ARXIV.2207.01964. https://arxiv.org/abs/2207.01964
50. Krüger, T., Mauerer, W.: Quantum Annealing-Based Software Components: An Experimental Case Study with SAT Solving (2020). Q-SE@ICSE. https://arxiv.org/abs/2005.05465
51. Lamata, L., et al.: Digital-analog quantum simulations with superconducting circuits. Adv. Phys. X **3**(1), 1457981 (2018). https://doi.org/10.1080/23746149.2018.1457981
52. Li, G., et al.: On the Co-Design of Quantum Software and Hardware. In: Proceedings of the Eight Annual ACM International Conference on Nanoscale Computing and Communication NANOCOM '21 Association for Computing Machinery, Virtual Event, Italy (2021). ISBN:9781450387101. https://doi.org/10.1145/3477206.3477464
53. Liu, J., et al.: Noise can be helpful for variational quantum algorithms (Oct. 2022). arXiv: 2210.06723 [quant-ph]
54. Lloyd, S.: Universal quantum simulators. Science **273**(5278), 1073–1078 (1996). https://doi.org/10.1126/science.273.5278.1073. eprint: https://www.science.org/doi/pdf/10.1126/science.273.5278.1073. https://www.science.org/doi/abs/10.1126/science.273.5278.1073
55. Lobe, E., Stollenwerk, T.: QUARK (Feb. 2022). https://quantum-computing-software.gitlab.io/quark/
56. Lubinski, T., et al.: Advancing hybrid quantum-classical computation with real-time execution. Front. Phys. **10**, (2022). ISSN:2296-424X. https://doi.org/10.3389/fphy.2022.940293. https://www.frontiersin.org/articles/10.3389/fphy.2022.940293
57. Marwedel, P.: Embedded System Design - Embedded Systems Foundations of Cyber-Physical Systems, Second Edition. Embedded Systems Springer (2011). ISBN: 978-94-007-0256-1. https://doi.org/10.1007/978-94-007-0257-8
58. Mauerer, W.: Semantics and simulation of communication in quantum programming (2005). https://doi.org/10.48550/ARXIV.QUANT-PH/0511145. https://arxiv.org/abs/quant-ph/0511145

59. Mauerer, W., Joblin, M., et al.: In search of socio-technical congruence: A large-scale longitudinal study. IEEE Trans. Software Eng. (01), 1–1 (May 2021). ISSN: 1939-3520. https://doi.org/10.1109/TSE.2021.3082074. https://www.computer.org/csdl/journal/ts/5555/01/09436025/1tJsglfkGru

60. Mauerer, W., Scherzinger, S.: 1-2-3 Reproducibility for Quantum Software Experiments. Q-SANER@IEEE International Conference on Software Analysis, Evolution and Reengineering (2022)

61. Medvidović, M., Carleo, G.: Classical variational simulation of the quantum approximate optimization algorithm. npj Quantum Inf. **7**(1), 101 (2021)

62. Miranskyy, A., Zhang, L.: On Testing Quantum Programs. In: 2019 IEEE/ACM 41st International Conference on Software Engineering: New Ideas and Emerging Results (ICSE-NIER), pp. 57–60 (2019). https://doi.org/10.1109/ICSE-NIER.2019.00023

63. Morgado, M., Whitlock, S.: Quantum simulation and computing with Rydberg-interacting qubits. AVS Quantum Sci. **3**(2), 023501 (June 2021). https://doi.org/10.1116/5.0036562

64. Nielsen, M.A., Chuang, I.L.: Quantum Computation and Quantum Information. Cambridge University Press, Cambridge (2000)

65. Pashayan, H., Wallman, J.J., Bartlett, S.D.: Estimating outcome probabilities of quantum circuits using quasiprobabilities. Phys. Rev. Lett. **115**(7), 070501(Aug. 2015). https://doi.org/10.1103/PhysRevLett.115.070501. https://link.aps.org/doi/10.1103/PhysRevLett.115.070501

66. Paudel, H.P., et al.: Quantum computing and simulations for energy applications: review and perspective. ACS Eng. Au **2**(3), 151–196 (2022). https://doi.org/10.1021/acsengineeringau.1c00033

67. Peham, T., Burgholzer, L., Wille, R.: Equivalence checking paradigms in quantum circuit design: a case study. In: Oshana, R. (ed.) DAC '22: 59th ACM/IEEE Design Automation Conference, San Francisco, California, USA, July 10–14, 2022, pp. 517–522. ACM (2022). https://doi.org/10.1145/3489517.3530480

68. Perdomo-Ortiz, A., et al.: A quantum annealing approach for fault detection and diagnosis of graph-based systems. Eur. Phys. J. Special Top. **224**, 131–148 (2015)

69. Pérez-Delgado, C.A., Perez-Gonzalez, H.G.: Towards a Quantum Software Modeling Language. In: Proceedings of the IEEE/ACM 42nd International Conference on Software Engineering Workshops ICSEW'20, pp. 442–444. Association for Computing Machinery, Seoul, Republic of Korea (2020). ISBN:9781450379632. https://doi.org/10.1145/3387940.3392183

70. Poggel, B., et al.: Recommending Solution Paths for Solving Optimization Problems with Quantum Computing. In: Proceedings of the IEEE International Conference on Quantum Software. IEEE (2023)

71. Qiskit Contributors.: Qiskit: An Open-Source Framework for Quantum Computing (2023). https://doi.org/10.5281/zenodo.2573505

72. Quetschlich, N., Burgholzer, L., Wille, R.: Predicting good quantum circuit compilation options. In: 2023 IEEE International Conference on Quantum Software (QSW), pp. 43–53. IEEE (2023)

73. Ramsauer, R., et al.: Static Hardware Partitioning on RISC-V - Shortcomings, Limitations, and Prospects. In: 8th IEEE World Forum on Internet of Things (IEEE WFIoT2022) (July 2022). https://doi.org/10.48550/arXiv.2208.02703. https://arxiv.org/abs/2208.02703

74. Reich, J., Schneider, D., et al.: Engineering of Runtime Safety Monitors for Cyber-Physical Systems with Digital Dependability Identities. In: Casimiro, A., et al. (eds.) Computer Safety, Reliability, and Security, pp. 3–17. Springer International Publishing, Cham (2020). ISBN:978-3-030-54549-9

75. Reich, J., Wellstein, M., et al.: Towards a Software Component to Perform Situation-Aware Dynamic Risk Assessment for Autonomous Vehicles. In: Adler, R., et al. (eds.) Dependable Computing - EDCC 2021 Workshops, pp. 3–11. Springer International Publishing, Cham (2021). ISBN:978-3-030-86507-8

76. Resch, S., Karpuzcu, U.R.: Benchmarking quantum computers and the impact of quantum noise. ACM Comput. Surv. **54**(7), (July 2021). ISSN:0360-0300. https://doi.org/10.1145/3464420

77. Rice, J.E., et al.: Quantum computation of dominant products in lithium–sulfur batteries. J. Chem. Phys. **154**(13), 134115 (Apr. 2021). ISSN:0021-9606. https://doi.org/10.1063/5.0044068. eprint: https://pubs.aip.org/aip/jcp/article-pdf/doi/10.1063/5.0044068/15588046/134115_1_online.pdf

78. Roffe, J.: Quantum error correction: an introductory guide. Contemp. Phys. **60**(3), 226–245 (2019). https://doi.org/10.1080/00107514.2019.1667078

79. Safi, H., Wintersperger, K., Mauerer, W.: Influence of HW-SW-Co-Design on Quantum Computing Scalability. In: Proceedings of the IEEE International Conference on Quantum Software. IEEE (2023)

80. Saurabh, N., Jha, S., Luckow, A.: A Conceptual Architecture for a Middleware for Hybrid Quantum-HPC Application Workflows. In: Proceedings of the IEEE International Conference on Quantum Software. IEEE (2023)

81. Sax, I., et al.: Approximate Approximation on a Quantum Annealer. In: Proceedings of the 17th ACM International Conference on Computing Frontiers, pp. 108–117 (2020). https://arxiv.org/pdf/2004.09267

82. Schmale, T., et al.: Backend compiler phases for trapped-ion quantum computers. In: 2022 IEEE International Conference on Quantum Software (QSW), pp. 32–37. IEEE Computer Society, Los Alamitos, CA, USA (July 2022). https://doi.org/10.1109/QSW55613.2022.00020. https://doi.ieeecomputersociety.org/10.1109/QSW55613.2022.00020

83. Schönberger, M., Franz, M., et al.: Peel — Pile? Cross-Framework Portability of Quantum Software. In: 2022 IEEE 19th International Conference on Software Architecture Companion (ICSA-C), pp. 164–169 (2022). https://doi.org/10.1109/ICSA-C54293.2022.00039

84. Schönberger, M., Scherzinger, S., Mauerer, W.: Ready to Leap (by Co-Design)? Join Order Optimisation on Quantum Hardware. In: Proceedings of ACM SIGMOD/PODS International Conference on Management of Data (2023)

85. Schönberger, M., Trummer, I., Mauerer, W.: Quantum Optimisation of General Join Trees. In: Proceedings of the International Workshop on Quantum Data Science and Management, QDSM '23 (Aug. 2023)

86. Schreiber, F.J., Eisert, J., Meyer, J.J.: Classical surrogates for quantum learning models (2022). arXiv: 2206.11740 [quant-ph]

87. Schuld, M., Sweke, R., Meyer, J.J.: Effect of data encoding on the expressive power of variational quantum-machine-learning models. Phys. Rev. A **103**(3), 032430 (Mar. 2021). https://doi.org/10.1103/PhysRevA.103.032430. https://link.aps.org/doi/10.1103/PhysRevA.103.032430

88. Schulz, M., et al.: Accelerating HPC with quantum computing: It is a software challenge too. Comput. Sci. Eng. **24**(04), 60–64 (July 2022). ISSN:1558-366X. https://doi.org/10.1109/MCSE.2022.3221845

89. Serrano, M.A., Perez-Castillo, R., Piattini, M., (eds.): Quantum Software Engineering. Springer (2022). ISBN:978-3-031-05323-8. https://doi.org/10.1007/978-3-031-05324-5

90. Sitdikov, I., et al.: Middleware for Quantum: An orchestration of hybrid quantum-classical systems. In: Proceedings of the IEEE International Conference on Quantum Software. IEEE (2023)

91. Sivarajah, S., et al.: t|ket⟩: a retargetable compiler for NISQ devices. Quantum Sci. Technol. **6**(1), 014003 (Nov. 2020). https://doi.org/10.1088/2058-9565/ab8e92

92. Sommerville, I.: Software Engineering, 9th edn. Addison-Wesley, Harlow, England (2010). ISBN:978-0-13-703515-1

93. Steiner, L., et al.: An LPDDR4 Safety Model for Automotive Applications. In: The International Symposium on Memory Systems MEMSYS 2021 Association for Computing Machinery, Washington DC, DC, USA (2022). ISBN:9781450385701. https://doi.org/10.1145/3488423.3519333

94. Stollenwerk, T., Lobe, E., Jung, M.: Flight gate assignment with a quantum annealer. In: International Workshop on Quantum Technology and Optimization Problems, pp. 99–110. Springer, Berlin (2019). https://elib.dlr.de/123777/. https://doi.org/10.1007/978-3-030-14082-3_9

95. Stollenwerk, T., O'Gorman, B., et al.: Quantum annealing applied to de-conflicting optimal trajectories for air traffic management. IEEE Trans. Intell. Transp. Syst. 21(1), 285–297 (2019)

96. Streif, M., Leib, M.: Training the quantum approximate optimization algorithm without access to a quantum processing unit. Quantum Sci. Technol. 5(3), 034008 (May 2020). https://doi.org/10.1088/2058-9565/ab8c2b

97. Tilly, J., et al.: The Variational Quantum Eigensolver: A review of methods and best practices. Physics Reports, 986 The Variational Quantum Eigensolver: a review of methods and best practices, pp. 1–128 (2022). ISSN:0370-1573. https://doi.org/10.1016/j.physrep.2022.08.003. https://www.sciencedirect.com/science/article/pii/S0370157322003118

98. Trummer, I., Koch, C.: Multiple query optimization on the D-wave 2X adiabatic quantum computer. Proc. VLDB Endow. 9(9), 648–659 (May 2016). ISSN:2150-8097. https://doi.org/10.14778/2947618.2947621

99. Ufrecht, C., et al.: Cutting multi-control quantum gates with ZX calculus (2023). https://doi.org/10.48550/ARXIV.2302.00387. https://arxiv.org/abs/2302.00387

100. Wang, S., et al.: Noise-induced barren plateaus in variational quantum algorithms. Nature Commun. 12(1), 6961 (2021). https://doi.org/10.1038/s41467-021-27045-6

101. Weder, B., et al.: Quantum software development lifecycle. Quantum Software Engineering, pp. 61–83. Springer (2022)

102. Weimer, H., et al.: Digital quantum simulation with Rydberg atoms. Quantum Inf. Process. 10(6), 885 (2011). https://doi.org/10.1007/s11128-011-0303-5

103. Wille, R., Hillmich, S., Burgholzer, L.: Tools for quantum computing based on decision diagrams. ACM Trans. Quantum Comput. 3(3), 1–17 (2022)

104. Wintersperger, K., Dommert, F., et al.: Neutral Atom Quantum Computing Hardware: Performance and End-User Perspective (2023)

105. Wintersperger, K., Safi, H., Mauerer, W.: QPU-System Co-Design for Quantum HPC Accelerators. In: Proceedings of the 35th GI/ITG International Conference on the Architecture of Computing Systems (Aug. 2022). Gesellschaft für Informatik

106. Xia, S., Zhao, J.: Static Entanglement Analysis of Quantum Programs (2023). arXiv: 2304.05049 [cs.SE]

107. Yamaguchi, M., Yoshioka, N.: Design by Contract Framework for Quantum Software (2023). arXiv: 2303.17750 [cs.CL]

108. Yarkoni, S., et al.: Multi-car paint shop optimization with quantum annealing. In: 2021 IEEE International Conference on Quantum Computing and Engineering (QCE), pp. 35–41. IEEE (2021)

109. Ying, M.: Toward automatic verification of quantum programs. Formal Aspects Comput. 31(1), 3–25 (2019). https://doi.org/10.1007/s00165-018-0465-3

110. Yue, T., et al.: Challenges and Opportunities in Quantum Software Architecture. In: Weber, I., Kazman, R., Pellicione, P. (eds.) Software Architecture Research Roadmaps from the Community. Springer (2023)

111. Zhao, J.: Quantum Software Engineering: Landscapes and Horizons. CoRR. abs/2007.07047 (2020). arXiv: 2007.07047. https://arxiv.org/abs/2007.07047

112. Zhao, P., Wu, X., Li, Z., et al.: QChecker: Detecting Bugs in Quantum Programs via Static Analysis (2023). arXiv: 2304.04387 [cs.SE]

113. Zhao, P., Wu, X., Luo, J., et al.: An Empirical Study of Bugs in Quantum Machine Learning Frameworks. In: Proceedings of the IEEE International Conference on Quantum Software. IEEE (2023)

114. Zhou, L., et al.: Quantum approximate optimization algorithm: performance, mechanism, and implementation on near-term devices. Phys. Rev. X 10(2), 021067 (June 2020). https://doi.org/10.1103/PhysRevX.10.021067. https://link.aps.org/doi/10.1103/PhysRevX.10.021067

Quantum Software Engineering Issues and Challenges: Insights from Practitioners

Manuel De Stefano, Fabiano Pecorelli, Fabio Palomba, Davide Taibi, Dario Di Nucci, and Andrea De Lucia

Abstract Quantum computing is an emerging field in which theoretical principles are being transformed into practical applications, largely due to the efforts of the developer community. In order to ensure that quantum software engineering continues to advance, it is vital to understand the experiences, challenges, and aspirations of developers. This chapter is a continuation of our previous work, which provided a comprehensive survey exploring the adoption patterns and common challenges in quantum software engineering. In addition to the survey, we conducted in-depth, semi-structured interviews with practitioners in the field to gain a deeper and more detailed understanding of their perspectives. Through the interviews and survey findings, we have gained nuanced insights into the motivations, hurdles, and outlook of developers toward the rapidly evolving quantum computing landscape. We describe the research methodology in detail, including the tools and techniques used, in order to provide a comprehensive understanding of the research process. Furthermore, we present critical insights from both the survey and interviews, enriching the narrative with fresh perspectives obtained from the post-publication interviews. This chapter is a blend of academic investigation and real-world practitioner insights, aiming to provide a comprehensive understanding of the current state of quantum software engineering. By illuminating the path for future research and development in this dynamic field, we hope to guide the way toward continued progress and innovation.

M. De Stefano (✉) · F. Palomba · D. Di Nucci · A. De Lucia
SeSa Lab, University of Salerno, Fisciano, Italy
e-mail: madestefano@unisa.it; fpecorelli@unisa.it; ddnucci@unisa.it; adelucia@unisa.it

F. Pecorelli
Jheronimus Academy of Data Science, s-Hertogenbosch, Netherlands
e-mail: fpalomba@unisa.it

D. Taibi
University of Oulu, Oulu, Finland
e-mail: Davide.Taibi@oulu.fi

© The Author(s) 2024
I. Exman et al. (eds.), *Quantum Software*,
https://doi.org/10.1007/978-3-031-64136-7_13

Keywords Quantum computing · Software engineering · Developer
community · Quantum software engineering

1 Introduction

Quantum computing (QC) stands at the forefront of technological advancements, with developers serving as the linchpin of this revolution [6]. While the conceptual roots of quantum mechanics are deeply entrenched in theory, the tangible impacts are most discernible in the realm of quantum software engineering (QSE), where this theory translates into real-world applications [8, 9]. Thus, gauging developers' experiences and insights is paramount [12]. Our study, initiated in our foundational work [2] and further elaborated in this chapter, seeks to bridge this gap.

Our seminal work [2] embarked on this challenging quest, offering an exploratory analysis of quantum software engineering. Through a thorough survey, we dissected the prevailing state of the field, elucidating adoption strategies, recurrent challenges, and potential avenues necessitating deeper probes. The inferences drawn provided a pragmatic perspective on quantum computing, grounded in the experiences of its primary actors—the developers.

Augmenting the initial insights, this chapter extends our exploration by delving deeper into the experiences of three quantum software field practitioners through semi-structured interviews. This granular approach captures the intricacies of developers' motivations, challenges, and aspirations. Such a comprehensive examination underscores a pivotal realization: while quantum computing is intertwined with intricate physics, its real-world application is unmistakably human-centric.

With its inherent challenges and experiences, the developer community's feedback holds the potential to sculpt the trajectory of quantum technologies [2, 10]. Their shared concerns spotlight the areas needing more refined tools and frameworks, elucidate existing knowledge chasms, and chart out the path for prospective research endeavors.

This chapter embarks on a systematic journey through the terrain of quantum software engineering. An extensive review of the current literature emphasizes practitioners' trials and tribulations, with our foundational work [2] serving as a pivotal reference. This approach encompassed a dual strategy: a macroscopic view of the QSE ecosystem through software repository mining, interspersed with a nuanced, ground-level perspective sourced directly from practitioners via an expansive survey. This congruence of theoretical and practical viewpoints carved a holistic image of QSE's current state. Our approach underscored the indispensability of aligning academic exploration with tangible, on-ground experiences, bridging a crucial literature gap.

Our research quest was anchored in discerning the real-world applications of quantum programming technologies, pinpointing quantum developers' challenges, and assessing software engineering (SE) techniques' relevance and applicability. This encompassed insights from researchers, practitioners, and tool vendors, each striving to decode the intricate dance between software engineering and quantum programming.

Our exploration pivoted on two central research queries:

1. *How and to what purpose are quantum programming frameworks predominantly utilized?*
2. *What predominant hurdles do quantum developers encounter when interfacing with quantum frameworks?*

Our investigation was guided by a series of fundamental questions that aimed to encapsulate the nuances of adopting quantum programming. Our goal was to achieve a deep understanding of these subtleties, as they play a crucial role in uncovering the primary challenges that quantum programming developers face. By shedding light on these challenges, we hoped to empower tool creators and academic researchers to craft innovative strategies that can help overcome these obstacles.

In this chapter, we take a two-pronged approach to our investigation. We first explore the current literature on quantum programming adoption, seeking to identify trends, patterns, and gaps in existing research. We then provide a comprehensive analysis of both the mining study and the broad survey we conducted, which allowed us to gather detailed insights directly from developers.

Our analysis of the mining study and the comprehensive survey builds on this foundation, providing a more granular view of the challenges that developers face. We examine issues such as debugging, testing, and community issues, as well as the challenges of working with quantum hardware and the need for better documentation and education. By exploring these issues in detail, we aim to provide actionable insights that can help guide the development of new tools and strategies for quantum programming.

2 Bridging the Gap in Quantum Software Engineering

Quantum software engineering (QSE) has burgeoned as a pivotal discipline within the quantum computing domain, with the *Talavera Manifesto* marking a significant milestone in its evolution [10, 11, 12]. This manifesto delineated core tenets and principles, laying a roadmap for researchers and developers. However, it inadvertently overlooked the practical challenges practitioners face at the quantum software development forefront.

A recent systematic mapping study by De Stefano et al. [3] delved into the current state of QSE research, aiming to outline the most investigated topics, the types and number of studies, and the primary reported results alongside the most studied quantum computing tools/frameworks. This study also aimed to gauge the research community's interest in QSE, its evolution, and any notable contributions preceding the formal introduction through the Talavera Manifesto.

Employing a meticulous methodology, De Stefano et al. searched for relevant articles across various databases, applying inclusion and exclusion criteria to select the most pertinent studies. Following a quality evaluation of the selected resources, relevant data were extracted and analyzed. The findings underscored a predominant focus on software testing within QSE research, with other crucial topics like software engineering management receiving scant attention. Among the technologies for techniques and tools, Qiskit emerged as the most commonly studied, although many studies either employed multiple technologies or did not specify any. The research community interested in QSE showcased interconnected collaborations, with several strong collaboration clusters identified. Interestingly, most QSE articles were published in non-thematic venues, with a preference for conferences, indicating a burgeoning interest in the domain.

The implications of this study are manifold, serving as a centralized information source for researchers and practitioners, facilitating knowledge transfer, and contributing significantly to QSE's advancement and growth. The study highlighted the nascent stage of QSE research, primarily centered around software testing, leaving other knowledge areas like software engineering management relatively unexplored. A notable uptick in published papers between 2020 and 2021 reflects a growing interest in QSE within the research community. The study also shed light on the most productive authors, the main collaboration clusters, and the distribution of researchers across different Software Engineering (SE) topics, which could catalyze the identification of potential collaborators and foster further research in QSE.

Furthermore, the study accentuated the need for more empirical studies and a better distribution of research efforts across diverse SE topics. It advocated for a broader acceptance of QSE papers in non-thematic publication venues to expand the research community's knowledge and reach. The insights gleaned from this study are instrumental in understanding the development and evolution of the research community, thereby significantly contributing to the advancement and growth of QSE.

The systematic mapping study also illuminated potential avenues for future research in QSE, particularly in the overlooked realms of software engineering management practices and quantum software maintenance. The call to action is for future research to focus on devising effective strategies and tools for managing the software development process and ensuring the reliability and performance of quantum software over time. The unique challenges and opportunities inherent in quantum software engineering warrant a thorough exploration to identify effective strategies for managing the development process and evaluating the efficacy of different software engineering practices and tools.

Despite the academic rigor marking the journey of QSE, the crucial component of practitioners' voices and experiences has often been overlooked. The academic literature has largely remained aloof from the day-to-day challenges and innovative solutions that practitioners often develop. While several studies have delved deep into the theoretical challenges and potential solutions in QSE from a high-level perspective [16, 10], they have missed out on the granular details and real-world manifestations of these challenges.

Among the myriad studies in this domain, the work by El Aoun et al. stands out for its empirical approach [5]. By analyzing QSE-related discussions on platforms like Stack Exchange and GitHub, they tapped into a rich vein of practitioner experiences. Their methodology employed automated topic modeling to distill the myriad discussions into coherent themes and challenges, providing a window into the world of quantum developers. However, the limitations of automated topic modeling sometimes missed out on the nuances and subtleties of human communication, and their passive approach did not allow for deeper, engaging discussions with practitioners.

3   Current Usage of Quantum Technologies

The mining study [2] focused on identifying and analyzing quantum software repositories to understand the extent and purpose of quantum programming frameworks usage. Our study's scope was primarily defined by the quantum technologies considered. We focused on three state-of-the-practice universal gate quantum programming technologies, namely QISKIT [1], CIRQ [4], and Q♯ [13], which are developed and maintained by IBM, Google, and Microsoft respectively. These frameworks are recognized as more mature and stable, each having unique functionalities and allowing the execution of quantum programs on both local simulators and real quantum devices provided by their vendors. We employed a software repository mining approach to identify projects on GITHUB that use at least one of the considered technologies. This process yielded a total of 731 unique repositories.

The data analysis phase for the mining study aimed at addressing the first research question using information from the repository mining. We employed Straussian Grounded Theory for a systematic approach to constructing theories from the data collected. This methodology involved a cyclical process of open, axial, and selective coding to derive a taxonomy that serves as the foundation for answering our research question.

We provided a data-driven perspective on how quantum technologies are employed in real-world scenarios.

As shown in Fig. 1, the mining revealed distinct usage patterns among quantum developers. Many repositories were dedicated to didactic purposes or personal experimentation with quantum technologies. This suggests that many developers are in the early stages of their quantum journey, using repositories as learning tools or platforms for experimentation.

An interesting facet of the mining study was the analysis of contributors to these repositories (Fig. 2). The distribution of contributors varied based on the type of repository. For instance, toy projects, which are typically smaller and more experimental, had a distribution skewed toward fewer contributors. In contrast, framework-related repositories, which are more extensive and foundational, had a broader distribution of contributors.

The mining study's results underscore the developing nature of quantum programming. While there is evident enthusiasm and interest in the field, as seen by the proliferation of didactic and experimental repositories, large-scale, collaborative

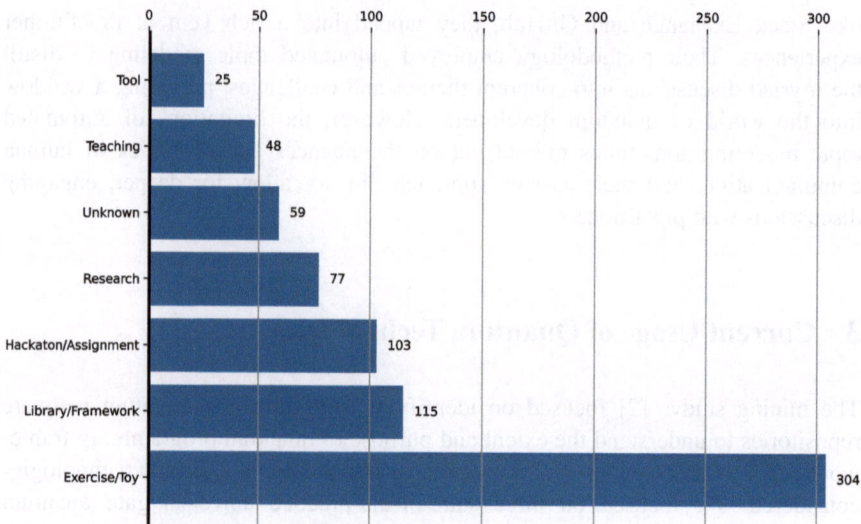

Fig. 1 Main task for which quantum repositories are created [2]

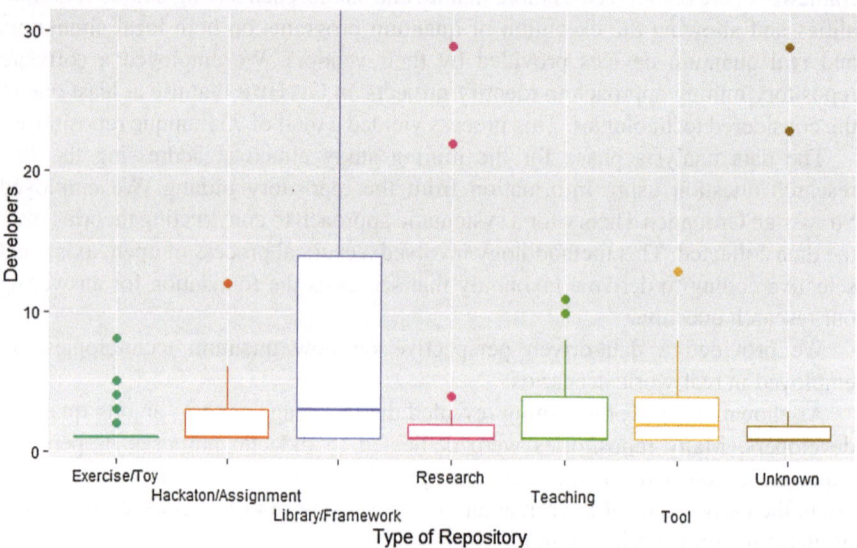

Fig. 2 Distribution of contributors per type of repository [2]

projects still have a long way to go. The contributor analysis further reinforces this, highlighting the need for more collaborative platforms and community-driven initiatives to foster growth in quantum software engineering.

4 The Practitioners' Voice

The survey study aimed to gather insights from quantum developers regarding their challenges and perspectives on the current and potential future adoption of quantum programming technologies (Table 1).

To engage with quantum software developers, we utilized the mined repositories to obtain a list of eligible candidates for our survey, ensuring the involvement of developers with real experience in quantum programming. We employed an *opt-in* strategy for recruitment, sending initial emails to gauge interest before providing additional instructions to willing participants. This strategy led to the recruitment of 56 *volunteers*.

The survey was structured into three main sections: gathering background information, understanding the current use of quantum technologies, and assessing their longer-term adoption and challenges.

The data analysis phase for the survey study aimed at addressing our second question by using the responses provided in the third part of the survey. Similar to the mining study, we employed Straussian Grounded Theory for a systematic approach to constructing theories from the data collected. This methodology involved a cyclical process of open, axial, and selective coding to derive a taxonomy that serves as the foundation for answering our research question.

Based on the practitioner feedback, we built a detailed taxonomy of their main challenges while working with quantum computing. This taxonomy, represented in Fig. 3, was developed through a rigorous Straussian Grounded Theory exercise. Some challenges are independent, while others lead to more specific sub-challenges.

4.1 The Quantum Environment: Hardware and Software

The quantum environment, encompassing both hardware and software, presents its own set of unique challenges. Software infrastructure issues can be related to frameworks, integration, and execution.

- **Framework.** Developers often grapple with the ever-changing API designs of quantum technologies. A significant number of our interviewees, 15 to be precise, lamented the frequent and unpredictable changes in API. Others highlighted the lack of support for certain operations, like those in QISKIT, and the absence of standardization across frameworks.
- **Integration.** Integrating quantum systems with traditional ones is no easy feat. Some developers mentioned the complexities of integrating classical algorithms into their quantum counterparts or connecting quantum computers to blockchain networks.
- **Execution.** Setting up execution environments and simulators or interfacing with classical systems can be daunting, as 11 of our participants reported.

Table 1 Questions asked in the survey

Question Text	Answer Type	Possible Answers
Part 1—Background		
What is your current employment status?	Multiple Choice	BSc Student; MSc Student; PhD Student; Researcher; Open Source Developer; Industrial Developer; Other
What is your educational background?	Single Choice	Computer Science; Chemistry; Physics; Other
What is your age range?	Single Choice	18–24; 25–34; 35–44; 45–54; 55+
What is your gender?	Free Text	–
Please indicate your expertise (in years) in Software Development.	Single Choice	None; 0–3; 3–5; 5–10; 10+
Please indicate your expertise (in years) in Industrial Development.	Single Choice	None; 0–3; 3–5; 5–10; 10+
Please indicate your expertise (in years) in Quantum Programming.	Single Choice	None; 0–3; 3–5; 5–10; 10+
What is your country?	Free Text	–
Part 2—Current Adoption		
Which quantum technology are you most confident with?	Single Choice	QISKIT; CIRQ; Q♯; Other
Which other quantum technology do you use?	Multiple Choice	QISKIT; CIRQ; Q♯; Other
In which context are you using quantum computing?	Multiple Choice	Academic Study; Hackaton; Industry; OSS; Personal Study; Research; Other
Could you please tell me more about the tasks you perform with quantum computing?	Long Free Text	–
Part 3—Potential Adoption and Challenges		
Consider the technology you are most confident with. What are the top three challenges that you have faced?	Multiple Free Text	–
Based on your experience, have you ever solved (or tried to solve) a problem using quantum programming that has no "traditional" solution (or the solution is intractable)?	Single Choice	Yes; No
If yes, could you please elaborate on the problem and why you had to use quantum computing?	Long Free Text	–
Based on your experience, have you ever solved (or tried to solve) a problem that has a "traditional" solution using quantum programming?	Single Choice	Yes; No
If yes, could you please elaborate on what it was and explain why you chose to use quantum computing?	Long Free Text	–

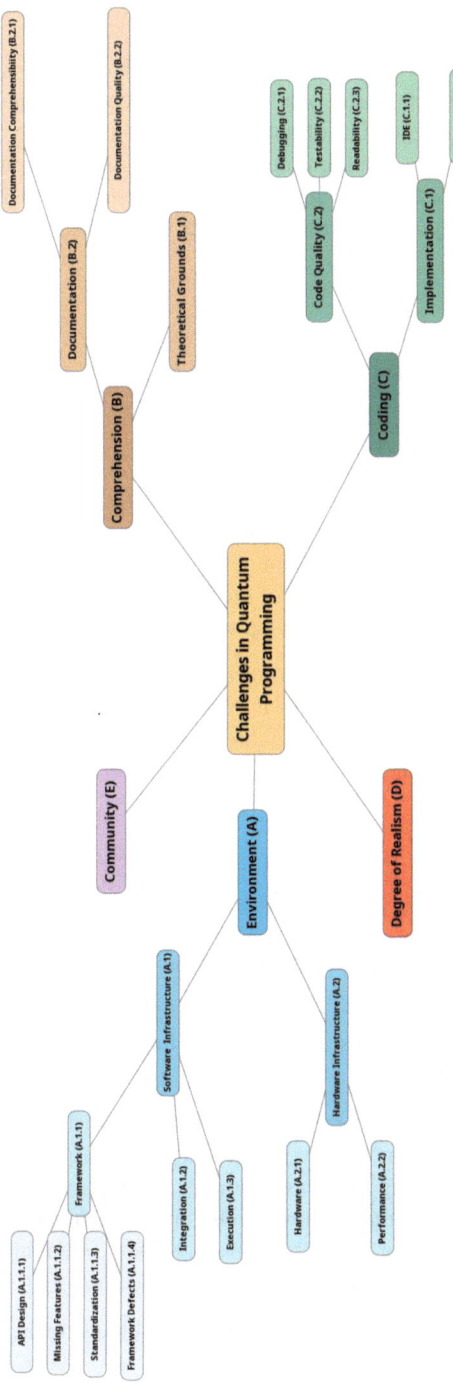

Fig. 3 Taxonomy of quantum programming challenges identified by practitioners [2]

Hardware infrastructure issues attain the developmental nature and availability of the hardware and the related performance.

- **Hardware.** The specialized nature of quantum hardware, which is still in its developmental phase, poses challenges. Developers often find themselves restricted by the limited number of qubits available in quantum computers.
- **Performance.** Emulating quantum programs on classical computers brings forth several performance issues. Emulators can be resource-intensive, and running programs on actual quantum devices can be time-consuming due to vendor-imposed job queues.

4.2   Comprehending the Quantum Realm

Understanding quantum programs is a challenge in itself.

- **Theoretical Grounds.** A significant number of our respondents (20) emphasized the steep learning curve associated with quantum programming, especially the need for a strong foundation in linear algebra.
- **Documentation.** These issues concern the comprehensibility and quality of the documentation related to quantum frameworks and code.

  - **Comprehensibility.** Inconsistent tutorials and documentation can hinder the learning process, a sentiment echoed by three participants.
  - **Quality.** Sixteen participants highlighted issues with outdated, incomplete, or missing documentation.

4.3   Quantum Coding Challenges

Coding in the quantum domain presents its own set of unique challenges related to implementation and code quality.

- **Implementation.** These issues are related to integrated development environments and compilation.

  - **IDE.** A good Integrated Development Environment (IDE) can be a game-changer. However, some developers found existing quantum IDEs lacking, especially when working with environments like Q♯.
  - **Compilation.** Translating quantum circuits into executable code for quantum computers is a complex process, with developers often struggling to adapt ideal quantum circuits to available device architectures.

- **Code Quality.** Code quality issues include problems related to debugging, testing, and readability of quantum code.

- **Debugging.** Deciphering error messages and debugging quantum programs can be particularly challenging due to the unique nature of quantum programming.
- **Testability.** Ensuring that a quantum program functions as intended is not straightforward. Some developers found it challenging to verify the correctness of their circuits.
- **Readability.** With quantum code primarily defining qubit registers and applying gates, creating readable code becomes challenging.

4.4 The Realism Quotient

While quantum computers promise groundbreaking solutions, their practical application remains a challenge.

- **Degree of Realism.** Developers often find it challenging to design quantum programs that can address real-world problems. The limitations of current quantum applications make it difficult to find problems that quantum solutions can address better than traditional technologies.

4.5 Building a Quantum Community

The early stage of quantum programming means a small community of developers.

- **Community.** Many developers desired a more robust community for peer support and collaboration. Slow code reviews and the effort required to understand quantum programs further compound the challenges.

5 Deepening the Practictioners' Insights

This chapter comprehensively analyzes the challenges of using quantum software development technologies in various fields. To achieve this, we took a unique approach of directly interviewing experts specializing in quantum technologies. These experts come from diverse backgrounds and working ecosystems.

During our interviews, we discussed practitioners' particular difficulties when working with quantum technologies. We covered a range of topics from the taxonomy of challenges we established [2], such as the shortcomings of existing quantum technologies, the requisite for more sophisticated hardware and software, and the struggles in creating quantum algorithms.

The insights provided by these experts were priceless, as they offered a wealth of knowledge and experience from their respective fields. We present the extracts of each interview in the following sections, accompanied by detailed analysis and commentary on the valuable insights provided by these practitioners. By doing so, we hope to shed more light on the challenges of working with quantum technologies and provide a better understanding of the field.

5.1   First Interview

In the first of our series of interviews, we engaged with an expert deeply involved in the practical application of quantum mechanics. This individual, currently affiliated with a consultancy company, has been actively working on the lattice Boltzmann method for quantum computing. Their experience primarily revolves around using platforms like Qiskit and Penny Lane, and they are keenly interested in the challenges and opportunities of quantum hardware and software. Throughout our discussion, they shared insights on the evolution of quantum computing, its challenges, and the real-world implications of integrating quantum solutions with classical systems.

Our first expert acknowledged the ever-evolving nature of APIs in quantum computing, emphasizing their appreciation for the consistent updates. They lauded the community's supportive character, particularly around a specific platform, which they described as responsive and invaluable.

Much of the discussion revolved around the practical application of quantum programming. While some in the field find it challenging to harness quantum programming for tangible tasks, this expert has successfully navigated these waters in their projects.

When discussing software infrastructure, the expert highlighted the seamless integration of quantum software with traditional software, primarily through Python. However, they also brought to light a theoretical challenge: the intricate process of mapping classical input to quantum.

The conversation then veered toward hardware challenges. The inherent noise in quantum mechanics was identified as a natural obstacle in quantum computing. Despite this, the expert recognized the commendable progress made in recent years, especially by a leading tech company, in mitigating this noise. But they also pointed out that this noise currently restricts the depth of circuits on real devices, leading them to use simulators often.

On the coding front in quantum computing, the expert found the process straightforward, especially with the support for various gates in specific platforms. They also shared their unique approach to testing, which involves juxtaposing quantum results with classical methods or analytical solutions.

The expert addressed the prevailing hype around quantum computing and the inherent challenge of achieving a quantum advantage. They proudly mentioned their company's significant strides, especially with specific models.

5.2 Second Interview

The individual shared their experiences of and insights into quantum computing during the interview. They emphasized the importance of grasping the fundamentals before delving into more complex frameworks and languages. They preferred a bottom-up approach, utilizing more straightforward tools like NumPy to build a foundational understanding. They believed this mitigated the challenges posed by the steep learning curve associated with quantum computing, especially when compared to the more mature field of machine learning.

The interviewee found that existing frameworks like Qiskit were more geared toward professional deployment rather than aiding in learning or debugging. They mentioned the difficulty in debugging in quantum computing, attributing it to the complexity added by these frameworks. They advocated a more straightforward approach to coding and debugging to understand and learn quantum computing.

Drawing parallels between the evolution of machine learning and quantum computing, the interviewee noted hype and venture capital involvement similarities. They observed that while machine learning has found broad applications and has become integral to many fields, quantum computing might find its niche in more specific areas like chemistry and physics, particularly in quantum simulation. They believed this could lead to significant advancements, such as discovering new pharmaceuticals.

The interviewee also touched on the potential for quantum computing to become a significant part of data center infrastructure in the future. However, they expressed skepticism regarding the timeline for such developments, likening the anticipation around quantum computing to the long-standing expectation around fusion energy.

Exploring various quantum computing languages, the interviewee found that understanding the underlying mechanics was crucial for making sense of these languages. They mentioned having examined various quantum computing languages and found that having a foundational understanding aided in making sense of how these languages and compilers were implemented.

Looking toward the future, the interviewee foresees a potential hype cycle for quantum computing, similar to what machine learning experienced. They anticipated initial excitement, followed by a period of disillusionment and, eventually, the emergence of practical applications as the field matures. They stressed the need for real impact or significant advancements in quantum computing to sustain momentum in the area, expressing cautious optimism for the potential of quantum computing to contribute to specific scientific and technological advances.

5.3 Third Interview

The interviewee is a professional in the field of quantum computing with several years of industry experience. They specialize in the interface aspect of quantum computing projects and have actively created educational resources for the community. Their work primarily focuses on software engineering within quantum computing, and they have a dedicated team to ensure code quality.

During the discussion, the interviewee highlighted several challenges and considerations in the quantum computing field. One primary concern is the lack of adequate documentation, which can be a barrier for newcomers or those not deeply versed in the science behind quantum computing. They emphasized the importance of understanding the input and output of specific modules in quantum computing projects, which is crucial for effective implementation and debugging.

The conversation also touched on the accessibility of the quantum computing community. The interviewee believes that while the community is robust, it may not be well advertised or easy to find for newcomers. They suggested that better communication and information distribution could help bridge this gap, making the community more accessible to those interested in quantum computing.

Regarding realism and expectations, the interviewee acknowledged that the field is not yet usable, and much of the work is about paving the way for future usability. They compared the hype around quantum computing to machine learning in its early stages, indicating that the field might face similar challenges in meeting high expectations.

Regarding code quality and debugging, the interviewee mentioned the challenges when code is written by scientists who might not have strong coding practices. They highlighted the difference in code quality when a dedicated software engineering team is involved versus when researchers or academics write the code.

Regarding the accessibility to quantum computers, the interviewee mentioned that they have never actually run anything on a real quantum computer but have used simulators instead. They speculated about the future accessibility of quantum computers to the public, comparing it to the current accessibility of supercomputers.

The interviewee also mentioned creating educational resources, such as blog posts and podcasts, to help others in the quantum computing community. They are willing to share these resources, indicating a collaborative spirit within the community.

Lastly, the interviewer expressed interest in the open-source software the interviewee is working on, indicating a willingness to share and collaborate within the community, further emphasizing the collaborative nature of quantum computing.

6 Synthesizing Academic Findings and Practical Insights

Exploring the quantum software engineering landscape involved conducting a mining study, a practitioner survey, and expert interviews. The mining study involved analyzing vast amounts of data to identify patterns and trends in quantum programming. The practitioner survey was conducted to gather feedback from professionals working in the quantum programming domain. Lastly, expert interviews were conducted to gain insights from knowledgeable individuals well versed in the field.

The findings from these diverse sources provide a rich tapestry of insights into the current state and challenges of the quantum programming domain. These insights include the tools and technologies currently being used, the challenges practitioners face, and the potential for future advancements.

This section synthesizes these findings to understand the quantum programming domain fully. By doing so, we hope to provide a comprehensive overview of the current state of the field as well as its potential for future growth and development.

Early Adoption and Experiments The study on quantum programming revealed that the field is still in its early stages, with many repositories dedicated to didactic purposes or personal experimentation. This early experimentation is further supported by the first interviewee, who discussed the challenges in practical application, and the second interviewee, who emphasized the need for a solid foundation before tackling complex frameworks. Moreover, the survey results of 20 participants, along with the second interviewee's comments, highlighted the steep learning curve in the current quantum programming landscape, which further underlines the experimental nature of this field. The findings indicate that, at this stage, quantum programming is primarily used for educational and exploratory purposes, with few practical applications. However, with further research and development, quantum programming could have significant implications for various industries.

Community and Collaborative Initiatives The importance of building a stronger and more collaborative community platform was a recurring theme that emerged from all sources. The mining study revealed a skewed distribution of project contributors toward a limited number of toy projects, denoting a lack of collaboration on a larger scale. This finding underscores the need for better community-building and collaboration platforms. Practitioners also expressed their desire for a more robust community to provide peer support, facilitate collaboration, and improve communication within the quantum computing field. The third interviewee emphasized the importance of information distribution and better communication within the quantum computing community. The first interviewee appreciated the supportive nature of the community around specific platforms, which further highlights the significance of a collaborative ecosystem in advancing the field. In summary, building a collaborative and supportive community is crucial for advancing the quantum computing field, and there is a need for better platforms to facilitate communication, collaboration, and information sharing.

Software and Hardware Infrastructure Challenges The survey and interviews with practitioners in the quantum computing field have brought to light several key challenges in the software and hardware infrastructure. A prominent concern among practitioners is the frequent and unpredictable changes in quantum computing APIs, as highlighted by 15 survey participants. This issue complicates the process of keeping software up to date with the latest developments. Another significant challenge is the integration of quantum systems with traditional computing systems.

This was particularly emphasized by the first interviewee, who stressed the importance of seamless integration of quantum software with conventional software. For effective integration, software developers must comprehensively understand both quantum and traditional software systems, along with their distinct characteristics. The hardware challenges in quantum computing were also addressed, particularly the limited availability of qubits and the inherent noise in quantum mechanics. These factors restrict the complexity of calculations that can be performed and limit the depth of circuits on real quantum devices, posing a hurdle for practitioners undertaking complex quantum computations. A possible future direction for the hardware support might be seen in co-design [14]. Co-design has been a foundational element in the evolution of computer architecture since the inception of the first systems. This concept, where end-user applications influence the design and capabilities of the hardware and vice versa, is crucial in quantum computing (QC). Especially in its resource-constrained early stages, QC heavily relies on co-design strategies. This approach involves tailoring the quantum hardware and software to optimize performance and functionality. The article explores the significance of co-design in the QC context, illustrating its benefits and proposing essential attributes for effective QC co-design strategies moving forward. This perspective suggests a future direction where addressing the current challenges in quantum computing infrastructure could involve a more integrated and co-evolutionary approach between software and hardware, aligning with the principles of quantum co-design.

Real-World Application and Quantum Advantage The concept of realism quotient, explored in a survey conducted among practitioners, seems to align with expert opinions on the practical implementation of quantum programming. Introducing the concept of "quantum utility, " which measures the effectiveness and practicality of quantum computers in various applications, provides a more holistic view of the field's progress. This new metric, focusing on achieving a quantum advantage in terms of speed, accuracy, or energy efficiency compared to classical machines of similar size, weight, and cost, enhances the realism quotient by considering the physical footprint and industrial value of quantum processors [7, 15]. The first interviewee's insights on achieving quantum advantage echo the goals set forth in the quantum utility concept [7, 15], and the second interviewee's doubts regarding the timeline for quantum computing to become a significant part of data center infrastructure indicate that the field is still struggling to establish a strong foothold in real-world applications. Moreover, the proposed application readiness levels (ARLs) and extended classification labels further refine the criteria for assessing quantum computing's practical applications in fields like quantum chemistry and machine learning [7, 15]. The second interviewee's expectation of a hype cycle similar to that experienced by the machine learning industry reflects a cautious optimism toward the potential of quantum computing to contribute to specific scientific and technological advancements. Overall, the survey and interviews highlight the ongoing challenges and possibilities that quantum programming presents for the future of computing, and underscore the importance of structured analysis and tooling, as emphasized in the concept of quantum computing optimization middleware (QCOM) [7, 15].

Educational Resources and Code Quality During the third interview, the interviewee's efforts in creating educational resources and ensuring code quality were discussed at length. It was noted that these efforts resonate with the concerns of practitioners in the quantum programming community regarding the comprehensibility and quality of documentation. Interestingly, when written by scientists, as opposed to a dedicated software engineering team, the mention of challenges in code quality reflects a broader concern in the community regarding the accessibility and readability of code. This highlights the need for collaborations between scientists and software engineering teams in the quantum programming community to ensure the development of high-quality, understandable, and readable code.

Future Usability and Accessibility During the third interview, the interviewee expressed their opinion on the field's current state, highlighting its unusability and speculating on the future accessibility of quantum computers to the public. This encapsulates the overall sentiment of cautious optimism prevalent in the field. While the field is full of potential and possibilities, it faces substantial challenges that need addressing before it can transition from a stage of experimentation to one of significant real-world impact. These challenges include infrastructure, community collaboration, and real-world application. Addressing these challenges is crucial for the field to realize its potential and significantly impact the real world.

7   Conclusion and Future Directions

The field of quantum software engineering is still in its nascent stages, facing a range of potential and significant obstacles that pose challenges to the development and application of quantum computing. However, combining the results of a comprehensive mining study, practitioner survey, and expert interviews provides a detailed and thorough understanding of the current state of the field, as well as its trajectory.

A closer look at the opportunities and challenges identified in this study reveals a range of factors shaping the field of quantum software engineering. For instance, there is great enthusiasm and interest in quantum programming, with abundant educational and experimental repositories indicating a fertile ground for innovation. The potential applications of quantum computing, especially in fields like chemistry, physics, and cryptography, are promising, and this has led to a growing community of developers and researchers eager to explore and contribute to this emerging field.

However, many challenges must be overcome before the full potential of quantum software engineering can be realized. These challenges include a steep learning curve, a lack of standardized frameworks, hardware limitations, and a nascent stage of community collaboration. Developers face significant hurdles in integrating quantum systems with traditional ones, frequent API changes, and complexities.

The lack of large-scale collaborative projects and robust community support further exacerbates the challenges in advancing quantum software engineering. Moreover, the struggle in harnessing quantum programming for tangible real-world tasks remains a significant concern.

Addressing the identified challenges requires a concerted effort from academia, industry, and the quantum computing community. Standardizing frameworks, improving documentation quality, and fostering a collaborative ecosystem are essential for nurturing the growth of quantum software engineering. Investments in educational initiatives to lower the entry barrier and nurture a new generation of quantum programmers are crucial. Creating platforms facilitating large-scale collaborative projects can accelerate the transition from experimentation to substantial real-world impact.

Moreover, continued research and development are vital in overcoming hardware limitations and enhancing the software infrastructure. Establishing partnerships between academia and industry can expedite the translation of academic findings into practical solutions, driving the field closer to achieving quantum advantage. In addition, managing the hype around quantum computing and setting realistic expectations can help navigate the hype cycle, ensuring sustained momentum in the field. The cautious optimism expressed by the interviewees and survey participants reflects a collective acknowledgment of the long yet promising journey ahead.

In conclusion, the quantum software engineering landscape presents a frontier of opportunities awaiting exploration and innovation. The insights garnered from the current state of the field provide a compass for navigating the uncharted waters of quantum software engineering, steering toward a future where quantum computing realizes its transformative potential.

Acknowledgments This work has been partially supported by the project 'QUASAR: QUAntum software engineering for Secure, Affordable, and Reliable systems, grant 2022T2E39C, under the PRIN 2022 MUR program funded by the EU NextGenerationEU.

References

1. Aleksandrowicz, G., Alexander, T., Barkoutsos, P., Bello, L., Ben-Haim, Y., Bucher, D., Cabrera-Hernández, F.J., Carballo-Franquis, J., Chen, A., Chen, C.F., et al.: Qiskit: An open-source framework for quantum computing. Accessed on: Mar **16**, (2019)
2. De Stefano, M., Pecorelli, F., Di Nucci, D., Palomba, F., De Lucia, A.: Software engineering for quantum programming: How far are we? J. Syst. Softw. **190**, 111326 (2022)
3. De Stefano, M., Pecorelli, F., Di Nucci, D., Palomba, F., De Lucia, A.: The quantum frontier of software engineering: a systematic mapping study. Preprint (2023). arXiv:2305.19683
4. Developers, C.: Cirq (2021). https://doi.org/10.5281/zenodo.4750446. See full list of authors on Github: https://github.com/quantumlib/Cirq/graphs/contributors
5. El aoun, M.R., Li, H., Khomh, F., Openja, M.: Understanding quantum software engineering challenges: An empirical study on stack exchange forums and github issues. In: 37th International Conference on Software Maintenance and Evolution (ICSME) (2021)

6. Galitski, V.: Quantum computing hype is bad for science. https://www.linkedin.com/pulse/quantum-computing-hype-bad-science-victor-galitski-1c. Accessed: 2021-07-21

7. Herrmann, N., Arya, D., Doherty, M.W., Mingare, A., Pillay, J.C., Preis, F., Prestel, S.: Quantum utility–definition and assessment of a practical quantum advantage. Preprint (2023). arXiv:2303.02138

8. Hoare, T., Milner, R.: Grand challenges for computing research. Comput. J. **48**(1), 49–52 (2005)

9. Knight, W.: Serious quantum computers are finally here. What are we going to do with them. MIT Technol. Rev. **30**, 2018 (2018). Retrieved on October

10. Piattini, M., Peterssen, G., Pérez-Castillo, R.: Quantum computing: A new software engineering golden age. ACM SIGSOFT Softw. Eng. Notes **45**(3), 12–14 (2020)

11. Piattini, M., Peterssen, G., Pérez-Castillo, R., Hevia, J.L., Serrano, M.A., Hernández, G., de Guzmán, I.G.R., Paradela, C.A., Polo, M., Murina, E., et al.: The talavera manifesto for quantum software engineering and programming. In: QANSWER, pp. 1–5 (2020)

12. Piattini, M., Serrano, M., Perez-Castillo, R., Petersen, G., Hevia, J.L.: Toward a quantum software engineering. IT Prof. **23**(1), 62–66 (2021)

13. Quantum Development Kit.: https://azure.microsoft.com/it-it/resources/development-kit/quantum-computing/ (2021). Accessed: 2021-06-05

14. Tomesh, T., Martonosi, M.: Quantum codesign. IEEE Micro **41**(5), 33–40 (2021)

15. Tsymbalista, M., Maksymenko, M., Katernyak, I.: Approaching quantum utility by leveraging quantum software stack. In: 2023 IEEE 13th International Conference on Electronics and Information Technologies (ELIT), pp. 210–215. IEEE (2023)

16. Zhao, J.: Quantum software engineering: Landscapes and horizons. Preprint (2020). arXiv:2007.07047

Correction to: Trapped-Ion Quantum Computing

Albert Frisch, Alexander Erhard, Thomas Feldker, Florian Girtler, Max Hettrich, Wilfried Huss, Georg Jacob, Christine Maier, Gregor Mayramhof, Daniel Nigg, Christian Sommer, Juris Ulmanis, Etienne Wodey, Mederika Zangerl, and Thomas Monz

Correction to:
Chapter 10 in: I. Exman et al. (eds.), *Quantum Software*, https://doi.org/10.1007/978-3-031-64136-7_10

The original version of the chapter "Trapped-Ion Quantum Computing" was inadvertently published with an incorrect acronym, which has now been corrected as follows:

- On page 251, the acronym "Advanced Query Tool (AQT)" has been corrected to "Alpine Quantum Technologies (AQT)" in the "Abstract and Keywords" section.

- On page 252, the acronym "Advanced Query Tool (AQT)" has been corrected to "Alpine Quantum Technologies (AQT)" in the third paragraph.

The updated version of this chapter can be found at
https://doi.org/10.1007/978-3-031-64136-7_10